AMERICA: WHO REALLY PAYS THE TAXES?

★ $ ★ $ ★ $ ★ $ ★ $ ★ $ ★ $ ★

BY DONALD L. BARLETT
AND JAMES B. STEELE

A TOUCHSTONE BOOK

Published by Simon & Schuster

New York   London   Toronto   Sydney   Tokyo   Singapore

TOUCHSTONE
Rockefeller Center
1230 Avenue of the Americas
New York, New York 10020

TOUCHSTONE and colophon are registered trademarks of Simon & Schuster Inc.

Designed by Irving Perkins Associates

Manufactured in the United States of America

10 9 8 7 6 5 4 3 2 1

Library of Congress Cataloging-in-Publication Data is available.

ISBN: 0-671-87157-9

ACKNOWLEDGMENTS

We incurred many debts in writing this book, but perhaps our greatest is to those readers of our last book, *America: What Went Wrong?* who urged us in public meetings across the country and in articulate, thoughtful letters to continue pursuing the story of Middle America's economic decline. Time and again, people from all sections of the country and from all walks of life pointed to a tax system that they perceived to be unfair, a system that they believed was contributing to their falling standard of living, accelerating the drift toward inequality, and eroding the essential trust between citizen and government. To all of you who took the time to write or to seek us out, we want to express our thanks for your encouragement and for planting the seed that has grown into this book.

We would like to thank all those we interviewed, many of whom are quoted in the book, but many others who are not, yet whose observations were of great value to us in understanding the complexities of taxes and their impact on daily life. We would like to thank many tax lawyers with whom we had the good fortune to discuss some of the broad themes that run through the book. We are most grateful for both their time and their insights.

We would also like to express our appreciation to employees of local, state, and federal agencies and of state and federal courts who assisted in the time-consuming task of locating records, reports, and other documents. The number of individuals who helped in the research runs into the hundreds. While we cannot thank them all personally, we would like to extend a special word of gratitude to several who have been most patient and helpful in seeking out answers to our many questions over the years, including Johnell A. Hunter and her colleagues in the IRS public affairs office in Washington; Ruth Davis and her staff at U.S. Tax Court; and Carolyn Cheezum at the Social Security Administration.

We would also like to thank Bing Mark, a *Philadelphia Inquirer* staff member who assisted with some of the research, and Minta K. Steinberger of Speed Service Couriers in Washington, D.C. Minta's unfailing good humor and professionalism in having documents and reports retrieved for us and sent speedily on their way helped us immeasurably.

As always, we are indebted to librarians at public, private, and university libraries across America, including those at the Lippincott Library of the University of Pennsylvania, the government publications room of the Free Library of Philadelphia, the Jenkins Law Library of the Philadelphia Bar Association, and at numerous small libraries, like the Kinderhook Regional Library in Waynesville, Missouri. We owe special thanks to members of the library staff of the *Inquirer* who for more than two decades have good-naturedly sought out answers to our many tedious queries.

The experience of working with everyone at Simon & Schuster has been most gratifying. We want to offer special thanks to Alice Mayhew, for her enthusiasm and support for the book from the start and for her thoughtful suggestions for improving the manuscript. We also want to express our appreciation to senior editor Ed Walters for his counsel and dedication to this project; Marjorie Horvitz for her copyediting, Lydia Buechler for her patience with our never-ending revisions, and Sarah Baker and Beverly Smith for their help and many courtesies. In addition, we are especially appreciative of all the effort by the Simon & Schuster production department staff, whose lives were made most difficult by our repeated attempts to convert a book-publishing deadline into a daily-newspaper deadline.

Last, a word of thanks to a longtime friend and colleague at the *Philadelphia Inquirer,* Mary Lowe Kennedy, who has now had a direct hand in three of our four books. Mary Lowe read the manuscript and made her usual thoughtful suggestions on organization, word usage, and writing. We will always be in her debt.

While many have contributed to this book, any mistakes are ours and ours alone.

For America's librarians—a dedicated group of people who have helped so much through the years

CONTENTS

CHAPTER 1

★ $ ★ $ ★

WHERE DID ALL THE MONEY GO?

The Two-Tax, Two-Class Society

So you have a feeling that you're paying taxes at a higher rate than a lot of millionaires?

That when politicians start talking about how they are going to tax the rich they mean—you?

That for your struggling family, the overall tax bill—local, state, and federal—has gone up, while for your more affluent friends it's gone down?

You have a feeling that your children are paying out a larger share of their income in federal, state, and local taxes than you did at their age—and aren't living nearly as well?

That the Social Security tax being withheld from your paycheck is going to someone whose income far exceeds yours?

That when members of Congress talk about cutting entitlements they mean yours—not theirs?

You have a feeling that as a single working parent you're paying a larger share of your income in taxes than some wealthy foreign investor who buys up American companies and eliminates jobs?

That the small business you run pays a higher percentage of its revenue in taxes than a *Fortune* 500 company?

That you and your spouse are paying comparatively more in

real estate taxes on your three-bedroom home than the couple across town in the six-bedroom, six-bathroom mansion?

Are those your feelings?

If so, trust them.

For over thirty years, members of Congress and Presidents—Democrats and Republicans alike—have enacted one law after another to create two separate and distinct tax systems: One for the rich and powerful—call it the Privileged Person's Tax Law; another for you and everyone else—call it the Common Person's Tax Law.

As a result, they have transferred the tax burden:

- From people who can most afford to pay to those less able to pay.
- From corporations to individuals.
- From foreign corporations to domestic corporations.
- From foreign investors to American workers.
- From multinational companies to medium-sized and small businesses.
- From the federal government to state and local governments, whose taxes already fall most heavily on those in the middle and at the bottom.

They have provided tax incentives for corporations to close plants in this country and export the jobs offshore. They have provided tax incentives to foreign corporations operating in the United States that they have denied to U.S. businesses. They have provided tax incentives to encourage corporate takeovers and restructurings that eliminate jobs. They have given foreign governments veto power over state tax laws. And they have exempted select corporations from payment of any income tax.

In short, they have taken tax and economic policies that once nurtured the growth of history's largest middle class, and replaced them with policies that are driving the nation toward a two-class society, eroding living standards for most Americans, and causing—for the first time since the Great Depression—a decline in the population sandwiched between the haves and the have-nots.

The people in Washington, as might be expected, would have you believe otherwise. To this end, they have crafted tax laws so complex that only the powerful and the influential can use them to their advantage. At the same time, that complexity enables the defenders of moneyed interests to confuse, mislead, and, when necessary, lie to citizens about the consequences of those laws.

Along the way, the politicians have created one tax myth after another:

- That they are soaking the wealthy.
- That those at the top of the economic pile are paying stiffer taxes than ever before.
- That corporate America is hobbled by an onerous tax load.
- That hefty taxes are discouraging investment and job-creation.
- That high taxes are undermining individual initiative.
- And, finally, that there is a desperate need for shared sacrifice.

Don't believe it.

If you are called upon by lawmakers and policymakers to make a shared sacrifice for the good of the country, you may fairly assume that this means a strengthening of the two tax systems, with comparatively little or no sacrifice for the privileged and yet more for you.

If you are a member of America's shrinking middle class—no matter whether you are a married wage earner, a single parent, an unmarried worker, a small-business owner, or whatever—you may fairly assume that you are paying taxes at a substantially higher rate than your parents or grandparents did—and have less money left over for housing, food, clothing, and other essentials.

If you are among the 91 million individuals and families who earn less than $75,000 a year and derive most of their income from a weekly paycheck, you may fairly assume that you are picking up a disproportionate share of the nation's tax burden.

And if you have just left high school or college to enter the job market, or will do so in the next few years, you may fairly assume that you will pay taxes at a higher rate than those starting out in any preceding generation since the turn of the century.

Nonetheless, the myths persist, fostered by both political parties, each playing to longtime constituencies. Such was the case during debate over President Clinton's budget bill in the summer of 1993. Opponents said the bill would cruelly soak the rich; its supporters said no, it would just make the tax code fair once again.

"The President and my Democrat colleagues are proud, even ecstatic, over the progressivity of [the] tax structure in this bill. . . . It is, in fact, nothing less than the politics of envy," said Rick A. Lazio, Republican representative from New York.[1]

"I make no apology for the fact that we are finally getting the wealthiest 1 percent in this country to pay their fair share for a change, no apology whatsoever," said David R. Obey, Democratic representative from Wisconsin.[2]

In fact, when measured in historical terms, neither was true.

Which might help to explain the rising level of frustration expressed by citizens everywhere. On August 6, 1993, as the Senate prepared to vote on the budget bill, reporters for *CBS Evening News* interviewed people at random on city streets, asking what they thought would happen if the measure was approved. One earnest woman, wearing a pained expression, stared into the camera and said:

"I don't know who to believe any longer."

Indeed.

With those eight words she summed up the feelings of millions of Americans. For today, when it comes to the interwoven issues of the American economy, the budget deficit, and the federal tax system, no one seems trustworthy. Democrat or Republican. Incumbent or challenger. Economist or bureaucrat. Member of Congress or President.

And there are solid reasons for the distrust.

For instance:

In 1986, when Congress passed that year's Tax Reform Act, overhauling the Internal Revenue Code, the Joint Committee on Taxation, the congressional committee that oversees all tax legislation, offered this explanation:

"After extensive review of virtually the entire prior tax statute, Congress concluded that only a thorough reform could assure a fairer, more efficient, and simpler tax system. Congress believed that the act, establishing the Internal Revenue Code of

1986, will restore the trust of the American people in the income tax system and lead the nation's economy into greater productivity."[3]

That "fairer" tax system produced America's most expensive social welfare program ever, measured in dollar benefits received by the average participant. From 1987 to 1991 alone, the cost to the U.S. government totaled more than $150 billion. By the end of 1994, it will top $200 billion.

Where did all the money go? To feed hungry children, perhaps? To create desperately needed middle-class jobs? To build new bridges, highways, or sewer systems? Or, maybe, to provide medical care to the working poor?

Not at all.

The $200 billion represents the federal income tax money that Congress decided to return to the nation's most affluent individuals and families—a tax break for the well-to-do.

How many people benefited from the windfall?

About 150,000 individuals and families with annual incomes over a half-million dollars. That's fewer than one-fifth of 1 percent of all taxpayers. Overall, from 1987 to 1991, they came away with an extra $200,000 a year in newfound spending money, thanks to the Privileged Person's Tax Law.

To understand how the two tax laws work, to understand who benefits from them, to understand why millions of people who are hurt by them are losing their middle-class lifestyles, let's look at two families: one that pays taxes under the Privileged Person's Tax Law; another that pays taxes under the Common Person's Tax Law.

First, the prosperous family: George H. W. Bush and his wife Barbara, the former President and First Lady. The Bushes reported adjusted gross income of $1,324,456 for 1991. They paid $194,594 in federal income tax. Their tax rate: 14.7 percent.

For some comparison, that same year 12.3 million individuals and families filed tax returns on which they reported adjusted gross income of $30,000 to $40,000, and paid income tax. (Median family income that year was $35,939, meaning half of all families earned more, half earned less.) The average tax bill was $3,679, or 10.6 percent of income—4.1 percentage points less than the Bushes paid.

But there is more. Next, add in the Bushes' Social Security tax payments, a maximum of $15,370. This brought their total federal tax payments to $209,964, for a combined tax rate of 15.9 percent.

Again, by way of comparison, families in the median-income range, with earnings between $30,000 and $40,000, paid $2,437 in Social Security taxes, bringing their total federal tax payments to $6,116. That worked out to a combined tax rate of 17.6 percent for the heart of working America.

Thus, the working middle-class family with an income of $35,000 paid federal taxes at a rate 1.7 percentage points higher than President Bush and his wife, whose income was more than $1.3 million.

That's the good news.

The bad news is that those numbers did not include local and state income taxes, or real estate taxes. The Bushes again fared quite nicely. With an income of $1.3 million, they paid $4,312 in state and local income and personal property taxes. That tax rate: three-tenths of 1 percent. The Bushes also paid $24,807 in real estate taxes, bringing their total tax payments—federal income tax, Social Security tax, state and local income tax, personal property tax, and real estate tax—to $239,083.

Their overall tax rate: 18.1 percent.

That's the Privileged Person's Tax Law.

Now the Common Person's Tax Law, as applied to Jacques Cotton and his children.

Cotton, forty-seven, is raising a son and a daughter, Clinton, seven, and Leslie, six, in the small town of Battle Ground, Washington, on the outskirts of Portland, Oregon. A ruddy-faced man with a deep, resonant voice, Cotton represents one of the fastest-growing categories of income tax filers—heads of household.

Most are women, but a growing number are men like Cotton, who are raising children. After he and his wife were divorced, Cotton was granted custody of their son and daughter and has assumed financial and emotional responsibility for rearing them.

Cotton works the night shift at a busy truck terminal—loading and unloading freight coming into or out of the Pacific Northwest. Working nights, he finds himself in a constant struggle to balance the demands of his job with the needs of his children. "Basically, I don't have much choice," he said. "If one of them is sick, I miss work."[4]

On a typical day, Cotton awakens the children at 7:00 A.M. to be dressed, fed, and sent to school. His son rides a bus to a nearby elementary school. Cotton drops his daughter off for a half day of kindergarten classes. Early in the afternoon he picks up Leslie and takes her to the home of a woman who looks after the children while he works. The bus discharges his son at the same home later in the afternoon. Cotton drives to Portland to work the 3:00–11:00 P.M. shift, then returns at midnight to pick up his sleepy children. He puts them to bed and turns in about 2:00 A.M. Five hours later he is up, repeating the process.

Child care is Cotton's largest expense, about $300 to $400 a month per child. "That's the going rate," he said. "That's me taking them to the sitter's home and dropping them off. And this was hard to find because I work nights."[5] Child care costs him more than his rent, which is $425 a month for a modest duplex in Battle Ground, a town of 3,800 north of Portland.

His other major expense is occupational therapy for his son, Clinton, who suffers from a birth defect, which Cotton describes as incorrect development of the nervous system. The problem has affected Clinton's coordination and ability to perform certain common functions. Cotton's employer-paid health plan has paid most, but not all, of Clinton's medical expenses. Some months Clinton's therapy bills range from $200 to $300.

"Money has been tight because of the situation with Clinton," Cotton said. "There are not a lot of doctors who know about this or who have even heard about it, so there are not a lot of therapists who are knowledgeable in this area. So there has been a lot of trial and error and visits to different doctors. That's been a lot of expense."[6] Yet Cotton believes it has been money well spent. His son has worked hard, and Cotton is proud of him. "He's getting better," he said.[7]

In 1992, Cotton earned $33,499. When it came time to fill out his tax return, he did not itemize but, like most Americans, took the standard deduction—$5,250. Personal exemptions for himself and his two children—$6,900—brought his taxable income to $21,349. On that amount, $3,199 in federal income tax was due.

Cotton did have one write-off—a tax credit for part of his child care expenses. The credit is for 20 percent of those expenses, up to a maximum of $2,400 per child. For many families who need child care full time, it covers only a portion of out-of-pocket costs. Cotton is typical.

In 1992, he paid about $8,000 for both children. Because of the ceiling imposed by Congress, Cotton could claim only $2,400 for each child—$4,800 total. Twenty percent of $4,800 gave him a tax credit of $960, which he subtracted from the $3,199 in federal income tax he owed. This brought his federal income tax bill to $2,239.

In addition to federal income tax, he paid $2,562 in Social Security and Medicare taxes. As is true for many middle- and lower-income people today, Cotton's Social Security and Medicare taxes exceeded his federal income tax. On top of his total outlay of $4,801 to the federal government, Cotton paid an additional $1,817 in Oregon state income tax. All told, Cotton paid $6,618 in Social Security tax and federal and state income taxes in 1992.

That was 19.8 percent of his income.

George and Barbara Bush's tax rate, remember, was 18.1 percent.

Thus, the Bushes, whose income was forty times greater than Cotton's, paid taxes at a rate 9 percent below his—courtesy of the Privileged Person's Tax Law.

Actually, the real tax load was even higher on Cotton, the disparity with the Bushes even greater. That's because the figures do not take into account state and federal excise taxes on gasoline, the federal telephone excise tax, sales taxes, and other such taxes, all of which fall more heavily on those in the middle and at the bottom. In Cotton's case, counting them in would boost the tax collectors' take to more than 20 percent.

For Cotton the last few years have been "a real grind," with virtually every penny coming into the house going back in taxes and expenses to keep his household running. Even so, Cotton considers himself more fortunate than many he knows—families who have no health coverage and who earn less money.

"I don't know how some people do it," he said. "Basically, I'm established. I work at a pretty good job. I make more money

than the average person. A single mother making less than me
—how do they get by? I can't imagine the kinds of pressures
that go on inside people's heads."[8]

Squeezing the Middle Class

The pressures abound. And they are unraveling the nation's
social fabric, as the longtime social contract between employer
and employee, citizen and government, is canceled.

Most Americans undoubtedly share a belief that businesses
should be encouraged to do the things that sustain the nation's
economy and its people: to hire American workers, invest in
American plants and equipment, create products that the
United States can export to bring money into the country. Instead, businesses today are rewarded as they eliminate jobs,
substitute minimum-wage or lower-paid workers for those who
once earned middle-income wages, employ part-time rather
than full-time workers, trim or eliminate health care benefits,
slice into pensions and other benefits, and move their manufacturing plants offshore.

The federal government rewards investors who seek short-
term profits at the expense of long-term growth that would
create jobs. It talks of retraining the newly unemployed to fill
high-tech jobs that don't exist. It encourages people to secure
an advanced education to qualify for jobs at companies that are
not hiring or are paying wages that make the degree a poor
economic investment.

Many factors, to be sure, have contributed to America's economic decline—a chronic trade imbalance, a perpetual federal
deficit, a failed educational system, the fraying of the traditional
family. But even if all these problems were resolved overnight,
the nation's tax system, which is so out of balance, would continue to force the nation toward a two-class society.

Just what kind of a system is this?

Very simply, a system that is rigged by members of Congress
and the executive branch. A system that caters to the demands
of special-interest groups at the expense of all Americans. A
system that responds to the appeals of the powerful and influential and ignores the needs of the powerless. A system that

thrives on cutting deals and rewarding the privileged. A system that permits those in office to take care of themselves and their friends.

It was not always this way. To understand just how different it used to be, let's look at four sets of statistics contrasting the 1950s with the 1980s and 1990s. In the 1950s, the tax system was designed to encourage the growth of a broad-based middle class. Which it did. In the 1980s and 1990s, the tax system has been designed to restrict middle-class growth, to force people down the economic ladder, and to keep people at the bottom trapped there.

SQUEEZING THE AMERICAN FAMILY—PART ONE. In the early months of 1954, when individuals and families began filing their tax returns for income received in 1953, they could claim personal exemptions that represented a significant percentage of their income.

Median family income in 1953 was $4,233—meaning that half of all families earned more, half less. The income was earned usually by one working spouse. It was enough to allow families who had never owned a home to buy one, enough to establish a middle-class lifestyle. Millions did just that.

The individual exemption that year was $600. For a family of four, that added up to $2,400. The $2,400, along with itemized or standard deductions, was subtracted from their $4,233 in earnings to determine the amount of income on which they had to pay taxes.

Forty years later, as Americans filed tax returns for 1993, the median family income was an estimated $38,000. The personal exemption was $2,350, so for a family of four, the exemptions totaled $9,400.

That $9,400, along with itemized or standard deductions, was subtracted from their $38,000 in earnings to determine the amount of income on which they had to pay taxes.

Examine carefully the relationship between the numbers in 1954 and 1994. In 1954, the average family's exemptions amounted to 57 percent of its income. That means more than half of the family's income escaped taxation. But in 1994, the average family's exemptions amounted to 25 percent of its income. Only one fourth escaped taxation.

If the 1994 exemption bore the same relation to income as 1954's, it would be worth $5,386. Per person. That would mean that the family of four with an income of $38,000 could deduct $21,544 in exemptions.

The bottom line: A tax cut of nearly $2,000.

SQUEEZING THE AMERICAN FAMILY—PART TWO. In 1953, the Social Security tax rate was 1.5 percent. It applied to only the first $3,600 in wages. This meant that Social Security taxes were withheld from the median-income family's paycheck for forty-five weeks. For seven weeks, the family received its full check. No withholding. The family's effective Social Security tax rate was 1.3 percent. Its total Social Security tax bill: $54.

In the years that followed—and especially in the 1970s and 1980s—Congress played with the numbers. Sometimes it raised the tax rate. Sometimes it raised the amount of income subject to tax. Sometimes it did both.

In 1993, that estimated $38,000 in median family income was earned, for the most part, by two working spouses. The Social Security tax rate was 7.65 percent. But it was applied to $57,600 in wages.

As a result, Social Security taxes were withheld from the median family's paycheck for fifty-two weeks. The family paid the full 7.65 percent rate—all year. Its total taxes: $2,907.

Let's review. From 1953 to 1993, median family income went up 798 percent. But the median family's Social Security tax bill spiraled 5,283 percent. While the 1993 family earned nine times more than the 1953 family, its Social Security taxes were more than fifty times greater.

If income had gone up at the same pace as Social Security taxes, the average family in 1993 would have earned $228,000.

That's $228,000. Or more than $4,000 a week.

SQUEEZING THE AMERICAN FAMILY—PART THREE. In 1954, corporations paid seventy-five cents in taxes for every dollar paid by individuals and families. In 1994, they will pay about twenty cents for every dollar paid by individuals and families.

Here is another way to look at it: In 1954, the national total of corporate income taxes matched the sum paid by individuals in twenty-one states, from New York to California, from Florida to Oregon. The other seventeen are Connecticut, Georgia, Kentucky, Maryland, Massachusetts, Minnesota, Missouri, Nebraska, New Jersey, North Carolina, Ohio, Oklahoma, Pennsylvania, Texas, Virginia, Washington, and Wisconsin.

In 1994, the total taxes paid by corporations nationwide will be less than that paid by individuals and families living in just three of those states—California, Ohio, and New York.

Looked at from still another perspective: If corporations paid taxes in the 1990s at the same rate they did in the 1950s, nearly two thirds of the federal deficit would disappear overnight.

All of this brings us to Tax Rule No. 1: If someone does not pay taxes, or pays less than his or her share, someone else will have to make up the difference. That someone else is you.

Now, keep in mind that so far we have been talking only about the federal tax system.

Next, throw in the tax systems of fifty states and thousands of local governments—from cities to counties, from school districts to townships—and the result is an overall national tax structure that is more hostile to ordinary Americans than any since the Robber Baron era a century ago.

One reason: With few exceptions, state and local taxes hit middle-income and lower-income workers harder than federal taxes. They also are weighted more heavily in favor of the affluent and of some—but not all—businesses than are federal taxes.

Again, consider a sampling of the results of tax policies—this time those of state and local governments.

SQUEEZING THE AMERICAN FAMILY—PART FOUR. In 1953, a median-income family—usually one wage earner—living in Philadelphia paid a wage tax of 1.25 percent. Total tax: $53.

By 1993, the Philadelphia wage tax rate had shot up to 4.96 percent. The median-income family's tax bill from the city—just on wage income—was $1,885. That represented an increase of 3,457 percent. Yes, median income also rose during that period—but only by 798 percent, remember.

Next, add on the Pennsylvania income tax. For 1953, that's easy. There was none. In 1993, the state income tax was 2.8 percent. It applied to virtually all income—wages, interest, dividends. No exemptions. No deductions. The median-income family's state tax bill went from $0 to $1,064.

Now combine just these two taxes, the Philadelphia wage tax and the Pennsylvania income tax, keeping in mind that there are many other taxes—sales taxes, real estate taxes, personal property taxes.

In 1953, a family moving into the middle class paid $53 in Philadelphia wage tax. There was no state income tax. In 1993, a family struggling to remain in the middle class paid $2,949 in Philadelphia wage tax and Pennsylvania income tax.

That worked out to a tax increase of 5,464 percent.

Once more, if the family's income had gone up at the same pace as its city and state taxes, its earnings in 1993 would have been $236,000.

That's $236,000 for the average family.

SQUEEZING THE AMERICAN FAMILY—PART FIVE. At the same time that middle-income and lower-income individuals and families in 1994 are shouldering a far heavier local and state tax burden than did their parents and grandparents, those in the upper-income classes are enjoying some of their lowest tax bills ever. Take, for instance, real estate taxes in California.

Consider first a working-class neighborhood in west Los Angeles. Along a street of modest single-family ranch homes, the real estate tax bill was $3,248 for a typical house with two bedrooms and one bath. For another house with two bedrooms and two baths, it was $3,267.

Now consider the homes in Beverly Hills, where the motion picture stars, the entertainment industry executives, and business leaders live. There, on a street with manicured lawns and gardeners at attention, the real estate tax bill for one multi-million-dollar dwelling—seven bedrooms, seven baths—was $4,743. For another home, with six bedrooms and eight baths, it was $6,664.

What the numbers mean is this: If you are a middle-income family, you may pay nearly as much in real estate taxes as a wealthy family whose home has a market value ten to fifteen times what yours is worth. And in some cases, you may even pay more.

For middle-income folks and the working poor, these are but a few of the consequences of the nation's two tax systems, explaining why you will not fare nearly so well as your parents or grandparents did in their day. In historical terms, more of your income is subject to federal income tax, thanks to smaller personal exemptions. More of your income is subject to a flat Social Security tax, which is bad for you, good for those above you on the income scale. More of your income is subject to largely flat local and state taxes.

What's more, the growing percentage of your money going to federal, state, and local tax collectors is coming out of a shrinking paycheck, when income is adjusted for inflation. In 1992, median family income amounted to $36,812. That was slightly less than thirteen years earlier, in 1979, when median family income was $37,136 in 1992 dollars. And it was up a scant 4.8 percent from twenty years earlier, in 1972, when income was $35,126 in 1992 dollars.

Subsidizing the Haves

The folks who brought you the middle-class squeeze have fashioned quite another tax system for the very wealthy over the last two generations.

In addition to the slash in tax rates that produced an extraordinary windfall for the nation's richest taxpayers, they preserved existing preferences, or arranged new ones, enabling those at the top to further trim their tax bills. For all the talk about ending tax shelters and closing loopholes, Congress has preserved some of the biggest and the best—from the long-standing tax exemption on capital gains at death to the exemption for gifts of appreciated property from stocks to works of art.

While many people in and out of government maintain that taxes are too high overall—that the combined federal, state, and local tax burden is crushing—the real problem is not the size of the burden, but how it is distributed. It is possible to structure a tax system that imposes taxes in such a way that people at the top are left with sufficient money to buy several houses, and everyone in the middle can buy one house. Or it is possible to structure it in such a way that people at the top are left with sufficient income to buy many houses, and a large number of the people in the middle cannot buy one.

In the 1950s, the United States had the former tax system. In the 1990s, it has the latter.

Why? Because Congress effectively jettisoned the progressive income tax—which held that tax rates should rise along with income—and replaced it with comparatively low rates plus a generous mix of preferences, and exceptions, and deductions that are designed to benefit the more affluent individuals and families: the Privileged Person's Tax Law.

Like the deduction for investment interest.

In 1990, the latest year for which these figures are available, 1.7 million individuals and families deducted investment interest expense on their tax returns. The total write-off came to $11.6 billion. That was the interest paid on money borrowed to speculate in gold futures or to buy shares in Wall Street's latest hot investment. In a word, it was the interest paid by people who had enough left over after taking care of food, clothing, shelter, insurance, education, and the like to gamble with a bit of it.

And let's put the number of beneficiaries in perspective. A total of 113.7 million returns were filed that year, including 96.7 million by persons reporting wage and salary income. In other words, fewer than 2 percent of working people profited from the deduction.

Actually, the numbers are even more tilted when they are broken down further. Of the $11.6 billion deducted for investment interest expense, $9.4 billion—or 81 percent of the total —was claimed by 669,000 individuals and families with incomes over $100,000.

The bottom line: Fewer than seven-tenths of 1 percent of working Americans derived any benefit from the deduction. For those at the very top, nearly 32,000 persons with incomes over $1 million, the investment interest expense write-off averaged $115,000.

For some, the write-off can be most advantageous. Consider the deduction claimed by Joe L. Allbritton, a Washington, D.C., banker listed in the *Forbes* magazine directory of the 400 richest

Americans. Born in Mississippi in 1924, Allbritton made his early money in Texas real estate and banking before moving on to Washington in the 1970s.

His holdings over the years have included a life insurance company (California regulators in 1991 ordered him to repay $12 million in improper dividends), a chain of funeral homes and cemeteries (the final resting places of Marilyn Monroe, Natalie Wood, and John Wayne), banks, television stations, newspapers, and horses (Hansel, his three-year-old Thoroughbred, retired in 1991 after winning the Belmont and the Preakness and was sold to Sheik al-Maktoum for something "less than the $12 million" asking price).[9] Allbritton now presides over Riggs National Bank, a Washington financial institution with a rich history—Abraham Lincoln banked there. It sits opposite the U.S. Treasury Building, down the street from the White House.

But the bank has not been doing well of late. It lost $57 million in 1990. It lost $63 million in 1991, and $21 million in 1992. Because of its 1990 loss and the size of Allbritton's salary that year—$1.4 million—*Barrons,* the weekly financial publication, designated him as America's most overpaid banker.

Some years ago, Allbritton described his personal financial situation as "comfortable," rather than "rich rich."[10] *Forbes* calculated that in 1993 he was worth about $300 million. Like many "comfortable" people, Allbritton at times has paid federal income tax below the rate paid by people at the bottom of the middle-income range. His bank, by the way, doesn't pay corporate income tax, since it is losing money. It collects refunds instead. In 1991 and 1992, it picked up a total of $14 million in refunds. That was tax money the bank had paid in earlier years when it was profitable.

As for Allbritton's personal taxes, when he and his wife completed their tax return for 1985, they reported adjusted gross income of $18.3 million. This placed them among the top one-tenth of 1 percent of the 87.2 million working Americans who filed tax returns that year.

Allbritton's investment interest expense deduction totaled $16.4 million. The write-off was so large—90 percent of income —that it reduced the Allbrittons' tax bill to just $179,800, or less than 1 percent of adjusted gross income.[11]

As a result, on the taxpaying scale the Allbrittons came in well below the 24.5 million individuals and families with incomes between $10,000 and $20,000, who paid taxes at a rate of 8 percent.

One other note: That $16.4 million in interest expense? The interest had not been paid entirely in 1985, the year it was deducted. Some of it actually had been paid in 1984. But the tax code limits the amount of the deduction in any given year, and Allbritton had reached that limit for 1984. So he carried over the unused amount to 1985 and wrote it off on that year's return. And because he still had some leftover interest expense, he carried that over to his 1986 tax return.

While the merits of such a deduction are debatable, what is not debatable is that Congress tends to enact preferences that benefit a limited number of persons. Hence, one tax law for the privileged person, another for the common person.

In theory, some preferences can be used by all taxpayers. In practice, it never works out that way. Only a comparatively small number of taxpayers are able to make use of them. Take, for example, another perennial topic, the capital gains tax rates.

Capital gains means the profit you get from selling something for more than you paid for it. What you sell could be stocks, bonds, your house, a painting or other piece of art work, a tract of vacant land. The idea is that this kind of income should be taxed just as wage or salary income is. But some people, especially in Washington, believe that a capital gains dollar is better than a paycheck dollar.

Under the 1993 tax-law changes, the new top rate on ordinary income—wages, tips, salaries—goes to 39.6 percent on the taxable amount over $250,000. But capital gains income will continue to be taxed at the more favorable rate of 28 percent—11.6 percentage points below the top income rate. In certain situations, the maximum capital gains rate is even lower—just 14 percent. Here is how it works:

An investor buys $1 million worth of stock in a new company. Seven years later, it's worth $9 million. The investor sells the stock and collects an $8 million profit. The tax on that income: $1,120,000, for a tax rate of 14 percent. A single professional woman, on the other hand, who earns $40,000 and accumulates money in a savings account, must pay tax at a rate of 28 percent. Different dollar bills; different rates.

Many lawmakers and policymakers believe that the capital gains rate should be further reduced—some would like to see it eliminated entirely. They say that a rate reduction would create jobs and lead to prosperity by fueling entrepreneurial advances, encouraging risk taking, and benefiting the stock market. Everyone, they say, would benefit. But who really does?

You may draw your own conclusions, based on the following statistics compiled from IRS tax data.

For the years from 1989 to 1991, capital gains income averaged $126 billion annually. Of that amount, $87 billion—or 69 percent—went to 1.2 million individuals and families with incomes above $100,000. Among that group, people with incomes above a half-million dollars got the lion's share, $51 billion. At the very top, 40,000 individuals and families with incomes of more than $1 million reported $40 billion in capital gains income in each of the three years.

In short, one twenty-fifth of 1 percent of working Americans collected 32 percent of all capital gains income. And they will benefit most from any further cuts in the tax.

Perhaps the most telling statistic that illustrates the two tax systems: In any given year, 93 percent of all persons filing tax returns receive no capital gains income.

The IRA Flimflam

Every so often, Congress, sometimes by accident, sometimes by default, extends a benefit reserved for the privileged to everyone. It never lasts. A case in point: retirement savings plans.

Before 1981, only workers whose employers did not provide pensions could establish Individual Retirement Accounts (IRAs). They could contribute 15 percent of their earnings, up to a maximum of $1,500 a year, and deduct the money from taxable income. People covered by pension plans where they worked were barred from having an IRA.

Congress, naturally, had provided a more attractive alternative for wealthier professionals—lawyers, physicians, accountants, and others—who could contribute up to 30 percent of their income (in certain situations much more) to a retirement plan called a Keogh account. A lawyer who earned $100,000 could deposit $30,000 in the tax-free account and reduce his taxable income by $30,000.

The professional could set aside 30 percent for retirement; the average worker with no pension, 15 percent. Interest in both accounts accumulated tax-free.

In 1981, after Ronald W. Reagan moved into the White House, he unveiled his first master plan for tax reform. This included a proposal that all workers be allowed to establish IRAs, even those already enrolled in a company pension plan. While many of the President's tax recommendations provoked strong opposition, the universal IRA concept won wide bipartisan support. One after another, lawmakers tossed their own bills into the legislative hopper.

Representative William Frenzel, Minnesota Republican, who introduced an IRA measure with John H. Rousselot, California Republican, and James J. Pickle, Texas Democrat, explained the importance of broadening the retirement program:

"Under current law, many employees are barred from making contributions to an Individual Retirement Account because they are active participants in an employer sponsored pension plan, even though the benefits that they eventually will receive from the plan are very small, or they are not vested in the plan at all. Therefore, these individuals are denied the opportunity to prepare adequately for their retirement by receiving a tax deduction for their contributions to a retirement savings plan." [12]

Treasury Secretary Donald F. Regan concurred. Allowing all workers to establish IRAs, Regan said, would "help the Social Security problem. Remember that Social Security was originally designed as a supplement and we have failed to follow through on the other part of that, that is, have people more self-reliant as far as their pensions are concerned." [13]

Other lawmakers pushed more sweeping changes, urging that IRAs be extended to housewives. "Many homemakers cannot invest in an Individual Retirement Account today," said Paul S. Trible, Jr., Republican representative from Virginia, "because they do not earn any wages. I think that is wrong. Paycheck or not, you and I know how hard homemakers work and how valuable is their work. I believe it is time to recognize the economic value of a homemaker's contribution to society."[14] Over in the Senate, David Durenberger, Minnesota Republican, agreed: "Wives and mothers should not be forced to choose between pension security and raising a family."[15]

With such widespread support among lawmakers in both parties, Congress handily enacted the new retirement law, which permitted any employed person to contribute up to $2,000 a year to an IRA and deduct that amount from taxable income. Wives who devoted their lives to rearing children were still treated as second-class citizens. They were prohibited from establishing an IRA, although their working husbands could increase contributions to a joint IRA by $250 for a maximum annual investment of $2,250.

The carrot of the IRA sent working Americans to their banks by the millions. Their response far exceeded expectations.

The numbers: In 1980, before IRAs were expanded to all workers, 2.6 million people contributed $3.4 billion to IRA accounts. In 1982, when the plan was offered to every worker, the number of contributors soared to 12 million, their contributions to $28.3 billion. From 1982 to 1985, an average of 14.3 million taxpayers set aside $134 billion for retirement. Note that most of the savings belonged to Middle America. Less than 6 percent came from persons with incomes over $100,000.

The Treasury Department was stunned. When the 1981 law was enacted, Congress's Joint Committee on Taxation had estimated that the expanded IRA would cost $3.3 billion in tax revenue in 1984. But the actual loss turned out to be $15.9 billion—a $12.6 billion mistake.

Despite the unanticipated revenue drain, federal officials held fast to the idea of encouraging people to save for retirement. Their attitude stemmed in part from an uneasy feeling that the Social Security system eventually would be unable to pay the promised benefits. As a result, in November 1984, when the Treasury Department issued its historic tax reform plan— the proposal that set the legislative wheels grinding toward the Tax Reform Act of 1986—it called for further expansion of IRAs.

To correct the bias against housewives, the Treasury tax writers recommended that "eligibility for IRAs be extended on equal terms to those who work in the home without pay and to those who work in the labor market."[16] Furthermore, they urged that the maximum contribution be boosted from $2,000 to $2,500 for a single person and to $5,000 for a husband and wife.

The expanded IRA was one of scores of provisions in a massive Treasury proposal intended as a genuine step toward fairness in the tax system. The plan retained the progressive rate structure and closed many blatant loopholes. Naturally, it was doomed. The suggestion that loopholes should be closed while rates remained progressive touched off a frenzied attack by special interests. President Reagan then disavowed many of the recommendations.

In May 1985, Reagan put forth his own reform plan. It was a shadow of the original, but it did retain the Treasury Department's idea of allowing housewives to establish IRAs—although the President suggested that contributions be limited to $2,000 for a single person, $4,000 for a husband and wife. "The existing limitations on IRA contributions," he said, "are illogical and inequitable as applied to married couples."[17]

And then something happened that was seemingly inexplicable.

Quietly, without any public debate, the President, Treasury officials, and many of the same lawmakers who once ardently championed IRAs began backing away from them. Members of Congress who six years earlier had tripped over one another in the rush to make tax-deductible IRAs available to all working people—except housewives—now scrambled to explain why they were unnecessary. In 1981, lawmakers had deemed the IRA crucial to let workers "prepare adequately for their retirement." In 1986, they labeled the same IRA a tax shelter—just like buying into a Santa Gertrudis cattle partnership in Texas or investing in jojoba oil in Costa Rica.

People didn't really need IRAs, the reasoning went. Not only were the tax-free retirement accounts a cheap shelter, but they stifled people's initiative in investing their money. Senator Bob Packwood, the Oregon Republican who coauthored the 1986 tax act, gave a typical argument:

"What I'm going to try to do over and over, whether it's the IRA deduction, whether it's the real estate tax shelters, whether it's the interest deduction on automobiles, what I'm going to try to convince people is that they are better off to have rates as low as possible and then they make the investments they want at a very low tax rate, whether that be in IRAs or automobiles or real estate or grocery stores or duplexes." [18]

When the Tax Reform Act of 1986 was finally signed into law, the tax-deductible IRA disappeared for millions of workers.

Single persons whose employer provided a pension—no matter how small or how secure—lost part of the deduction when their income reached $25,000, and they lost the full deduction at $35,000. Married couples lost part of the deduction when their income reached $40,000, and they lost the full deduction at $50,000. Housewives, naturally, remained second-class citizens and were barred from establishing an IRA.

Why did politicians revoke for most Americans the tax deduction that they had introduced with such fanfare only five years before?

The Joint Committee on Taxation, which has the task of explaining congressional intent on such matters, provided the official reason:

Congress determined that, since 1981, the expanded availability of IRAs had no discernible impact on the level of aggregate personal savings . . .

Further, Congress determined that data had consistently shown that IRA utilization was quite low among lower-income taxpayers who could be the least likely to accumulate significant retirement savings in the absence of a specific tax provision. For example, for the 1984 tax year, only 7.8 percent of returns with adjusted gross income (AGI) under $30,000 (who represent 76 percent of all taxpayers) made IRA contributions, whereas 59 percent of returns with AGI of $50,000 or more made IRA contributions. It was clear to Congress, therefore, that utilization of the IRA deduction increased substantially as income increases. [19]

In other words, the committee said Congress was doing away with IRAs because they were largely a tax write-off for the affluent.

Nothing could have been further from the truth. In 1985,

16.2 million individuals and families claimed a deduction for contributions to an IRA. Of that number, 14.5 million—or 90 percent of the total—had incomes below $75,000. A full 71 percent had incomes below $50,000.

No, the unstated reason Congress canceled IRAs for working persons was to help offset the tax revenue lost by cutting the top rate on the wealthiest from 50 percent to 28 percent. This was, remember, a keystone of Reaganomics.

But what about those other retirement savings plans, the Keogh accounts available to professionals—as well as to members of Congress? After all, those, too, were tax write-offs for retirement—just bigger ones than IRAs. Revised slightly, the Keogh plans remained firmly in place. Once more, IRS statistics tell the story of the two tax systems.

In 1980, the year before Congress enacted the universal IRA, 2.6 million individuals and families, mostly middle-income workers, contributed $3.4 billion to their IRAs. In contrast, 569,000 individuals and families, mostly upper-income professionals and self-employed persons, contributed $2 billion to Keogh accounts. IRA contributions exceeded Keogh contributions by $1.4 billion.

Five years later, in 1985, contributions to IRAs, again largely from middle-income Americans, had soared 1,024 percent, from $3.4 billion to $38.2 billion. Contributions to Keogh accounts also had climbed, although not so sharply, rising 160 percent, from $2 billion to $5.2 billion. Now IRA contributions exceeded Keogh contributions by a whopping $33 billion.

Middle America had had a taste of the Privileged Person's Tax Law and responded accordingly.

Not to worry. Congress recognized the error of its ways. The Tax Reform Act of 1986 would restore the proper balance between the Privileged Person's Tax Law and the Common Person's Tax Law.

From 1985 to 1991, the number of returns showing an IRA deduction plummeted 73 percent, falling from 16.2 million to 4.3 million. Contributions paralleled the decline, plunging 76 percent, from $38.2 billion to $9.2 billion. This was, of course, because millions of Americans were now ineligible to take the deduction they'd so eagerly sought before.

The Keogh statistics, as you might have guessed, were going

in the other direction. The number of returns with Keogh contributions rose 24 percent, from 675,800 to 841,100. Contributions followed the upward trend, climbing 31 percent, from $5.2 billion to $6.8 billion.

Consider what happened to different income groups under the two tax laws between 1985 and 1991:

The number of persons with incomes between $50,000 and $75,000 who claimed an IRA deduction fell 88 percent, dropping from 3 million to 375,000.

At the other end, the number of persons with incomes between $200,000 and $500,000 who contributed to a Keogh account went up 217 percent, from 27,100 to 86,000.

The number of persons with incomes between $40,000 and $50,000 who claimed an IRA deduction fell 78 percent, dropping from 2.6 million to 560,000.

At the other end, the number of persons with incomes between $500,000 and $1 million who contributed to a Keogh account went up 63 percent, from 8,100 to 13,200.

The number of persons with incomes between $30,000 and $40,000 who claimed an IRA deduction fell 75 percent, dropping from 3.2 million to 807,200.

At the other end, the number of persons with incomes of more than $1 million who contributed to a Keogh account went up 135 percent, from 2,000 to 4,700.

Hence, the two tax systems. While Congress curtailed or eliminated the tax-deductible retirement plan for individuals making more than $25,000 and families making more than $40,000, it preserved the tax-deductible retirement plan for the affluent.

But wait, only those persons who work for a company that provides a pension lost their tax-deductible IRA. At least they still will receive a pension when they retire. Right?

Perhaps.

But the sweeping changes in the American workplace, which started in the 1980s with corporate buyouts and will continue through the 1990s and beyond with restructurings attributable to the so-called global economy, make those pensions less certain.

Under the new economic order, as envisioned by both Democrats and Republicans, few persons will ever find lifetime employment with one company and collect the guaranteed pensions those companies once provided. Instead, they will join a nomadic workforce that moves from city to city, from company to company, from occupation to occupation, sort of itinerant electronic-age tinkerers.

Lynn Martin, secretary of labor during the Bush administration, once put it this way: "The days when job security could be guaranteed by a company, a union, or even government are largely over. Today, job security can only be achieved when workers have the willingness and the opportunity to learn and are not discouraged from moving from job to job and career to career."[20]

In the end, the pension may be there. Or it may not.

But there will certainly be a nest egg waiting for the Keogh contributors.

And who might they be? Doctors, dentists, investors, accountants, and writers, among others.

There is yet a third group of retirement plan beneficiaries not counted in either the Keogh or the IRA statistics. They are members of partnerships. Arrangements between two or more persons to share profits and losses, partnerships are engaged in operating all sorts of businesses—farming, manufacturing, wholesale trade, real estate, motels, construction, banking, retail stores, securities and commodities trading. But when it comes to partnership retirement plans, one group stands out above all the others—lawyers.

The law partnership typically establishes a retirement plan and makes contributions on behalf of the individual members. Such is the case at Wachtell, Lipton, Rosen & Katz, the large New York law firm that was at the center of the corporate takeover wars during the 1980s.

In 1986 and 1987, Herbert M. Wachtell, a senior litigator and name partner in the firm, had a total of $500,740 contributed to a tax-deductible retirement plan on his behalf. Remember, that's $500,740 that otherwise would have been part of his taxable income.[21]

Martin Lipton, who developed the legal strategies used to thwart takeovers, had a total of $481,875 contributed to a retirement plan on his behalf. Bernard W. Nussbaum, the firm's other senior litigator, who went on to become counsel to President Clinton, had $345,665 contributed to his retirement plan.[22]

Let us summarize: If you work for a company that promises to pay you a pension, and where you may or may not have a job five years from now, you are barred from making a tax-deductible contribution to a retirement plan. If you are a lawyer (or any other professional), you may make a tax-deductible contribution of a quarter-million dollars or more. Hence, one tax law for the privileged person, another for the common person.

There is a darker side to all this. For in the process of fashioning two tax laws, Congress has successfully fed a mean-spirited antagonism by playing off one individual against another, one family against another. At the heart of the two systems is an overall tax-rate structure that assigns to the same income class people with markedly dissimilar incomes, people confronted with markedly different economic problems.

Think about it.

A family that earns $40,000 a year is not faced with the same obstacles to improving its standard of living as a family that earns $20,000. The family with the larger income has, for example, the option of renting or buying a house. For the family with the smaller income, the only option—except in isolated cases—is to rent. Yet members of Congress consider both families equal, in economic terms, and tax them at the same rate— 15 percent.

A family that earns $100,000 a year is not confronted with the same financial choices as a family that earns $60,000. The family with the larger income may own its home, buy a gilt-edged health insurance policy, and send a child to Harvard University. The family with the smaller income will be compelled to make choices among the three alternatives. Yet members of Congress consider the families equal, in economic terms, and tax them at the same rate—28 percent.

A family in Austin, Texas, with an income of $250,000 is not faced with the same financial uncertainties as a family in New York City with an income of $175,000. Yet members of Congress consider the families equal and tax them at the same rate —36 percent.

A family in Miami with an income of $3 million is not faced

with the same financial decisions as a family in San Francisco with an income of $300,000. Yet members of Congress consider both families equal and tax them at the same rate—39.6 percent.

Tax-Free Millionaires

Then, of course, there are the most favored families of all. They are the people whose income puts them in the top 39.6 percent tax bracket, but who pay taxes well below the rate imposed on middle-income and lower-income working folks. And some pay no tax at all.

For this you can thank Congress, which year after year boasts loudly that it is revoking the tax privileges of the wealthy and will force them to pay higher taxes. You can judge for yourself the truth of the lawmakers' claims, by weighing their words against the results in their never-ending quest to ensure that every affluent person pays income tax. Call it the elusive millionaires' tax.

It all began on January 17, 1969, when Treasury Secretary Joseph Walker Barr marched up to Capitol Hill to sell the tax program of outgoing President Lyndon B. Johnson. Barr, a Harvard-trained economist with a flair for congressional string-pulling, wanted to stir interest in a new way of looking at tax policies—the concept of "tax expenditures," meaning money that would no longer be collected in taxes if Congress enacted a given deduction or write-off.

As part of his sales pitch, he told the lawmakers:

"Our income tax system needs major reforms now, as a matter of importance and urgency. That system essentially depends on an accurate self-assessment by taxpayers. This, in turn, depends on widespread confidence that the tax laws and the tax administration are equitable, and that everyone is paying according to his ability to pay."[23]

He then warned that the country faced the real possibility of a taxpayer revolt. "The middle classes," he said, "are likely to revolt against income taxes not because of the level or amount of the taxes they must pay, but because certain provisions of the tax laws unfairly lighten the burdens of others who can afford to pay."[24]

To illustrate the inequities, Barr pointed to 155 tax returns filed by wealthy Americans for 1966 with incomes above $200,000, "on which no federal income taxes were paid, including 21 with income above $1 million."

Newspapers, magazines, radio, and television seized on the disclosure. "Treasury Secretary Warns of Taxpayer's Revolt," exclaimed the *New York Times*.[25] "Treasury Chief Warns of Taxpayer Revolt," echoed the *Wall Street Journal*.[26] "It now appears that the nation's middle class . . . may be fed up," asserted *Time*, adding:

"What upsets Americans most is the feeling that they are being cheated."[27]

The drumbeat of news accounts about millionaires who paid no taxes fueled official Washington's greatest fear: That large numbers of ordinary individuals and families would lose faith in the system and avoid paying their taxes.

Congress responded with the most extensive overhaul of the Internal Revenue Code since 1954. The centerpiece was a new concept—the minimum tax. Now nobody could get away without paying taxes, the lawmakers bragged. Sure, the affluent had used the existing rules and regulations to escape payment of income taxes—but now Congress would create a second batch of rules and regulations overlaying the first, to ensure that everyone would have to pay something.

To reassure a skeptical public, members of Congress's two tax-writing bodies, the House Ways and Means Committee and the Senate Finance Committee, were loud in voicing displeasure that people with seven-figure incomes were paying no taxes. A report prepared by the Senate committee, then headed by Russell B. Long, Louisiana Democrat, put it this way:

Increasingly in recent years, taxpayers with substantial incomes have found ways of gaining tax advantages from the provisions that were placed in the code primarily to aid limited segments of the economy. In fact, in many cases these taxpayers have found ways to pile one advantage on top of another.

The committee agrees with the House that this is an intolerable situation. It should not have been possible for 154 individuals with adjusted gross incomes of $200,000 or more to pay no federal income tax.[28]

By the time the House and the Senate had worked their will, never again would the rich be excused from paying a penny in federal income tax. Lawmakers said so.

"Million dollar incomes without tax liability will become a thing of the past," said Representative Wilbur D. Mills, Democrat from Arkansas and the chairman of the tax-writing House Ways and Means Committee.[29]

"It was unconscionable that some 155 very wealthy persons paid no tax at all in prior years; the minimum tax and list of tax preferences should foreclose this opportunity," said Representative Ogden R. Reid, Republican from New York.[30]

"I do want to point out that this bill does represent a real accomplishment in three fundamental areas. First, it increases tax equity by substantially closing loopholes that have enabled some citizens to avoid paying their fair share of taxes while imposing unduly heavy burdens on other citizens," said Representative John W. Byrnes, Republican from Wisconsin.[31]

"As to those 155 or so individuals who supposedly had incomes in excess of $200,000 a year but, because they paid no federal income taxes thereon, set this whole matter in motion, it might be noted that most, and possibly all of them, from now on, will have to start paying at least something again in the way of federal income taxes as a result of this bill's passage," said Representative Howard W. Robison, Republican from New York.[32]

When President Richard M. Nixon signed the tax bill into law on December 30, 1969, he, too, assured working folks that everyone would now be required to pay income taxes:

"A large number of high-income persons who have paid little or no federal income taxes will now bear a fairer share of the tax burden through enactment of a minimum income tax comparable to the proposal that I submitted to Congress. . . ."[33]

The "fairer share" turned out to be more of the same—nothing.

In what has become one of those tax miracles so common in Washington, those at the top continued to escape the income tax. In 1974, the number of individuals and families with income over $200,000 who paid no tax stood at 244—up 57 percent from 1966.

So Congress enacted another "tax reform" law aimed in part, once more, at affluent citizens who paid no taxes. If the Tax Reform Act of 1969 was supposed to end the practice by which wealthy people could avoid payment of taxes, the Tax Reform Act of 1976 would really end it.

As Representative Christopher J. Dodd, Connecticut Democrat, explained during House debate in September 1976:

"The conference report also tightens up the minimum income tax provisions substantially, to insure that wealthy individuals will not be able to use tax shelters to get out of paying income taxes entirely." [34]

Over in the Senate, Paul J. Fannin, Arizona Republican, asserted that "actions taken by the conferees will assure that all taxpayers pay a reasonable amount of taxes as a result of curbing tax shelter devices and expanding the minimum tax." [35]

President Gerald R. Ford said so, too, when he signed the measure into law on October 4, 1976:

"This bill raises the minimum tax paid by high-income persons and eliminates or restricts many tax shelters. These actions are consistent with my firm support of measures designed to close the loopholes and ensure that each taxpayer bears his or her fair share of the overall tax burden." [36]

And two months later, the Joint Committee on Taxation emphasized Congress's reasoning for tightening the minimum tax provision:

The minimum tax was enacted in the Tax Reform Act of 1969 in order to make sure that at least some minimum tax was paid on tax preference items, especially in the case of high-income persons who were not paying their fair share of taxes.

However, the previous minimum tax did not adequately accomplish these goals, so the [1976] Act contains a substantial revision of the minimum tax for individuals to achieve this objective. [37]

Nevertheless, the numbers kept going the wrong way. By 1986, the number of high-income persons who paid not a penny in federal income tax had climbed to 659—up 170 percent from 1974 and up 325 percent from 1969, when the first of the tax laws was enacted to prevent such an occurrence.

But 1986 would be different. The tax reform act to end all tax reform acts would guarantee it. As lawmakers rushed to praise their handiwork before voting on the Tax Reform Act of 1986, they spoke passionately of what it would achieve in fairness—how never again would the people at the top be granted immunity from paying taxes.

Listen to their words:

"This bill adopts a tough certain exacting minimum tax. We are not going to see stories about this corporation or this rich fellow or this rich woman earning a major amount of money and paying nothing in taxes. . . . What is at stake here is us demonstrating to the American people that we are willing to take the tough choices, make the tough decisions and give them a tax system that they can count on, that is fair, that will finance this government in the right way," said Representative Byron L. Dorgan, Democrat from North Dakota.[38]

"Ordinary citizens—those people without the use of high-paid lawyers and fancy tax shelters—have had to witness a parade of newspaper headlines heralding the . . . hundreds of millionaires who paid no federal income taxes. This proposal will make that kind of unfairness a thing of the past," said Senator John F. Kerry, Democrat from Massachusetts.[39]

"Madam Speaker, the vote today is for fairness and equity. For decades, the Congress has called for tax reform. This is our chance. We have railed against the abuses of a tax code that allows millionaires and the rich to escape tax-free, while the working men and women of this country pay for everything," said Representative William B. Richardson, Democrat from New Mexico.[40]

"By instituting a tough, inescapable minimum tax, we have assured that no matter what special tax incentives wealthy individuals or profitable corporations use, they will be required to pay a minimum amount of tax," said Senator John H. Chafee, Republican from Rhode Island.[41]

"Fairness is the hallmark of this bill. We have strengthened the minimum tax for corporations and individuals. No longer will we hear about those who escape their tax responsibility.

Taxpayers and corporations alike will pay their fair share," said Representative Frank J. Guarini, Democrat from New Jersey.[42]

"It wasn't too long ago that my constituents were outraged because of news stories that detailed how wealthy individuals and corporations were escaping taxation by cleverly manipulating the law. Under the tax bill, this will no longer take place," said Representative George C. Wortley, Republican from New York.[43]

"It makes me angry that 250 families earned over $1 million last year and paid no taxes. . . . This bill makes sure that does not happen anymore," said Representative Richard A. Gephardt, Democrat from Missouri.[44]

"[This bill] includes a strong minimum tax provision that assures that wealthy individuals and profitable corporations will pay at least some taxes," said Senator Charles McC. Mathias, Jr., Republican from Maryland.[45]

And, finally, one of the two principal authors of the tax bill, Senator Bob Packwood, the Oregon Republican who headed the Senate Finance Committee:

"Every year, the story is printed in the papers—and I paraphrase—844 Americans last year made over $1 million and paid no taxes. That, justifiably, galls the average taxpayer who is making $15,000 a year and paying $1,000 in taxes. This bill closes those loopholes."[46]

It did not.

In 1989, the latest year for which statistics are available, the number of persons with incomes above $200,000 who paid not one penny in federal income taxes crossed the 1,000 mark for the first time, reaching 1,081.

That was up 64 percent from 1986.

Let us summarize:

In 1969, it was disclosed that 155 individuals and families, by employing a variety of perfectly legal tax-avoidance devices put into the Internal Revenue Code by Congress, paid no federal income taxes.

Congress said it would put an immediate halt to this intolerable practice by overhauling the tax code. Congress called its solution the Tax Reform Act of 1969.

It didn't work. Lawmakers, conveniently, left a good many tax preferences intact and created some new ones. As the years went by, the lucky people at the top continued to avoid payment of federal income taxes.

Congress said this was terrible and that it would fine-tune the law and end the preferences. This time, the solution was called the Tax Reform Act of 1976. It didn't work. Lawmakers, conveniently, left a good many preferences intact and created some new ones. As the years went by, the lucky people at the top continued to avoid payment of federal income taxes. Now there were more of them.

Congress said OK, now we'll roll up our sleeves and make the tough decisions to really halt this practice. Congress called this solution the Tax Reform Act of 1986. It didn't work. Lawmakers, conveniently, left a good many preferences intact and created some new ones. As the years went by, the lucky people at the top continued to avoid payment of federal income taxes.

Now there are more of them than when Congress enacted the first "tax reform" bill, or the second, or the third.

Oh, well, you may say—what difference does it make if a thousand or so rich people don't pay income taxes?

A lot. For four reasons.

ONE. At a cost to the economy of untold billions of dollars, Congress has amended, written, and rewritten the tax laws over and over to halt this one practice—without success. Multiply the minimum tax fiasco by the hundreds of other tax issues that lawmakers have dealt with in a similar fashion, and with the same results, and you begin to understand the current state of America's tax system.

TWO. The grandiose claims made by lawmakers each time they rewrote the law reflect one of the most enduring traditions in Washington: Say that you have fixed something even when you know—or certainly should know—that you have not. This practice, perhaps more than any other, is undermining the essential trust between those who govern and the governed.

THREE. As a result of that erosion of trust, coupled with the belief that Congress takes special care of certain taxpayers, a growing number of people are flouting the law. Some play the audit lottery, deliberately filing tax returns with questionable entries in the expectation that they will not be examined. (Only five of every hundred returns with income over $100,000 were audited in 1992.) Some file false returns by failing to report all income, inflating deductions, or claiming deductions to which they are not entitled. And some don't file returns at all—an estimated 7 million in 1992. The estimated loss of tax revenue for 1992: $135 to $150 billion, almost enough to eliminate the deficit.

FOUR. The comparatively few people at the top who pay no taxes are symptomatic of the two-class, two-tax system in which Congress has imposed one tax on the privileged, another on everyone else. The twin systems allow tens of thousands of affluent individuals and families to pay federal income taxes at a rate below that of a middle-class family, and, in some cases, of the working poor.

Once more, look at the numbers drawn from IRS records for 1989:

More than 1,000 individuals and families paid not one dollar in federal income tax that year—this even though their incomes exceeded $200,000. Their effective tax rate: 0 percent. During the same year, 9 million individuals and families with income between $20,000 and $25,000 paid $18.2 billion in income tax. Their average tax bill amounted to $1,983. Their effective tax rate: 8.9 percent.

More than 5,000 individuals and families with incomes over $200,000 paid some federal income tax in 1989—but at an effective rate of less than 5 percent. During that same year, 7.5 million individuals and families with income between $25,000 and $30,000 paid federal income taxes at an effective rate of 10 percent—double the rate levied on the most affluent citizens.

More than 6,000 individuals and families with incomes over $200,000 paid some federal income tax in 1989—but at an effective rate of between 5 and 10 percent. During the same year, 8.6 million individuals and families with income between $40,000 and $50,000 paid federal income taxes at an effective rate of 11.5 percent—from one to several percentage points above the rate levied on the most affluent citizens.

For lawmakers, Democrats and Republicans, the system that has perpetuated the myth that they are soaking the rich continued to work to perfection in 1993 during debate on the budget bill. The airwaves crackled as talk shows on radio and television bristled with angry accusations between groups. Newspapers and magazines fanned the antagonism. A *New York Times* headline on July 23, 1993, was typical:

CONFEREES ON BUDGET AGREE
TO RAISE TAX RATE ON RICH

During an appearance on the *Larry King Live* program on CNN television, Bill Bradley, the Democratic senator from New Jersey, defended President Clinton's budget bill and the decision to make the tax system "more progressive" by raising the top rate from 31 percent to 39.6 percent on families with taxable incomes of more than $250,000.

A caller from Princeton, New Jersey, expressed her frustration:

"I have a two-part question. I wanted to know if you wanted to tax the wealthy, why don't you go for a consumption tax or an asset tax? I live in New Jersey. I work in New York City. Our income is $250,000. By the time you're done with me, I'll be paying 60 percent of my income back. I don't mind paying fair share. But isn't this a little much? With New Jersey tax, New York tax, New York City's tax, state tax, municipal tax, Social Security, I won't have any money to run the economy because I'm being taxed to death. So I say go for the wealthy with an asset tax."[47]

Replied Senator Bradley:

"An asset tax would be unconstitutional at the federal level. You cannot tax property at the federal level. That's why we're left with the income, and the President wanted to have this as a progressive tax and that's what we're going to have. So indeed, if you make more than $250,000 a year you're going to be paying considerably more in taxes."[48]

And there it was, progressivity as defined by a majority of Democrats—if you earn $250,000, you are the same as someone who makes $25 million.

Neither the Princeton woman, nor anyone else, pays overall taxes at a rate even remotely close to 60 percent. Nevertheless, she echoed the views of many taxpayers who resent being lumped with people in other income groups with whom they have nothing in common—neither their economic circumstances nor their lifestyles, and least of all their assets.

A Princeton, New Jersey, family earning $250,000 may be considered "wealthy" by a New Jersey family earning $35,000. But the Princeton family is hardly in the same league as, say, New Jersey's Governor Christine Todd Whitman and her husband, John, of Far Hills, who in 1992 reported adjusted gross income of $3.6 million. The Whitmans, in turn, are not in the same class as Jacqueline Mars Vogel of Bedminster, New Jersey. She's a member of the Mars candy family (Milky Way and M&M's) and, according to *Forbes* magazine estimates, is worth $2.4 billion.

(The Whitmans' combined tax bill, by the way, totaled $1.2 million. Their overall tax rate—local, state, and federal—was 34 percent. The Princeton woman who complained to Larry King and Bradley about paying 60 percent was, like many upper-income taxpayers, grossly exaggerating.)

In any case, playing one group against another is not the exclusive preserve of Democrats. Republicans play the same game, albeit in a slightly different way.

Robert J. Dole, the Kansas Republican and Senate minority leader who directed the opposition to the 1993 Clinton budget bill, was especially critical of the plan to raise the top rate to 39.6 percent. Asked at one point if he thought the rich were paying their fair share of taxes, Dole replied:

"Well, I'd rather use the term 'successful' rather than 'rich,' if I had the preference. I mean a lot of people are insulted by the fact that if you're successful in America, somehow you're an enemy of the state and you have to be leveled off somehow with big taxes." [49]

And there it was—the view of the income tax seemingly held by a majority of Republicans. Anyone who earns $250,000 a year—about 1 percent of 89 million taxpayers in 1991—is "successful." Anyone who holds down two or three jobs to earn $35,000 or $45,000 a year is unsuccessful.

Business as Usual in Washington

So what about the Omnibus Budget Reconciliation Act of 1993—the legislation that Dole and every other Republican voted against because the burden would be too great for those at the top, the legislation that Democrats said would force the richest Americans to pay a fair share of government's costs?

If you think that the budget bill so heatedly debated will improve the fortunes of ordinary working Americans—think again.

If you think the bill will seriously reduce the runaway federal deficits—think again.

If you think the bill will stem the mounting tax burden on middle-class taxpayers—think again.

If you think the bill really socked it to the most affluent citizens—think again.

If you think the bill extracted ever more money from corporations—think again.

If you think things are going to change for the better in the foreseeable future—think again.

In fact, you may reasonably be assured that when it comes to taxes, things will get worse. Two events in 1993, political snapshots in time, offer a window into the tax future. One is the opening of debate over universal health coverage. The other concerned the global economy.

First, health care. Presumably, few people would suggest that medical care should be restricted to those who can pay for it. Yet there is wide disagreement on how to finance coverage for everyone—lawmakers and policymakers will argue the issue through 1994 and possibly into 1995. The one suggestion that keeps recurring, in one form or another, is for an employee contribution system. President Clinton's plan calls for a premium amounting to no more than 3.9 percent of a worker's wages.

In this case, "premium" is a Washington euphemism for "tax." Such premium collections could match corporate tax collections, which totaled $117.5 billion in 1993. A separate bureaucracy outside the IRS would be established to collect the premiums, but that's another matter.

The proposed "premium" has all the attributes of a tax. Payment would be mandatory for everyone with income above 150 percent of the poverty level, or about $22,000 for a family of four. Some people would receive benefits (health care) for which other people paid. And the money would be withheld from weekly paychecks. (Most employers would pay the other 80 percent of the cost of insurance, although small businesses would receive a subsidy.)

As proposed, middle-income workers and businesses in the Northeast would subsidize lower-paid workers and businesses in the South. Also, taxpayers in states that provide more generous health-care benefits to the poor would subsidize those states that provide less. That means middle-income taxpayers in many states would take a second hit, since they account for a disproportionate share of state tax collections.

One group of taxpayers, to be sure, will come out in good shape: the people at the top. If your income from investments totals $2 million, you may have to pick up the full premium, which would work out to about two-tenths of 1 percent of income.

The story is different at the other end of the income scale. If you are a family earning $35,000, the premium you pay could reach 3.9 percent of your income. Now add that to your current Social Security and Medicare taxes of 7.65 percent. Total tax rate: 11.55 percent. That's $11.55 off the top of every $100 in your paycheck, before you get to the federal income tax, and state and local income taxes.

And if you're a self-employed single parent earning $30,000, you would pay both the employee's and employer's share of the insurance. Although you could deduct the premium on your tax return as a business expense, your tax rate would still be about 7 percent. That, once again, is on top of all other taxes.

And since the insurance payments are classified as "premiums," they will not show up in official government statistics that calculate taxes paid by income groups, thereby understating the real burdens on middle and lower-income workers.

Next, the global economy—a term that has come to denote the practice by which American companies make and sell things in other countries while foreign companies make and sell things here, as goods and services move freely from one country to another.

Just as universal health care appears likely to mean higher taxes for the average person, so, too, does the global economy. The reason: As U.S. companies expand abroad, so do their tax payments to foreign governments. And as the taxes they pay abroad go up, the taxes they pay to the U.S. Treasury go down. When corporations don't pay their share of government's costs, you make up the difference.

Vice President Albert Gore provided a glimpse of the future, albeit unwittingly, in November 1993, after he debated Ross Perot on the merits of the North American Free Trade Agreement. Gore left Washington the next morning to dramatize support for the trade pact in appearances before pro-NAFTA audiences around the country. His first stop was near Denver, at Storage Technology Corporation, a company that designs, manufactures, and sells information storage and retrieval systems for computers.

To a crowd of several hundred StorageTek employees waving NAFTA banners in the company cafeteria at Louisville, Colorado, Gore pledged to carry the fight through to victory: "We have the momentum now."

He was right about that. NAFTA passed. But the company the Vice-President chose to showcase as a NAFTA beneficiary does not bode well for you and the taxes you pay. In recent years, StorageTek has closed domestic operations and slashed jobs in the United States, opened plants abroad, benefited from special U.S. tax provisions that encourage companies to shift production jobs to Puerto Rico, and paid more taxes to foreign governments than it does to the United States.

In 1992, for example, Storage Technology, with revenue of $1.5 billion, paid $17.1 million in income taxes to foreign governments, but just $300,000 to the United States, according to reports filed with the U.S. Securities and Exchange Commission. Thus, 98 percent of its tax payments were shipped overseas. In its annual report, the company explained why it was paying so much more in foreign taxes than U.S. taxes:

"The overall effective tax rate was 55% in 1992, compared to 12% in 1991 and 9% in 1990. The increase in the company's effective tax rate is principally due to a shift in the company's taxable earnings from its domestic operations, which are largely sheltered by U.S. federal income tax net operating loss carry-forwards, to the Company's international operations."[50]

In other words, the company paid more taxes in 1992, but only because foreign taxes went up. For previous years it was much the same story, and overall, from 1990 to 1992, the company paid a total of $35.7 million in foreign taxes, but only $9.4 million to the United States.

And StorageTek is likely to continue to pay taxes at a low rate in the United States for some time to come. That's because it will take years for it to use up the net operating loss (NOL) carryforward tax deduction. As of December 25, 1992, the company had $550 million in NOL tax benefits which it could use to reduce its U.S. taxes for years to come.

How did StorageTek get this tax break?

By losing millions of dollars.

After growing rapidly through the 1970s, the company over-extended itself in the 1980s, could not pay its bills, and was forced to seek protection from creditors in U.S. Bankruptcy Court in 1984. When it emerged in 1987, StorageTek was al-lowed to enter on its books hundreds of millions of dollars in losses from the years the company lost money. Which in turn could be used to offset future taxes when the company made a profit. Think of it as a tax break for bad management.

The reorganized StorageTek proceeded to sell assets, slash its workforce, and close a California plant. In Colorado alone, the company's workforce dropped from a high of 9,000 before bankruptcy to 4,500 in 1993.

All this has helped shore up the company's bottom line. But unlike the pre-bankruptcy year of 1979, for example, when it paid $8.8 million in federal taxes, StorageTek now pays very little in U.S. income tax. No wonder the company is optimistic about the future. As StorageTek noted in its 1992 annual re-port: "We are in a unique position to capitalize on changing technologies and markets."[51]

The hotly disputed Omnibus Budget Reconciliation Act of 1993 didn't disturb the tax break that lets StorageTek avoid most U.S. taxes, nor did it interfere with other tax breaks—

such as the virtually unlimited deduction for interest on corporate debt—that have allowed other businesses to escape most or all taxes. But Congress did tend to certain other parts of the tax law, in line with the age-old practice of looking after the needs of privileged constituents.

Especially caring was Daniel P. Moynihan, the New York Democrat who, as chairman of the Senate Finance Committee, helped write and shepherd the budget bill through Congress.

Among the provisions that Moynihan took a personal interest in was restoration of a tax break that had been crimped slightly by the Tax Reform Act of 1986: the charitable deduction of appreciated property. Call it the Moynihan Charitable Amendment for Millionaires.

Like all provisions of the Internal Revenue Code, this one is endlessly complex. But the bottom line is that the 1993 change in the law allows wealthy investors who donate artworks to museums to escape payment of lots and lots of taxes.

Were certain interests lobbying for the provision?

You bet.

The museums that receive the gifts and the people who donate them, like B. Gerald Cantor, a founding partner in the brokerage firm of Cantor, Fitzgerald & Co., Inc., with offices in New York and Beverly Hills. One of the top money-earners in the securities business year in and year out, Cantor placed No. 12 on *Financial World* magazine's 1993 list of the 100 highest-paid people on Wall Street. His income for the year: At least $28 million.

Cantor, who maintains homes on New York's Fifth Avenue and in Beverly Hills, has assembled one of the world's largest private collections of sculptures by Auguste Rodin, the French artist best known for *The Thinker*. Hence the interest in Senator Moynihan's tax-law amendment. Over the years, Cantor and his wife, Iris, have donated Rodin sculptures to various museums, which then named halls and exhibition areas in the couple's honor.

The Metropolitan Museum of Art in New York boasts an Iris and B. Gerald Cantor Exhibition Hall; the Brooklyn Museum has a Cantor Gallery, and Stanford University has the B. Gerald Cantor Rodin Sculpture Garden.

As you might guess, the charitable deduction was of interest to Cantor. Of so much interest that he retained the services of one of Washington's high-powered lobbying firms, Liz Robbins Associates, to lobby on behalf of "tax legislation related to charitable deductions," according to registration reports filed with the clerk of the U.S. House of Representatives.[52]

This is not the first time that Cantor has stood to benefit from a law engineered by Moynihan. And while many other wealthy art collectors will profit from the 1993 change in the law—and museums also lobbied strongly for it—the senator's previous effort benefited Cantor alone. You could call it a sort of designer tax bill. Basically, such tax provisions are crafted to allow some lucky person or business to avoid taxes that everyone else in a similar situation must pay.

Lawmakers go to great lengths to keep beneficiaries' names secret, since they are always wealthy people and influential companies with the right connections. But you can see what such a provision looks like just by visiting your local library. Ask to see the Internal Revenue Code. Turn to Section 543(b), the one that states:

> Special Rules for Broker-Dealers—In the case of a broker-dealer which is part of an affiliated group which files a consolidated Federal income tax return, the common parent of which was incorporated in Nevada on January 27, 1972, the personal holding company income (within the meaning of Section 543 of the Internal Revenue Code of 1986) of such broker-dealer, shall not include any interest received after the date of enactment of this Act with respect to (1) any securities or money market instruments held as inventory, (2) margin accounts, or (3) any financing for a customer secured by securities or money market instruments.

By happy coincidence, Cantor, Fitzgerald & Co., Inc., happened to be the one company in America that met those requirements—it was incorporated in Nevada on January 27, 1972—and thus could escape payment of taxes it otherwise would have been obliged to pay.

While Moynihan arranged for that section to be inserted in the Tax Reform Act of 1986, he limited his remarks during the final day of debate to a sweeping historical assessment of his and Congress's good deeds:

"I simply restate my view that this is not economic legislation, it is not a revenue measure, it is by contrast a profound statement concerning the requirements of citizenship and the ethical basis of the American Republic." [53]

Let's hope not. Because Moynihan's "profound statement" reflecting "the ethical basis of the American Republic" contained, in addition to Cantor's designer tax break, hundreds of other custom-tailored provisions for the affluent and the influential, allowing all to escape payment of billions of dollars in taxes. Which then had to be shouldered by other Americans— just one of the "requirements of citizenship," no doubt.

The man for whom Moynihan provided special tax relief has mined the tax code for his own benefit, and the benefit of his clients, for years.

Cantor has been structuring financial deals to escape payment of taxes since at least the 1950s. In those days, when the top individual tax rate was 91 percent on taxable income over $400,000, Hollywood's top entertainers and other well-to-do types invested in Cantor's tax-avoidance schemes. Danny Kaye and his wife, Sylvia; Doris Day and her husband, Martin Melcher; and Gordon MacRae and his wife, Sheilah, were among the singers, entertainers, and movie stars who took part in Cantor-arranged transactions to cut their taxes.

Cantor's securities firm offered the affluent a variety of tax-cutting packages aimed at reducing the amount of income subject to tax. Many of the transactions existed only on paper. Eventually, the Cantor, Fitzgerald firm attracted the attention of IRS auditors. One by one, Cantor's clients were hit with back tax bills, and when they took their cases to court they often lost. In one instance, the U.S. Tax Court described the interest deductions of a Cantor client this way: "The amount in question represents phantom interest on phantom notes in a phantom short sale." [54] In another case, the court observed: "Each transaction was without substance and reality and was a sham transaction. . . . The principal purpose of each transaction was the creation of deductions for tax purposes." [55]

Cantor himself has also run afoul of the IRS. One of the issues involved charitable deductions for artworks—the deduction of such interest to Senator Moynihan. In 1980, the IRS issued a deficiency notice contending that Cantor and his first wife, who had been divorced in 1976, owed an additional $64,925 in taxes on their 1973 return. Under challenge were portions of two Cantor deductions: a $100,000 write-off for his investment in a failed company that was to produce a motion picture, and $320,225 in charitable contributions.

Of the latter, the IRS told Cantor that "the claimed fair market value of the pieces of art, sculpture, etc. you contributed to charitable institutions was excessive by $84,700. Accordingly, your taxable income is increased by $84,700."[56] Cantor settled the dispute by paying an additional $33,309 in taxes.

The charitable deductions claimed by Cantor and other high-income taxpayers who donate artworks or other gifts of appreciated property—from real estate to stocks—reflect Congress's belief in one of the underlying principles of the two tax laws: that all dollar bills are not created equal and that the people who hold different dollar bills should be taxed differently.

Thus a dollar given to charity is worth more if the donor is an art collector who contributes a painting rather than a carpenter who contributes money. A dollar spent on interest for a loan to speculate in platinum futures is worth more than a dollar spent on interest for a loan to pay for kidney dialysis treatment. A dollar spent for health insurance is worth more if the beneficiary is a corporate executive rather than a self-employed traveling salesperson. A dollar spent on interest payments is worth more for the consumer who buys a yacht than the consumer who buys a college education. The dollar is worth more if it is put into a retirement account by a lawyer than by a housewife.

Similarly, a dollar earned by a speculator in a start-up company must be taxed more lightly than a dollar earned by a sales clerk at a department store. A dollar earned by a foreign corporation doing business in the United States must be taxed more lightly than a dollar earned by the proprietor of a neighborhood grocery store. A dollar earned by a foreign investor who plays the stock market must be taxed more lightly than a dollar earned by a single parent on a passbook savings account. A dollar earned by an investor who buys certain securities must be taxed more lightly than a dollar earned by someone who works with his or her hands.

Different dollar bills.

One tax law for the privileged person.

Another for the common person.

CHAPTER 2

★ $ ★ $ ★

THE TAX WAR YOU LOST

The Great Rate War

When Ronald Reagan was a Hollywood actor in the 1950s, he testified before Congress that high tax rates were confiscatory and thwarted movie production. At the time, the maximum rate was 91 percent on taxable income over $400,000. Asked by one lawmaker if he would consider 50 percent to be a more appropriate rate, Reagan, who was representing the Motion Picture Industry Council and the Hollywood AFL Film Council, replied:

"I can tell you that as far as I am concerned, you have chosen a good figure. If I could keep 50 cents on the dollar I earned, I would be too busy in Hollywood to be here today." [1]

Twenty-three years later, when Reagan was President, and the top rate was the 50 percent that he once termed "a good figure," he complained that it was killing American initiative and needed to be much lower. In his inaugural address on January 20, 1981, the new President declared:

"Those who do work are denied a fair return for their labor by a tax system which penalizes successful achievement and keeps us from maintaining full productivity." [2]

The two Ronald Reagans, separated by nearly a quarter century, sum up the most enduring struggle over the federal income tax:

Whatever the rate imposed at the top, it is too high for some of the people who pay it.

So it was when William Bourke Cockran, Democratic repre-

sentative from New York, took to the House floor to denounce
a pending income tax amendment:

> If the time should ever come when, in order to secure the
> enjoyment of property to its owners, it will be necessary to
> treat prosperity as a crime and to punish the rich by an abuse
> of the power of taxation, then the safety of this Republic will
> be endangered, its prosperity will be shattered, its glory will
> be dimmed, its days will be numbered . . .
>   The men who offer this amendment as a sop to the discon-
> tented will be swept away by the rising tide of socialism. They
> will discover, when too late, that in overturning the barriers
> which separate liberty from anarchy they have liberated ten
> thousand furies who will sweep over them and overwhelm
> them in a mad procession of anarchy and disorder.[3]

The time was exactly one hundred years ago—1894.

The proposed income tax rate that so agitated Cockran and
others: 2 percent.

It was to be levied only on incomes over $4,000, meaning that
it would be paid by about 1 percent of the population—people
like John D. Rockefeller, Andrew Carnegie, and J. P. Morgan.

Although Congress enacted the tax, the U.S. Supreme Court
agreed with Cockran and declared it unconstitutional. Justice
Stephen J. Field labeled it an "assault upon capital" and said it
would lead to "a war of the poor against the rich, a war con-
stantly growing in intensity and bitterness."[4] What's more, he
said, such a tax would reduce the salaries of judges in violation
of the Constitution. It took nearly twenty years and a constitutional amendment before the income tax became a permanent
fixture of U.S. government finances.

Much has changed since 1894—and much has not.

To understand why and how today's tax system has been
skewed heavily in favor of the privileged, why Congress has
created a system that pits one group of Americans against another, and why the middle class long ago lost a war it never
knew it was in, it is first necessary to understand the origin of
the progressive income tax—a tax built on the belief that as
income rises, so, too, should the rate at which it is taxed.

Vested interests have been fighting over tax rates for more

than a century. Those at the top, for whom rates are never low enough, have developed a litany of economic myths to try to keep them down. Whatever the top rate may be, they say that it stifles economic growth, kills initiative, discourages risk taking, curbs productivity, chokes investment, and inhibits savings.

It hasn't mattered whether the maximum tax rate was 91 percent on taxable income over $400,000, as it was in the 1950s; or 73 percent on taxable income over $1 million, as it was in the early 1920s; or 50 percent on taxable income over $106,000, as it was in the early 1980s; or 39.6 percent on taxable income over $250,000, as it is in the 1990s. The rates are always considered by some to be too high.

The rate battle goes back to enactment of the income tax in 1913. The tax owes its existence to neither major political party but rather to the populist and progressive third-party movement that flourished at the turn of the century, a time of sweeping social and economic change. Critics challenged the unbridled power of the business trusts, which controlled everything from beef to oil, from sugar to lead. Muckrakers exposed greed and corruption in powerful monopolies and political machines. Progressive societies sprouted everywhere. Consumer leagues, child labor committees, charitable societies, church organizations, and women's clubs focused national attention on social ills.

City slums were so overcrowded that the population density of some New York City neighborhoods exceeded that of Bombay, India. Unsafe and unhealthy conditions were commonplace in factories where women worked "for ten hours on five nights of each week, from 7 P.M. to 5:30 A.M., with a break of half an hour at midnight"—a crushing workload, but fewer hours than those worked by women in canneries, who put in ninety to a hundred hours a week. Sweatshops and tenement employment flourished with child labor—"one little girl of nine said she had to work in the daytime and had no time to play, but that sometimes she was allowed to go out at night 'to save the gas.' "[5] Amid all the poverty, an exponential growth in wealth was concentrated in the hands of a few. The rich were getting richer, and everyone else was falling behind.

Given the widening chasm between classes, the reformers found a receptive audience. Because the federal government derived most of its revenue from tariffs and excise taxes, poor and low-income families were saddled with a disproportionate share of the burden. The House Ways and Means Committee described America's tax policy this way:

> The amount each citizen contributes is governed, not by his ability to pay tax, but by his consumption of the articles taxed. It requires as many yards of cloth to clothe, and as many ounces of food to sustain, the day laborer, as the largest holder of invested wealth; yet each pays into the Federal Treasury a like amount of taxes upon the food he eats, while the former at present pays a larger rate of tax upon his cheap suit of woolen clothing than the latter upon his costly suit. The result is the poorer classes bear the chief burden of our customhouse taxation.[6]

Thus, the income tax was born, signed into law by President Woodrow Wilson on October 3, 1913. It was a far cry from the income tax we know today. To begin with, few had to pay it— less than 2 percent of the population. The law set rates from 1 percent on taxable income up to $20,000 to 7 percent on income above $500,000. It exempted the first $3,000 earned by a single person and $4,000 earned by a married couple. Since the overwhelming majority of Americans supported families on less than $1,000 a year, they were spared payment of any income tax. (The $4,000 exclusion, by the way, would translate into a $58,000 exemption in 1993 dollars. If you earned less than $58,000, you would not have to file a tax return. If you earned more, you would pay tax only on the amount over $58,000.)

When the United States entered World War I, in 1917, Congress sharply increased rates and broadened the base to pay for the war. The Revenue Act of 1917 reduced exemptions and established twenty graduated rates rising from 2 percent, levied on taxable income up to $2,000, to 67 percent on all income over $2 million. The maximum rate was up from 15 percent the year before. The act also imposed an excess profits tax on individuals and businesses.

Because of the lower threshold at which the income tax kicked in, the number of returns jumped from 437,000 in 1916 to 4.4 million in 1918. Even so, 95 percent of the population still paid no income tax. If there was any doubt about the tax's ability to generate revenue from the wealthy, the 1917 legislation put that to rest. The larger tax base and higher rates brought in more revenue in 1918 than the government had collected from all sources in any one year before the income tax was enacted.

After the war's end, in November 1918, individual taxpayers and corporations expected rates to fall. They didn't. The war had been costly in economic as well as human terms. By 1919, the nation's debt stood at a record $25 billion, up from $1 million in 1916. To reduce the debt, Congress continued the high rates. Among taxpayers—still limited to the nation's most affluent citizens—disappointment gave way to resentment.

The man who would crystallize opposition to what he viewed as oppressive tax rates, lead the campaign against them, and develop the philosophy that opponents have kept alive to this day was Andrew W. Mellon, the Pittsburgh industrialist, who sat on the boards of nearly sixty corporations and who had amassed one of the half-dozen largest fortunes in the nation. So effective was his leadership that even today, when lawmakers and other officials debate tax policy they often sound as if they are reading Andrew Mellon's speeches.

The First Great Rate War began in March 1921, when Mellon, then little known outside of Pittsburgh, took over as secretary of the Treasury. Mellon had been recommended for the job by Harry M. Daugherty, the manager of Warren G. Harding's 1920 presidential campaign. When Daugherty suggested Mellon to Harding, the new president replied:

"Mellon . . . Mellon. I don't know him."[7]

Within months, everyone would.

Mellon was obsessed with tax rates. So were his business associates and his friends, who had to pay taxes. One month after taking office, he set the single-minded goal of cutting rates. Mellon had accumulated his fortune during the years when there was no individual income tax and a small corporate income tax, or none at all. He preferred to return to those days when the government derived most of its revenue from tariffs and excise taxes. But if there had to be an income tax, Mellon's idea of an appropriate rate dated back two thousand years.

"It is not too much to hope," he said, "that some day we may get back on a tax basis of 10 percent, the old Hebrew tithe, which was always considered a fairly heavy tax."[8] Much as he would have liked a flat tax of 10 percent, Mellon was a realist. He knew it was unacceptable politically. So he settled for a plan with top rates ranging from 15 percent at the bottom to 25 percent at the top. (Notice that the 1986 tax writers virtually copied the Mellon plan, setting the bottom rate at 15 percent and the top rate at 28 percent.)

To sell his tax cuts in the days before television, when radio was still in its infancy, Mellon came up with what would be described today as sound bites. They were pithy statements rooted in a little bit of truth, a lot of distortion, and some fiction. They have survived down through the years.

It was Andrew Mellon, in 1924, who suggested that lower rates produce more revenue: "It seems difficult for some to understand that high rates of taxation do not necessarily mean large revenue to the government, and that more revenue may often be obtained by lower rates."[9]

Half a century later, in 1979, Jack Kemp, then Republican representative from New York and a driving force behind the 1980s tax cuts, repeated the theme: "The idea that lower marginal tax rates can produce higher tax revenues seems too good to be true to some people. It seems to promise something for nothing. Indeed, the whole line of reasoning is not readily accepted, or even fully understood, by the older economics establishment of either political party."[10]

It was Andrew Mellon, in 1924, who argued that if rates were too high, wealthy people would avoid paying taxes: ". . . since the close of the war people have come to look upon [high taxes] as a business expense and have treated them accordingly by avoiding payment as much as possible. The history of taxation shows that taxes which are inherently excessive are not paid."[11]

More than sixty years later, during debate on the Tax Reform Act of 1986, Robert J. Dole, Republican senator from Kansas, sounded eerily like Mellon: "Some members [of Congress] contend that higher tax rates are the only way to tax the well-to-do. But that argument already has been proven wrong. Chairman Packwood has made the point time and time again in this debate —high tax rates are an illusion because everyone with any skill at financial planning finds a way to avoid them."[12]

It was Andrew Mellon, in 1924, who maintained that rates were destroying business initiative: "Anyone at all in touch with affairs knows of his own knowledge of buildings which have not been built, of businesses which have not been started, and of new projects which have been abandoned, all for the one reason —high surtaxes." [13]

Years later, Ronald Reagan said motion pictures were not being made because of high rates: "The [motion picture] producer, faced with the risk of no return on his investment, seeks to minimize the gamble by featuring one of those artists of proven box office value. The artist in a 75 to 91 percent tax bracket raises his price because the only way he can keep a dime is to make a dollar. Or, if he has done his one or two pictures, he turns down the picture entirely. The result is unemployment in our industry." [14]

It was Andrew Mellon, in 1924, who complained that the income tax was part of a socialist-communist conspiracy: "Taxation should not be used as a field for socialistic experiment, or as a club to punish success." [15]

Which sounded like Ronald Reagan in 1961: "We have received this progressive tax direct from Karl Marx, who designed it as the prime essential of a socialist state. . . . There can be no moral justification of the progressive tax." [16]

While Mellon talked about helping the poor and the middle class, and about the need to encourage economic growth—as would others years later—there was but one objective: dramatically reducing taxes on the rich.

Tax Reform for the Wealthy

Although Republicans controlled Congress, Mellon had only limited success after he took over Treasury in 1921. Republicans were more interested in revising tariffs than in rewriting the income tax law. Still, in that year, they slimmed the maximum individual rate from 73 percent to 56 percent—far short of Mellon's goal, but a beginning.

Meanwhile, Mellon, once a near recluse in Pittsburgh, developed into a master manipulator of public opinion. With a big assist from the nation's largest newspapers, which championed lowering rates for the wealthy—another pattern that would be repeated decades later—he gradually built a base of support for his plan.

When Calvin Coolidge succeeded Harding, who died in 1923, he embraced Mellon's theories and campaigned for reelection on them in 1924. As for Mellon, he came up with a new strategy to enlist support for his cause—a more lofty motive than merely reducing taxes. The real problem, he said, "is not so much one of tax reduction as of tax reform." [17]

This was one of the first times—if not the very first—that the phrase "tax reform" was used to justify a tax cut for the affluent. It would not be the last. Other secretaries of the Treasury, other Presidents, other lawmakers, would adopt the same tactic, especially in the 1970s and 1980s. Over time, much of the debate concerning tax rates would boil down to two phrases. Tax legislation that would increase the rate on the wealthy was called "class warfare." Tax legislation that would reduce the rate on the wealthy was called "tax reform."

Once again, Congress responded, this time shaving the maximum rate from 56 percent to 46 percent. In three years, Mellon had engineered a rate cut from 73 percent to 46 percent.

Still, more work remained. He continued his one-man lobbying effort through 1924 and 1925, emphasizing the importance of cutting taxes for the rich to create jobs for the poor. It was the Roaring Twenties version of the supply-side economics of the 1980s. "A reduction in the surtax," Mellon declared, "increases the amount of capital which is put into productive enterprises, stimulates business, and makes more certain that there will be more $5,000 jobs to go around. . . . What we mean by tax reform is to make more of these jobs." [18]

Mellon collected his thoughts on taxes and the need for lower rates in a little book called *Taxation: The People's Business*. Lobbying organizations, like the American Bankers League, distributed thousands of copies to businessmen. They responded predictably. Albert H. Wiggin, president of Chase National Bank in New York, wrote Mellon:

"We were fortunate in seeing an advance copy of your [book], and were so enthusiastic over it that we could not resist the impulse to distribute quite a large number of copies to customers and friends of the Chase National Bank. The men to whom copies of your book were sent included presidents and other officials of larger banking institutions throughout the country, treasurers of important business concerns, stockholders of this bank and many other influential and intelligent men among our clientele." [19]

Mellon had carefully targeted his audience, focusing on persons who could exert influence on the legislative process. When an admirer suggested distributing one million copies to the public at large, he rejected the idea, saying that "the subject is one which might not appeal to the ordinary working man, and I am not certain that there would be any real demand for the book from this class of readers." [20] Weighty matters like taxation, Mellon believed, were beyond the understanding of the average person.

Mellon's persistence paid off. On February 26, 1926, President Coolidge signed the Revenue Act of 1926. As congressional leaders and other government officials looked on, news accounts noted that "Secretary Mellon appeared to be the happiest man in the group. He smiled continually while the movie and news camera men were busy in catching the scene for presentation to the world on the screen and in newspapers." [21]

And smile he should. The legislation, sold as "tax reform," slashed the maximum individual rate from 46 percent to 25 percent on all taxable income above $100,000. It cut the maximum estate tax from 40 percent to 20 percent on estates of more than $10 million. It abolished gift taxes. At the other end of the income scale, the reform legislation nudged down the bottom rate from 2 percent to 1.5 percent on the first $4,000 of taxable income.

America's wealthiest citizens profited handsomely. J. P. Morgan, the financier who frequently complained about high taxes, saved a quarter-million dollars. Mellon himself saved more than $800,000. Henry Ford saved $1.1 million. John D. Rockefeller, Jr., saved $2.8 million, thus acquiring an extra $54,000 a week in spending money.

All seemed to be going according to Mellon's grand scheme. More than $1 billion gushed from Washington in refunds and rebates. Additional millions flowed out of the tax cuts. For a tiny segment of the population, lower taxes had created unparalleled abundance. The number of persons who filed returns with incomes of more than $1 million spiraled from 33 in 1920 to 511 in 1928—a 1,448 percent increase. The ranks of the near rich also swelled. The number of persons with returns showing incomes between $100,000 and $1 million rose from 3,616 in 1920 to 15,466 in 1928—a 328 percent increase.

But something was amiss. The money was not trickling down as predicted. The $5,000 jobs were not materializing as Mellon had promised. The number of persons reporting incomes under $10,000 went down, plummeting from 7 million in 1920 to 3.7 million in 1928—a 47 percent decline. Part of the falloff could be attributed to increased exemptions. Yet those numbers should have been offset by a rising level of prosperity—if the trickle-down theory had any merit. It didn't.

Instead, Mellon's tax cuts pumped too much money into too few hands. That money, in turn, fueled a frenzied speculation in the stock market. Wall Street loved it. Bankers, brokers, and businessmen formed pools. They sold securities among themselves, forcing prices up, and then unloaded the stocks at inflated values.

It all ended in the great Wall Street crash, followed by the Great Depression. With America sinking deeper, Mellon set sail for Europe as ambassador to Great Britain—and to escape a looming congressional impeachment inquiry on an array of charges. Among them: Mellon-owned companies received millions of dollars in tax refunds while he was Treasury secretary. And his Pittsburgh bank peddled bonds for $98 that turned out to be worth pennies.

Reality had discredited Mellon's theory of low rates. The businesses that Mellon had said were crippled by high rates and required significant relief to invest in new plants and equipment did *not*. The wealthy who Mellon had said urgently required a substantial tax reduction to invest in productive businesses did *not*. The benefits of the tax cuts that Mellon said would funnel down the income scale to office and factory workers did *not*. The Depression that Mellon said would run its course did *not*.

With factories silent and more than 12 million Americans unemployed, tax rates were raised once again. The top bracket went back up to 63 percent in 1932, to 79 percent in 1936. Individual income tax revenue rebounded sharply, rising to $1.1 billion in 1937, the third-highest collection in history. The returns offered convincing evidence, again, that higher rates produced higher revenue, even when the country was gripped by a Depression.

Birth of Withholding

Soon everyone, not just the affluent, would be concerned about rates. For the tax system Americans know today was created in World War II, when the income tax was transformed from one that applied only to the affluent to one that touched virtually every working person. In World War I, well-to-do individuals and corporations picked up a large share of the cost. World War II would require taxes from most everyone.

With passage of legislation in 1940, 1941, 1942, and 1943, the bottom tax bracket was cut in half, from $4,000 to $2,000. The personal exemption for married couples was sliced from $2,500 to $1,200. The bottom rate shot up from 4 percent to 19 percent. The maximum rate was kicked up to 81 percent and then 88 percent. The income level at which that top rate kicked in was cut from $5 million to $200,000.

For most Americans, the greatest change came in 1943, when withholding was instituted. Never again would the average worker receive a full paycheck. The number of individual returns filed soared from 4 million in 1939 to 40 million in 1943. On the revenue side, income tax collections spiraled from $1 billion in 1939 to $19.7 billion in 1944—a 1,870 percent increase.

It was the largest tax increase in American history. You may have thought that the 1993 budget bill was the largest, given the debates in Congress and all the media attention growing out of those debates. Remember the rhetoric?

"The Democrat plan imposes the largest tax increase in American history," said Jim Ramstad, Republican representative from Minnesota.[22] "The president is proposing the largest tax increase in history," said Dan Miller, Republican representative from Florida.[23] "This legislation will impose the largest tax increase in history," said Jack Kingston, Republican representative from Georgia.[24] "This is the largest tax increase in the history of this country," said Craig Thomas, Republican representative from Wyoming.[25]

It wasn't even close.

In the five years from 1939 to 1944, overall general fund revenue from individual and corporate income taxes, excise taxes, and other levies shot up from $4.8 billion to $40.5 billion —a 744 percent increase.

To put that in perspective, in 1992 general fund revenue totaled $657 billion. If all taxes were raised at the same rate as the 1939–44 years, government revenue would total $5.5 trillion in 1997. That's trillion. In one year. Enough money to eliminate, not deficits, but the entire national debt in a single year. By that yardstick, the 1993 tax increase was historically insignificant.

In any event, with World War II raging, with 12 million American men and women deployed around the world, with a U.S. war-related death toll heading toward 300,000, a few people were still concerned about the top tax rate. Among them were Thomas W. Phillips, Jr., a Pennsylvania oil and gas operator who was active in state Republican circles and who had served in Congress during the Mellon years, and Frank E. Gannett, the owner of a string of New York newspapers that today is Gannett Co., Inc., publisher of *USA Today* and more than eighty newspapers.

Hoping to duplicate Mellon's achievement—but make it permanent—Phillips, Gannett, and their allies sought to persuade state legislatures to petition Congress for a constitutional convention. Their goal was a constitutional amendment that would forever limit the top tax rate to 25 percent. During the war years, they signed up fourteen states.

They owed their early success to two factors—the country's preoccupation with the war, and secrecy. Although Gannett was a newspaper publisher, the amendment proposal received scant publicity. Resolutions were introduced near the end of a legislative session, when it was too late to hold public hearings, and the interest of both legislators and the news media waned.

By the early 1950s, the amendment drive stalled as government officials and prominent citizens denounced the idea. One of the leading tax authorities of the time, Erwin N. Griswold, dean of the Harvard University Law School, was especially critical:

"It is very clear that the benefits of such a change would redound to the relatively rich, and the burdens would have to be borne by the relatively poor. Not only would the change in effect eliminate progressive income and estate taxation . . . but it would confer the financial benefits almost exclusively on persons of very large incomes." [26]

Representative Wright Patman, the Texas Democrat who pursued Mellon with the threat of impeachment until he took off for Great Britain, and who was among the first to call attention to the amendment drive, said that any ceiling "restricts the tax on the rich only, without any limitation on the middle-income groups or on the poor. This will result in two classes—the very rich and the very poor." [27] Two congressional committees reached similar conclusions. The Treasury Department, which under Mellon had enthusiastically endorsed low rates, now strongly opposed them.

The shift in sentiment in Washington benefited the country. From the end of the war through the 1950s and into the 1960s, the ranks of Middle America swelled as never before. Even the definition of middle class changed. At the turn of the century, membership was confined to teachers, shopkeepers, doctors, lawyers and other professionals. By the 1950s, it had grown to include everyone from steelworkers in Levittown, Pennsylvania, to autoworkers in Detroit.

Over the course of two decades—from 1940 to 1960—the changes were evident in virtually every aspect of American life. The percentage of owner-occupied homes surged from 44 percent to 62 percent. Automobile registrations more than doubled, from 27 million to 62 million. The number of households with telephones more than doubled, from 37 percent to 78 percent. The number of college degrees awarded more than doubled, from 217,000 to 477,000. All this at a time when population rose just 36 percent, from 133 million to 181 million. During these same years, average family income, produced largely by one wage earner, far outstripped inflation. And taxes were comparatively low.

Except at the top. Throughout the 1950s and into the early 1960s, the maximum tax rate was 91 percent. It applied to all taxable income over $400,000. While no one paid an overall rate even approaching that figure, wealthy individuals and families did see a substantial portion of their income go to taxes. In 1951, for example, persons with million-dollar-plus incomes paid, on average, more than $1.2 million in income tax. In 1991, those with million-dollar-plus incomes paid half as much —$629,000.

The tax system, to be sure, was but one of the factors contributing to the growth of history's first broad-based middle class. Mortgage programs of the Federal Housing Administration and the Veterans Administration encouraged home ownership. The GI Bill enabled millions to go to college. The interstate highway program created jobs and opened a new era of transportation and mobility. Factories provided jobs that paid middle-class wages. Growing consumer demand led to ever more jobs. And because Europe and Japan were still rebuilding from the war, the nation had little competition.

Nonetheless, the progressive income tax played a critical role. If the tax system had been comparable to one in place in the 1920s, or in the 1980s and 1990s, the middle-class expansion never would have occurred on the scale that it did.

Throughout the 1950s and early 1960s, there was no broad public support for rewriting the tax laws. And with good reason. Most people were doing reasonably well. (Obviously, one glaring gap was the failure to include blacks in the upward movement. Soon after opportunities were opened to blacks in the 1970s and 1980s, the membership doors of Middle America began to swing closed—for both blacks and whites.) Still, there was discontent among some in the upper brackets. A collection of economists and politicians talked about the gross national product and savings rates and productivity and the need for more investment capital. They mounted the argument that the statistics would look better if tax rates were substantially lowered.

From this group, a most unlikely tax-cutter emerged. He was not a conservative Republican, in the mold of Mellon, but a liberal Democrat—John F. Kennedy. Within three months of taking office in 1961, Kennedy sent an urgent message to Congress:

"I am directing the secretary of the Treasury, building on recent tax studies of the Congress, to undertake the research and preparation of a comprehensive tax reform program to be placed before the next session of the Congress."[28]

There it was again—the phrase "tax reform" used to promote

a tax cut for the affluent. The major sections of the Kennedy tax reform plan were not implemented until 1964. But the legislation enacted that year—which cut the top rate from 91 percent to 70 percent—paved the way for sweeping tax changes through the 1980s.

The new law not only dropped the maximum rate from 91 to 70 percent; it also cut the top tax bracket in half. Under the old law, the 91 percent rate took effect after taxable income exceeded $400,000. Under the new law, the 70 percent rate began at $200,000.

The importance of the Kennedy tax-law change would be little noticed at the time. But it was basically a new way of manipulating the tax system. Once the lawmakers, policymakers, and lobbyists had seen the possibilities, they were more than eager to use it again and again. The result: Over the next twenty years, Congress would enact tax law after tax law that gutted the progressive structure of American taxes while throwing the doors of the U.S. treasury open to those who could pay for access.

Although it may have been unintended, the Kennedy tax philosophy ushered in a new era. Previously, the emphasis in tax debate had been on rates; now tax partisans could focus on the amount of income subject to taxation, the other half of the income tax equation. The original proposal had been to lower rates slightly while at the same time making more income taxable; that way revenue would not be lost. But what happened was the opposite. The rates were lowered—and then new loopholes were opened for the wealthy, new ways were found to exploit existing ones. The amount of income placed off-limits —not subject to tax at any rate—skyrocketed. And then the rates were lowered some more.

This permitted future Presidents and lawmakers to argue that because ever more income was escaping taxation due to tax breaks granted by other Presidents and lawmakers, the rates had to be further eased. The process began in earnest in January 1981.

Sixty years after Mellon, President Reagan set out to turn back the clock. Rather than eliminate all shelters and write-offs, Reagan and a seemingly unlikely group of Democratic allies— among them Senator Bill Bradley of New Jersey and Representative Richard A. Gephardt of Missouri—concentrated on reducing rates. At the time, the maximum rate was 70 percent on income over $212,000.*

That first year, the top rate was lowered to 50 percent. Like Mellon, the new generation of "tax reformers" was unsatisfied. Democrats and Republicans alike wanted to bring back the 1920s. There was but one nagging obstacle. Unlike the 1920s, everyone now paid income tax. One public opinion poll after another found a broad-based support for progressive rates. Americans were decidedly opposed to rate reduction.

A survey by the Roper Organization, Inc., a public opinion polling firm, showed an overwhelming commitment to the progressive tax system. Those queried opposed reducing the number of brackets—then more than a dozen—and rejected even a maximum tax of 35 percent as being too low, let alone the 28 percent under consideration.

"We find absolutely no support among the public," the Roper study said, "for such drastic reductions in the top tax bracket. To the contrary, a whopping two-thirds of the public say it is a 'bad idea' to lower the maximum rate even to 35 percent."[29]

Capitol Hill Magic Show

So how do you sell something that most taxpayers don't want, indeed that they realize will not be in their best interest? Simple. You resort to a time-honored tradition in the nation's capital. Call it the Capitol Hill Magic Show.

To understand the way Congress goes about enacting tax legislation, in particular tax laws that most taxpayers oppose, you might want to think of lawmakers as legislative magicians—members of the Capitol of Magic, who can reach into a bag of inexhaustible tricks and with a little sleight of hand enact tax legislation that looks as if it will do one thing but does quite another.

Although the repertoire has been refined over the last thirty years, the illusions growing ever more sophisticated, there is

---

* The 70 percent rate applied only to unearned income—such as money from interest and dividends. Wage and salary income was taxed at a maximum of 50 percent. Thus even the 70 percent rate applied to very few taxpayers.

nothing new about the practice itself. Down through the decades, members of each Congress have passed along the secrets of their magic to a new generation of lawmakers, enabling them to carry on the tradition. Before we consider how it was done in 1986, let's look at one typical magic act that lawmakers have perfected through the years and still perform over and over again before an ever credulous public.

It's called the loophole-closing routine. Here, even the word "loophole" is an illusion. It suggests that a preference or tax break was written into the law by mistake and that sharp-eyed lawyers and accountants then exploited the language of innocent legislative draftsmen, using the law in a way that was never intended. Some loopholes certainly were accidental. The vast majority were not. They were put there as part of the magic act.

Thus, the most enduring routine of all is the perennial performance during which lawmakers announce they have plugged the loopholes. With all eyes fixed on the mystical plugging, the Capitol Hill magicians with one hand close a loophole and—while promising that such evil practices are now over for good—use the other hand, deftly unseen, to open a new one.

Listen as members of one Congress after another close loopholes.

1934—"I think we have completely blocked that loophole of tax escape," said Representative Samuel B. Hill, Washington Democrat.[30]

1937—"With respect to these loopholes, it is felt that the pending legislation . . . will prove an effective bar to their further use," said Representative Robert L. Doughton, North Carolina Democrat.[31]

1954—"The bill also closes many loopholes through which skillful taxpayers can avoid paying their just share of the tax burden," said Representative Daniel A. Reed, New York Republican.[32]

1969—"When we pass this tax legislation we will not read again about these millionaires who do not pay taxes because we have examined in detail all of the procedures that have been used by

[them], and by thousands of others who are in a similar category, and we have systematically attacked the problem and plugged the loopholes," said Representative Al Ullman, Oregon Democrat.[33]

1976—"This tax package is deserving of support. . . . The bill makes the most significant changes in the tax law since 1969. It closes loopholes used by the wealthy," said Representative Jonathan Bingham, New York Democrat.[34]

1986—"By plugging loopholes for the rich . . . we are able to cut the top individual tax rate nearly in half, from 50 to 28 percent," said Senator Mark Andrews, North Dakota Republican.[35]

1993—"This budget plan closes tax loopholes that have favored special interests and a fortunate few," said William J. Coyne, Pennsylvania Democrat.[36]

One might think that after Congress had closed loopholes for more than a half century, there couldn't possibly be any left. But that's the power of congressional prestidigitation. The stories of real people show the results of the Capitol Hill Magic Show.

In the depths of the Depression, with unemployment rising to 25 percent of the workforce, destitute families standing in breadlines on street corners, and the United States grappling with the most serious economic crisis in its history, the wealthy partners of J. P. Morgan & Co., the august private bank of Wall Street, achieved the seemingly impossible. The partners paid less than $50,000 in taxes in 1930, and none at all in 1931 and 1932, even though they earned millions of dollars in those years.

How did they do it?

By juggling the books of the partnership to create paper losses to offset their considerable personal incomes. No one in their set considered this improper. To tax lawyers and accountants, the Morgan partners were simply practicing shrewd tax management.

J. P. Morgan & Co. was a partnership of twenty wealthy men,

including J. Pierpont Morgan, the son of the founder. From an unmarked stone building at 23 Wall Street, the House of Morgan exerted vast influence on the financial life of the nation. Every year, the partners embarked on a year-end paper-shuffling exercise to minimize their taxes. They officially terminated the partnership and launched a new one of the same name, selling off the assets of the old to the new.

As paper losses mounted in 1930 from the stock market plunge, the partners took advantage of the situation. Rather than wait until year's end to dissolve, they terminated the partnership in midyear to write off the losses incurred in the first half of the year. As the stock market continued to fizzle in the second half, they dissolved the partnership again six months later, waiting until January 2, 1931, the first business day of the new year, to actually disband it.

Waiting until 1931 enabled the partners to write off $21 million in paper losses from the last half of 1930, reducing their taxes nearly to zero.

All this was perfectly legal, and Morgan had no qualms about it. "If the government objects to tax evasion," he said later, "it should change the laws, which can be done by Congress, but the taxpayers must not be insulted. . . . Congress should know how to levy taxes, and if it doesn't know how to collect them, then a man is a fool to pay the taxes. If stupid mistakes are made, it is up to Congress to rectify them and not for us taxpayers to do so."[37]

However, when Congress made noises about rectifying its mistakes, Morgan warned the lawmakers that taxing the rich would only hurt America: ". . . if you destroy the leisure class, you destroy civilization," he told reporters outside a congressional hearing room where he had been called to testify on February 4, 1936. Asked to define the leisure class, Morgan described it as people "who can afford to hire a maid."[38]

The disclosure of the Morgan partners' tax-free status led Congress to adopt the Revenue Act of 1934, to close loopholes like the one that Pierpont Morgan had exploited. "We have plugged the big holes," Representative Hill, a Democratic congressman from Washington, told colleagues on February 16, 1934. "The committee believes it has absolutely plugged that avenue through which taxes were escaping by manipulation of capital investments, purely for the purpose of creating paper losses in order they might offset those losses against ordinary income, and thereby reduce the taxes of the taxpayer." [39]

Not really. There were so many others to choose from, as attested by Alfred P. Sloan, Jr.

The president of General Motors Corporation, Sloan was fond of saying that he had no hobbies. He believed only in work. "Without hard work, nothing real can be accomplished," he once said. The exception to Sloan's strict regimen was his yacht, the *Rene,* a breathtaking $1.1 million vessel 235 feet long, which he moored on Long Island Sound near his Great Neck, New York, home.

Having powered GM past Ford Motor Company in the race to manufacture more cars, Sloan was in 1936 the nation's highest-paid chief executive. When his $565,311 annual salary from GM was coupled with dividends, stock benefits, and other income, he and his wife had a total income of $2.9 million for the year. The *Rene* cost roughly $150,000 a year for upkeep and crew, an expense easily within Sloan's means. Nevertheless, he found a way to cut costs: He incorporated his yacht and wrote off its operating expenses as a business deduction, thereby reducing his federal income tax bill.

Sloan turned over title to the vessel and common stock valued at more than $1 million to a paper company he had created, the Rene Corporation. He executed a lease between himself and his newly formed company, in which he agreed, in effect, to pay Rene Corporation—his own company—an annual fee to rent the good ship *Rene*—his own yacht.

The charter fees never covered annual upkeep and costs. No matter. The deficit was made up by income from dividends on stock Sloan had given to the Rene Corporation, thereby reducing the holding company's taxable income and the amount of federal income tax Sloan would owe.

In 1934, Rene Corporation showed gross income of $153,864, of which $63,750 represented dividends received and $90,114 charter fees paid principally by Sloan to his own corporation to use his own yacht. Total deductions, however, were $223,219, resulting in a net loss of $69,353 to the corporation. From 1931 to 1936, Sloan saved $222,647 in federal income taxes—the equivalent of about $2.3 million today. [40]

Sloan was doing what the privileged excel at—converting personal expenditures to tax deductions, an option not available to ordinary taxpayers. As Henry Morgenthau, Jr., secretary of the Treasury under Franklin D. Roosevelt, explained in 1937: "These transactions partake of the same unreal character as if a small taxpayer incorporated his household kitchen as a restaurant and deducted the expenses and losses from his taxable income because he had so few customers."[41]

Congress enacted more loophole-plugging legislation following revelations about the tax-avoidance practices of Sloan and others. Yet avoidance continued as before. The wealthy still had ways to reduce their taxes. Meet Ben W. Heineman, Sr.

One of the first of the conglomerate builders, Heineman was a Chicago lawyer who in the 1960s created Northwest Industries, Inc., with 41,000 employees and products from batteries to underwear. Heineman spent most of the year managing his far-flung empire from an office in the Sears Tower in Chicago. In the summer, however, he adopted the kind of schedule most people can only dream about.

Each year, Heineman and his wife left Chicago in mid-June to sail the Great Lakes for six weeks. Afterward, they put in at Sister Bay, Wisconsin, where they owned a summer home on sixty acres atop a bluff overlooking scenic Green Bay. The Heineman summer retreat was a two-story frame house with five bedrooms and three baths, plus a "cottage for help," a garage, and a storage house. Below the bluff was the family's private beach on the bay.[42]

Heineman spent all of August there, working, as he later explained, on company business. This was his time to "think," away from constant interruptions at the office. Even so, Heineman later said, the house was not conducive to quiet reflection. His work space on the front porch overlooking the bay was less than ideal. As Heineman explained, he would spread his papers "on a lunch table on the front porch, and would work, and then I would gather up my papers and put them in a briefcase, so that we could have lunch, and I would spread them after lunch, and work and gather them up and put them away. . . ." Then there were phone calls for his wife, Natalie, visits by friends, and other interruptions. When guests stayed at the house, the problems intensified. Heineman found it all "very unsatisfactory, very inconvenient."[43]

Heineman could have used one of the four upstairs bedrooms for a study. But that "would have deprived the house of guest capability," he said. Or he could have returned to his office in Chicago. But that did not appeal to him either. "To come back to Chicago would be to come back to heat," he said. "Heat is very distasteful to me."[44]

To make himself more comfortable, Heineman built separate quarters on the face of the cliff overlooking the bay, some 100 yards from the main house. Equipping the cliffside room with a desk, a conference table, chairs, and a bath and shower, Heineman called his perch above Green Bay his "office."[45]

Built as it was on the side of the cliff, Heineman's retreat was expensive to construct, costing some $250,000. But no matter. He wrote off the annual maintenance costs and charged off depreciation as "necessary and ordinary" business expenses, claiming the deductions on his personal income tax return. For the three years from 1976 to 1978, Heineman deducted $50,448, saving $33,287 in federal income taxes at a time when his annual income exceeded $1 million.

The IRS later challenged the deductions, contending that they were personal expenses that were made for Heineman's own convenience, not as a requirement of his job. The U.S. Tax Court disagreed, siding with Heineman:

"After weighing and balancing the relevant considerations, we conclude and hold that the expenses of constructing and maintaining the petitioner's Wisconsin office were appropriate and helpful to the performance of his duties as the chief executive officer of Northwest and that therefore such expenses are deductible . . . and the depreciation attributable thereto is deductible."[46]

As you may have guessed by now, deductions are very important to upper-income taxpayers. Just how important—and how large—can be seen in the amount claimed from 1987 to 1991 by people with incomes over $200,000. On average, 723,000 individuals and families claimed $75,000 in deductions apiece in each of the five years. Their total write-offs came to more than $270 billion.

What does a quarter-trillion dollars in deductions translate to in taxes saved? Enough to wipe out all the income taxes paid by everyone earning less than $50,000 a year in Oregon, Massachusetts, Washington, and North Carolina—every year for the five years.

On top of the deductions are all the assorted credits and adjustments and sources of tax-free income. Taken all together, they can have a dramatic impact on the bottom line of a tax return. Meet Dr. Earl O. Bergersen.

Bergersen is an orthodontist who began practicing in the Chicago suburb of Winnetka, Illinois, in 1959. In addition to maintaining his practice, Dr. Bergersen invented orthodontic devices, including "several types of appliances intended to prevent the need for children to wear braces."[47] To manufacture them, Dr. Bergersen and his wife, Evelyn, incorporated a company called Ortho-Tain, Inc., in 1974 and opened a small plant in Winnetka.

Two years later, the Bergersens moved the Ortho-Tain plant to Puerto Rico, taking advantage of one of the more lucrative tax loopholes in the Internal Revenue Code—Section 936. Originally intended to promote industrial development in Puerto Rico, Section 936 has become instead an incentive for American corporations to lay off factory workers in the United States and replace them with lower-paid production workers on the island.

Much of the relocation to Puerto Rico has been by major pharmaceutical companies. But the same tax benefits they enjoy are available to small companies such as Ortho-Tain.

In 1976, Ortho-Tain opened a plant in the town of Toa Alta, twenty miles southwest of San Juan. The company became a "possessions corporation"—meaning that its profits would not be taxed by the United States. As is customary with such corporations, Ortho-Tain, which had seven employees, also received "a grant of industrial tax exemption from the Puerto Rican government." That meant no taxes in Puerto Rico either.[48]

Five years after Ortho-Tain switched operations to Puerto Rico, the Bergersens made plans to relocate there too. They bought a lot in exclusive Dorado Beach, west of San Juan. Bergersen sold his dental practice and severed his relationship with three universities in Illinois. After construction began on the Puerto Rican home, the couple sold their Winnetka house for $545,250.

By late 1986, the new house, all 15,000 square feet of it—it was twice the size of the Ortho-Tain manufacturing plant—was completed at a cost the Bergersens estimated "exceeded $1,500,000."[49] The couple hired a "housekeeper and gardener to live and work at the Puerto Rico home."[50] While building the island home, the couple purchased, in March 1986, a furnished town house for $229,800 in Glenview, Illinois, "as a place to stay when visiting the Chicago area."[51]

All this buying and selling of houses required a good deal of cash. The Bergersens had a ready source—Ortho-Tain, their tax-free Puerto Rican company. While the Dorado Beach house was under construction in 1985, the couple borrowed $812,558 from Ortho-Tain. The next year, when they bought the Glenview town house and moved to Dorado Beach, they borrowed $770,672. In 1987, they borrowed an additional $699,861. For the three-year period, they received loans totaling $2,283,091 from their tax-free corporation. Then, in 1987, Ortho-Tain paid the couple dividends of $2,799,500, which the Bergersens used to repay the loans.

As you might expect, the assorted financial transactions led to some pretty complicated tax returns. Along with other dealings, they resulted in substantial deductions claimed by the Bergersens for the three years from 1985 to 1987.

For example, the couple wrote off $320,287 for interest that they paid to their own company on the money they had borrowed. They wrote off $16,031 for advertising. They wrote off $11,317 for travel and meetings. And there was a deduction of $1,317 for preparation of their tax returns. Because the Bergersens and Ortho-Tain were located in Puerto Rico, the $2.8 million in dividends they received from the company was considered to be exempt from the federal income tax. All told, the deductions and other tax breaks resulted in losses of more than a quarter-million dollars.[52] (The IRS later challenged certain deductions and transactions. The issue is pending in U.S. Tax Court.)

During these years—when the Bergersens built a $1.5 million home in Puerto Rico, sold their Winnetka house for $545,000, purchased a town house in Glenview for $229,800, borrowed $2.3 million from Ortho-Tain, and received $2.8 million in dividends from Ortho-Tain—exactly how much did the couple pay in federal income taxes?

Not a cent.[53]

Helping the Rich by Helping the Poor

The loophole-closing bit is the oldest act in the Capitol Hill Magic Show. But as time has passed, lawmakers have worked newer, equally successful material into their performances, with even more spectacular results. Which brings us back to 1986.

To overcome public indifference, if not opposition, to another round of Washington-style tax reform that year, lawmakers launched an extraordinary media campaign. The American public was told that the new tax law would hit the special interests hardest. That it would extend the largest tax cuts to the hardworking, middle class. That it would bestow generous benefits on the poor. That those at the top would profit ever so slightly.

At the same time, lawmakers reached into their bag of tricks for the helping-the-poor sleight of hand. In this routine, all eyes focus on one hand bearing cash as lawmakers and Presidents assure citizens that the latest tax bill will help the poor. And with the other hand, unwatched, they help the rich. The routine worked so well the first time it was used, back in the 1960s, they decided to try it again. No one seemed to notice that the ranks of the poor continued to swell, while the people at the top grew ever more prosperous.

Listen to what those who make the tax laws have said over the last quarter century. Let's begin in 1969 with Representative Wilbur D. Mills, the Arkansas Democrat who stamped his imprint on the Internal Revenue Code from the day he joined the Ways and Means Committee, in January 1943, until his legislative career ended prematurely in October 1974, when the congressman looked on as his companion, a Washington stripper who performed as Fanne Fox, the Argentine Firecracker, went swimming at 2:00 A.M. in the Tidal Basin near the Washington Monument. In urging passage of the Tax Reform Act of 1969, Representative Mills told his colleagues:

"The pending legislation provides for a new low income allowance which is specifically designed to concentrate tax relief on low income individuals living at poverty or near-poverty levels. . . . This provision when fully effective will give over $2 billion of relief and will completely exempt from tax many millions of taxpayers at or near poverty levels."[54]

Other lawmakers were swept up in the save-the-poor fervor.

Representative James A. Burke, Massachusetts Democrat, said that "the bill is unprecedented in the generosity of its relief provisions for our low-income citizens, and for that reason, if for no other, the conference report deserves prompt approval by the House. The provision which has the greatest salutary impact on those at or near the poverty level is the low-income allowance in the bill, which will remove some 5.2 million returns from the tax rolls in 1970."[55]

Representative John W. Byrnes, Wisconsin Republican, noted that "this bill does represent a real accomplishment in three fundamental areas" and pointed in particular to the "low income allowance that will remove over 5 million low-income individuals from the tax rolls."[56]

And Representative Al Ullman, Oregon Democrat, reaffirmed that "the low income allowance provision will remove from the rolls 5 million taxpayers, representing the poverty level of the nation."[57]

President Richard M. Nixon seized on the theme when he signed the tax reform act into law on December 30, 1969, though by some miracle of Washington mathematics the number of indigent to be helped had swollen from 5 to 9 million in one week. Said the President:

"More than 9 million low-income people who pay taxes will be dropped from the tax rolls. This results primarily from the special low-income allowance that I proposed last April as a means of making sure that people at or below the poverty level do not have to pay federal income taxes."[58]

Whatever the precise figure, all agreed that millions of working poor would never again pay taxes. Never, at least, until it was time to enact another tax bill, when another Congress and another President could repeat the process.

Like in 1986.

To marshal votes for a tax bill that polls showed the public opposed, supporter after supporter rose during debate in September of that year to talk about the one feature of the legislation that no lawmaker could possibly object to—eliminating taxes for the needy. Senator Bill Bradley, who was a principal backer of the legislation, explained:

"The one thing that everyone said they liked is that this bill takes 6 million low income people off the tax rolls. But then they dismiss it as something that is as sure or unsurprising as the fact that the sun will rise tomorrow morning. If it is so unexceptional, if it is something that is so taken for granted, Mr. President, why has it not happened before?"[59]

But of course it had happened before. Bradley, a former Rhodes scholar, either was unaware of this or chose to pretend that it had not. Whatever the case, Democrats and Republicans sounded as though they were reading from a Hollywood script as they recited their lines on saving-the-poor-from-taxes:

"A vote for this tax reform bill is a vote to free 6 million Americans, who are currently living below the poverty level, from the tax rolls," said Senator John H. Chafee, Rhode Island Republican.[60]

"It [the bill] is also an antipoverty program, as it increases the earned income credit for lower income taxpayers with children and removes 6.5 million working poor from the tax rolls. I believe this will be an incentive for many to get off welfare and into the work force," said Representative John S. McCain III, Arizona Republican.[61]

"It helps people at the bottom; 6 million people off the tax rolls, at the bottom," said Representative Richard A. Gephardt, Missouri Democrat.[62]

"Most important, the legislation will take more than 6 million working poor off the tax rolls," said Representative John R. McKernan, Jr., Maine Republican.[63]

"Over 6 million lower income Americans will no longer be liable for income tax," said Senator Robert J. Dole, Kansas Republican.[64]

"By removing approximately 6 million of the working poor from the tax rolls, it provides needed relief for those who can least afford to lose a portion of their income to taxes yet who have faced a rapidly rising tax burden in recent years," said Representative Tim Valentine, North Carolina Democrat.[65]

"The bill takes 6 million low-income individuals off the tax rolls. This is perhaps the most frequently touted virtue of the package, and it should be—for when was the last time we in this Congress had the chance to vote to give benefits to the poor rather than vote to cut them back?" said Senator John F. Kerry, Massachusetts Democrat.[66]

"This bill takes 6 million working poor off the tax rolls. This really makes sense. History may look back and record this initiative as one of the most successful welfare programs that benefits the most needy in our society," said Senator Pete V. Domenici, New Mexico Republican.[67]

"This bill will take 6 million of our nation's working poor off the tax rolls, giving them an extra incentive to pursue productive employment," said Senator Mitch McConnell, Kentucky Republican.[68]

"The first and perhaps most important elemental fact is that we have taken some 6 to 7 million Americans out of poverty by the simple expedient of ceasing to tax them into it," said Senator Daniel P. Moynihan, New York Democrat.[69]

"The legislation will remove 6 million poor persons from the tax rolls—700,000 of whom are the elderly," said Representative Robert J. Lagomarsino, California Republican.[70]

"Again, may I say this conference report takes 6 million working poor folks in America off the tax rolls completely, Mr. President, a monumental task of great significance to ordinary working people in the country," said Senator Alan J. Dixon, Illinois Democrat.[71]

"This tax bill will provide the greatest relief for the working poor. Six million taxpayers are dropped from the tax rolls," said Senator Charles E. Grassley, Iowa Republican.[72]

"Over 6 million of the working poor will be taken off the tax rolls. This includes nearly a million of our senior citizens," said Representative Frank J. Guarini, New Jersey Democrat.[73]

"Tax reform will mean that over 6 million working poor Americans will be removed from the federal income tax rolls altogether," said Representative Willis D. Gradison, Jr., Ohio Republican.[74]

"Over 6 million of our nation's poor will be given a boost up the economic ladder by being taken off of the tax rolls altogether," said Senator Robert W. Kasten, Jr., Wisconsin Republican.[75]

"There are other features of the bill which are equally positive. It removes over 6 million low-income Americans from the tax rolls, making it possible for them to provide for themselves without resort to welfare," said Representative Jim Kolbe, Arizona Republican.[76]

"An estimated 6 million working poor, living at or below the poverty level, will no longer have to pay income taxes," said Representative Olympia J. Snowe, Maine Republican.[77]

"Under this bill, 6 million of the working poor will be taken off the tax rolls. This is only right. In some cases, the tax burden they currently face is enough to force them to use food stamps in order to make ends meet. It is time we let those people keep their entire paycheck," said Senator Mack Mattingly, Georgia Republican.[78]

Here, then, is how the numbers add up:

In 1969, Congress relieved either 5 million poor folks—or 9 million, depending on whose numbers you use—from paying income tax.

In 1986, Congress removed another 6 million poor folks from the tax rolls, bringing the total spared to either 11 million or 15 million.

But even those figures are understating the extent of Congress's largesse. That's because not only do lawmakers and Presidents remove the poor from the tax rolls outright, they also pare taxes over and over again in such a way as to make the leftover poor disappear too. If you take their word for it, that is.

In the 1969 Tax Reform Act, Congress proclaimed that it had cut the taxes of persons with incomes below $3,000 by 69.8 percent. Six years later, in the 1975 Tax Reduction Act, Congress boasted it had cut the taxes of that same group by 237.5 percent. Thus, by 1976, Congress had chopped the taxes of individuals and families earning less than $3,000 by a total of 307.3 percent. In 1986, Congress said it had trimmed the taxes of Americans earning less than $10,000 by another 65 percent.

Now consider some numbers that Congress does not tell you about:

Individuals and families with incomes below $15,000 paid an average of $585 in taxes in 1986. By 1991, the average tax bill for that income group had dropped to $512—a savings of $73.

By way of contrast, individuals and families with incomes above a half-million dollars paid an average of $505,518 in taxes in 1986. By 1991, their average bill had plunged to $312,007—a savings of $193,511.

For the people at the top, Congress had provided a 38 percent tax cut—three times the 13 percent tax cut bestowed on those at the bottom.

And one final set of numbers. Remember Senator Mattingly talking about people forced to use food stamps?

In 1972, three years after Congress first saved the poor from taxes, 11 million people received food stamps. (It was in 1972 that eligibility rules became the same in all states.)

In 1986, the second year that Congress saved the poor, 21 million people received food stamps—up 91 percent in fourteen years.

In 1993, about 27 million people received food stamps—up 29 percent in seven years. Or an overall increase of 145 percent over two decades.

For Congress, there are certain practical advantages to this process, both economic and political. Eliminating taxes at the bottom carries a low price tag. In 1986, individuals and families with incomes below $10,000 paid $4.9 billion in income taxes. That amounted to 1 percent of all personal income taxes collected ($367 billion). The revenue loss from cutting taxes for those people would not be missed.

More important, the $4.9 billion was paid by 15.1 million individuals and families. That worked out to 18 percent of the nation's 84 million taxpayers and potential voters—large numbers to incumbent lawmakers who are looking forward to the next election. By reducing or eliminating the taxes of 15.1 million persons who accounted for 1 percent of government revenue, lawmakers achieved maximum political gain at the smallest unit cost.

But of greater value, the process diverted attention from the real beneficiaries of tax reform. They, of course, were the same class of taxpayers who had benefited in the 1980s and 1990s as well as the 1920s—those at the top.

Class Warfare

Who picks up the tab for this—the staggering cost of tax cuts for the wealthy? You guessed it—the middle class. They do so in income taxes, new excise taxes, and other levies imposed by federal, state, and local governments, in inflated Social Security taxes that are used not for retirement benefits but to offset the loss of other tax revenue, and in interest payments on a runaway national debt.

Congress, to be sure, paints a different picture. To make tax-law changes more palatable, lawmakers routinely try to show how the middle class, like the poor, will benefit. So it was that in 1986, Democrats and Republicans talked about the good things that were going to happen to middle-class taxpayers. Listen, once more, to what they had to say.

Representative Dan Rostenkowski, the Illinois Democrat who heads the House Ways and Means Committee and was one of the two principal drafters of the 1986 tax bill: "I began the campaign for tax reform with the premise that middle-income families should be the big beneficiaries—and that every private interest across the country should ante up a small part of the tab. . . . About the only people I have not heard from are the very people this bill does the most for. And that is the middle-income taxpayers."[79]

"The winners are the middle class, who will generally see tax relief," said William B. Richardson, Democratic representative from New Mexico.[80]

"Overall, the tax bill benefits the majority of middle-income taxpayers by reducing the tax rate, making the whole tax process simpler and increasing standard deductions," said Cardiss Collins, Democratic representative from Illinois.[81]

"We have to assure the honest, middle-class worker that he is not being a sucker for paying taxes on his wages, and that he is not paying a great deal more in taxes than those who are far better off than he. This bill does that," said Russell B. Long, Democratic senator from Louisiana.[82]

Others, like Robert Dole, a member of the Senate Finance Committee, which helped write the tax bill, were more specific about the benefits: "Most individuals and particularly lower-

and middle-income taxpayers will have major decreases in tax liability. It is worthy of note that, even though we will reduce the top individual tax bracket to 28 percent, lower- and middle-income taxpayers will receive a larger percentage tax reduction than higher income individuals. Taxpayers with incomes over $100,000 will have a tax cut of less than 2.5 percent."[83]

Some lawmakers took a slightly different tack. Listen to Representative Jack Kemp:

"It used to be in America that you could earn a significant amount of money and get to keep only 30 cents on the dollar. When this tax reform is complete, American families will pay no more than 30 cents to the federal government."[84]

Guy Vander Jagt, Republican representative from Michigan, sounded the same refrain:

"The centerpiece of the Reagan revolution will be the dramatic cut in tax rates. Think of it. When the President came riding into this city, the top rate was 70 percent. When he rides out of this city, the top rate will be 28 percent. Back then, any extra dollar that your extra effort earned for you, you kept one-fourth; the government took three-fourths away. Now we are turning that around and you keep three-fourths of the extra dollar. That is called incentive. That is at the heart of our American free enterprise system."[85]

Warming to the cause, Vander Jagt went on to say that "if you are a percolate-up economist, believing that the economic health of people with more after-tax dollars percolates through the whole economy, benefiting all, then you will vote for tax reform. . . . This tax bill is good for the American taxpayer. Truly, it is tax reform of the people, for the people, and certainly by the people."[86]

But was it?

In 1980, less than 1 percent of the 74 million individuals and families who paid income tax were taxed at 70 percent on the last dollar earned. In other words, getting to keep seventy cents of every dollar of income had no impact whatsoever on 99 percent of the taxpaying population. In fact, a full 85 percent of taxpayers that year were not taxed at the 50 percent rate, or 45 percent, or 40 percent. The overwhelming majority of American taxpayers already got to keep seventy cents on every dollar. The great rate-cut deception was intended, from the beginning, to provide the most generous benefits to those at the very top. Just as had been the case a half century ago.

So what did the numbers look like after five years? Consider the following, compiled from IRS tax statistics for the years 1986 and 1991:

Senator Dole said that people with incomes over $100,000 would see a scant 2.5 percent reduction in their taxes. As it turned out, their tax cut was 34 percent. In 1986, individuals and families with incomes over $100,000 paid, on average, $71,595 in income taxes. In 1991, they paid $47,215—a tax savings of $24,380.

By contrast, the heart of Middle America, individuals and families with incomes between $20,000 and $50,000, received a 15 percent tax cut. In 1986, they paid, on average, $3,888 in income taxes. In 1991, they paid $3,302—a tax savings of $586. Thus, those in the middle did not come close to receiving the larger tax reduction promised by Dole. Their 15 percent cut was less than half of the 34 percent reduction granted to the top. As for the 2.5 percent cut that Dole said more affluent taxpayers would enjoy, it turned out to be thirteen times greater.

If ordinary working Americans did not receive the kind of tax cuts promised by Congress, lawmakers and other government officials did. When President Reagan signed the tax bill into law on October 22, 1986, he told the assembled crowd on the White House lawn: "I feel like we just played the World Series of tax reform—and the American people won." [87]

Some, like the President, won more than others.

In 1981, the Reagans, with an adjusted gross income of $412,730, paid $165,291 in income taxes. Their tax rate: 40 percent. By 1987, still a year before all the provisions of the 1986 act were in effect, the Reagans' tax rate had plunged to 25 percent. Their income that year totaled $345,359; their taxes, $86,638.

While the Reagans' income declined by 16 percent between the two years, their tax bill plummeted 48 percent. Actually, the true tax rate in 1987 was even lower. That's because they also had $91,807 in tax-exempt interest income. When that was added in, their tax rate dropped below 20 percent.

In looking at those two years, members of Congress also profited handsomely. In 1981, many lawmakers were in the 44 percent tax bracket or higher. That is, they paid tax at a rate of 44 percent or more—many at 50 percent—on the last dollar earned. In 1989, they all paid taxes at a 28 percent rate.

The Tax Reform Act of 1986 accomplished what disciples of Andrew Mellon had been struggling to recapture for decades —it gave wealthy taxpayers the same rate as middle-class Americans. By 1988, a schoolteacher, a factory worker and his working wife, and billionaire investor Warren E. Buffett were all in the same tax bracket—taxed at 28 percent on the last dollar of income.

Representative Jim Kolbe summed up the achievement: "At last we have made a step, and a large one at that, toward a tax code which is based upon economic growth rather than income redistribution."[88] Kolbe was not alone. A number of lawmakers believed the move away from progressive rates would end what they considered to be the unfair redistribution of income.

Which brings us to Tax Rule No. 2: All tax laws redistribute income. The issue is in which direction. Will money be channeled up, so that wealth may be concentrated more at the top? Or will it be funneled down, so that a middle class can grow?

During the 1920s, when a series of tax cuts sent the top rate plunging from 73 percent to 25 percent, income was redistributed up, fueling speculation in the stock market rather than the creation of jobs that paid meaningful wages. From the 1940s through the 1950s and into the early 1960s, lawmakers and Presidents—Democrats and Republicans—enacted tax laws that redistributed income down, thereby helping to fuel the largest growth of a middle class ever. But in the 1960s, lawmakers and Presidents—again Democrats and Republicans —enacted tax laws to tilt the tax system back toward the top.

That process continued, albeit gradually, in the 1970s. By the 1980s and into the 1990s—the 1993 tax increase notwithstanding—the system once more was weighted heavily in favor of the affluent. Not surprisingly, for the first time in this century, the middle class is shrinking rather than expanding. The people at the top are doing better than ever.

One acute observer of America, Akio Morita, chairman of Sony, who spent part of his early career here and expresses a fondness for the country, has marveled at the U.S. practice of throwing huge amounts of money to a comparatively small number of people, so much money that they are unable to spend it. On this, Morita has written:

"A corporate chairman with whom I am acquainted complained that he has no use for all the money he receives. His company is doing well and his income is in the multi-million dollar a year range. His children are all grown and he and his wife already have vacation villas, a yacht and a private airplane; he said they just have no way to spend any more money on themselves."[89]

This redistribution to folks at the top has come at the expense of others. The federal government's tax-return data tells the story. In 1951, it took the wages and salaries of 6 million individuals and families at the lower end of the income scale to match the wages and salaries of the top 1 percent. By 1991, it took the wages and salaries of 33 million individuals and families at the bottom to equal the wages and salaries of the top 1 percent.

In 1951, the average wage and salary in the top 1 percent was slightly under $20,000—or sixteen times greater than the average at the bottom. By 1991, the average wage and salary of the top 1 percent was more than $220,000—or thirty-four times greater than the average at the bottom.

That's the bottom contrasted with the top. What about middle-income families? In 1951, it took the wages and salaries of 2 million median-income families to equal the earnings of the top 1 percent. By 1991, it took the wages and salaries of 6 million median-income families to equal the earnings of the top 1 percent.

Keep in mind, also, that during the explosive growth of the middle class in the 1950s, wages and salaries came largely from one working spouse. In 1991, it came largely from two working spouses. As you might guess, the bulging wage and salary income of the people at the top has been accompanied by a steadily growing concentration of wealth. Remember, too, they are likeliest to have significant income from investments.

But in Congress, where tax law is made, you would think it was the rich—not the middle class—that were under siege.

Look no further than a chapter in the debate that swirled around the Clinton budget package in 1993.

One of the recurring themes of opponents was that the proposed increase in income tax would pit one group of Americans against another. Over and over, on the floor of the House and Senate, on television talk shows, and in newspaper columns, the notion of raising the top rate was portrayed as class warfare. This even though the proposed increase—from 31 percent to 39.6 percent for individuals and families with taxable incomes of more than a quarter-million dollars—still left the rate lower than at any time since the 1920s.

Alfonse M. D'Amato, Republican senator from New York, set the tone: "There is something that I think is very dangerous taking place in this nation. Let me tell you what it is. It is class warfare under the theory of 'let's get the rich guy, the richest 1 percent.' So we set them up, target them; those are the people we are going to get."[90]

Senator William S. Cohen, Republican from Maine, put it this way: "We are talking about taxing the rich. Once again, we are engaging in classic class warfare."[91]

Others joined in. "I do not know how long we can continue that kind of class warfare," lamented Senator Dole.[92]

"While reducing the budget deficit may be the most important issue before this Congress, the President and his allies in Congress are offering this country what amounts to class warfare. . . . I object to these higher taxes," said Senator Slade Gorton, Republican from Washington.[93]

Over in the House, representatives expressed the same concern. Robert K. Dornan, Republican from California, said that "to sell this program of higher taxes, Clinton and his liberal allies here in the House have turned to the standard liberal theme of class warfare, though they have couched it in terms of 'progressivity,' 'fairness,' and 'equality.' "[94] Representative Jim Bunning, Republican from Kentucky, labeled the legislation "a historic class warfare scheme."[95] And Gerald B. H. Solomon, Republican from New York, observed that "as young Russians cover Marx's statue in Moscow with flippant slogans such as 'workers of the world, forgive me,' America is awash in the Marx-Leninesque rhetoric of class warfare."[96]

The news media echoed the theme. The *Wall Street Journal* published editorials on "The Class Warfare Economy."[97] On CNN's *Inside Business* report, David Jones, chief economist at Aubrey G. Lanston and Company, said that "taxing the rich may sound good politically, at least when we're talking about class warfare, but economically it's a very dangerous exercise."[98] On CNN's *The Capital Gang,* Robert Novak, political columnist and commentator, said that "the Republicans are gun shy. They should have come out for—against this class warfare, this class hatred, which is going to hurt the economy, when you say, we are going to tax the successful people in the country."[99]

They were right about one thing. There has been class warfare. But it didn't start with the introduction of the Omnibus Budget Reconciliation Act of 1993. Nor was it directed against the rich. In truth, it began quietly in the 1960s, and continued through the 1970s and 1980s. And the target was the middle class.

It was a war that Middle America lost.

Resoundingly.

CHAPTER 3

★ $ ★ $ ★

WHY YOU PAY MORE

Washington Trickery

Suppose, for a moment, that Congress came up with a new tax to help pay for running the U.S. government and to reduce the federal deficit.

Suppose that everyone who holds a job and earns less than $60,600 would be required to pay the tax on the full amount of his or her earnings.

Suppose, furthermore, that everyone who earns more than $60,600 would be excused from paying the tax on part or nearly all of his or her earnings.

And suppose, finally, that everyone whose income is derived from investments and capital gains from speculating in the stock market would be entirely exempt from the tax.

How would you feel about such a proposal?

What's that? You think such a tax could never be implemented, that the lawmakers who proposed it would be voted out of office?

Think again.

In fact, the tax already is in place.

It's called Social Security.

If you earn less than $60,600 in 1994, you pay it every week.

If you earn a lot more—say, $606,000—you pay it for only five weeks of the year.

But at least it's going for a good cause, right?

Your retirement, right?

Wrong again.

A chunk of your Social Security tax is being spent, every day, to pay for the cost of running the U.S. government. By decade's end, a half trillion of Social Security tax dollars will have gone to pay for everything from military hardware to congressional junkets, from state dinners at the White House to the interest on the national debt.

How can this be?

In simplest terms, the people in Washington who write the tax laws and spend the money have substituted a portion of the Social Security tax for the federal income tax—without ever explaining what they were doing. That means that the U.S. government derives general operating revenue from a tax that does not apply to anyone who earns more than $60,600—the maximum salary subject to Social Security tax in 1994.

An analysis of a half century of tax and economic data shows that to pull off the sleight of hand, a succession of Congresses and Presidents has issued a blizzard of sometimes obscure, sometimes misleading, and, increasingly, false statements on government finances. What it means is this:

If you are a working couple with two children, earning $40,000 in combined salaries, you are paying 6.2 percent of your income, in part, to fund government operations.*

If you are a single man or woman with a salary of ten times that amount, or $400,000, you are paying nine-tenths of 1 percent of your income, in part, to fund government operations.

And if you are a corporate executive like, say, Daniel P. Tully, chief executive officer and chairman of the board of Merrill Lynch & Company, Inc., the Wall Street investment house, who earned $5.2 million in 1992, you are paying seven-hundredths of 1 percent of your income, in part, to fund government operations.

In other words, the middle-income family pays taxes to support government at a rate eighty-nine times greater than the chief executive of the world's largest brokerage and investment firm.

Try viewing this in reverse. If you earn $30,000 at your job

---

* The total Social Security tax rate is 7.65 percent. Of that figure, 6.2 percent is for Old-Age, Survivors, and Disability Insurance (OASDI), which provides monthly benefits to retired and disabled workers, and 1.45 percent is for Medicare.

this year, and pay Social Security taxes at the same rate as the top officer of Merrill Lynch, the amount withheld from your weekly paycheck would total forty cents.

That's forty cents.

So it is that while politicians and economists each year argue over the proper mix of spending cuts and tax increases to curb the federal deficit, they have concealed a much larger issue: For more than two decades, a collection of Congresses and Presidents of both parties have transferred the overall tax burden in the United States from the people at the top of the economic ladder to those in the middle and, in many cases, at the bottom. They have done this in two ways:

First, by dramatically increasing Social Security tax rates and then using the money for ordinary government programs—not Social Security—while simultaneously cutting the tax bills of the nation's most affluent citizens by billions of dollars.

Second, by shifting the cost of billions of dollars in programs once underwritten by the federal government to state and local governments, whose tax systems impose a much heavier burden on people in the middle and at the bottom.

These are big issues. But taxes are paid by people. Real people like Alan Greenspan and Sean McKinney.

The sixty-eight-year-old Greenspan charts the financial direction of the country as chairman of the board of governors of the Federal Reserve System. In 1991, his salary was $125,100. His income from investments was between $200,000 and $1.2 million.

McKinney is an eighteen-year-old freshman at St. Joseph's University in Philadelphia, who hopes to run his own business one day. One of five children, he worked during the years he attended Malvern Preparatory School in Chester County, Pennsylvania—from which he was graduated in 1993—to save money and help pay part of his $16,000 yearly college tuition bill. In 1991, he earned $2,244. He had no income from investments.

Guess who paid the larger percentage of his income in Social Security tax to help pay the interest on the national debt?

If you picked the 1993 high school graduate, score yourself 100. McKinney, who earned an average of $43 a week, paid Social Security taxes at two and one-half times the rate of

Greenspan, who earned $2,406 a week. Now, you may think that all this will change as a result of the tax increases and spending cuts in the 1993 budget bill that lawmakers debated so heatedly.

Think again.

The budget package continues business as usual. What's more, several of the proposals to raise revenue for overhaul of the nation's health care system would worsen the disparities if enacted.

As might be expected, the people who formulate the government's economic policies would like business as usual to continue. People like Greenspan, the Federal Reserve chairman who headed the National Commission on Social Security Reform, which came up with the plan back in 1983 that has led to sharply higher Social Security taxes on middle-class workers.

Several years ago, when it was recommended that Social Security should be placed outside the federal budget and the tax cut, Greenspan objected. During an appearance before the House Budget Committee in February 1990, he told lawmakers:

"I fear that adopting a system that draws attention to the surpluses in the [Social Security and other] trust funds might foster the illusion that saving already is great enough to meet future obligations."[1]

Translation: The present system, which imposes a disproportionate share of the government's tax burden on middle-income and low-income workers, is just fine.

Greenspan's statement was in keeping with his personal views on matters economic. In past hard times, the Federal Reserve chairman saved his deepest concern for the fortunes of Wall Street brokers. That was the case in 1974 when Greenspan, then chairman of the President's Council of Economic Advisers, took part in a summit conference on inflation called by President Gerald R. Ford. When it was suggested during the conference that working folks were especially hard hit by double-digit inflation, Greenspan took exception. Said he:

"Everybody is hurt by inflation. If you really wanted to examine who, percentagewise, is hurt the most in their incomes, it is the Wall Street brokers. I mean their incomes have gone down the most. So if you want to be statistical, I mean let's look at what the facts are."[2]

The facts, indeed.

To understand how the Social Security tax came to be used as a substitute for the income tax, it's first necessary to realize that official explanations of government policies often bear little resemblance to the actual policies that are finally implemented.

So it was with Social Security. From the very beginning, government officials fostered the mistaken notion that employees and employers were paying Social Security taxes into a trust fund, where the money would accumulate until the day workers would begin receiving their retirement benefits.

As the Social Security Board explained in 1940: "You pay a tax to the federal government, and so does your employer. These taxes go into the fund out of which your benefits will be paid later on. The tax is a sort of premium on what might be called an insurance policy, which will begin to pay benefits when you qualify at age 65 or over, or in case of your death."[3]

In truth, as the Social Security tax money came into the U.S. Treasury, it went right back out again in the form of retirement checks. It was pay-as-you-go, with the money transferred from a current generation of workers to a retired generation of workers. The program was built on faith. Those paying taxes to support yesterday's workers trusted that tomorrow's workers would pay taxes to support them.

And for a long time it worked. During the 1940s, 1950s, and early 1960s, a balance was maintained so that the amount of tax revenue collected was about equal to the amount of benefits paid. In those years, the only casualty was truth, as the government continued to push the deceptive idea of a trust fund.

Things began to change by the mid-1960s.

The ambitious social programs of President Lyndon B. Johnson, combined with the escalating Vietnam war, took a toll on government finances. In 1967, the government ran up a $15.7 billion deficit—the largest since World War II—and faced the prospect of a deficit twice that size the next year.

At the same time, Social Security tax revenue was growing faster than payments to retirees. The annual surplus topped the billion-dollar mark for the first time in 1966, reaching $2.5

billion. Projections called for further increases. Unfortunately, at least from official Washington's viewpoint, the oversupply of Social Security dollars was outside the federal budget.

How better to mask the deficits than to merge Social Security revenue and expenditures from other so-called trust funds with general fund revenue and expenditures in a single budget? The general fund revenue came from individual and and corporate incomes taxes, excise taxes, and other miscellaneous sources. But at the moment, every bit of it, plus a lot of borrowed money, was going out to pay for the Great Society programs, the Vietnam war, and all other government operations.

Against that background, in January 1968, President Johnson proposed a new way of reporting government income and spending. He called it the "unified budget." Social Security and other trust fund tax dollars would be rolled in with all other government revenue.

In adopting the new plan, Johnson said he was only following the advice of a high-level panel that he had appointed—the President's Commission on Budget Concepts—which had called for the unified accounting to make the budget "a more understandable and useful instrument of public policy and financial planning" and to "bring this document abreast of the times."[4]

If the stated purpose was to modernize the budget, the practical effect was quite different. By commingling "trust fund" accounts such as Social Security with general revenue, the new system reduced the federal deficit by billions of dollars overnight, and thus obscured the mounting cost of the war. Under the old way of keeping the books, the federal deficit had been pegged at $19.8 billion. Under the new accounting, the deficit appeared to be only $8 billion.

Congress liked the results. Mike Mansfield, the Montana Democrat who was the Senate majority leader, said the President's revised budget had a number of "striking advantages" over the old one, adding that "the new, higher figures may be hard for us to get used to, but they are a truer reflection of the facts of government finance."[5]

A few lawmakers disagreed, among them John J. Williams, the Republican senator from Delaware who was sometimes called "the conscience of the Senate." Williams was blunt:

"If any privately operated bank issued such a report to its stockholders, the officials of that bank would be in the penitentiary. It is equally misleading for the federal government to resort to such backhanded accounting methods, which can have but one purpose and that is to deceive the American people as to the serious state of our financial situation."[6]

Williams lost.

Deception won.

Which brings us to Tax Rule No. 3: What Washington says it is doing about taxes, and what it really does, are seldom the same.

In 1969, the unified budget, Washington's idea of Creative Math, worked as anticipated, and the government reported a $3.2 billion surplus. It was possible to finance a war, pay for social programs, and balance the budget, all at the same time.

The following year, in his annual message to Congress, President Johnson took note of the "budget surplus," saying it would relieve inflationary pressures and reduce federal borrowing: "In my first budget message five years ago, I stated: 'A government that is strong, a government that is solvent, a government that is compassionate is the kind of government that endures.' I have sought to provide that kind of government as your President. With this budget I leave that kind of government to my successor."[7]

In fact, what Johnson left was the first of the make-believe budgets. If Social Security and other "trust fund" surpluses had been excluded, the government would have reported a deficit of $4.9 billion.

Even with the more generous accounting rules, lawmakers and policymakers were unable to produce a surplus two years in a row. The 1969 surplus of $3.2 billion would be the last the U.S. government would report in this century. And for the foreseeable years in the next century.

Raising Taxes on Wage Earners

By 1970, the unified budget notwithstanding, the government posted a deficit of $2.8 billion, which climbed to $23 billion the following year. More important, Johnson's financial gimmickry put in place a system that eventually would be used to impose an ever greater tax burden on middle-income and lower-income working Americans. Here is how it came about.

Though the Social Security tax had produced excess revenue in the Johnson years, that rosy situation didn't last. The gap between taxes collected and payments to retirees closed quickly. The annual surplus, which hit $4.8 billion in 1969, fell to $400 million in 1973. By 1975, more money was going out than was coming in.

Social Security was in trouble.

Concern began to grow over its precarious financial condition. Jimmy Carter turned it into a campaign issue when he ran for President in 1976, vowing "to restore the financial integrity of the Social Security system."[8]

After the election, the President and Congress hammered out legislation that called for a series of Social Security tax increases. On Capitol Hill, supporters ignored the impact of the higher taxes on working Americans and focused instead on assuring the program's solvency.

Al Ullman, Democratic representative from Oregon, who was chairman of the House Ways and Means Committee, urged his colleagues to approve the legislation: "I am glad to be able to report to the House that your committee has fashioned a financing bill . . . which will restore Social Security to a sound basis and enable us to tell our constituents that we have met the problems that have caused their justified concerns."[9]

Over in the Senate, William D. Hathaway, Democratic senator from Maine, echoed the view: "We cannot renege on the promises and commitments which have been made to those who are retired and those who will retire. Acceptance of the [bill] will keep faith with the American people."[10]

With that, Congress enacted the Social Security Act Amendments of 1977. The legislation raised the combined tax rate paid by employers and employees over several years from 11.7 percent to 15.3 percent, and increased the amount of wages and salaries on which Social Security taxes would be levied from $16,500 in 1977 to $42,000 in 1987.

During a bill-signing ceremony, President Carter praised lawmakers for their "sound judgment and political courage," adding: "This legislation is wise. It's been evolved after very careful and long preparation. It focuses the increased tax burdens, which were absolutely mandatory, in a way that is of least burden to the families of this nation, who are most in need of a sound income. The level of payments were raised for those who are wealthier in our country where they can most easily afford increased payments." [11]

Americans, Carter said, could rest assured that Social Security had been saved: "This legislation will guarantee that from 1980 to the year 2030, the Social Security funds will be sound."

The President was wrong on both counts.

Middle America—not the wealthy—would pay the higher taxes.

And the year 2030 would arrive forty-eight years ahead of time.

By 1982, Social Security was in deeper trouble than ever. That year, the amount of benefits paid exceeded the taxes collected by nearly $11 billion—the largest gap ever.

Not to worry. Once again, Congress, with another President in the White House, this time a Republican, came to the rescue. Another package of Social Security amendments was enacted in 1983. It accelerated the tax hikes provided in the 1977 law and brought new federal workers into the system.

As usual, self-praise rang through the House and Senate. Dan Rostenkowski, Democratic representative from Illinois, set the tone:

"The passage of this bill through Congress over the last two months is as remarkable as it is monumental. In the face of crisis we have shown that we can rise above partisan differences; that we can withstand enormous pressure from special interest; that we can raise the level of national confidence in government. We have reason to be proud of ourselves tonight. Beyond these doors we may never receive the recognition we have earned. But we know that when we must work together—we can." [12]

An upbeat President Ronald Reagan, on signing the bill at a White House ceremony in April 1983, said the legislation struck "the best possible balance between the taxes we pay and the benefits paid back. This bill demonstrates for all time our nation's ironclad commitment to Social Security. . . . Our elderly need no longer fear that the checks they depend on will be stopped or reduced. These amendments protect them. Americans of middle age need no longer worry whether their career-long investment will pay off. These amendments guarantee it. And younger people can feel confident that Social Security will still be around when they need it to cushion their retirement." [13]

As promised, the 1983 amendments, when coupled with the 1977 law, took Social Security out of the red. The system went from an $11 billion shortfall in 1982 to a $12 billion surplus in 1986. But there was a darker side to the two legislative packages. Both furthered development of the two tax systems.

ITEM. From 1977 to 1990, the Social Security tax rate was raised nine times on Middle America. It went from 5.85 percent to 7.65 percent—where it remains in 1994—an increase of 31 percent. By way of contrast, the top income tax rate of the wealthiest Americans was slashed from 70 percent in 1977 to 39.6 percent in 1994.

ITEM. In 1993, a median-income family with earnings of $37,800 paid out 7.65 percent of its income in Social Security taxes. A more affluent family, earning ten times median family income, or $378,000, paid Social Security taxes at a rate of 1.46 percent. And a rich family, with income 100 times greater than the median family income, or $3.78 million, paid Social Security taxes at a rate of one-tenth of 1 percent.

ITEM. Over the two decades from 1971 to 1991, the combined Social Security and income tax bills of median-income families shot up 329 percent, while the combined tax bills of individuals and families with incomes of more than $1 million fell 34 percent.

ITEM. A middle-class family in which both spouses worked, earning $75,000 in combined salaries during 1993, not only paid more in Social Security taxes as a percentage of their income; they paid more in actual dollars than a wealthy executive who was single or whose spouse didn't work. The executive, who earned, say, $2 million, paid the maximum Social Security taxes of $5,529. That was three-tenths of 1 percent of his pay. The middle-class family earning $75,000 paid a total of $5,738. That was 7.65 percent of their pay. Not only were they taxed at a rate 25 times greater than the executive, but they also paid more in total dollars—$209 more.

ITEM. The higher Social Security rates have generated as much as $50 billion a year in surplus revenue, largely from middle-income and lower-income workers. This has allowed lawmakers and policymakers to use Social Security taxes as a substitute for income taxes and to help pay for the income tax cuts given to affluent taxpayers.

Over the last several years, about 12 percent of the money withheld from your paycheck for Social Security, and the same amount contributed by your employer, has gone to pay for other government programs. While that may not represent a huge amount for one person, you might want to think of it as one piece of a jigsaw puzzle. Millionaires who pay no tax are another piece. Wealthy individuals who pay tax at a rate below the working poor and middle-income folks are another. Corporations that contribute a shrinking share to the tax pie are another. Tax write-offs for donations of appreciated stocks and works of art are another. In all, the puzzle has several hundred such pieces.

Alone, the individual pieces do not count for a lot. When they are all put together, the picture shows a beleaguered middle-income family and individual amid a sea of hands grabbing for the money in their wallets. And taking it. Title it The Great Tax Rip-off.

In any event, besides being unfair, the inflated Social Security tax rates, when combined with the unified budget, have allowed members of Congress and Presidents—again, both Democrats and Republicans—to mislead the public about the state of government finances. Just as Senator Williams had warned.

Consider, for example, how the government announces, and the news media dutifully report, the size of the annual deficits. You can pick any year. The stories are always the same. But let's look at what they said on October 29, 1992.

Atlanta Constitution—"The Department of the Treasury announced Wednesday that the federal budget deficit for fiscal 1992, which ended last month, was $290.2 billion, less than expected but still a record."

Chicago Tribune—"In another government report, the Treasury Department said Wednesday the U.S. budget deficit swelled to a record $290.2 billion in the fiscal year that ended September 30."

Houston Post—"The federal budget deficit soared to a record $290.2 billion over the past 12 months, the government said Wednesday. The gap between what the government spent and what it took in easily surpassed the previous record of $269.5 billion, reached in fiscal 1991."

Los Angeles Times—"The Treasury Department said the budget deficit for the fiscal year 1992 hit a new record—$290.2 billion—breaking the 1991 record of $269.5 billion."

New York Times—"The gap between federal spending and revenues widened to a record $290.2 billion in the year ended September 30, the government said today."

Philadelphia Inquirer—"The federal budget deficit soared to a record $290.2 billion over the last 12 months, the government said yesterday."

USA Today—"The federal budget deficit widened to a record $290.2 billion the fiscal year ended September 30, the Treasury Department said Wednesday."

Wall Street Journal—"The federal deficit set another record, coming in at $290.2 billion for the fiscal year that ended September 30."

That "$290.2 billion" the U.S. Treasury announced and the news media reported—that was the pretend deficit.

The real deficit was $386.2 billion.

That's $96 billion—or 33 percent more—than the deficit that everyone read or heard about.

The artificial deficit was arrived at this way:

First, Social Security and other "trust funds" collected $96 billion more in taxes than they needed. The general fund spent $386.2 billion more than it collected in taxes. So, the government spent the $96 billion in trust fund revenue and subtracted it from the $386.2 billion general fund deficit. That produced the pretend deficit so widely reported—$290.2 billion.

The real deficit of $386.2 billion went unnoticed.

If that's not bad enough, there are all the IOUs.

IOUs? Yes.

Each time the government takes a Social Security tax dollar and spends it for, say, a new submarine, it puts an IOU into the

Social Security "trust fund," which is really just a bookkeeping device, not a true trust fund. The same practice is followed with the other so-called trust funds—for airports, unemployment, Medicare, highways, and federal employees' retirement.

In all, the IOUs total a staggering $1.1 trillion—and they are growing daily. The government also pays interest on its IOUs. The interest, naturally, is more IOUs.

If all the markers were to be redeemed, it would take every dollar in federal income tax paid in 1994 by the 80 million or so individuals and families earning less than $75,000. And every dollar in income tax paid by those 80 million people next year and the year after and the year after that.

By then there would be a new batch of IOUs.

Indeed, the federal government issues IOUs as fast as it can print them. In five years, from 1988 to 1993, the dollar value of IOUs stuffed into "trust funds" soared 105 percent, spiraling from $536 billion to $1.1 trillion. The biggest holder of all, as you might have guessed, is the Federal Old Age and Survivors Insurance Trust Fund, better known as Social Security, which is sitting on $356 billion worth of IOUs.

What difference does any of this make? What difference does it make if the true deficit is $100 billion more than the pretend deficit? What difference does it make if Social Security and other trust funds are filled with IOUs?

A great deal. For a number of reasons, all related to your taxes.

At some point, the IOUs will have to be replaced with money to pay Social Security benefits to retirees. That was the justification for the tax-rate increases in 1977 and 1983—to put away extra money in the trust fund so it would be there when the baby boomers begin to retire early in the next century. Except that the only things in the trust fund are markers.

When benefit checks begin to exceed Social Security tax revenue, Congress will have to make a decision: Increase the income tax to redeem the IOUs, raise Social Security taxes, reduce retirement benefits, raise the retirement age, eliminate early retirement, do nothing and allow the deficit to grow, or invoke some combination of those options.

The day of reckoning is approaching sooner than expected. That's because the gap is beginning to narrow, as it did in the

1970s, between Social Security taxes collected and retirement benefits paid out. Once the taxes fail to cover benefits, Congress will be compelled to choose.

One reason why this decision will have to be made sooner than expected—possibly before the turn of the century—is that Social Security tax collections are slowing—dramatically. From 1987 to 1988, tax collections jumped 13 percent, rising from $213 billion to $241 billion. In 1989, collections rose 9 percent, then the growth trailed off to 7 percent in 1990, to 4 percent in 1991, to 3 percent in 1992 and in 1993.

While the growth rate in Social Security tax collections fell, the growth rate in benefits paid to retirees and the disabled rose. From 1987 to 1988, benefits paid went up 6 percent, from $204 billion to $217 billion. Benefits went up another 6 percent in 1989, 7 percent in 1990, 8 percent in 1991, and 7 percent in 1992. This trend will most likely continue as more workers join the retirement pool and more persons receive disability insurance. The ranks of the latter group are swelling because of AIDS.

The decline in the growth rate of Social Security tax collections is attributable in part to the ongoing restructuring of American business, with its emphasis on ever higher quarterly profits and increasing shareholder value. These goals are being achieved by eliminating jobs and rejecting long-term investments that would lead to expanded employment. Add to that the nation's overall failure to develop new industries. Three trends have emerged from these developments that spell trouble for Social Security.

TREND NUMBER ONE. Higher-paying manufacturing jobs are being eliminated; lower-paying service jobs are being created. In 1993, a total of 17.8 million persons were employed in manufacturing, making things with their hands. That was down from 18.4 million in 1983, down from 20.2 million in 1973, and not far above 17.0 million in 1963. In 1963, 30 percent of the workforce was employed in manufacturing. In 1993, it was 16 percent and falling. While $20-an-hour steelworkers are disappearing, $8-an-hour security guards are replacing them. Lower wages mean reduced Social Security tax revenue.

TREND NUMBER TWO. A majority of middle-income workers whose jobs have been eliminated have been unable to find comparable work and have been forced into lower-paying jobs. That, too, translates into lower Social Security revenue. Others have been forced into early retirement, which means reduced Social Security revenue, or none at all.

TREND NUMBER THREE. Another group of displaced middle-income workers, unable to find good jobs elsewhere, have started up their own businesses, or work as independent contractors (often for the same companies that once employed them), for less money and no benefits. The self-employed person must pay both the employer's and employee's share of Social Security taxes. That's a full 15.3 percent coming off the top of already reduced income. Not surprisingly, growing evidence suggests that tax avoidance is rampant.

All these factors add up to higher taxes or larger deficits. Growing deficits, in turn, mean a still higher national debt and more of your tax dollars going for interest payments. Since 1980, such interest payments have represented the largest transfer of wealth ever, from the people who pay taxes to the people who own the debt and collect the interest on it.

More accurately, the money goes from middle-income and lower-income taxpayers to upper-income investors. While affluent individuals and families pay taxes that go, in part, to pay interest, they as a group are more likely to own a piece of the debt, and hence are merely exchanging money with one another.

You may decide for yourself which side of the transfer you are on. If you do not own Treasury securities, you are turning over a large slice of your income tax payments to those who do.

How much money, exactly, are we talking about?

During the 1980s, the transfer of wealth totaled $1.1 trillion. In the 1990s, it will hit $2 trillion—and that's after the 1993 budget bill, hailed as the biggest deficit-reduction measure in history.

To put $2 trillion in more understandable terms, it represents every dollar in income tax that will be paid each year through the 1990s by individuals and families earning less than

$100,000 a year in New York, Massachusetts, North Carolina, Ohio, Oregon, Pennsylvania, Texas, Colorado, Arkansas, Georgia, Indiana, Kansas, Louisiana, Maine, Minnesota, Missouri, Nebraska, New Hampshire, Tennessee, and West Virginia.

Remember now, if you live in one of those states, and your income remains under $100,000 a year during the 1990s, every dollar in income tax you pay will go to the people, businesses, and institutions who own the national debt.

From 1980 to 1993, spending for the food stamp program rose from $9 billion to $25 billion—an increase of 178 percent. During the same period, interest payments on the national debt shot up from $53 billion to $199 billion—an increase of 275 percent. More significantly, in 1980 the U.S. government paid out six times as much in interest to the people who own the national debt as it did to feed the needy. In 1993, it paid out eight times as much in interest.

Robin Hood in Reverse

At the same time that Congress has diverted Social Security tax dollars to mask the deficit, it has turned to some seemingly unlikely sources to raise new income tax revenue.

Meet Randall L. Conaway of Mount Vernon, Missouri.

He is the future—a middle-class American who represents the fastest-growing source of potential tax revenue for the U.S. government. Just what did the forty-four-year-old Conaway do that made him so attractive to the people who write the nation's tax laws?

Well, he was unemployed.

Unemployed?

A source of tax revenue?

That's right.

Conaway lost his longtime job as an $8.19-an-hour electronics assembler in 1992 when the company where he had worked for nearly nineteen years, Zenith Corporation, closed and moved to Mexico. Like millions of other working Americans whose middle-class existence is slipping away, Conaway began collecting unemployment compensation. And like millions of other unemployed working Americans, he paid federal income tax on his unemployment benefits.

Workers who are reporting unemployment compensation payments are the fastest-growing group of tax-return filers. Their numbers are shooting up at a faster rate than those reporting wage and salary income. They are going up at a faster rate than those reporting dividend income. Faster than those reporting interest income. Faster than those reporting income from a business or profession.

From 1987 to 1991, the number of individuals and families reporting jobless benefits on their tax returns jumped 35 percent, rising from 7.4 million to 10 million returns. During the same years, the number of individuals and families with dividend income went up just 4 percent, from 22.3 million to 23.3 million returns. The number reporting income from a business or profession climbed 16 percent, from 9.9 million to 11.5 million returns.

Only one group of tax-return filers came close to matching the growth rate of the unemployed: individuals and families with income from tax-exempt securities. That's income on which they pay no federal income tax. Their numbers increased 31 percent from 1987 to 1991, going from 3.2 million to 4.2 million. Thus, the two fastest-growing groups of tax filers were those who had lost their jobs and those who didn't need a job.

In the case of tax-exempt securities, nothing better illustrates the hollowness of Washington claims about plugging loopholes than the fact this age-old tax break of the wealthy is still part of the tax code. Upwards of $15 billion in interest income flows untaxed to the nation's wealthiest families each year because interest paid on state and local bonds is exempt from federal taxation.

To be sure, much of the revenue from the sale of tax-exempt securities is put to good use—building schools, highways, bridges, auditoriums, water treatment facilities, and other civic projects. No one disputes that. The problem is one of fairness, and it is threefold: First, the tax benefits flow overwhelmingly to wealthy individuals. Second, people who live in communities and states that issue few such securities ultimately subsidize people living in communities and states that issue large numbers of bonds. And third, the loss of tax revenue at the federal level offsets the tax savings at the local level.

Nevertheless, the tax break remains one of the longest running in the code and has withstood every effort at repeal. More than a half century ago, during debate on the Revenue Act of 1934, Representative Martin F. Smith, Democrat from Washington, condemned the inequities created by tax-exempt bonds and the misuse of the language to promote them: "The term 'tax-exempt securities' is a misnomer, for such a thing does not in fact exist. The bondholders are exempted from paying the tax, but the rest of the community has to pay the tax, which is shifted from the tax dodger to the taxpayer." [14]

Three decades later, in December 1969, when lawmakers enacted the first in a series of tax reform laws, Representative John V. Tunney, Democrat from California, criticized Congress's failure to deal with the issue. Said Tunney: "There are taxpayers with income from tax-free bonds in excess of $1 million who pay no tax at all, and who do not even have to file a return." [15]

Nothing has changed.

In 1986, two decades after Tunney's lament, after Congress had enacted yet another tax bill that it called reform, Sheldon S. Cohen, a former IRS commissioner, explained what the latest tax-code revision would mean for the affluent.

Cohen, who headed the IRS from 1965 to 1969, spoke from personal knowledge: "After tax reform, is it still possible to be rich and avoid paying income taxes? Yes, if you invest in certain tax exempt bonds. We have a client who owned investment real estate, retired, and sold out for about $8 million. He invested every penny in tax exempt bonds.

"He is a millionaire many times over—he did not pay any taxes before tax reform, and he still won't pay taxes after tax reform." [16]

What effect will all the tax-law changes incorporated in the 1993 budget bill, formally called the Omnibus Budget Reconciliation Act, have on this practice?

None.

As for the hotly debated increase in the top tax rate from 31 percent to 39.6 percent on families earning more than $250,000, 39.6 percent of nothing is still nothing.

The result has left intact a tax privilege that benefits the upper 2 percent of Americans. Just who are these people?

They are people like James Jarrell Pickle, the Democratic

congressman from Texas and a senior member of the House Ways and Means Committee—the committee that determines what income will be taxed and what income will be exempt from taxes, who will pay taxes and who will be excused from paying taxes.

Consider a sampling of his tax-free investments: Rowlett (Texas) bond, RMA Tax Free Fund, University of Texas bond, North Central Austin bond, Royce City (Texas) School bond, Eanes (Texas) School bond, Lake Travis School bond, City of San Antonio bond, City of Austin bond, Pearland (Texas) bond, Lower Colorado River bond, Fort Bend (Texas) bond, and Dennison (Texas) Waterworks bond.

In 1992, Pickle's income from his tax-free investments amounted to between $70,000 and $200,000. That's just the money on which he paid no federal income tax.

Forget the higher figure for a moment. Look just at the $70,000. That $70,000 in tax-free income exceeded the wages and salaries of 84 million individuals and families who were required to pay taxes. Or 93 percent of all taxpayers.

Pickle, of course, did pay some tax on other income. The money he received from taxable investments totaled at least another $25,000. His congressional salary that year amounted to $129,500.

Oh, yes, one other source of income: Social Security. In 1992, Representative Pickle picked up $20,000 in Social Security benefits.

You might want to think of that sum in terms of who pays the largest share of Social Security taxes, keeping in mind that as the government collects the Social Security taxes withheld from your paycheck, it immediately transfers that money to retirees like Pickle.

It took the Social Security taxes of more than a dozen clerks working full time at Wal-Mart to pay the $20,000 to Pickle. Or, if you will, the Social Security taxes of a dozen Randall Conaways.

Representative Pickle, by the way, was among that group of senior citizens who many members of Congress worried about because they would have to pay slightly more in taxes on their Social Security income as a result of the 1993 budget act. During debate on the legislation, lawmaker after lawmaker fretted about the increased tax burden on the elderly. Senator Orrin Hatch, the Utah Republican, was typical:

"Over five million senior citizens will see much of their effort to save for their retirement go directly to the tax collector. This plan places an unfair burden of tax not on Social Security benefits, but on the fruits of the lifelong labors of those seniors whose initiative led them to work and save for retirement." [17]

Senator Hatch need not have worried about his congressional colleague, or, for that matter, all the other high-income Social Security recipients. In Pickle's case, his overall income added up to somewhere between $230,000 and $410,000—with about one third of the money exempt from federal income taxes. This means that Representative Pickle paid combined federal income taxes and Social Security taxes at a rate roughly comparable to that paid by a family with a total income between $40,000 and $50,000.

Pickle's tax-free income, whether $70,000 or $200,000 a year, is little more than pocket change when compared with that of serious investors in tax-exempt securities.

Like H. Ross Perot.

The entries in Perot's tax-free investment portfolio for 1991 read like the gazetteer for the United States. Based on a financial disclosure report that he filed with the Federal Election Commission in 1992, his holdings at the time covered forty-four of the fifty states. From Alabama (Alabama Municipal Electric bonds) to Wyoming (Sublette County bonds), from Alaska (Anchorage bonds) to Florida (Lakeland bonds).

Perot's investments covered all governmental jurisdictions: From states (State of Connecticut bonds and Louisiana State General Obligation bonds) to counties (Baltimore County, Maryland, bonds and Butler County, Ohio, bonds). From cities (Denver, Colorado, bonds and Jacksonville, Florida, bonds) to school districts (Philadelphia School bonds and Austin, Texas, Independent School District bonds).

They touched all aspects of public life: From water (California Department of Water bonds and Wichita Water Utility bonds) to airports (Greater Orlando Aviation bonds and Tulsa Airport bonds). From health care (Delaware Health bonds and Illinois Health bonds) to public buildings (Michigan State Building bonds and Texas Public Building Authority bonds). From electricity (Muscatine, Iowa, Electric bonds and Tallahassee Electric bonds) to universities (University of Texas bonds and Nevada State University bonds).

From highways (Kentucky Turnpike bonds and New Jersey Turnpike bonds) to transit systems (Metro Atlanta Rapid Transit Authority bonds and Massachusetts Bay Transit bonds). From hospitals (Salt Lake City, Utah, Hospital bonds and Lake County, Indiana, Hospital bonds) to schools (Arapahoe, Colorado, School District bonds and Cobb County, Georgia, School bonds). From rivers (Lower Colorado River Authority bonds and Grand River, Colorado, Dam Authority bonds) to economic development (Mobile Industrial Development bonds and Ohio Economic Development bonds).

Perot's income from the scores of tax-exempt holdings ranged from a few thousands dollars a year on some bonds to more money in one year than many families will earn in a lifetime on others. From upwards of $5,000 from his Minneapolis Mortgage bonds and Metropolitan Government of Nashville bonds to more than $50,000 from his South Columbia Basin bonds and Oregon State bonds. From more than $100,000 from his Vermont Education bonds and North Carolina Municipal Power bonds to more than $1 million from his Texas Turnpike bonds and South Carolina Public Service bonds.

The bottom line:

Perot's total tax-free income in 1991 fell somewhere between $18 million and more than $87 million. (The FEC requires only that candidates report income within ranges, rather than precise amounts. Thus, candidates need only say if they had income between, say, $50,000 and $100,000, or more than $1 million.)

Whatever the exact figure, whether $18 million or more than $87 million, it was money on which Perot—perennially ranked near the top of *Forbes* magazine's list of the 400 richest Americans—paid no federal income tax. For 1991, that was a tax savings of between $6 million and upwards of $27 million. Remember now, if Perot—or anyone else—doesn't pay his share of income tax, someone else must make up the difference. So who is that someone else?

You might answer that from the vantage point of the 14,000 people who work or live in Fulton County, Pennsylvania, in the mountains of the south-central part of the state, along the Maryland border. Its county seat, McConnellsburg (population 1,200), sits between Pittsburgh and Philadelphia.

As in so much of the rest of the country, job opportunities in Fulton County have dwindled over the years. The county's largest private employer, JLG Industries, Inc., which manufactures cranes and aerial work platforms, reduced its global workforce by 15 percent between 1990 and 1993. Nonetheless, the number of families collecting welfare remains well below the statewide average, and many husbands and wives travel to neighboring counties to work. Of the 5,000 individuals and families who filed tax returns, better than 99 percent reported incomes of less than $100,000.

It took every dollar they paid in federal income tax in 1991 to make up for the income tax that Perot escaped paying by virtue of his tax-exempt investments.

And perhaps then some.

But what do the overall numbers look like? How much interest income goes untaxed? And in contrast, how much unemployment compensation income is subject to tax?

In 1991, tax-exempt interest income totaled $44.3 billion. That money was excluded from adjusted gross income. It was free of federal income tax. That same year, Americans who had lost their jobs reported receiving $23.3 billion in unemployment benefits. That money was added into their adjusted gross income to determine, after deductions, the amount of income tax they were required to pay.

Of those reporting tax-free income, 32,000 millionaires received a total of $4.8 billion. That worked out to an average of $150,000 per millionaire. No tax due.

At the other end of the economic ladder, 1.8 million individuals and families with incomes in the $20,000 to $30,000 range received $4.9 billion in unemployment benefits. That worked out to an average payment of $2,700. It was subject to federal income tax.

Over the five years from 1987 to 1991, some 30,000 individuals and families with incomes of more than $1 million received a total of $21.4 billion tax-free. There were 55,000 people with incomes between $500,000 and $1 million who received $14.8

billion tax-free. And some 200,000 people with incomes between $200,000 and $500,000 received $28.6 billion tax-free.

Falling Behind

While Congress has preserved the tax privileges of the very rich, it has been imposing more taxes on middle-class Americans. Which brings us back to the story of Randall Conaway of Mount Vernon, Missouri.

The Conaway family knows all about the two-class society. They just joined it. The onetime factory worker whose job was transferred to Mexico, Conaway is one of those Americans for whom the tax system has gone awry. To appreciate just how far awry, we need look no further than the taxes now imposed on his unemployment compensation.

For most of its history, unemployment compensation was looked upon as a benefit to help temporarily unemployed persons get through a difficult time. It was not seen as a source of tax revenue. Unemployment assistance dates from 1935, when it was signed into law in the same bill that created Social Security. Over time, Social Security would affect more people, but in 1935, with the Depression raging, unemployment compensation got equal, if not greater, billing. As President Roosevelt put it on signing the benefits into law on August 14, 1935:

"We can never insure one hundred percent of the population against one hundred percent of the hazards and vicissitudes of life, but we have tried to frame a law which will give some measure of protection to the average citizen and to his family against the loss of a job and against poverty-ridden old age." [18]

Neither members of Congress nor the President could have foreseen Social Security's eventual impact. And neither, it is safe to say, could they have foreseen that a future Congress and President would target jobless benefits as a source of tax revenue.

But in 1978, another President—also a Democrat—and another Congress—also Democratically controlled—altered the social contract among worker, employer, and government. This new generation of politicians believed that unemployment compensation was contributing to—unemployment. They reasoned, therefore, that the tax exemption for jobless benefits should be ended.

When he submitted his proposal to Congress that year, President Jimmy Carter, a Democrat, sounded much as President Ronald W. Reagan, a Republican, would sound a decade later:

"Unemployment compensation is a substitute for wages that generally provides needed relief to persons in financial distress. But, in some cases, the unemployment compensation system discourages work for taxable income. Since unemployment benefits are tax free, they are more valuable than an equivalent amount of wages. . . . There can be no justification for conferring this tax-free benefit upon middle and upper-income workers." [19]

Congress agreed.

With passage of the Revenue Act of 1978, unemployment benefits became taxable for the first time. Still, the change affected comparatively few. Only half the benefits could be taxed. And the benefits were not subject to tax until a family's total income exceeded $25,000. (In 1979, median family income was less than $20,000.)

But the door was open. When another President moved into the White House, and another team of policymakers began setting the national agenda, the concept of taxing jobless benefits fit neatly into their view that unemployment compensation was undermining American society and encouraging unemployment.

The idea surfaced on Thanksgiving Day, 1982, while President Reagan was vacationing at his Santa Barbara, California, ranch. Reagan press secretary Larry Speakes said the administration was weighing proposals to tax jobless benefits "to make it less attractive" to stay unemployed. Taxing benefits, Speakes contended, would "encourage [the unemployed] to get into training programs." White House counsel Edwin Meese ventured: "When unemployment benefits end, most people find jobs very quickly." [20]

The proposal came under immediate attack. "People on unemployment aren't goldbricks or loafers," fumed Henry S. Reuss, a Democratic congressman from Wisconsin. "They're usually people who are down on their luck, through no fault of their own. . . . It would be unconscionable to, in effect, reduce unemployment compensation for the poor by taxing it." [21]

The uproar was so intense that an embarrassed White House backed away from the idea a day later, protesting that the press had given the public the wrong impression of President Reagan's intentions.

The notion that the administration wanted to tax jobless benefits, Speakes said, "tends to contribute to an image of not caring about people, which is totally false." Reagan passed the word to his staff, the press was told, that the idea was dead. "This is not the type of thing I want to do," he said. [22]

As events showed, though, it was. Rather than dying, the plan to tax unemployment compensation merely moved to a back burner. When the Treasury Department released a blueprint for revamping the tax code called Tax Reform for Fairness, Simplicity, and Economic Growth, in 1984, one of the proposals to make the code "fairer" called for taxing unemployment benefits. Once again, the idea was to make the unemployed look harder for another job. "Any wage replacement program will reduce work incentives by reducing the net gain from returning to work," the Treasury report theorized. "This effect is greatest when such payments are nontaxable." [23]

Taxing unemployment benefits became a standard feature of the tax-revision bill that worked its way through Congress in 1985–86 to become the Tax Reform Act of 1986. To back it up, the House Ways and Means Committee, chaired and dominated by Democrats, issued a report that dusted off the explanations the White House had offered a few years earlier: "The committee believes that unemployment compensation benefits, which essentially are wage replacement payments, should be treated for tax purposes in the same manner as wages or other wage-type payments. Also, when wage replacement payments are given more favorable tax treatment than wages, some individuals may be discouraged from returning to work. Repeal of the present law exclusion contributes to more equal tax treatment of individuals with the same economic income and to tax simplification." [24]

The committee had Randall Conaway in mind.

The events that took him off the assembly line and put him

on the unemployment line are part of a broader story of what is happening to America, the erosion of the nation's once preeminent manufacturing base.

Conaway worked for eighteen years at a color-television assembly plant of Zenith Corporation in Springfield, Missouri, near the Missouri Ozarks. When the plant opened in 1966, it was one of dozens in the United States, owned by such familiar American names as Motorola, Magnavox, and Philco. Covering 1.7 million square feet, the Springfield plant employed more than 3,000 workers at its peak and was the largest private employer in town. Conaway went to work there in 1973 as a machine operator on the assembly line, which turned out 5,000 color television sets a day. "Working at Zenith was one of the best jobs you could have," Conaway said.[25]

His and his wife's life was a snapshot of middle-class Americana from the 1950s to the 1970s. They bought a modest, one-story home in Mount Vernon, a small town thirty miles southwest of Springfield. They began raising a family of four—two boys and two girls. The couple's life revolved around their children, their community, and Conaway's job at Zenith, where he earned $19,000 a year by the mid-1980s.

While the pay fell short of median-family income, Conaway's job provided a crucial benefit—health insurance. The Zenith plan picked up most of the medical costs of caring for their oldest son, Chris, who suffered from cerebral palsy. "I will say this for Zenith," Conaway said, "they never once refused anything my son needed in all those years."[26]

All that was before Zenith began to move jobs to factories outside the United States, including a new plant in Reynosa, Mexico, just across the Rio Grande from McAllen, Texas. The relocation failed to stem the red ink. Nor did the pay cuts and wage freezes that Zenith workers agreed to in later years. In October 1991, the company announced that it would shut down the Springfield facility—the last American-owned television plant in the United States—and move operations to Mexico.

May 1, 1992, was Conaway's last day. From $8.19 an hour, or roughly $350 a week, his take-home check dropped to $175, the amount Missouri paid in unemployment compensation.

Even with his wife working as a cook in a nursing home at "right above minimum wage," it meant a dramatically lower standard of living for the couple and their children, who ranged in age from nine to sixteen. Conaway and his wife began to deal with the challenge. First, "I just had some financial obligations to get out of the way so we could even survive and live on what little bit we have coming in."[27]

To pay off some of the family's debt, Conaway withdrew $30,000 that had accumulated in a Zenith retirement plan. He reinvested $15,000 in a bank account, then used $5,000 of what remained to pay taxes on the withdrawal—including a penalty for taking the money out of a retirement plan at a plant that had eliminated his job.

Conaway was bewildered: "We agreed with normal taxes, but that 10 percent penalty we got hit with because we drew it out earlier, that really got a lot of us. The government opened up the border and made it easy for Zenith to go down there. They open up the border, we get laid off, and then we get hit with the 10 percent penalty."[28]

But there were still more taxes to pay—this time federal income tax on the unemployment compensation. Once more, Conaway was bewildered: "We've lost a good job. We're getting unemployment of $175 a week. And then . . . to pay income taxes on those unemployment benefits. It just doesn't seem fair. People are already behind."[29]

As for the retirement money left over after paying taxes, it went to pay off debts, including medical bills. The Conaways' oldest son died in 1990, at the age of eighteen. Even with the Zenith health plan, the Conaways incurred substantial medical expenses because they had kept Chris at home in his last months rather than institutionalize him. "We didn't want him dying in a hospital," Conaway said.[30]

By now the family's savings are virtually wiped out. Although he looked hard, Conaway was unable to find another job with the pay and benefits he received at Zenith.

"The job market I'm sure is pretty much like the rest of the country: it's bad," he said. "There are a lot of jobs for $4 and $5 an hour. But a person can't make a living on that. You only exist. If you are a young kid living at home and only have a car payment to worry about, yeah, you can do it. But if you're married or trying to survive as an adult, you can't do it."[31]

It was just that kind of job, though, that Conaway eventually was forced to accept, to keep food on the family table. He went to work as a nurse's aide in a nearby veterans' home. To shuttle people between bed and bathroom, to deliver food, to do all the other chores required to help the elderly, Conaway earns about $230 a week, some $55 more than he received in unemployment compensation. He likes doing the work, but "I don't see this as a permanent situation. I can't afford it. I've got kids looking at college, and it takes more than this. Maybe down the road I can come up with something. Only time will tell."[32]

This sequence of events would plunge some people into a mental depression. But not Randall Conaway. He is, after two years of reversals, upbeat and hopeful.

His wife, Susan, has changed jobs. As a seamstress in a small company that makes men's and women's clothing, she works four ten-hour days, earning $5.50 an hour. If she successfully completes the company's training program, Conaway said, she can earn from $6 to $7 an hour.

Conaway does not have a trace of bitterness about the course his life has taken, but he is perplexed by the federal policies that contributed to the elimination of his job and those of his coworkers:

"To me it seems, since so many companies are adamant on leaving, that every company that stays in the United States should have every tax benefit of the companies that move. But they don't. . . . Make it fair right across the board. It doesn't matter if you are south of the border or north of the border, make it the same for everybody. If you are going to give Joe Blow a million-dollar tax benefit for going south, then give the same to the one who stays here in the states. Make it fair."[33]

Conaway doesn't know what the future holds. He's not concerned about himself or Susan, but he *is* anxious about his children.

"My wife and I will survive," he said. "I will be successful in whatever I do. But I do worry about my kids. I don't know what their quality of life will be. I have life better than my mother and father ever had it. But what about my kids? What in the hell are they going to have?

"I know many kids who are holding down two jobs just to be able to afford to buy a house. What's it going to be like five years from now, ten years from now? And a lot of them can't even get the down payment for a house working two jobs now. What's going to happen for, say, my kids? If I can't help them, what are they going to have? What are they going to have to look forward to?"[34]

Let us summarize: Congress raises Social Security tax rates only on middle-income workers so that it can use the excess money to pay for other government programs and disguise the size of the true deficit. It seeks out the unemployed, mostly middle-income and lower-income workers, and taxes their benefits. At the other end, anyone who makes more than $60,600 escapes the Social Security tax. And lastly, 300,000 persons with incomes above $200,000 received $64.8 billion—that's billion—in tax-free interest income between 1987 and 1991.

Just a couple more contrasts between the two tax laws, one for the privileged person, another for the common person. But lest you still have some lingering doubt about the two-tiered system, let's take a look at one other area of the tax law to see how the beliefs of lawmakers and policymakers have changed over the years, to see how they have categorized American taxpayers, to see how they have come to treat them differently.

The tax issue: charity. Or more precisely, the tax deduction for charitable contributions.

The Philadelphia Nun's Write-off

Like so many preferences in the tax code, it began with the warning that the end was near—in this case the end of charitable, humanitarian, and educational endeavors as they had been known. The year was 1917. Congress was preparing to raise tax rates to finance World War I. A freshman Democratic senator from New Hampshire, Henry F. Hollis, warned that the rush to increase taxes would undermine the nation's churches, educational institutions, and charitable organizations.

When "we impose these very heavy taxes on incomes," Hollis told his Senate colleagues, "that will be the first place where the wealthy men will be tempted to economize, namely, in donations to charity. They will say, 'charity begins at home.' "[35] Hollis proposed a temporary solution—an amendment that would allow taxpayers to deduct up to 20 percent of their taxable income for charitable contributions. The deduction would be eliminated once the war was over and tax rates were lowered.

Remember that at the time, 95 percent of all working Americans did not earn enough money to pay income tax. The beneficiaries of the provision would be the country's most affluent citizens. As would be the case for the rest of the century, much of the news media rushed to support the tax break.

"This country," declared the *Washington Post,* "cannot abandon or impoverish the great structure of private charity and education that has been one of the most notable achievements of American civilization. Therefore, with every additional dollar the government finds it necessary to take in taxation it becomes increasingly necessary to accept the principle of the pending amendment and leave untaxed that part of every citizen's income which he may give voluntarily to the public good." [36]

The *Boston Transcript* declared that "in simple justice and for the national welfare the United States Senate should promptly write the Hollis amendment into the taxation bill." Failure to do so, the newspaper said, would strike "at America's whole organization for social progress and education, the relief of distress, and the remedy of evils." [37]

And the *New York Times* warned that "there is a necessary social effect to this taxation of great incomes. It diminishes or dries up the springs of philanthropic, eleemosynary and educational life. The foreign calls on charity and benevolence since the war began have reduced contributions to American educational and humane works." [38]

When the Revenue Act of 1917 emerged from Congress, the charitable deduction had been scaled back slightly, to 15 percent of taxable income. It was the first in a long line of temporary tax deductions that would become permanent.

Although tax rates fell, thanks to Andrew Mellon, the charitable deduction, designed only to see philanthropy through the war, lived on. And as usually happens in tax matters, the new deduction provided the opening for yet another tax provision that would provide a windfall worth tens of billions of dollars to the richest Americans.

The provision, one of the earliest special-interest tax bills on

record, was inserted into the Revenue Act of 1924. The beneficiary was a most unlikely special interest—Mary Katharine
Drexel, a Philadelphia nun.

Born in 1858, she was the second daughter of Francis Anthony Drexel, a Philadelphia banker. Mary Katharine was
raised in the style befitting wealthy Philadelphians—a town
house in the city, an estate in the country, private tutors, fre-
quent trips to Europe.

It was assumed that the outgoing Kate would become another
Drexel pillar of the Philadelphia establishment. She loved the
social whirl and once told a friend, "Oh, I love those parties.
I'm never going to stop going to parties as long as I live." [39]

Thus, it came as something of a shock when Kate quietly
entered a convent at the age of thirty-one in 1889 to become a
nun. Two years later, she took the vows of poverty and soon
afterward received the Pope's permission to establish her own
order, the Sisters of the Blessed Sacrament. Known as Mother
Drexel, she embarked on what would become her life's work—
establishing schools for poor black and Indian children in the
West and South.

In New Orleans, she founded Xavier University, the nation's
first Catholic university for blacks. She started a school for poor
black and Indian children on the grounds of the mother house
of her order, north of Philadelphia. The money to fund these
works came from a $6 million trust fund left by her father. It
yielded an income estimated at $1,000 a day, making Mother
Drexel, as newspapers were fond of saying, "the richest nun in
the world."

Mother Drexel's practice of underwriting good works posed
no problem until the federal income tax was enacted in 1913.
Even though she was spending all her money to feed, clothe,
and educate the poor, she was required to pay a modest amount
in federal income tax. Enactment of the deduction in 1917 offered little help, since it was limited to 15 percent of income.

That Mother Drexel should have to divert a portion of her
income from meeting the needs of the poor to the U.S. Treasury upset her brother-in-law, Walter George Smith, a Philadelphia lawyer. Smith took up Mother Drexel's tax problem with
another Philadelphia lawyer, George Wharton Pepper. Both
prominent members of the Philadelphia bar, Smith and Pepper

lunched together at the Lawyers Club, near Independence Hall. Pepper was in a good position to remedy the situation. He was a freshman member of the U.S. Senate.

Smith proposed an amendment that would exempt from taxation persons who in any year gave away "90 percent or more" of their income to charity. Pepper approached colleagues on the Senate Finance Committee. There was no opposition. The committee dropped into the Revenue Act of 1924 sixty words that afforded an exception to the 15 percent charitable deduction in cases where a taxpayer gave away 90 percent of his or her income. That person would be entitled to an unlimited charitable deduction.

Still, since most working Americans paid no income tax, there was little interest in the deduction for charitable contributions. Little interest, that is, until Congress manufactured its next charity crisis. Like the first one, it was war related.

As Congress expanded the income tax from a levy on the affluent to a mass tax on almost all working Americans to finance the Second World War, and at the same time introduced withholding, alarms were sounded once more about charitable giving. This time it was argued that withholding should not apply to a percentage of income the worker said was going to charity.

Carl T. Curtis, the Republican representative from Nebraska, was concerned that since a portion of every worker's paycheck would be withheld to cover the taxes owed, these people would cut back on their charitable donations. Said Curtis:

"Because men give a few dollars to support the Boy Scout movement a community may be saved the expense of a costly trial and a prison term. Because men give of their substance to support a church that inspires people to high living and restrains their bent for evil, homes are saved, and children are not sent to public institutions supported by taxation. Because men give of their substance to provide charity and philanthropy the taxpayers of America are saved millions of dollars."[40]

James L. Baldwin, research director of the Institute for Capital Conservation and a self-described tax specialist, repeated the theme in a letter to Curtis, who reprinted it in the *Congressional Record*:

"It [withholding] will dry up and bankrupt our churches,

hospitals, colleges, and other voluntarily supported institutions of benevolence. Already, their receipts are the lowest in American history in ratio to national income."[41]

Congress rejected the proposal for two reasons: First, the government needed every penny of revenue to pay for the war. The second reason, far more significant for the long term, involved the beginning of the two tax systems. Hollis's original deduction sailed through Congress in 1917 because it benefited a comparatively small number of high-income taxpayers. Curtis's provision, on the other hand, would have benefited the great mass of taxpayers.

As it turned out, income tax withholding had no effect on charity in America. Churches flourished. Charitable organizations continued their good deeds. The Boy Scouts prospered. And another group prospered even more—affluent individuals and families who capitalized on Mother Drexel's vow of poverty.

The exception to the tax code that enabled Mother Drexel to spend all her money on the needy became an ingenious scheme that allowed persons who never had a nodding acquaintance with indigence—and who certainly had never taken vows of poverty—to avoid payment of tens of billions of dollars in federal income taxes.

As time went by, a growing number of high-income taxpayers discovered they could qualify for the Philadelphia nun's write-off without actually giving any cash to charity. The trick was to donate an asset, usually securities or real estate, sometimes a work of art, to a foundation, often one under the donor's control. The asset typically had been acquired years before, at a fraction of its current value. But the charitable contribution was calculated on its current market value.

This meant an artwork bought years before for $50,000, which had increased in value to $1 million, could be given to a tax-exempt organization and the donor could claim a $1 million charitable deduction. If the donor had an annual salary of $1 million, he would pay no income tax on that money.

In 1963, a Treasury Department study showed how one millionaire had escaped payment of $6.2 million in tax one year, thanks to the unlimited charitable deduction. The unnamed individual acquired stock for $466,000. He later donated the securities, then valued at $21.6 million, to a foundation. He wrote off the $21.6 million as a charitable deduction on his tax return, thereby offsetting the tax owed on all other income that year.

His story was not unusual. By the 1960s, more than a hundred wealthy persons with annual incomes exceeding $1 million were using the deduction to "pay little or no tax on their income." Among the beneficiaries: John D. Rockefeller III, grandson of the founder of Standard Oil, now Exxon Corporation.

When Treasury Secretary Joseph Barr announced in January 1969 that 155 individuals and families with incomes above $200,000 paid no federal income tax, in part because of the unlimited charitable deduction, and lawmakers disclosed self-dealing transactions between tax-exempt organizations and their founders, the pressure built to overhaul the tax code and eliminate abuses.

Bills were introduced to compel foundations to distribute a percentage of their income every year instead of accumulating it, as many were; to impose a small tax on their investment income; to prohibit a foundation from owning a controlling interest in a business; and to end the unlimited charitable deduction. Officials of philanthropic institutions rushed to Capitol Hill to defend their way of doing business. Among them was John D. Rockefeller III.

The oldest and most anonymous of the third generation of Rockefellers—Nelson, Laurance, Winthrop, and David were his brothers—John D. III was a formal, retiring person, even in relationships with family members, as attested to by this entry in his diary at age fifty-one: "Had lunch with Brother Laurance —a sort of 'get acquainted' talk."[42]

With interests in Asian affairs, population control, and the arts, John D. III, more than his brothers, had assumed the family mantle of philanthropist, moving into positions on many of the boards that his father had created, and serving as chairman of the Rockefeller Foundation. It was in that capacity he appeared before the House Ways and Means Committee in February 1969.

Rockefeller began by reciting the family's efforts in private philanthropy; the contributions of the Rockefeller Foundation to the fields of public health and agriculture; the Population Council; Lincoln Center; and Colonial Williamsburg. He stressed the importance of such work:

> My experience with these organizations has made me increasingly aware of the importance of private philanthropy in our pluralistic American society. It supplements the work of government. It often pioneers the difficult or controversial field for government. It provides a channel through which individual initiative can be expressed effectively.[43]

Then he summoned up Alexis de Tocqueville, the French political scientist and politician who set down his observations on American life following a tour of the country in 1831 and 1832, at the age of twenty-six:

> These Americans are the most peculiar people in the world. You'll not believe it when I tell you how they behave. In a local community in their country a citizen may conceive of some need which is not being met. What does he do? He goes across the street and discusses it with his neighbor. Then what happens? A committee comes into existence and then the committee begins functioning on behalf of that need, and you won't believe this, but it's true: all of this is done without reference to any bureaucrat; all of this is done by the private citizens on their own initiative.[44]

Rockefeller acknowledged abuses that needed to be corrected, but he opposed the remedies, especially the proposal to end the unlimited charitable deduction:

> This provision makes available for public service an important source of philanthropic funds. As is well known, a relatively few people give a high proportion of the total in major fund-raising campaigns. Many of these large donors are able to do so only because of the unlimited deduction.[45]

Then Rockefeller went on to explain his own situation, his own views on taxation:

I, personally, believe that all individuals who are able should pay some reasonable tax, including those who have become entitled to the unlimited deduction privilege. A figure of 10 to 15 percent of adjusted gross income occurs to me as a reasonable amount for such individuals to pay in these circumstances, recognizing that the balance of what would otherwise be paid in taxes is being contributed to projects and programs in the public interest.

In my own case, although I have qualified for the unlimited deduction privilege during every year since 1961, I have deliberately paid a tax of between 5 and 10 percent of my adjusted gross income each of those years.[46]

And there you had it, what one of the country's richest citizens considered a "reasonable" tax, one that he paid voluntarily.

Interestingly, not one member of the Ways and Means Committee, which writes the tax laws, took note publicly that John D. Rockefeller III's idea of a fair tax on the wealthy was a rate below that levied on the country's median-income families—families who did not have the option of paying the tax voluntarily. It was a quiet affirmation of America's two-tiered tax system—one for those at the top, another for everyone else.

Although Rockefeller made no mention of it during his Washington appearance, he and his brothers wrote off more than their cash contributions on their tax returns. In addition to the direct outlays, the brothers and their employees at the Rockefeller Family office in Rockefeller Center provided "services" to tax-exempt groups. For tax purposes, the Rockefellers called these services "unreimbursed expenses."

That included salaries paid to employees and "travel, entertainment, and other miscellaneous expenses" incurred by the Rockefellers or their employees while performing services for a charitable organization. If one of the brothers flew to Washington to take part in the deliberations of a national study group, stayed there several days, entertained fellow panel members during the proceedings, and employed his personal staff to assist the group, the expenses and salaries were written off as a charitable deduction.

Most of the services for which John D. III claimed the unlimited charitable deduction were to groups or causes to which he had long given money. A longtime advocate of population control, he served in 1970–71 as chairman of the presidential Commission on Population, Growth and the American Future. For trips to Washington and for using Rockefeller Family employees on commission business, he deducted $233,169 on his income tax returns in 1970 and 1971 for "services" under the unlimited charitable deduction.

The brothers also deducted expenses for "services" to the family's foundations or other tax-exempt institutions. David wrote off $24,106 of unreimbursed expenses for Rockefeller University in 1970. He and John D. III wrote off $21,882 for services to the Rockefeller Brothers Fund, the philanthropic venture they oversaw with their other brothers. For services to his own foundation, the JDR3rd Fund, Inc., John D. III wrote off $101,061 from 1969 to 1971. All told, John D. III claimed "unreimbursed" expenses of $708,623 for the years 1969 to 1971. David's totaled $155,251 for 1970–71.

When the Tax Reform Act of 1969 finally became law, it contained many of the provisions Rockefeller had spoken against, including a gradual phaseout of the unlimited charitable deduction. But what Congress took away with one hand, it returned with the other, raising the allowable charitable deduction from 30 percent to 50 percent of adjusted gross income, a benefit of value only to the nation's most affluent citizens.

No Deduction for Doing Good

For some special interests, this was not enough. The Tax Reform Act of 1969, followed by the Tax Reform Act of 1976, reduced the number of taxpayers filing itemized returns, just as intended. In all, 12 million individuals and families stopped writing off deductions—including charitable contributions—between 1969 and 1977. Officials of America's tax-exempt organizations responded as their predecessors had in the early 1940s, forecasting the demise of charity. They had friends in both parties.

In 1978, two senators, Daniel P. Moynihan, a Democrat, and Robert Packwood, a Republican, took up their cause. As lawmakers have done for years, they said they were concerned about inequities, that the overwhelming majority of individuals and families received no tax benefit from their charitable gifts.

The solution: a Moynihan-Packwood bill that would permit everyone to write off charitable contributions on their tax returns, regardless of whether they itemized other deductions. Moynihan explained:

"The principal effect of this amendment is to benefit low- and middle-income persons, most of whom do not itemize, and to encourage charitable giving by providing all taxpayers with this effective and human incentive." [47]

As always in matters of taxation, economists were standing by to provide the requisite data in support of the need for the legislation. In this case, Moynihan cited Harvard Professor Martin Feldstein, former chairman of the Council of Economic Advisers and "perhaps the most distinguished economist who has addressed himself to these issues." Feldstein had estimated that "charities have lost about $5 billion in contributions since 1970, primarily as a consequence of changes in the tax code." [48]

Taking a leaf out of John D. Rockefeller III's book, Moynihan turned to Tocqueville to sell his colleagues on the worthiness of the proposal. Indeed, he turned to the very same words recited by Rockefeller, although apparently from a different translation.

Packwood was more precise about which organizations were suffering as a result of the inability of low- and middle-income persons to deduct their contributions:

"Upper-income persons traditionally support a somewhat different range of nonprofit organizations than middle-income persons. For example, wealthy donors often emphasize higher education and cultural activities. In contrast, middle-income givers have more traditionally supported community-based charities such as the United Way, the Red Cross, the Salvation Army, Meals-on-Wheels, as well as the varied activities of churches." [49]

Packwood, too, cited Harvard Professor Feldstein as the authority and concluded: "Individuals taking the standard deduction should not continue to be taxed on private dollars contributed to nonprofit organizations for public purposes; 77

percent of our taxpayers currently pay tax on their voluntary contributions. This bill corrects that inequity."[50]

The news media rushed to support the cause. *Time* magazine and the *Washington Post* published columns calling for passage of the legislation. Both invoked Professor Feldstein. Both invoked Tocqueville—the same passage.

During hearings held later in 1978, representatives of various tax-exempt organizations paraded before congressional committees to urge passage of the Moynihan-Packwood bill and to predict dire consequences if the measure failed. Jack Moskowitz, vice president of the United Way, was typical.

"There is a real danger that charitable giving may become the province of the wealthy elite instead of the open, shared expression of concern for others that has maintained our pluralistic way of life for 200 years,"[51] Moskowitz warned, adding:

"If Congress does not accept the Moynihan-Packwood proposal, United Way may not flourish, but it will survive. The large universities, museums, and other long-standing institutions will survive also. But all of those financially fragile entities so important to American life, such as local community centers, small colleges, day-care centers, halfway houses, co-ops, little theaters, will surely go under."[52]

All the lobbying was to no avail. Congress—in 1978, at least—was unwilling to extend the charitable deduction to all taxpayers. That would soon change.

In 1981, as President Reagan pushed the first of his tax-cuts-for-the-wealthy through Congress, Moynihan and Packwood resurrected their charitable deduction for nonitemizers. Once more, the two senators cited the unfairness of the existing system. As Packwood put it:

"It is unfair, however, that we allow those who itemize—quite frankly those are usually people in upper-income brackets—those who itemize the deductions to take a deduction for contributions to charity, but those who do not itemize to be prohibited from deducting a contribution to charities."[53]

President Reagan opposed the idea. While he often spoke wistfully of the rich American tradition of volunteerism and support of charitable efforts, the President personally was not big on contributions. Indeed, that year, 1981, the Reagans' cash contributions would total $5,965, or 1.4 percent of their adjusted gross income of $412,730.

The Reagans claimed another $5,930 in noncash charitable contributions. That was the value assigned to Nancy Reagan's designer clothing, which she donated to the Fashion Institute of Design and Merchandising Museum and the Los Angeles County Museum of Art.

But Reagan was, if anything, flexible. When it became clear that he needed every vote for his tax-cut package, he threw his support to the charitable write-off for nonitemizers, and the provision passed into law as part of the Economic Recovery Tax Act of 1981. Truth to tell, the provision—like most of those that lawmakers champion as a boon to middle-income taxpayers —was all show and no substance.

As is the case with all deductions, the more prosperous enjoyed a disproportionate share of the benefits. With a top tax rate of 50 percent, a wealthy family that donated $200,000 to a foundation was actually giving only $100,000 of its money. The family gave 50 percent, the other 50 percent came from the U.S. Treasury. By contrast, a middle-income family in the 19 percent bracket that donated $500 to a church gave $405—or 81 percent—from its own pocket, with the remaining $95, or 19 percent, coming from the U.S. Treasury.

The Moynihan-Packwood provision had other limitations. For 1982 and 1983, the deduction was limited to 25 percent of contributions totaling no more than $100. Thus, no matter how much money was donated, the deduction could not exceed $25. In 1984, the law raised the maximum write-off to $75. In 1985, the nonitemizer could deduct 50 percent of all contributions, with no limit, and in 1986, 100 percent of all contributions.

Then came the bill's fine print. From the beginning, the provision had been sold on the basis of fairness. If the rich could deduct their contributions, the average taxpayer should have the same right. But for nonitemizing beneficiaries of the Moynihan-Packwood provision, fairness was only temporary. It would expire on December 31, 1986. After that, nonitemizers would once again lose the deduction for charitable contributions. The two-tax system would be fully restored: The affluent could write off their contributions; the average worker could not.

Four years later, in May 1985, President Reagan unveiled his plan "to overhaul our tax code based on the principles of simplicity and fairness, opening the way to a generation of growth." The proposal, he said, "will help fulfill America's commitment to fairness, hope, and opportunity for all its citizens."[54]

Among the President's recommendations: Eliminate a year ahead of time the charitable deduction for anyone who did not file an itemized return. Why the abrupt reversal in tax policy? Listen to the explanation offered by President Reagan's tax advisers:

"The allowance of a charitable contribution deduction for nonitemizers is administratively burdensome for the Internal Revenue Service and complicated for taxpayers. In particular, it is extremely difficult for the IRS to monitor deductions claimed for countless small donations to eligible charities; the expense of verification is out of proportion to the amounts of tax involved. Dishonest taxpayers are thus encouraged to believe that they can misrepresent their charitable contributions with impunity."[55]

In other words, the 25.4 million individuals and families who did not itemize deductions were prone to cheating when it came to writing off their charitable contributions. But the 36.2 million taxpayers who itemized deductions were more likely to be honest. The average charitable contribution claimed by nonitemizers in 1985, by the way, was $186. The average charitable contribution claimed by those who filed itemized returns was seven times as much, or $1,326. For those with incomes over $1 million, the average charitable gift was $147,000.

When the Tax Reform Act of 1986 emerged from Congress, the charitable deduction for nonitemizers, the deduction once labeled critical to the survival of community centers and little theaters, the deduction that restored Tocqueville's vision of America, the deduction that Moynihan and Packwood had said was needed to make the system more fair, had been eliminated. Neither Packwood nor Moynihan thought it important enough to keep, although Moynihan was distressed about subjecting rich people who donated artworks and stocks that had appreciated in value to a slight increase in taxes.

Congress apparently subscribed to the views put forth by President Reagan's tax experts, who had concluded that the deduction for nonitemizers did not really encourage increased charitable contributions—the opposite view to that put forth by the expert on the other side, Harvard Professor Feldstein. The President's experts said:

> There is little data indicating whether the charitable contribution deduction for nonitemizers has significantly increased the level of charitable giving. Because nonitemizers generally have lower incomes and thus lower marginal tax rates than itemizers, their contributions generally are not affected significantly by tax considerations. Rather, contributions made by nonitemizers are influenced far more by non-tax considerations such as general donative intent. Therefore, any adverse effect of the proposal on charitable giving is not expected to be significant.[56]

Translation: Low- and middle-income individuals and families contributed to churches and charities because they were motivated to do good, and therefore did not need a tax deduction. Itemizers, on the other hand, contributed because they received a tax deduction.

CHAPTER 4

★ $ ★ $ ★

WHY CORPORATIONS PAY LESS

The Potato Chip Deduction

When you sit down to calculate the amount of taxes you owe the U.S. government, how would you like to have a new deduction? A write-off, say, for the value of your good family name?

Here is how it would work:

Let's say that in 1993 you married and are now preparing your first joint tax return. You and your new spouse had combined income for the year of $35,000. You subtract from that $4,700 in personal exemptions. That leaves $30,300. Next, you subtract $8,000 in itemized deductions for interest on the home mortgage, real estate and other taxes, and contributions to your church and charities. That leaves you with $22,300 on which you must pay taxes.

But you get one more deduction. For the merger of the family names. It's a tough call deciding just what that name might be worth. Pick a round number, say $150,000. You'll have to spread the write-off over fifteen years, for $10,000 a year.

So you deduct $10,000 for the family name. That further reduces the amount of income on which you must pay taxes to $12,300.

Total tax due: $1,845.

The deduction for your name knocked 45 percent off the family tax bill, saving you $1,500 in federal income tax.

When, you ask, can you begin to claim this new deduction?
You can't.
Corporations can.

Buried in the 1993 Omnibus Budget Reconciliation Act—the Clinton budget bill that Democrats and Republicans fought over furiously during the spring and summer of 1993—was a tax-law revision that permits merging corporations to write off the value of their names and other so-called intangible assets on their tax returns.

Businesses have always been permitted to depreciate the value of physical assets—a building, a piece of equipment, a car. The reasoning is this: Such items wear out over time and ultimately have to be replaced. Moreover, the price paid for a piece of machinery, for example, is known. So it is easy to figure the deduction for that equipment over a period of years. The same is true for a building or a car.

But what is the name of a potato chip worth? Or a recipe for pizza? Or a formula for wax? Or the secret ingredient in a hair tonic? Since no one really knows the value of "Dorito" when it is attached to corn chips, or "Kellogg's" to raisin bran, or "Skippy" to peanut butter, or "Quaker" to oats, or "Thomas's" to English muffins, businesses had been barred from deducting the estimated worth of brand names.

Now, thanks to Dan Rostenkowski, chairman of the House Ways and Means Committee and Washington's most powerful tax writer, all that has changed. His work prompted one financial publication to label the budget legislation "The Investment Bankers Relief Act of 1993."[1]

Under the new law, when one company acquires another— say, a food company—it will be permitted to write off the estimated worth of the brand names involved over fifteen years. This tax giveaway will allow corporations to escape payment of tens of billions of dollars in income taxes. It also raises the possibility of another round of corporate takeovers—with accompanying job losses.

Better still, although the tax break is not exactly retroactive, it sort of is. The courts have been clogged with cases in which businesses have challenged the Internal Revenue Service's refusal to allow such deductions. The budget act encourages the

IRS to settle these cases in keeping with the spirit of the new law. In other words, let corporations keep their write-offs even though they may not have been legal when first claimed.

Curiously, lawmakers who were silent about this retroactive tax giveaway for corporations were among the loudest in denouncing the act's retroactive increase in tax rates on the wealthy. "I wonder what would have happened last November if they [freshmen senators] announced during the campaign they would not only raise taxes once they took office but they would even raise taxes that would be effective before they took office," asked Senator Robert Dole.[2] Over in the House, Robert K. Dornan, California Republican, put it this way: "Probably the worst feature of Clinton's tax-hike plan is that the higher tax rates are retroactive to the beginning of this year, twenty days before Clinton was even inaugurated."[3] By way of comparison, the retroactive tax break for deducting intangible assets goes back not just days or months, but many years, for those companies that went to court.

So what difference does it make if companies get a deduction for the name of their potato chips?

Remember how lawmakers take care of the rich, closing one loophole while opening another, all the time preserving the most generous ones? Well, they do the same for corporations. Lawmakers and Presidents have provided businesses with a catalog of tax preferences that allow them to pay taxes at a rate below that imposed on middle-income and working-poor individuals and families. Sometimes preferences can be used by all businesses. Others are tailor-made for certain businesses or industries.

There are preferences that permit banks, which make billions of dollars in loans to foreign countries that go bad, to write off the unpaid debt on their tax returns. There are preferences that allow foreign-owned companies to pay taxes at rates below U.S.-owned businesses. There are preferences that allow oil companies to write off imaginary costs. There are preferences that allow poorly run businesses to get tax refunds from earlier years. There are preferences that allow unlimited deductions. There are preferences that encourage corporations to restructure and avoid taxes completely.

The cumulative impact of all the preferences—plus the lowest tax rate in a half century—means corporations pay much less in tax, and you make up the difference. How much less?

If corporations in 1994 paid taxes at the same rate as corporations did through the 1950s, the U.S. Treasury would collect an extra $250 billion a year. That's two and one-half times as much money as corporations presently pay in taxes. Let's put that $250 billion in more personal terms.

It would be enough money to nearly eliminate the federal deficit.

It would be enough money to provide a 60 percent tax cut for everyone with an income below $200,000.

It would be enough money to pay for health care for everyone who is uninsured—and still have enough left over for a tax cut for individuals.

Business conditions in the 1990s, to be sure, are not the same as they were in the 1950s. And while it might be difficult to generate an equivalent amount of tax revenue, the $250 billion figure provides some insight into just how much taxes corporations once paid, and how little they pay today.

Which brings us to Tax Rule No. 4: When corporations pay a smaller share of overall taxes, individuals must make up the difference.

During the 1940s, corporate taxes accounted for 33 percent of the federal government's general fund tax collections. The corporate share slipped to 31 percent in the 1950s and to 27 percent in the 1960s. Then it plunged to 21 percent in the 1970s, continuing its free fall in the 1980s to 15 percent, where it remains in the 1990s.

At the same time corporations were contributing an ever smaller share of the cost of running the government, individuals were picking up a growing portion. During the 1940s, individual income taxes accounted for 44 percent of the government's general fund tax collections. This figure rose to 49 percent in the 1950s, to 57 percent in the 1960s, to 66 percent in the 1970s, to 72 percent in the 1980s, and to 73 percent in the 1990s. (Excise taxes and other miscellaneous revenue make up the difference.)

This is not to say that every company gets a break on its taxes. Far from it. There are wide disparities among corporations.

Some businesses, like some individuals, shoulder a disproportionate amount of the corporate tax. Some companies pay taxes close to the maximum rate. Many pay very little. But overall they are sharing less of the burden.

Tax-Free Cruising

On April 15, 1993—the deadline for filing federal income tax returns—a full-page advertisement appeared in *USA Today* and other newspapers. The ad showed a bearded Uncle Sam, wearing a uniform with epaulets and a top hat fashioned out of stars and stripes. On his left breast was a name tag, UNCLE SAM, CAPTAIN, and he was pointing at the reader in the time-honored "I Want You" fashion. Only this time, the message in large type was:

"Taxpayers, you've got some Royal Caribbean Coming."

And in smaller letters:

"Long forms, short forms and the refund you thought would be a lot bigger. Holy withholding, don't we all have some Royal Caribbean coming? Forget your IRA—you couldn't ask for a better shelter than being under an umbrella on the deck on one of our ships. . . . We even have a wonderful kids' program—so bring the little tax deductions."

Sunny skies aside, American taxpayers might well wish they had "some Royal Caribbean coming." That's because Royal Caribbean—a cruise company with its headquarters and ships based in Miami, a company that had former First Lady Rosalynn Carter launch one of its vessels in 1988, a company that makes tens of millions of dollars in profits, largely on the basis of its U.S. customers—pays not one cent of U.S. income tax.

Royal Caribbean Cruises, Ltd., which describes itself as "one of the leading providers of cruises to North American passengers," offers cruises to more than one hundred destinations on four continents.[4] In 1993, the company, by its own account, operated "nine ships with a total of 14,228 passenger berths, making it the largest cruise line brand in the world based on passenger berths."[5]

Its fleet includes the *Majesty of the Seas* (capacity: 2,354 passengers), featuring "a five-deck atrium with glass elevators, two dining rooms, a bi-level show lounge, a nightclub, a casino, a cinema, children's facilities, twin swimming pools, a two-level indoor-outdoor café, an exercise facility, a conference center and a library. . . . Many cabins have private balconies and verandas."[6]

To recruit passengers for cruises, ranging in price from $180 to more than $600 a night per person, Royal Caribbean emphasizes its shipboard services:

> It's no mystery why Royal Caribbean is an award-winning cruise line. You'll get your first clue when you meet our service staff. Take your room steward. When you see how neat and tidy he keeps your room, by making the bed, changing the linens, cleaning the bath and doing extra little things like lining your shoes up all in a row, you might begin to think of him as your personal butler. . . .
>
> Friendly waiters flavor every meal with refined hospitality and easygoing good humor (some of them really should be listed as part of the entertainment). Although they've won plenty of awards for service, they're never too impressed with themselves—not until you're happy with every aspect of your meal.[7]

They'd better be friendly. Their livelihood depends on it.

Waiters and busboys, for example, were hired to provide that "refined hospitality and easygoing good humor" at a salary that placed a premium on tips. "We extend to you the opportunity of employment with our company in the capacity of busboy-waiter at a salary of U.S. $50 per month," according to a 1992 employment contract with a waiter and busboy. Actually, the company guaranteed $700 a month, but that figure included all tips. While the cruise line had a good deal on its taxes, the benefits did not extend to employees. According to the employment agreement: "Salary payments will be made on the fifteenth (15) and the last day of the month in cash onboard the vessel. Federal Income Taxes will be withheld from all United States citizens-residents."[8]

Employment practices aside, business has been brisk for Royal Caribbean. Each year, its ships have operated at between 98 and 100 percent of capacity. Royal Caribbean says its "share of the overall North American market in terms of passengers carried has increased from 13.3 percent in 1987 to 19.7 percent in 1992."[9]

Royal Caribbean's revenue rose accordingly. From 1989 through 1992, revenue from the cruise business totaled more than $3 billion. Its operating profit—or profit before interest expense and taxes—was $395 million. After interest payments of $237 million, the company's net income came to $158 million.

On those profits, Royal Caribbean paid no U.S. income tax. As the company explained in a report filed with the U.S. Securities and Exchange Commission:

"Income taxes are not significant to the company since the company and its subsidiaries are not subject to United States corporate tax on income generated from the operation of their ships."[10]

Royal Caribbean is essentially an American company, but according to SEC reports it is incorporated in Liberia and registers its ships in the Bahamas, Liberia, and Norway. It is known in the tax code as a "controlled foreign corporation," which is exempt from U.S. income tax.

Now, who controls this company that produces more than $1 billion in revenue a year and pays no income tax? The principal owners are the Wilhelmsens, a wealthy Norwegian shipping family, and Cruise Associates, a partnership formed in the Bahamas to represent the interests of one exceedingly rich Chicago family—the Pritzkers.

The actual investors in the Bahamian partnerships are various trusts established primarily for the Pritzker family. The Pritzkers themselves rank near the top of *Forbes* magazine's list of the 400 richest people in America, with an estimated fortune of $4.4 billion. Their holdings include scores of businesses, from the Hyatt Hotel chain to the Union Tank Car Company, which leases railway tank cars. Jay A. Pritzker, chairman of the board of Hyatt Corporation, became a Royal Caribbean director in 1993.

Is Royal Caribbean's tax-free status a cruise line aberration? Not at all.

Its chief competitor, Carnival Cruise Lines, Inc., also is immune from the corporate income tax on its cruise business. Like Royal Caribbean, Carnival is basically an American company. It is headquartered in Miami, and its Caribbean-bound ships sail from Miami. But the company is incorporated in Panama. And its subsidiaries were established in the Bahamas, the British Virgin Islands, Liberia, and the Netherlands Antilles.

During the seven years from 1986 to 1992, Carnival reported profits of $1.2 billion. On its noncruise operations, it made tax payments totaling $29 million. That worked out to an overall tax rate of 2.4 percent.

By way of contrast: In 1991, a total of 17.3 million individuals and families with income between $20,000 and $30,000 paid $38 billion in income tax. Their average tax rate: 8.9 percent—nearly four times the rate levied on Carnival.

Another way to look at Carnival's preferential tax rate is from the viewpoint of the 11.4 million individuals and families who earned between $50,000 and $75,000 in 1991. They paid, on average, $7,735 in taxes. If they had been taxed at Carnival's rate, they would have paid $1,444—a savings of $6,291. The 2.6 million individuals and families in the $100,000 to $200,000 income group would have paid $3,128—a tax savings of $21,139.

Carnival, by the way, is controlled by another member of the *Forbes* directory of 400 richest Americans—Ted Arison. The magazine estimates his fortune at $3.65 billion.

Surely, though, the tax situation of Royal Caribbean, Carnival, and other cruise lines must be an exception. Right?

Wrong.

It is true they benefit from a tax preference Congress designed especially for them. But other companies keep their taxes low—often below the rate imposed on middle-income individuals and families, and far below the 34 percent corporate rate in effect from 1987 to 1993—through other preferences. Consider these approximate tax rates paid by a few companies, based on information drawn from reports filed with the SEC.

CHASE MANHATTAN CORPORATION. Based in New York, Chase is the parent company of Chase Manhattan Bank, the global banking institution. For the years 1991 and 1992, Chase reported income before taxes of $1.5 billion. The company paid $25 million in U.S. income tax, for a tax rate of 1.7 percent. The official corporate tax rate in those years was 34 percent.

By contrast, individuals and families with income between $13,000 and $15,000 paid taxes at a rate of 7.2 percent—or four times the Chase rate.

Of course, Chase did pay $170 million in income taxes in other countries, or $145 million more than it paid in the United States. Even when the foreign taxes are added in, the Chase income tax bill still came in at just 13.3 percent—slightly above the 12.9 percent paid by individuals and families earning $50,000 to $75,000.

But the family tax rates are calculated on total income before expenses—like food, housing, and clothing—are subtracted. The corporate tax rates are calculated on income after expenses —like wages, rent, and bad loans in the United States and over-seas—are subtracted.

BAXTER INTERNATIONAL, INC. A global manufacturer and marketer of health care products, Baxter is based in Deerfield, Illinois. For 1991 and 1992, Baxter reported income before taxes of $1.4 billion. The company paid $75 million in U.S. income tax, for a tax rate of 5.4 percent. Baxter also paid $101 million in income taxes to foreign governments, bringing its overall United States–foreign tax rate to 12.6 percent. That was a little more than the 11.1 percent rate paid by individuals and families earning between $40,000 and $50,000.

TEXACO, INC. One of the major international oil companies, Texaco is headquartered in White Plains, New York. For 1991 and 1992, Texaco reported income before taxes of $2.7 billion. The company paid $237 million in U.S. income tax, for a tax rate of 8.8 percent. Texaco also paid $103 million in income taxes in other countries, bringing its global tax rate to 12.6 percent.

OGDEN CORPORATION. A diversified supplier of aviation, building, energy, and waste management services, Ogden is headquartered in New York. For 1991 and 1992, Ogden reported income before taxes of $217 million. The company paid less than $200,000 in U.S. income tax, for a tax rate of less than one-tenth of 1 percent.

That was well below the 10.6 percent rate paid by 12.3 million individuals and families earning between $30,000 and $40,000. They paid taxes at 100 times the rate imposed on Ogden Corporation. To look at it another way, if they had been taxed at Ogden's rate, their average tax bill would have totaled $35, instead of the $3,679 they paid.

SOCIETY CORPORATION. A bank holding company with more than four hundred branches in Ohio, Indiana, and Michigan, Society is based in Cleveland, Ohio. For 1991 and 1992, Society reported income before taxes of $548 million. The company paid $86 million in U.S. income tax, for a tax rate of 15.7 percent. That was about the same as the 15.5 percent rate paid by 3.6 million individuals and families earning between $75,000 and $100,000.

SONAT, INC. A diversified energy company with interests in oil and gas exploration and development, offshore drilling, and natural gas pipeline, Sonat is headquartered in Birmingham, Alabama. For 1991 and 1992, Sonat reported $237 million in income before taxes. The company paid $20 million in U.S. income tax, for a tax rate of 8.4 percent.

Let us summarize. Six companies—Chase, Baxter, Texaco, Ogden, Society, and Sonat—reported income before taxes of $6.6 billion for 1991 and 1992. They paid $443 million in U.S. income tax. That worked out to a tax rate of 6.7 percent. Add in foreign taxes, and the overall rate comes to 12.4 percent, a little below that paid by persons in the $50,000 to $75,000 income group. And then, of course, there were Royal Caribbean and Carnival Cruise Lines, which paid no U.S. income tax on their cruise profits.

You might be forgiven if you thought that no U.S. corporation could earn millions in profits and pay little or no income tax. After all, members of Congress themselves assured you, over and over, that they were putting an end to such practices when they passed the Tax Reform Act of 1986. Refresh your memory and listen to the words of a few of them, urging their colleagues to enact the pending bill.

"We have put a tough minimum tax in the tax bill. Never again will people be able to point to huge corporations making hundreds of millions of dollars and not paying any taxes. All profitable corporations are going to have to pay their share," said Democratic Senator Lloyd Bentsen of Texas.[11]

"This minimum tax, Mr. President, is, I think, inescapable once it is in full effect. There will not be a profit-making corporation in the country that can escape taxation, and believe me, there are lots of corporations that wanted out from under this provision," said Republican Senator Bob Packwood of Oregon.[12]

"No longer will middle-income families pay a higher tax rate than some multi-billion dollar corporations," said Democratic Senator Bill Bradley of New Jersey.[13]

"For the first time, there is a minimum tax so everyone will be paying a fair share of the tax burden. No longer will we read of multi-billion dollar corporations avoiding any tax payment whatsoever," said Republican Senator Mack Mattingly of Georgia.[14]

"A tough minimum tax will make it impossible for individuals and corporations with true income to avoid paying taxes," said Republican Senator Steve Symms of Idaho.[15]

"Mr. President, for too long, large corporations in our country have been paying no taxes. It has destroyed the faith of too many of our people in the tax code and in the fairness of our society. This bill changes the law that allows large corporations to pay nothing in taxes," said Democratic Senator Thomas R. Harkin of Iowa.[16]

"Included in this legislation is a stiff minimum tax provision. Corporations will no longer be able to dodge paying their fair share of taxes," said Republican Senator Robert W. Kasten, Jr., of Wisconsin.[17]

"What about these major corporations who have billions to buy each other, but not one dime for their fair share of taxes? Is it legal on their part? Certainly. Past congresses have made it legal, but it is immoral and we will stop it in this bill with a tough, fair minimum tax," said Democratic Representative Barbara Boxer of California.[18]

"It makes me angry that corporations in this country that make millions of dollars get by with paying no taxes. . . . This bill makes sure that does not happen anymore," said Democratic Representative Richard A. Gephardt of Missouri.[19]

The speechmaking was all part of the Capitol Hill Magic Show. Lawmakers knew—or certainly should have known—that years before, they had specifically exempted certain corporations from payment of any income taxes, and they had preserved those exemptions. They knew, or certainly should have known, that over time, they had provided a mix of deductions, write-offs, credits, preferences, and assorted loopholes to permit any number of other corporations to avoid payment of income taxes, or to pay taxes at rates below those imposed on middle-class individuals and families.

Further, an analysis of a half century of tax and economic data contradicts claims that higher taxes discourage job creation. During the 1950s, a time when corporations paid taxes at a much higher rate than now, they also created jobs that paid middle-class wages. By contrast, since corporate tax rates began to tumble in the 1980s, the nation's corporations have been steadily eliminating jobs that paid middle-class wages. During the 1950s, the corporate tax rate was 52 percent, half again as high as the 1994 rate of 35 percent.

Fat City

Where does the money go that corporations once paid in U.S. income tax? A growing chunk of it is paid in income taxes to support foreign governments. (More about this later.) But much of it is written off in ever larger deductions.

You may better appreciate the benefits of this practice by looking at your own tax return. See the top of page two of your Form 1040, the line for adjusted gross income? From that figure you subtract either the standard deduction or itemized deductions to arrive at the income on which you must pay tax. Now multiply your deduction by two or three, and see how the tax you must pay melts away.

Over the years, that's what corporations have done. Deductions have soared for failed business practices (net operating loss deduction), for bloated executive salaries, for runaway interest payments on money borrowed to fund the manic takeovers of the 1980s. Of all these, the latter has proved especially destructive for working Americans.

A part of the tax code for decades, the interest deduction once served a useful purpose. That was back in the years when corporations borrowed money to build and equip new plants, and thereby create middle-income jobs. But beginning in the 1980s, many corporations borrowed money to finance restructurings, takeovers, or buyouts of other companies, leading to closed factories and the elimination of middle-income jobs. Running at $200 billion a year, the virtually unlimited deduction for interest on corporate debt has enabled companies to transfer an increasingly larger share of the income tax burden onto individuals. Middle America is thus getting hit twice—first, in the loss of good-paying jobs; second, by having to pay higher taxes.

For many companies the deduction has virtually wiped out their federal tax bill. Witness Playtex Family Products.

One of the most recognizable brand names, Playtex has been caught up in the financial frenzy that has gripped much of corporate America and Wall Street. For years, it was part of a Chicago-based conglomerate called Esmark, Inc., a holding company with interests ranging from food to automotive products. In 1984, Esmark was taken over by Beatrice Foods, one of the giants of the food and personal services industry.

As a division of the two conglomerates, Playtex paid federal income tax on its operating profits as part of the consolidated tax return filed by its corporate parent.

Then in 1986, Beatrice was taken over by the Wall Street leveraged buyout firm Kohlberg Kravis Roberts. Since then, Playtex has gone through a succession of restructurings and buyouts that have eliminated its federal income tax payments.

After the Beatrice takeover, Kohlberg Kravis Roberts began selling off parts of Beatrice. One of the properties was International Playtex, Inc., a division headquartered in Stamford, Connecticut. The maker of products from lingerie to rubber gloves to tampons, Playtex had annual sales of $600 million and had long been a profit center for Esmark and then Beatrice.

In December 1986, Beatrice spun off Playtex in a leveraged buyout by Playtex's management. The purchase price was $1.25 billion, financed largely by borrowed money again. The new company was called Playtex Holdings.

Another spin-off followed in 1988 as separate companies were created for the intimate apparel and family products divisions. Again, borrowed money, much of it raised by the junk bond machine of Drexel Burnham Lambert, financed the deals.

A look at the income statement of one of these companies, Playtex Family Products, Inc., shows what happens to a corporation's taxes when it loads up with debt.

For the four years from 1989 to 1992, Playtex Family Products recorded operating profits—or profits before payment of interest and taxes—of $461 million. During the same period, the company's interest payments totaled $474 million, thereby wiping out its operating profits and reducing its federal income tax bill to zero.

Or how about Stone Container Corporation of Chicago, a global paper-products company that went on a buying spree in the 1980s, financed in part by Michael Milken, the king of junk bonds.

As a result of all the debt, Stone Container in 1991 and 1992 paid no U. S. income tax. The company's income before interest and tax payments totaled $493 million. But its interest expenses added up to $784 million, wiping out any U.S. tax bill.

Stone Container and Playtex are representative of the hundreds of companies that have either eliminated or dramatically reduced their corporate tax payments by way of the virtually unlimited write-off for interest payments. Money that once went to the U.S. Treasury in taxes now goes to the people and institutions that own the corporate debt. They include wealthy foreign investors, pension funds, and others who are exempt from payment of the individual income tax.

In short, the Treasury—which means you—loses twice. The first time when the company escapes payment of the corporate income tax because of the interest deduction. The second time when the owners of the corporate debt escape payment of the individual income tax on the interest they collect. Actually, you lose three times. Since the companies report earnings losses because of the inflated interest payments, they can use those losses to offset taxes they may owe in future years when they are profitable.

For most companies, the swollen interest deductions have grown out of corporate restructurings. A few, though, have polished and refined the write-off, elevating it to a new level. They claim it for money borrowed to pay dividends to their stockholders. If that sounds strange, you're right—it is. Dividends are supposed to come from earnings. But a resourceful corporation knows how to shift the cost to taxpayers.

Assuming that you, too, would like to pick up a quick $25 million, here is how you might work it. The only requirements are a little knowledge of modern business math and the Internal Revenue Code, plus a willingness to allow other people to pay your taxes.

Begin by acquiring a company—something, perhaps, like the All-American Fat Rendering Company, which has been around since shortly after the Civil War. Naturally, you—and a few partners—do this with mostly borrowed money. Then, over the next year or two, you borrow even more money, to buy more companies in the fat-rendering business.

Now you have assembled an empire of fat, which, you conclude, is worthy of some reward in itself. So you borrow some more money and pay yourself a special dividend of $25 million.

You now have $25 million.

Your fat empire has a mountain of debt.

But the company gets to write off the interest payments on its debt. Which means it doesn't have to pay taxes anymore. Even better, the company gets the U.S. Treasury to write it a refund check for the taxes it paid a few years earlier. Of course, there is some danger that your company won't be able to make such high payments and will go bankrupt, throwing people out of work. But that's a risk you're willing to take.

You say this will never work? That nobody's going to lend you money so you can pay yourself a special dividend? And then forgive your taxes to boot?

Don't be so sure.

This very plan worked nicely for a small group of Texas businessmen and Wall Street investors. In fact, SEC records show that they walked away with a special dividend of $180 million from their company, which was, indeed, a fat-rendering business. That was a return of about 1,400 percent in two years. For you, it would be the same as if you had put $1,000 in your savings account two years ago and went back this week and picked up $15,000.

The company, Darling-Delaware Company, Inc., a fat-rendering business founded in 1882 at the stockyards on Chicago's South Side, collects grease and animal by-products from butcher shops, restaurants, poultry houses, farms, meatpackers, and slaughterhouses. At the company's rendering plants in two dozen states, these raw materials are converted into meat and bone meal, yellow grease and tallow. These commodities, in turn, are sold as feed for livestock and as ingredients for cosmetics, soap, pet food, rubber, lubricants, paint, polishes, and other consumer and industrial products.

Darling-Delaware was family owned until 1986, when a group of investors bought it for $96 million—mostly borrowed money. The new owners moved the business from Chicago to Dallas and went on a buying spree. They acquired fat-rendering plants across the country and added them to Darling-Delaware, making it the nation's largest independent renderer.

Before it changed hands, Darling-Delaware had been both profitable and a tax-paying member of corporate America. In 1984, when the company was still family owned, it recorded net sales of $246 million. Earnings from operations—before interest payments and taxes—totaled $21 million. After paying $2 million in interest on borrowed money and $5 million in federal income tax, Darling-Delaware was left with a profit of $13 million.

But all this changed when the company was sold. Five years later, the new owners, through acquisitions, had boosted sales 70 percent, from $246 million to $417 million. Earnings from operations, though, were up only 29 percent, from $21 million to $27 million. More important, the company ended the year with a loss of $16 million. How did this happen?

By 1989, Darling-Delaware's interest payments had soared to $43 million—a 2,100 percent increase over 1984. That meant that the company's earnings from operations ($27 million) did not cover its interest obligations ($43 million).

Which meant that Darling-Delaware paid no federal income tax.

In fact, it collected a multimillion-dollar refund from the U.S. Treasury, or, more accurately, from you and all other taxpayers.

What accounted for the huge jump in debt and interest?

Darling-Delaware's new owners had borrowed $300 million. Some of the money went to buy other rendering companies. And $180 million went into their own pockets. They called it a "special dividend." Indeed it was a special dividend. Unlike most dividends, which are paid out of corporate profits, it was funded by U.S. taxpayers.

Of course, Darling-Delaware was merely doing what hundreds of other companies were doing, borrowing money to pay investors and passing the cost along—albeit indirectly—to all other taxpayers. So who were the investors who picked up the $180 million dividend? They included:

EDWARD W. ROSE III of Dallas, who collected $25.8 million. Rose, who owned 14.3 percent of the company, holds an MBA from Harvard. He is a general partner with George W. Bush, the eldest son of the former President, in the partnership that owns the Texas Rangers baseball team.[20]

Rose also was president and sole stockholder of Cardinal Investment Co., Inc., a Dallas investment and brokerage firm, which received $2.2 million from Darling-Delaware for consulting and investment banking services over a twenty-six-month period.

DORT A. CAMERON III of Greenwich, Connecticut, who, with other investors in a limited partnership, shared $62.4 million from Darling-Delaware. The partnership, Investment Limited Partnership, owned 34.7 percent of Darling-Delaware's stock. Cameron was a protégé of Michael R. Milken at Drexel Burnham Lambert, Inc., and was quoted once as describing the convicted junk bond swindler as "the most important individual who has lived in this century."[21]

Cameron was a general partner in Investment Limited Partnership, whose limited partners have included various Drexel Burnham executives, the Equitable Life Assurance Society, and the billionaire Bass family of Texas.

RICHARD E. RAINWATER of Fort Worth, Texas, who collected $9.5 million. Rainwater, who owned 5.3 percent of the company's stock, holds an MBA from Stanford University. He is credited with devising the investment strategy that transformed the oil-rich Bass family from mere millionaires in the 1970s to billionaires in the 1980s and 1990s.[22]

Rainwater set out on his own in 1986, establishing an investment firm in the office building that houses the Bass operations. With Cameron, he, too, was a general partner in Investment Limited Partnership. He also is an investor in the Texas Rangers baseball team and appears in the *Forbes* directory of the 400 richest Americans, with an estimated worth of $470 million.

WILLIAM A. SHIRLEY, JR., of Dallas, who collected $28.4 million. He owned 15.8 percent of the company's stock. Shirley had owned Valcar Enterprises of Texas, Inc., a rendering business, when he joined with Rainwater, Rose, and Cameron in 1986 to buy Darling-Delaware.[23] As president of Darling-Delaware in 1988, Shirley was paid $483,750. He also is an investor in the Texas Rangers.

STEVEN F. SPIRITAS of Dallas, who collected $15.2 million. He owned 8.5 percent of the company's stock. Spiritas was the chief executive officer of Supreme Beef Processors, Inc., a beef supplier whose biggest customer was the U.S. government, notably the Defense Department and the Agriculture Department.[24]

How, you might ask, is it possible for a company to borrow money to pay a dividend when it is unable to generate enough cash to pay the interest on the money it borrows?

No problem at all if you had access to the greatest American money machine of all time—the junk bond apparatus of Drexel Burnham Lambert. Like so many others, Darling-Delaware's investors turned to Drexel Burnham, which along with Wall Street investment firms that followed, raised billions of dollars by peddling bonds regardless of whether there was an economic need or a sound business reason for doing so.

The overriding consideration was how much money could be made in the shortest possible time with the greatest cost being allocated to others—from employees to taxpayers. Here is what Darling-Delaware's investors did, courtesy of the tax code:

In December 1988, the company secured $240 million in bank loans and arranged with Drexel Burnham for the private placement of $165 million in notes. Proceeds from the notes and part of the bank loans paid off existing debt, including the money that had been borrowed to buy the company. The rest went for the $180 million dividend.

But the Drexel Burnham private notes carried a stiff interest rate, which escalated sharply, beginning at 14⅜ percent and going up ½ percent every three months the first year alone.

To pay off the Drexel Burnham notes, Darling-Delaware's owners sold $165 million in new notes to the public. By Drexel Burnham, of course. To assure potential buyers of the soundness of the investment, Drexel Burnham offered this explanation of how the company intended to meet its debt obligations:

"Darling's business currently provides a stable cash flow base with potential for increases through additional acquisitions and continued cost savings through centralization."[25]

It didn't work.

In the first quarter of 1990, the last time that Darling-Delaware filed documents with the SEC, the company reported a $5.4 million loss. As in the previous year, the company actually had a profit from the operation of its business. But the $5.6 million profit was wiped out by $11.1 million in interest payments.

A once profitable company that paid taxes was turned into an unprofitable company that paid generous dividends to its investors—but no income tax. The company also later defaulted on its interest payments.

The unlimited write-off for corporate interest is just one more piece of the jigsaw puzzle, The Great Tax Rip-off. A law that exempts cruise lines from the payment of all tax is another piece. So, too, is the uncontrollable desire of lawmakers and Presidents to look after the needs of other special interests.

Like oil wells and trees.

Tax-Free Trees

The story begins not with oil or trees but—once again—with people who devote their lives to finding new ways to pay taxes at a lower rate than you do. In the early 1980s, they added another chapter to their book of tax-avoidance innovations—the make-believe corporation.

It looked like a corporation. It acted like a corporation. It earned money like a corporation. But it didn't pay taxes like a corporation. Better yet, it paid no taxes at all. It was called a master limited partnership.

Traditional partnerships—law firms, accounting firms, small groups of investors—pay no federal income tax. Rather, the profits and losses of the business flow directly to the tax returns of the individual partners, on the theory that partnerships are loose confederations of individual investors or professionals, and not really operating corporations.

But the master limited partnership was an entirely different animal. For all practical purposes, it was a corporation. It often had thousands of employees. Its business was conducted on a wide scale. Its "shares"—called partnership "units"—were bought and sold publicly on stock exchanges just like the common stock of a corporation.

Publicly traded partnerships were corporations in virtually every way except one—they paid no corporate income tax. "This idea is so damn good," said Bromley DeMeritt, vice president of McRae Consolidated Oil & Gas, a Houston company that converted to a limited partnership in 1983, "it's hard to believe."[26]

Indeed it was. But it was true.

The first was Apache Corporation, a Minneapolis-based oil and gas driller, in 1981. But it was T. Boone Pickens, Jr., the predatory oilman from Mesa Petroleum Co. of Amarillo, Texas, who popularized the scheme. Having struck fear into the oil industry by threatening to take over a number of oil companies in the early 1980s, Pickens moved on to greener pastures— harvesting the federal tax code.

In 1985, Pickens turned Mesa into a master limited partnership, in a move widely hailed for its tax ingenuity. The advantage, Pickens noted, would be that "net available cash flow from [Mesa's] properties, unburdened by income taxes at the corporate level," could be distributed to the MLP's own shareholders, providing "substantially higher cash flow than Mesa's current common stock dividend."[27]

Commenting on Pickens's gambit, *Forbes* said: "In terms of outmaneuvering the IRS, the proposed metamorphosis of Mesa Petroleum is nothing short of a masterpiece."[28]

Soon publicly traded limited partnerships began replacing

corporations in many fields. They were in gambling casinos (Sahara Casino Partners, L.P.), fast-food chains (Burger King Investors Master Limited Partnership and Winchell's Donut Houses, L.P.), snowmobile makers (Polaris Industries Partners, L.P.), cable television distributors (Jones Intercable Investors, L.P.), professional sports teams (The Boston Celtics Limited Partnership), gas stations (Power Test Investors, L.P.), cellular phones (United Cellular Master Limited Partnership), nursing homes (Angell Care Master Limited Partnership), and motel chains (Motel 6 Holdings, L.P., and Days Inn Company).

By 1986, more than a hundred had been formed, with a total value of $15 billion. Rough estimates put the taxes lost at more than half a billion dollars a year and growing. All of which had the professionals in the Treasury alarmed.

And with good reason. Let's say the American Casino Company had an operating profit of $100 million and no debt. At the time, the maximum corporate tax rate was 46 percent. American Casino paid $46 million in corporate income tax, leaving the company with a net profit of $54 million. It kept $4 million to invest in new slot machines and distributed the remaining $50 million in dividends. Those investors subject to the individual income tax then paid tax on their dividends. But if American Casino converted to an MLP, the Treasury was out $46 million up front.

To tackle the problem, the Treasury Department urged Congress to pass legislation imposing the corporate tax on large partnerships. In June 1986, J. Roger Mentz, assistant Treasury secretary for tax policy, appeared before a House Ways and Means subcommittee and urged Congress to correct what he called a "defect" in the tax system.

"The treatment of entities not as corporations that function in a manner similar to corporations, and compete with corporations, results in an inequity," Mentz told committee members.[29]

But something funny happened on the way to tax reform. By the time Mentz returned to the committee with specific recommendations a year later, he was singing a different tune. Treasury still believed that large, publicly traded partnerships should be taxed just like corporations. But not all of them. Mentz asked the committee to make an exception for partnerships in the oil, gas, and other natural-resource industries, sectors of the economy that he claimed were "different" from partnerships in the hospitality, health care, and sports industries. Why were they different? Because, Mentz said, natural-resource developers had long used partnerships as a way of doing business.

"Given the importance of natural-resource development to the nation's security," he stressed, "Congress should consider carefully whether such traditionally noncorporate activities should be subjected to corporate level tax."[30]

Score one for the lobbyists.

In the year following Mentz's original proposal to tax publicly traded limited partnerships, the Treasury Department and the tax-writing committees had been besieged by lobbyists for the oil and gas industry seeking a special exemption. It worked.

Not only did Mentz endorse an exemption, but the House Ways and Means Committee agreed. When the committee drafted the Revenue Act of 1987, it came down hard, as expected, on publicly traded limited partnerships, declaring that they should be taxed in the same way as corporations—except for a few. Those few consisted of "certain partnerships, 90 percent of whose gross income . . . [is] income and gains from certain natural resource activities." The justification: "The committee considers that disruption of present practices in such activities is currently inadvisable due to general economic conditions in these industries."[31]

It turned out that the "natural-resource exception" offered some new ways to mine the tax code. If oil investors could pony up money for tax-free partnerships, why couldn't an existing corporation in the "natural-resource" field spin off some of its assets into a partnership, manage them as if they were a division of the corporation, but escape payment of income taxes on the profits?

No reason at all.

Which is just what one of the giants in the timber industry did. Burlington Resources, Inc., a natural-resources holding company, spun off its longtime timber holdings in 1989 to create the Plum Creek Timber Company Limited Partnership.

Burlington did this in a $550 million deal that resembled a public stock offering, except that partnership units, rather than shares of stock, were offered to investors. Burlington received cash from the sale and also retained an 11 percent ownership stake in Plum Creek Timber as the company's general partner. Which meant that, for all practical purposes, nothing changed with Plum Creek operations.

It had the same employees. The same managers. It served the same clients. It cut trees in the same forests. The only difference was its tax status. Plum Creek, the corporate subsidiary, had paid income tax as part of the consolidated income tax return of Burlington Resources. Now Plum Creek, the limited partnership, paid no income tax because it qualified for what it called the "Natural Resource Exception" in the tax code.[32]

Transformed into a partnership, Plum Creek proceeded to make the most of its tax-free status. Its operating profit nearly doubled—from $52.4 million in 1990 to $97.8 in 1992. Another statistic also was going up: the number of trees cut. By 1992, the number of board feet produced was running at a record 586 million.

Not going up so fast, however, was the amount of timber the company was reproducing each year in its own forests. In a report filed with the SEC in 1989, Plum Creek, which cuts more than 500 million board feet of timber a year, estimated that its forest reserves would produce "an average annual growth of approximately 210 million board feet of timber for the next several years."[33]

Bolstered by its natural-resource exception, Plum Creek was cutting down trees twice as fast as it was replacing them. What's more, its forest reserves included some of America's most pristine timberland—magnificent stands of old-growth Douglas fir and western hemlock, trees that have been part of America's natural heritage for more than two centuries.

Plum Creek's 1.4-million-acre private forest—second in size in the Pacific Northwest to Weyerhaeuser's—dates back to a Civil War land grant from Abraham Lincoln, who wanted to induce a forerunner of the current company to extend rail lines to the West. It is timber from these rich hardwood groves, with their highly prized grains and colors, that are falling to the chain saw amid Plum Creek's rush for operating profits.

To environmentalists and conservationists, the name Plum Creek has become synonymous with evil. The company has been accused of engaging in indiscriminate clear-cutting—the practice by which mature forests are literally reduced to fields of stumps. "Within the industry, they're considered the Darth Vader of the State of Washington," Rod Chandler, a Republican congressman from Washington, told the *Wall Street Journal*. "And I think they've earned it." [34]

The reason behind Plum Creek's insatiable appetite for old-growth timber is to feed a lucrative consumer market for logs.

Not in the United States.

In Japan.

Trees that once went to sawmills in the Northwest, to be fashioned into lumber or wood products, now are trucked as raw logs to busy ports on Puget Sound or the Pacific Ocean for shipment to Japan and other Asian countries.

Exports of raw logs to the Far East have increased sharply in the last generation. As recently as 1960, the U.S. exported virtually none of its raw timber. By the late 1980s, log exports were big business. In the five years from 1980 through 1984, the U.S. exported an average of 3.2 billion board feet of logs per year. From 1985 to 1989, the last year for which figures are available, the number jumped to an average of 4.2 billion board feet a year—a 31 percent increase.

But surely this is good news for the United States, facing a chronic trade deficit with Japan? A bright spot in an otherwise dismal international trade picture?

Wrong.

Exports of finished products—manufactured items or finished wood products such as lumber—are indeed good for the nation's trade balance and domestic economy. But the export of raw logs doesn't help the United States domestically. In fact, it means fewer jobs.

When logs are exported, there is less raw material to be processed in U.S. sawmills, where most timber-industry workers are employed. Not surprisingly, as log exports to the Far East have risen, mills have closed in record numbers throughout the Pacific Northwest.

From 1980 through 1992, a total of 313 mills closed and 30,464 timber-industry workers lost their jobs, according to Paul F. Ehinger and Associates, a Eugene, Oregon, forest-industry consultant. The pace appears to be accelerating, as most of the mills (177) and the bulk of the jobs (17,074) were lost in the last five years.[35]

By contrast, mills are humming in Japan. The Japanese have long preferred to import raw logs and turn them into finished products in their own factories. Indeed, the Japanese have gone to great lengths to protect their domestic wood-products industry, so much so that the U.S. trade representative criticized the Japanese in 1989 for restricting access to their internal market for U.S. wood products:

"Access of Japan's market for forest products is impeded by a variety of tariff and non-tariff measures, including technical standards which favor Japanese producers. These practices include wood grading requirements which discriminate against U.S. wood products, as well as a variety of testing standards which impede U.S. exports."[36]

No company has been more accommodating than Plum Creek. Exports to Pacific Rim countries are its bread and butter, as the company noted in a report filed with the SEC:

"Plum Creek generally realizes higher profit margins on sales of logs in such markets, particularly in the Japanese markets, because of the demand for higher quality logs for use in residential construction."[37]

For Plum Creek, chainsawing its forests and sending the logs abroad—when coupled with its federal tax exemption—have produced a financial bonanza. "We posted record earnings during a year of continued economic and political uncertainty," the company said in its 1992 annual report. "Revenues for the year were a record $439.9 million, up 13 percent compared to 1991. Our record earnings totaled $64.2 million or $4.02 per Unit [share], compared to $18.7 million or $1.10 per Unit in 1991. We also ended the year with a strong balance sheet with approximately $70 million in cash and cash equivalents."[38]

On the record earnings, of course, the company paid no corporate income tax. Instead, the profits flowed straight to the limited partners. And who might they be?

They are, among others, Robert M. Bass of the wealthy Bass family of Texas. Listed as one of the *Forbes* 400 richest Americans, Bass is worth an estimated $2.2 billion. He holds a stake in Plum Creek through SPO Partners & Co., a San Francisco private investment firm, which has served as an umbrella for a number of investors and limited partners in Plum Creek. The Bass-affiliated group bought into Plum Creek in 1990. Apparently pleased by the returns, they acquired control in 1993, purchasing Burlington Resources' remaining interest for $70 million and becoming Plum Creek's new general partner.

By cashing in on a tax-free deal, Robert Bass was merely keeping up a family tradition. The Basses have been making use of preferences in the tax code with great success for decades. The family fortune grew out of one of the earliest and largest tax giveaways—the oil depletion allowance, which provided many millions to the Bass clan's patriarch, the legendary Texas wildcatter Sid W. Richardson.

The depletion allowance is a tax break designed to recoup drilling costs. Originally a product of oil-industry lobbying in World War I, it was expanded in the 1920s and paved the way for fortunes to be made in the Texas oil fields.

Depletion is the oil industry's answer to the manufacturing industry's depreciation. If a manufacturer can write off the cost of purchasing new machinery, why shouldn't an oilman be allowed to write off the cost of drilling an oil well? It sounds fair enough. But there is a difference. Tax benefits from depreciation cease when the cost of the machinery has been recovered. The tax benefits from depletion never dry up: they just go on and on, as long as the well pumps oil. Because oilmen can recover their costs many times over, a Columbia University law professor once dubbed the depletion allowance "the special deduction for imaginary costs." [39]

Thanks to depletion and other assorted oil-industry tax breaks, Sid Richardson died a very wealthy man in 1959, leaving millions to the Basses and his tax-exempt charity, the Sid W. Richardson Foundation of Fort Worth. The Basses used Richardson's bequest as leverage to elevate themselves into the front rank of America's wealthiest families by investing in a myriad of other enterprises, from entertainment to real estate to timber.

For Robert Bass and other limited partners who enjoy Plum Creek Timber's special tax status, the future looks bright. Operating income keeps going up. The loophole that enables Plum Creek to avoid all federal income tax remains intact.

No wonder stock market analysts and financial publications

are enthusiastic. In a September 1993 article, *Financial World* observed that shares in the partnership "have tripled in price from $20 in January 1991 to a recent 60⅝" and that "barring a sharp rise in interest rates, Plum Creek Timber is still headed up for the foreseeable future."[40]

Financial World said the timber partnership "surprised even bullish analysts" when it reported 1993 second-quarter earnings of $28.2 million—"a 93 percent jump over the same period in 1992."[41] And why not. For every $10 million in profit that it earns, Plum Creek avoids paying $3.5 million in federal income tax.

Keep in mind, once more, that Plum Creek's special status is only one of hundreds upon hundreds of preferences that lawmakers have seeded through the Internal Revenue Code to allow select businesses to escape payment of income tax. Those preferences show why, when members of Congress talk about taxes, what they say is so often far removed from reality.

Remember 1986 and the Tax Reform Act? The year when lawmakers said they were going to transfer the tax burden off the backs of working Americans? The year when lawmakers said corporations would begin picking up a larger share of that burden? Let's go back to that year and listen, once more, to what the lawmakers had to say.

"The bill shifts $120 billion of taxes from individuals to corporations over the next five years," said Representative James L. Oberstar, Minnesota Democrat.[42]

"By shifting approximately $120 billion of the overall federal income tax liability from individual taxpayers to corporations, this bill restores a balance in the tax code that has been upset over the years," said Senator William S. Cohen, Maine Republican.[43]

"The bill will increase corporate taxes about $120 billion over the next six years," said Representative William D. Lowery, California Republican.[44]

"This bill makes political sense because it reaches down and lifts a $120 billion tax burden off the backs of the poor, beleaguered, individual taxpayer, and puts it on the corporate ledgers, many of whom earned enormous profits and paid not one cent in taxation," said Representative Guy Vander Jagt, Michigan Republican.[45]

Newspapers and magazines, radio and television, repeated the theme, declaring that corporations now would pick up more of the cost of running the government.

"The new bill will increase corporate taxes by about $120 billion over five years, roughly restoring the corporate tax to its levels in the 1970s," reported the *Wall Street Journal*.[46] "A staunchly probusiness President has given his blessing to a tax plan that will shift about $120 billion of the tax burden from individuals to corporations over the next five years and put the corporate share of income taxes paid back at the levels of the 1970s," said *Business Week*.[47]

What do the real numbers look like eight years later?

During the 1970s, total income taxes paid by individuals and corporations averaged $178 billion a year. Of that amount, individuals paid 75 percent, corporations 25 percent.

From 1987 to 1993—the seven years after passage of the 1986 act—total income taxes paid averaged $550 billion a year. Of that sum, individuals paid 82 percent, corporations paid 18 percent. The corporate share was 7 percentage points below the 1970s level. It was a full 21 percentage points below the 1950s.

And what about all those claims by lawmakers and government officials of restoring the balance that existed in the 1970s, of transferring the tax burden from corporations to individuals?

It was just one more act in the magic show.

Consider, for example, the revenue forecasts prepared in 1986 by the economic experts in President Reagan's White House.

For 1987, the experts said, corporations would pay $105 billion in income tax. Instead, they paid only $84 billion—a $21 billion mistake.

For 1988, the experts said, corporations would pay $117 billion in income tax. Instead, they paid only $95 billion—a $22 billion mistake.

For 1989, the experts said, corporations would pay $129 billion in income tax. Instead, they paid only $103 billion—a $26 billion mistake.

For 1990, the experts said, corporations would pay $140 billion in income tax. Instead, they paid only $94 billion—a $46 billion mistake.

For 1991, the experts said, corporations would pay $149 billion in income tax. Instead, they paid only $98 billion—a $51 billion mistake.

For 1992, the experts said, corporations would pay $160 billion in income tax. Instead, they paid only $100 billion—a $60 billion mistake.

Total miscalculation: $226 billion. A mistake of nearly a quarter-trillion dollars.

Because the White House economic experts exaggerated corporate tax payments—along with a series of other miscalculations—their deficit forecasts were erroneous too. When President Reagan submitted his budget to Congress in 1987, he predicted the deficit would end by 1992, when the government would record a surplus of $12.3 billion.

The 1992 surplus turned out to be one more deficit—a deficit totaling $290 billion. Or just another $300 billion mistake—the equivalent of all the income taxes that residents of Ohio, Oregon, and Vermont will pay for the next ten years or so.

Is there any reason to think that Washington's trustworthiness on tax matters has improved, now that we are in the 1990s with a new administration and many new lawmakers? In 1993, during the hot debate over the budget bill, some of those lawmakers charged that raising the corporate tax rate from 34 percent to 35 percent would hurt American business, and that raising the top individual rate from 31 percent to 39.6 percent would cripple small businesses.

"Eighty percent of small businesses who file as individuals will be hit by these taxes. . . . This is a huge sacrifice for the most vibrant facet of our economy," said Representative Ron Packard, California Republican.[48]

"The second thing wrong with this package is the effect that it will have on small businesses in America. Most small businesses pay their taxes at the level of the individual owner, partner, or shareholder, and they will be subject to higher individual rates and to the so-called millionaire surtax. With effective rates slated to exceed 40 percent, many small businesses will find themselves subject to marginal rates well above those of the nation's largest and most profitable corporations. These small businesses will be paying higher taxes, instead of investing in new equipment and creating new jobs. . . . This tax package, Mr. Speaker, will kill the goose that lays the golden egg," said Representative William Emerson, Missouri Republican.[49]

"I think something else to be kept in mind is the injury this package inflicts on small business. It is important to bear in mind that small businesses—and I am talking about partnerships, proprietorships and subchapter S corporations, and they employ 80 percent of our workers, and they are people who are not legitimately in the classification of being rich and fat cats— and the fact of the matter is those individuals are going to experience a hit of a magnitude of up to 45 percent in their taxes, and that will cost employment," said Representative Philip M. Crane, Illinois Republican.[50]

"A plan that raises taxes and cuts jobs is not good for the economy and in this context I would stress the radicalness of the change in the tax code that applies to subchapter S corporations. While regular corporations will have top tax rates raised from 34 to 35 percent—or effectively 3 percent—subchapter S corporations will have top tax rates raised from 28 to 41 percent—an almost 50 percent increase in tax burden. Instead of small business being encouraged by government it will be stifled by the tax code," said Representative Jim Leach, Iowa Republican.[51]

Was all the gloom warranted? Or was it the 1993 equivalent of the 1986 corporate tax forecasts? Draw your own conclusions from the following IRS statistics.

The new maximum rate of 39.6 percent begins on taxable income exceeding $250,000. As it happens, not too many small-business owners fall into that bracket. For 1990, the latest year available, 14.8 million individuals and families filed returns showing income from sole proprietorships. Of that number, 14 million—or 95 percent of the total—reported gross receipts below $200,000. The higher top rate applied to fewer than 5 percent of the small businesses operated as sole proprietorships.

But what about the other small businesses that lawmakers

were so concerned about, the subchapter S corporations? And what are they anyway?

These businesses are named for a section of the Internal Revenue Code that Congress enacted in 1958 to encourage small-business growth. Many owners of small businesses wanted the legal protection from liability provided by corporate status, but preferred to report their profits and losses on their personal tax returns. This often allowed them to save on taxes, since a corporation's profits were taxed at the corporate level and the dividends it paid were taxed again at the individual level. Thus was born subchapter S.

In 1980, IRS statistics show, 20 percent of all tax returns filed by corporations came from subchapter S businesses. By 1985, the number had edged up to 22 percent. But between 1985 and 1990, it suddenly soared to 42 percent. What accounted for the explosive growth?

Tax avoidance.

When lawmakers rewrote the tax code in 1986, they cut the corporate tax rate from 46 percent to 34 percent, and they slashed the maximum individual rate from 50 percent to 28 percent. For the first time, the individual rate was below the corporate rate. All of a sudden, the S corporation had a little more appeal as a tax-savings device. Once more, the statistics tell the story.

From 1980 to 1985, the number of S corporation tax returns went up 33 percent, rising from 545,000 to 725,000. Over the same period, the number of returns filed by traditional corporations went up 18 percent, from 2.2 million to 2.6 million.

Now look at what happened between 1985 and 1990, when the new lower tax rates were in effect. The number of S corporation returns spiraled 121 percent, shooting from 725,000 to 1.6 million. In contrast, the number of returns filed by conventional corporations plunged 19 percent, falling from 2.6 million to 2.1 million.

Thus, much of the congressional hand-wringing over the plight of the small subchapter S businessman in 1993 was really directed at many people who had changed the form of their business to escape paying a portion of their taxes. Even so, the number of businesses paying at the higher rate remained small.

The Business of Beverly Hills

Let's take a look at one small business that operated through much of the 1980s as an S corporation. Let's look at its owners, their backgrounds, and some of their tax stories, as well as the business's own tax history. The business is the Beverly Hills Gun Club.

Gun club?

You may remember it from *Beverly Hills Cop II*. Moviegoers saw Axel Foley (Eddie Murphy) walk up the tree-lined drive and into the club, which looked like some period private club, with its rich wood paneling and elegant paintings, glass trophy cases and bouquets of flowers, white-jacketed waiters and hushed conversations, and a perfectly coiffed blond receptionist with finely clipped diction.

Well, any resemblance between the movie version and the real club is purely coincidental. The movie gun club was located in an appropriate tree-lined setting. The real gun club is across the street from Tom John Towing, "Official Police Impound," home to scores of wrecked, abandoned, and towed cars. The club is modeled along the lines of a used-car showroom—tile floor, fluorescent lights, drab walls, and framed photos. Racks of weapons line one wall. Along another are display counters and shelves with assorted merchandise—leather and satin jackets and cotton windbreakers (priced from $120 to $695), T-shirts, sweatshirts, and caps, all emblazoned with the Beverly Hills Gun Club logo.

There are racks of promotional literature—"Beverly Hills Gun Club Rules and Regulations," "Beverly Hills Gun Club—Responsibilities of the Security Guard," and announcements of upcoming classes, like the firearms training course for women ("Let's have some fun ladies while you learn a skill that may one day save your life; and remember—you don't have to be a victim—you have a choice") and the course in "citizen mace," which will entitle those students who successfully complete it to receive a permit enabling them "to purchase, carry and use tear gas for personal protection . . . the same tear gas used by police officers nationwide."[52]

The club's main entrance is protected by a steel-barred door. Admittance is by buzzer. A large sign atop the building says in red letters BEVERLY HILLS and in black letters GUN CLUB. In keeping with Hollywood's fantasy tradition, the gun club is not located in Beverly Hills. But many of the people behind the club live there.

The gun club, which opened in 1981, is the creation of Arthur M. Kassel and his wife, Tichi Wilkerson Kassel. Of Beverly Hills. And of inherited wealth. Back in 1930, Mrs. Kassel's previous husband, William R. Wilkerson, founded the *Hollywood Reporter,* the trade paper for the motion picture and entertainment industry. *Time* magazine once described Wilkerson as "a suave, natty Tennesseean with drooping lips and a dark moustache . . . as toughly handsome as a Central Casting Corporation gambler."[53]

The oft-wed Wilkerson—there were at least five Mrs. Wilkersons, and Tichi was the last and one of the youngest—enjoyed the good life. So much so that he attracted the attention of the Internal Revenue Service when he borrowed large sums of money from the parent corporation, some of which went to build a $160,000 home in Bel Air—that's $160,000 in Depression-era dollars. Over time, the staff to run the French Colonial mansion would include two maids, a cook, a chauffeur, a butler, and a couple of gardeners. Wilkerson sought, without success, to convince the U.S. Board of Tax Appeals that he purchased the house so that "he might conduct business at the dinner table."[54] The tax board took a dim view of his explanation, saying that "it seems a strain on a practical imagination to abide by Wilkerson's statement that the only reason for the purchase of the home was as a place for business contacts. . . . There seem to have been other places in which to talk business"[55] The tax board ordered Wilkerson to pay the back taxes assessed by the IRS.

In addition to running the *Hollywood Reporter,* Wilkerson operated several popular Los Angeles restaurants and nightclubs, and he was one of the original stockholders in the corporation that built the Flamingo Hotel and Casino in Las Vegas in 1946. His more prominent partner was Benjamin "Bugsy" Siegel, the organized-crime boss who met an untimely death a year later. Wilkerson had sold his stock two months before Siegel was blown away while sitting on the couch of his girlfriend's mansion in Beverly Hills.

When Wilkerson died in 1962, at the age of seventy-one, his fifth or so wife, Tichi, inherited the business. She later married Arthur Kassel, and the two became mainstays in the Hollywood–Beverly Hills social whirl. The newspapers recorded their presence at Hollywood and Beverly Hills parties (for the mayor of Cannes, for Gene Autry, for the French ambassador); Tichi received her own star along the Hollywood Walk of Fame; and they turned up in one news account of fashion-conscious men:

> Tichi Wilkerson Kassel, onetime editor of the *Hollywood Reporter,* also feels strongly that her husband, Arthur M. Kassel, chairman of the Beverly Hills Video Group, should tie his own [bow tie], which he does. He ties it once and then fastens it at the back of his neck with Velcro.
> "Tichi won't allow me to wear a red tie or cummerbund," sighed Kassel, who says that on average they attend two black-tie events a week. He owns nine tuxedos, including an Armani, a Bijan (the most expensive), a Gucci and three from C & R Clothiers, which he always packs for the Cannes Film Festival because "they don't wrinkle." [56]

In 1981, they established the Beverly Hills Gun Club, not in Beverly Hills, but several miles away at 12306 Exposition Boulevard in West Los Angeles. According to company reports, a partnership called High Caliber Enterprises Limited owned and operated the firing range. The Beverly Hills Gun Club, Inc., a subchapter S corporation, was the managing general partner. The partnership documents provided not only for the distribution of any profits but for the allocation of losses or expenses so that the gun club operations could be written off on the personal tax returns of the investors. At $200,000, Tichi Kassel was the largest single investor. [57]

Two years later, in 1983, the partnership agreement was amended to add a new investor, Sylvester Stallone of Rambo and Rocky fame. Partnership documents show that at various times Stallone was entitled to 19 percent to 25 percent of the gun club's profits—or losses to use as deductions on his own tax return. [58]

During the club's early years, when it enjoyed its small-business tax status, Kassel encountered some personal tax problems with the IRS. The agency issued a notice that on his 1978 return he had improperly written off $21,000 in paper losses from a trading scheme. Kassel challenged the claim in U.S. Tax Court. The case dragged on for a decade, until September 1992, when he agreed that he had underpaid his income tax that year by $8,277 and that there had been "a substantial underpayment attributable to tax-motivated transactions." [59]

As for the gun club itself, being a subchapter S corporation, it paid no income tax. As it reported in a document filed with the SEC: "The company was not subject to federal income tax." [60]

Over the years, the gun club, open until midnight seven days a week, became one of the trendy places to spot celebrities. In addition to Stallone, whose photo appears on a wall, there was the actress Jamie Lee Curtis *(Blue Steel),* whose photo and thank-you note also grace the wall. Other club shooters, identified by newspaper columnists, have included Robert Culp, Geena Davis, Arsenio Hall, Lisa Hartman, Rebecca De Mornay, Sean Penn, George Peppard, Mickey Rourke, Susan Sarandon, and Charlie Sheen. [61] By 1993, the club boasted 1,900 members, including 1,000 lifetime members. The annual membership fee was $195.

But Hollywood is just one source of patrons. As the club explains, among its customers are "foreign tour groups especially from Japan where the use of firearms is severely restricted." [62] Business also was boosted by the rioting that erupted after the first Rodney King verdict in Los Angeles. About that same time, Arthur Kassel decided to take the gun club public.

In May 1993, the old partnership and S corporation arrangement was scrapped and a new Beverly Hills Gun Club, Inc., filed a registration statement with the SEC. It offered 1 million shares of stock for sale, at $5.50 a share, and 1 million warrants to buy stock at a future date. The gun club explained the timing:

"As a result of the increased public concern for personal safety and the increased ownership of handguns, it is the company's strategy to expand its facilities and products to assist in meeting the safety needs of individuals at their homes and businesses. This includes the opening of three additional gun club facilities."[63]

The stock offering would bring to 2 million the number of shares outstanding, since Kassel, his wife, and other investors already owned 1 million shares. The Kassels themselves held 776,260 shares. Other stockholders included the actor Robert Wagner, who held 26,645 shares. Among those nominated to serve as directors of the publicly owned Beverly Hills Gun Club were Donald O'Connor, the song-and-dance man (*Singin' in the Rain*), who also happens to be the brother-in-law of Arthur Kassel, and Donald E. Santarelli, a former deputy U.S. attorney general, who headed the Law Enforcement Assistance Administration under President Nixon.

To market its stock, the Beverly Hills Gun Club turned to a new brokerage firm called American National Securities, Inc., which, unlike the gun club, was actually located in Beverly Hills. It was headed by one Jerome N. Schneider, who during the 1970s and 1980s established banks in overseas tax havens and sold them to people who wanted their very own financial institution. These weren't the kind of banks you're used to seeing. They didn't have vaults. Or cashiers. Usually, they consisted of little more than a mail drop, a plaque on the wall, and a file folder in a cabinet of some operative in places like the Cayman Islands and the Republic of Vanuatu. Schneider also wrote books titled *How to Profit and Avoid Taxes by Organizing Your Own Private International Bank in St. Vincent,* and *Using an Offshore Bank for Profit, Privacy and Tax Protection.*[64]

Let us review, now, the tax histories of these varied businesses. Royal Caribbean Cruises, with profits of $158 million, pays nothing in federal income tax. Carnival Cruise Lines, with profits of $1.2 billion, pays $29 million in income tax—for a tax rate of 2.4 percent. Darling-Delaware, a onetime profitable business that paid income tax, has been converted into an unprofitable business that pays no income tax. Plum Creek, with profits of $86 million, pays nothing in federal income tax. And the Beverly Hills Gun Club, during its years as an S corporation, not only paid no federal income tax itself but provided plenty of losses for its investors to write off on their personal tax returns—reducing the amount of income tax they paid.

Five businesses that pay little or nothing in U.S. income tax. Isolated examples, perhaps?

Not at all.

The list is endless. As we have seen, the tax rates of many large, multinational American corporations such as Chase Manhattan, Baxter International, Ogden Corporation, and Texaco, to name a few, are below the rates levied on middle-income families and individuals. And in just five instances, the beneficiaries of these tax policies include four families who hold membership on the *Forbes* magazine directory of 400 richest Americans, some people who live in one of America's most exclusive zip codes, and a collection of wealthy investors.

Members of Congress, to be sure, would have you believe otherwise. Charles E. Schumer, Democratic congressman from New York, spoke for a majority of his colleagues as they prepared to vote on the Tax Reform Act in September 1986:

"If this bill becomes law, the No. 1 issue on taxes that is vexing the American people: Why should I pay my share when the wealthy individual or wealthy corporation is not paying his share, will be gone." [65]

CHAPTER 5

★ $ ★ $ ★

FOREIGN TAX BREAKS

Low Rates—But Not for You

You say you would like to find a perfectly legal, surefire way to cut your federal income tax bill? That you're paying too much in taxes, what with the two children and the prospect of college tuition?

That with an income of $45,000 from your work and the spouse's part-time job, the money never seems to stretch far enough? That it seems as if every year you pay out more, more, more—and a lot of that more is taxes?

Boy, do members of Congress have a deal for you.

How would you like to pay about $300 in income tax on your $45,000 in earnings?

All you have to do is move to the Turks and Caicos.

Turks and Caicos?

That's a string of thirty islands, cays, and islets dotted across 5,000 square miles of ocean, north of Haiti and southeast of the Bahamas. Together, they add up to a land area about the size of San Jose, California.

What, you may ask, do a bunch of islands, some uninhabited year-round, have to do with paying U.S. income tax?

Well, some people there do earn U.S. income—but they don't pay nearly as much tax as you. In 1990, for instance, residents of the Turks and Caicos who received money from their investments in the United States paid U.S. income tax at a rate of seven-tenths of 1 percent. On an income of $45,000, that would amount to $315.

By way of contrast, that year the 8.8 million individuals and families in the $40,000 to $50,000 income group who lived in one of the fifty states paid an average of $5,090 in income tax. That was $4,775 more than the island residents. Their tax rate was 11.3 percent.

No wonder that in 1993 a Miami public relations firm began to promote the Turks and Caicos as a good place to conduct offshore business, urging tax consultants, bankers, lawyers, and insurance companies to consider the tax benefits of moving their offices there. Or at least their office addresses.

One *Fortune* 500 company, Texaco, Inc., chose the latter option. It established a company called Texaco Capital LLC on the Turks and Caicos to sell a new issue of securities offered late in 1993. While the Texaco subsidiary was organized on Grand Turk Island, "the principal executive offices of its manager" remained at Texaco, Inc.'s headquarters in White Plains, New York.[1]

How is it possible for the residents of islands 600 miles south of Miami to pay income tax at a rate of seven-tenths of 1 percent, and for a middle-class family living in Chicago to be taxed at a rate sixteen times higher, when all the money in both cases was earned in the United States?

Because Congress has cut special deals in tax treaties with countries around the world—in some cases, there are no treaties at all—so that wealthy investors get the kind of tax rate that you can only dream about.

It's a practice that takes on growing significance now that the 1990s buzzphrase "global economy" is used to justify all manner of decisions by government and business. In many cases, those decisions are contributing to a falling standard of living—from the elimination of jobs to reduced wages, from the trimming of pensions to forced part-time employment. And the "global economy" is also tightening the squeeze on U.S. taxpayers.

Actually, you can throw a dart at a world map and be sure that the people living almost anywhere it sticks who receive money from their U.S. investments are paying U.S. taxes at a rate below yours. In fact, many of them pay nothing at all—and on incomes running into the hundreds of millions of dollars.

So let's say you're not inclined to move to the Turks and Caicos—that the casual lifestyle on islands with miles of white, soft-sand beaches, where the days are spent scuba diving and deep-sea fishing and sailing, where interisland transportation can be erratic and other amenities lacking, is not what you had in mind.

How about Thailand?

Suppose that in 1990 you earned $35,000 at your job in Florida. If you were a typical U.S. taxpayer, you paid $3,708 in income tax. Your tax rate was 10.7 percent.

If you had lived in Thailand and collected that $35,000 on investments in the United States, you would have paid $52 in U.S. income tax. Your rate? Less than two-tenths of 1 percent.

Oh, Thailand isn't to your liking? How about Austria?

Suppose that in 1990 you earned $25,000 at your job in Ohio. If you were a typical U.S. taxpayer, you paid $2,268 in income tax. Your tax rate was 9.2 percent.

If you had just lived in Austria and picked up that $25,000 from your investments in the United States, you'd have paid only $25 in U.S. income tax—for a tax rate of one-tenth of 1 percent.

Other countries, to be sure, wouldn't work out quite so well for you. Like Japan. Persons living in Japan who received, say, $62,500 from their investments in America in 1990 paid $1,875 in U.S. income tax.

Of course, if you lived and worked in Massachusetts and earned $62,500 and were a typical U.S. taxpayer, you paid $7,986 in income tax that year—four times as much.

This tilt in favor of foreign investors applies at the higher end of the income scale as well. Within the United States, the 2.3 million individuals and families who reported incomes between $100,000 and $200,000 paid, on average, $24,865 in income tax—a rate of 19 percent. By contrast, residents of Ireland with the same income from American investments paid $5,903 in U.S. income tax—a rate of 4.5 percent.

But if you want the best deal of all, you will have to move not to the Turks and Caicos or Thailand or Austria or Ireland, but to the United Arab Emirates.

If you lived there in 1990 and collected $25,000 on your American investments, you would have paid $15 in U.S. income tax. On $45,000 of income, you would have paid $27. And on $150,000 of income, you would have paid $90.

The tax rate: six-hundredths of 1 percent.

Not bad, right? Practically tax-free. And if you happen to be one of these lucky foreign investors, the news is getting better all the time. Conversely, if you happen to be an American taxpayer whose income is derived from a weekly paycheck, the news is getting progressively worse.

In the years from 1985 to 1990, the amount of money that residents of foreign countries received from their investments in the United States surged from $17.5 billion to $79.4 billion —an increase of 354 percent. Of course, the total of U.S. income tax they paid went up too—but not nearly as fast. It rose from $900 million to $2 billion—an increase of 122 percent.

What this means is that for foreign investors, not only did their U.S. income rise but they got a tax cut too—a nice hefty one of 51 percent. Their tax rate fell from 5.1 percent to 2.5 percent.

For you, the story is quite different. Let's say that in 1985 your family income amounted to $28,000. (Median family income that year was $27,735.) If you had prospered at the same rate as foreign investors, by 1990 your income would have reached $127,000.

However, there was no tax-rate cut for you. Instead, your rate went up. On $28,000, you would have paid about $3,100 in income tax in 1985. On $127,000, you would have paid about $23,000 in 1990. While your income rose at the same pace as that of foreign investors—354 percent—the amount of taxes you paid would have spiraled 642 percent.

Thanks to Congress, investors living abroad generally escape payment of billions of dollars in U.S. income tax on their investments in America. Just a couple more pieces of the jigsaw puzzle. Nevertheless, they account for only a fraction of the tax dollars that are being lost each year as a result of a more disturbing trend for American taxpayers—a tax system that is increasingly reflecting what economists and people in Washington call the global economy.

That phrase has come to mean many different things to different people—from a lowering of wage rates in the United States to a flood of cheap imports into the American market, to increased business opportunities for American businesses abroad. But what has been overlooked in all this is the impact the global economy is having on the taxes American corporations pay. The evidence is everywhere. Even in intimate apparel.

Foreign Flight

The Warnaco Group, Inc., is a New York–based company that grew out of the takeover wars of the 1980s, one of the corporate offspring of the Drexel Burnham money machine. In typical fashion, the company's owners, a group of investors, purchased the business with mostly borrowed money. So much borrowed money that for the years 1988 to 1992 the company's interest payments on its debt totaled $317 million—or 94 percent of its $336 million in earnings before payment of interest and taxes.

Warnaco designs, manufactures, and markets "a broad line of women's intimate apparel, such as bras, panties and sleepwear, and men's dress and sport shirts, neckwear, sweaters and accessories."[2] The women's apparel is sold under such familiar trade names as Olga, Valentino, and Warner's. The menswear division sells apparel and accessories under the brand names of Christian Dior, Hathaway, Chaps by Ralph Lauren, and Puritan, among others.[3]

These products are carried nationwide in more than 15,000 department, specialty, and mass-merchandising stores, among them Wal-Mart, Victoria's Secret, Macy's, Kmart, and Federated Department Stores. In the United States, the company has nineteen manufacturing facilities and warehouses, from New York to California. It has an additional eighteen manufacturing plants and warehouses in other countries, from Costa Rica to Ireland.

Warnaco is run by Mrs. Linda J. Wachner, one of America's highest-paid female executives. Her salary and bonuses from 1990 to 1992 totaled $8.5 million, for an average annual income of $2.8 million. That was the smaller part of her compensation package.

As often happens in corporate takeovers, Warnaco was initially a private company. Later, stock was sold to the public. The offering provided Mrs. Wachner with far more lucrative opportunities than her salary and bonus: stock options.

She received options to buy 1.3 million shares of Warnaco

stock for $4.67 a share. To help make the purchase, the company loaned her the money. She put up one penny—yes, that's one cent—for each share. Warnaco loaned her the other $6 million—without interest. By 1993, with the stock trading as high as $38 a share, her paper profits added up to $43 million.

All this for an executive job that is not full time. When some of Warnaco's businesses were spun off in 1990 into yet another company, Authentic Fitness Corporation, Mrs. Wachner served as chairman and chief executive officer of that company as well. Her employment contract provided for a base salary of $675,000 for three years and other cash incentives, all in addition to her Warnaco agreement, where she was paid $2.8 million annually.

Overall, Mrs. Wachner received, on average, better than $4 million a year from 1990 to 1992. (That figure does not count the value of the stock options, which are worth far more.) This explains why Graef S. Crystal, an adjunct professor at the University of California at Berkeley Business School, who compiles lists of underpaid and overpaid executives, singled out Mrs. Wachner for special mention in January 1992:

"In these days of equal pay for equal work, it gives me great pleasure to announce that Linda J. Wachner, the 45-year-old CEO [chief executive officer] of the Warnaco Group Inc., passed all but two men to end up as the second runnerup for the most overpaid CEO of the year. Indeed, if you make the appropriate adjustments for her company's size and performance, she would even beat out the two men."[4]

Her salary and bonuses were so large that they exceeded the income tax paid by both companies. But take Warnaco alone.

From 1988 through 1992, Warnaco revenue totaled $2.8 billion. Its income before interest payments and taxes amounted, as we saw, to $336 million. As for its income tax payments, here's the breakdown based on company reports filed with the SEC:

Income tax paid to foreign countries—$11 million.

Income tax paid to the United States—$0.

And therein lies another trend in the global economy that is siphoning money from the wallets of ordinary taxpayers. Like Warnaco, a growing number of U.S. companies are paying more income taxes to support foreign governments than they are paying to support the U.S. government. Here is a sampling based on total revenue and tax payments for the years 1990 to 1992, as reported in SEC documents.

AMERICAN HOME PRODUCTS CORPORATION of New York, a major drug manufacturer, had revenue of $22 billion. The company paid $675 million in income taxes to foreign governments, and $545 million in local, state, and federal income taxes in the United States. More than five of every ten dollars in tax payments went overseas.

BLACK & DECKER CORPORATION of Towson, Maryland, a manufacturer of power tools and and small household appliances, had revenue of $14 billion. The company paid $151 million in income taxes to foreign governments, and $6 million to the United States. More than nine of every ten dollars in tax payments went overseas.

CITICORP of New York, the country's largest banking company, had revenue of $79 billion. The company paid $1.4 billion in income taxes to foreign governments, and $214 million to the United States. Four of every five dollars in tax payments went overseas.

COCA-COLA COMPANY of Atlanta, the world's largest soft-drink business, had revenue of $35 billion. The company paid $1.7 billion in income taxes to foreign governments, and $784 million to the United States. Seven of every ten dollars in tax payments went overseas.

EXXON CORPORATION of Irving, Texas, the world's largest oil company, had revenue of $351 billion. The company paid $6.9 billion in income taxes to foreign governments, and $2.1 billion to the United States. Three of every four dollars in tax payments went overseas.

FISCHER & PORTER COMPANY of Warminster, Pennsylvania, a manufacturer of process control instruments used by chemical, power, petroleum, and other industries, had revenue of $706 million. The company paid $13 million in income taxes to foreign governments, and $200,000 to the United States. More than nine of every ten dollars in tax payments went overseas.

FORD MOTOR COMPANY of Dearborn, Michigan, the country's second-largest car manufacturer, had revenue of $286 billion. The company paid $1.3 billion in income taxes to foreign governments, and $876 million to the United States. Three of every five dollars in tax payments went overseas.

GILLETTE COMPANY of Boston, the manufacturer and marketer of razors, razor blades, dental-care products, stationery, toiletries, and cosmetics, had revenue of $14 billion. The company paid $456 million in income taxes to foreign governments, and $339 million to the United States. Three of every five dollars in tax payments went overseas.

INTERNATIONAL FLAVORS & FRAGRANCES, INC., of New York, a developer and manufacturer of flavors and fragrances used in a variety of products, from perfumes to confectionery items, had revenue of $3 billion. The company paid $197 million in income taxes to foreign governments, and $102 million to the United States. Three of every five dollars in tax payments went overseas.

JOHNSON & JOHNSON of New Brunswick, New Jersey, the pharmaceutical and health care products company, had revenue of $37 billion. The company paid $1.2 billion in income taxes to foreign governments, and $483 million to the United States. Seven of every ten dollars in tax payments went overseas.

LOCTITE CORPORATION of Hartford, Connecticut, a manufacturer of specialty chemical products, sealants, and adhesives, had revenue of $1.7 billion. The company paid $68 million in income taxes to foreign governments, and $7 million to the United States. Nine of every ten dollars in tax payments went overseas.

UNITED TECHNOLOGIES CORPORATION of Hartford, Connecticut, a company that designs and manufactures high-technology products for the aerospace and other industries, had revenue of $65 billion. The company paid $789 million in income taxes to foreign governments, and $530 million to the United States. Three of every five dollars in tax payments went overseas.

Not too long ago, most of corporate America's tax dollars remained in this country. And that was at a time when businesses paid taxes at a much higher rate. From 1968 to 1970, Ford paid $1.2 billion in income tax to federal, state, and local governments, and $454 million to foreign governments. More than seven of every ten dollars in tax payments stayed in the United States. From 1966 to 1968, Gillette paid $103 million in income tax to federal, state, and local governments, and $48 million to foreign governments. Seven of every ten dollars in tax payments stayed in the United States.

To be sure, a portion of the growing tax payments abroad today are attributable to increased sales outside the United States. In some cases, though, foreign countries impose higher tax rates than the 35 percent levied in the United States. In other instances, companies hold down U.S. tax payments by manipulating revenue and expenses. Whatever the situation, American taxpayers end up subsidizing citizens in other countries through the U.S. tax system. For this, too, you may thank Congress, which has failed to adapt the Internal Revenue Code to a global economy.

While there are many complex rules, generally if a company pays $1 million in income tax to, say, Japan, it can subtract $1 million from its U.S. income tax bill. As recently as 1965, the foreign tax credits claimed by U.S. companies were comparatively small. That year, credits totaled $2.6 billion, or about 10 percent of the $25.5 billion that companies paid in U.S. income tax.

By 1990, however, the foreign tax write-off had swelled to $25 billion—reaching 27 percent of the $93.5 billion that companies paid in U.S. income tax. Over the twenty-five years, foreign tax credits—or taxes paid to foreign countries—had jumped 862 percent. Income tax paid in the U.S. went up just 267 percent.

What accounts for such a dramatic increase over the last twenty-five years in a tax write-off that has been on the books for seventy-five years? The answer is not simply increased sales abroad.

One major cause is a practice by which global corporations play off different nations' tax systems against one another, shifting expenses and profits—often through paper transactions—to achieve the lowest overall tax rate or to advance some other business goal. Another major cause is favorable tax decisions made by friendly U.S. policymakers.

Here's an example of such a decision. As so often happens with taxes, it grew out of a secret deal cut by special interests and government officials, this one made shortly after World War II. The results of such decisions are always the same—a transfer of the tax burden from them to you.

Deal in the Desert

The story begins in a most unlikely place, the Arabian desert, in the turbulent period after the war. It was there, in one of the most sparsely populated regions of the world, that American oil companies and officials of the U.S. Department of State talked a group of Bedouins into enacting an income tax. This in a country where a principal industry at the time was diving for pearls, where a main source of revenue was a head tax on Muslim pilgrims visiting holy shrines, where the population was overwhelmingly illiterate—only 5 percent could write their names. Why an income tax?

To learn why, turn back the clock a few more years, to 1933. It was in that year that King Ibn Saud of Saudi Arabia gave American companies permission to search for oil. Five years later, Standard Oil Company of California (Chevron) and the Texas Company (Texaco) made the great strike at Hasa, one of the most prolific oil fields ever discovered. The two companies were soon joined by Standard Oil Company of New Jersey (now Exxon) and Mobil Oil, in a consortium called the Arabian American Oil Company (ARAMCO), to develop the Saudi deposits.

ARAMCO drilled wells, laid pipelines, built storage tanks, and constructed maritime terminals to load crude oil onto tankers for shipment around the world. More important, ARAMCO

made certain that the king's every wish was fulfilled. At Ibn
Saud's bidding, ARAMCO built roads, schools, hospitals—even
air-conditioned a sun-baked terrace at the royal palace by en-
closing it in a plastic bubble. Whatever the king wanted, AR-
AMCO, the good corporate citizen, provided.

When World War II disrupted the oil trade and squeezed the
king's purse, ARAMCO rushed to the royal rescue. The company intervened with the U.S. State Department to make Saudi
Arabia eligible for wartime assistance through Lend-Lease,
President Roosevelt's program to supply money, food, and
arms to Great Britain in the war against Germany. Although
Lend-Lease was intended to help nations that were actually at
war with the Germans—and the Saudis were not—the State
Department got around that by having Roosevelt determine
that "the defense of Saudi Arabia is vital to the defense of the
United States," thereby opening the door for millions of dollars
in foreign aid to the Saudi royal family.[5]

After the war, Ibn Saud did not let his gratitude toward the
Americans interfere with his personal interests. He demanded
an increase in royalties from ARAMCO. Oil revenue had
greatly enriched the royal family, rising from $3 million in 1939
to more than $40 million by the late 1940s. The family's once
spartan desert existence was giving way to a life of profligate
pleasures, with cars, imported women, French chefs, lavish pal-
aces, and spending binges abroad. Nevertheless, the king
wanted more.

Raising the royalty was easier said than done. Much as AR-
AMCO wanted to keep the king happy, the company couldn't
increase his royalty without disrupting the industry's worldwide
pricing structure. The royalty was standard—12.5 percent of
the selling price of a barrel of crude oil. If ARAMCO raised
King Ibn Saud's royalty to 50 percent, it would have to do the
same for farmers, businessmen, state governments, and other
owners of oil lands in the United States—then the world's largest petroleum producer. Such an increase would, in turn, result
in lower profits.

What to do? Poring over arcane sections of the U.S. tax code,
oil-company lawyers came up with a novel way to keep the
Sauds stocked with cars, concubines, and cash. One section permitted American corporations doing business abroad to sub-

tract the income taxes paid to foreign governments from their U.S. tax bills. Saudi Arabia had no income tax, but if the king were to enact one, ARAMCO could channel more money to the royal family at no cost to the company. It would come from U.S. taxpayers.

The foreign tax credit was one of the oldest provisions in the Internal Revenue Code. Enacted in 1918, it was aimed at preventing a corporation operating abroad from being taxed twice on its foreign earnings—once by the country where it was doing business and again by the United States. The goal was to support expansion of U.S. interests.

For the oil companies, discovery of the tax credit was like making a second great strike in the desert. It would allow them to leave their worldwide royalty rate intact while satisfying the king's demands.

A few obstacles had to be overcome. To begin with, the income tax was usually levied in countries with advanced societies and economies. Saudi Arabia failed to qualify on either count. In the late 1940s, it was still a land of medieval customs and manners. The population was believed to be 3.5 million—no census had ever been taken—and about half were Bedouin nomads who drove flocks of sheep and goats from one watering hole to another, subsisting on camel's milk. Slave dealers flourished, with estimates of the number of slaves ranging up to 1 million or more. Runaway slaves were routinely beheaded. Disease was widespread. The life expectancy of the average Saudi was thirty-three years.

In the United States, the foreign tax credit was originally meant to help corporations that paid a legitimate foreign income tax—one also levied on most citizens and corporations in the other country—and not a tax that merely singled out one company, like ARAMCO. Most important, the credit was not supposed to allow an American corporation to shift the cost of doing business abroad to taxpayers at home.

Nevertheless, the oil companies lined up support for the idea with the State Department in Washington during the fall of 1950. They had little trouble winning approval. For State Department officials, keeping Ibn Saud and the oil companies happy was the first priority, not the U.S. Treasury.

As lawyers for the major oil companies drafted the proposed

Saudi statute in New York, the State Department arranged for a government expert on international taxation to go to Saudi Arabia to explain to the king why an income tax, as opposed to a higher oil royalty, would be more advisable from ARAMCO's standpoint. Of course, Ibn Saud did not care whether it was called a royalty, an income tax, or a tithe. He simply wanted more money. If enacting an "income tax" would produce the cash he sought, so be it.

On November 4, 1950, Ibn Saud signed the first of two royal decrees that purported to levy a 20 percent income tax on all individuals and corporations in the kingdom. A close reading showed that they applied to only one taxpayer—ARAMCO. The income tax assured King Ibn Saud of half of ARAMCO's operating profits—then about $100 million a year.

On December 30, 1950, after the decrees were final, a brief ceremony held on the outskirts of the Red Sea port of Jedda marked a historic turning point in the history of American taxes. There, Fred A. Davies, the tall, distinguished-looking ARAMCO executive vice president, and Sheik Abdullah Sulaiman, Ibn Saud's wily old minister of finance, raised earthenware cups of tea and coffee as they signed a three-page agreement in which ARAMCO agreed to "submit" to the new Saudi income taxes.[6] With the stroke of a pen, Sulaiman had greatly increased King Ibn Saud's annual income. Davies not only had resolved the impasse at no cost to his company but had guaranteed it long-term access to the greatest reservoir of oil on earth. The only losers that day were American taxpayers.

When the U.S. Treasury Department realized the magnitude of the giveaway to the oil companies, officials were livid. Treasury saw the Saudi tax for what it was—a device apparently "engineered" by the oil companies to funnel more royalties to the Sauds without any additional expense to ARAMCO.[7]

Treasury held up formal approval of the tax credit for four years. Finally, in 1955, the oil companies, with the help of the State Department, prevailed. A reluctant Treasury certified the Saudi income tax as qualifying for foreign tax credit treatment.

It is difficult to tell who benefited the most—ARAMCO or the House of Saud. It is quite clear who lost. Overnight, the Treasury surrender wiped out $350 million in federal income tax that ARAMCO had owed the U.S. government since 1950.

The long-term losses to the Treasury were much greater. In 1949, ARAMCO had earned $114 million and paid $43 million in U.S. income tax—a tax rate of 38 percent. In 1950, the company earned $110 million and paid $199,032 in federal tax —a tax rate of less than two-tenths of 1 percent. By the late 1950s, when ARAMCO was earning $300 million or more a year, the company paid no tax to the United States as a result of the Saudi foreign tax credit.

Naturally, American taxpayers had to make up for the lost revenue. Were they outraged? Not a bit.

As is so often the case with taxes, nobody told them about this tax giveaway. The behind-the-scenes battle between the Treasury and State Departments was kept secret. Thus, there was no public debate over the merits of a tax break that would ultimately cost American taxpayers tens of billions of dollars. Also, as so often happens when taxes are involved, what little information did seep out was misleading.

Shortly after ARAMCO and the Saudi government signed the tax accords, a *New York Times* story described the pact as a "profit sharing agreement," in which "ARAMCO agrees to pay an income tax on the net income, after payment of United States taxes . . . equal to one-half of the net operating income of the company."[8] It was, of course, the other way around, with the Saudis having first crack at ARAMCO's profits. After they took their cut, nothing was left for the United States.

This practice, perfected in Saudi Arabia, was quickly adopted elsewhere. Eventually, every oil-producing nation where American companies had a concession enacted an income tax law to increase its oil revenue by tapping the foreign tax credit provision of the U.S. Internal Revenue Code.

Kuwait, Iraq, Abu Dhabi, Bahrain, Qatar, Algeria, Nigeria, Libya, Gabon, Indonesia, and Ecuador all imposed income taxes on American multinational oil companies that operated concessions. Today, every country that discovers oil, or even thinks it might, immediately adopts an income tax acceptable to the American multinational oil companies—as well as to the U.S. State Department.

For example, when the Chinese discovered oil reserves off Canton in the South China Sea in 1981, foreign oil companies were invited to bid for concessions. Before drilling started, an important issue had to be resolved: The Chinese Communists needed to adopt an income tax law. Unlike their predecessors in Saudia Arabia, who relied on oil-company expertise in drafting an income tax statute, the Chinese turned to another source: the U. S. Internal Revenue Service.

A team of IRS officials was dispatched from Washington to Beijing in 1981 to brief Chinese officials on the intricacies of the U.S. foreign tax credit. The purpose was to make certain that the Chinese law, when adopted, would be a "creditable" tax, meaning it could be subtracted dollar for dollar from the United States tax bill of any American oil company that discovered oil in China. Armed with the technical advice of the IRS, China's National People's Congress followed through. In December 1981, the Chinese legislature approved the Foreign Enterprise Income Tax Law, and shortly afterward the bureaucracy issued regulations to administer it.

Those who had a hand in crafting the ARAMCO tax credit—from King Ibn Saud to officials in the State Department and oil-company executives—are gone. But their legacy lives on. The foreign tax credit and a host of related income-shifting strategies it helped spawn are alive and well. For U. S. taxpayers, the impact is greater than ever.

There is no better example of the legacy than the Internal Revenue Service's unsuccessful attempt to collect billions—that's right, billions—of dollars that it says the ARAMCO consortium owes in back taxes and penalties growing out of another major oil event in the Middle East—the 1979–80 Iranian oil crisis.

The international oil industry was thrown into turmoil in 1979 after the ouster of the Shah of Iran, the country's long-time ruler, and the subsequent fundamentalist Islamic revolution. Muslim clerics suspended Iranian oil sales abroad, throwing the world oil markets into chaos. To soften the impact of the Iranian cutoff, Saudi Arabia increased production and sold its oil below world prices. This benefited the ARAMCO partners—Exxon, Chevron, Texaco, and Mobil—which now had access to substantial supplies of Saudi crude at bargain basement prices.

The IRS later claimed that the four American oil companies profited in one other way: They diverted the oil to foreign subsidiaries out of the reach of U.S. tax laws, then resold the refined products at sharply higher prices, reaping huge profits.

The Texaco operations, as detailed by the IRS, show how the scheme worked.

In a thirty-month period from 1979 to 1981, one Texaco company (Texaco International Trader) transferred 72 million barrels of Saudi crude to another Texaco company (Texaco Overseas Limited), based in Bermuda. But no transfer actually occurred. The Bermuda company existed only on paper. It had no assets, no employees. The oil was transported a short distance down the Persian Gulf to Bahrain, where it was refined for a nominal price, and transferred to Texaco's Bermuda subsidiary. The refined products were sold at market prices, giving Texaco a substantial return on the low-cost Saudi oil. As the IRS spelled out:

"These profits were directly attributable to the ARAMCO advantage and were not subject to U.S. or Bermuda tax. [Texaco's Bermuda subsidiary] was a shell and performed no meaningful function other than the avoidance of U.S. tax. . . . The commercial arrangement . . . worked for the mutual benefit of all parties; however, it resulted in the shareholders artificially shifting income from U.S. to foreign entities not subject to U.S. tax."[9]

IRS ultimately sent deficiency notices totaling more than $15 billion to Exxon, Texaco, Chevron, and Mobil. The companies are contesting the notices in U.S. Tax Court, in the largest series of cases ever tried in that court. And all signs indicate they may never have to pay a dime. Late in 1993, a tax-court judge ruled in the first case on Exxon's behalf, in effect dismissing the IRS's claim. Judge Meade Whitaker, while acknowledging that the oil companies may well have earned huge profits, said that those profits were "irrelevant" to the case.

Transferring Taxes to You

What the oil companies do is a variation of a longtime game played by multinational corporations. It involves something called transfer pricing, and it works like this: A company loads up expenses in a high-tax country, thereby inflating its deductions and reducing or eliminating the taxes it must pay. At the same time, the company diverts its profits to a low-tax country, enabling it to keep a larger share of them.

Thus Tax Rule No. 5: For multinational corporations, the amount of taxes they pay is flexible; for small and medium-sized U.S. businesses, it is mandatory.

The practice of shifting income and expenses was patented by U.S. multinational companies long ago and has since been copied and refined by those based in other countries. As a result, foreign-owned businesses operating in the United States now pay much less in U.S. income tax than locally owned companies. Consider a few findings drawn from IRS statistics for 1989, the latest year for which data is available.

A total of 44,840 tax returns were filed by corporations that operate in this country but are controlled by foreign investors. Of that number, only 12,971—or 29 percent—paid any income tax. A whopping 71 percent of all foreign-owned businesses paid no U.S. income tax.

On their tax returns, the foreign-controlled corporations reported total revenue of $967.1 billion. They paid $6.2 billion in income tax—or six-tenths of 1 percent of revenue.

For some comparison, all other U.S. companies reported revenue of $9.2 trillion and paid $94.1 billion in income tax—or 1 percent of revenue.

If you think that differences in taxation measured by tenths of a percentage point are insignificant, consider this:

Each one-tenth of a point shaved off total corporate tax bills in 1990 translated into more than $11 billion in lost tax revenue for the U.S. Treasury. More personally, it meant that every dollar in income tax paid by everyone earning less than $50,000 a year in Illinois and South Carolina went to offset that lost revenue.

A study conducted in 1992 by the staff of a House Ways and Means subcommittee showed that eighteen electronics companies controlled by foreign investors reported revenue of $174.8 billion but paid taxes of only $755.2 million. Their tax rate based on total sales: four-tenths of 1 percent.

When you fill out your next Form 1040 and pay your income tax, you might want to think of that percentage in terms of your own household. If your total income was $200,000, you would pay $800 in income tax. If your total income was $50,000, you would pay $200 in income tax. If your total income was $40,000, you would pay $160. If your total income was $30,000, you would pay $120. And if your total income was $20,000, you would pay $80.

Take another look at your Form 1040. See the line that says: "This is your total tax." If it is larger than the above amounts, you are paying U.S. income tax at a higher rate than some of the world's largest and richest corporations.

But that's not too difficult, since—as the staff of the House Ways and Means subcommittee discovered—one foreign-controlled company "with sales in excess of $6.6 billion paid no tax." [10] Another year, with sales of $2.8 billion, the same company paid $156 in U.S. income tax. That's $156. Which means that if you were a single person earning $10,000, you paid more income tax than a global corporation.

For foreign-owned corporations in the automobile industry, the subcommittee found, "28 percent of the returns reviewed showed no tax due. Industry sales totaled close to $27 billion on those returns. One company had sales that totaled $3.4 billion over two years and paid no tax." [11]

During committee hearings, the findings by congressional investigators prompted this observation by Representative Paul E. Kanjorski, Democrat from Pennsylvania:

"U.S. corporations, in their overseas sales, show a profit of 9 percent [on assets]. But foreign corporations doing business in the United States show two-tenths of 1 percent of profit [over a three-year period]. Is it possible that American corporations are forty-five times more effective in making profits and doing business overseas than foreign corporations are in the United States? I think that is ludicrous. Somebody is cooking the books." [12]

From the other side of the aisle, Representative Duncan Hunter, California Republican, observed:

"The point is that this is an excellent strategy for our trading adversaries, because every dollar that they evade in U.S. taxes is a dollar that they can apply to their own research and development, their own industrial and manufacturing base. And even if they have to pay their tax back in their home country, the government in their home country can refund that tax in terms of an accelerated write-off for their critical industrial areas. As a result of that, they can be more effective in putting Americans out of work. So every dollar they evade is basically a bullet fired at the American worker." [13]

You might think that when a Democrat and a Republican line up like that on the same side of an issue, they must be reflecting the prevailing view in Washington and forces must be at work to reverse this process.

But you would be wrong.

And you might think—given all the forecasts by Washington's political columnists—that with the 1992 election of the largest slate of new members of Congress in forty-four years, there would be a heightened interest in changing such policies.

But you would be wrong again.

Democrats and Republicans alike, as well as some of the nation's largest news organizations, chided President Clinton in 1993 for suggesting that foreign-controlled companies in the United States should pay more taxes.

The attitude of a majority of the members of Congress may have been summed up by one incoming representative who joined other freshman lawmakers in a roundtable discussion on the *CBS This Morning* program in January 1993.

The show's coanchor, Paula Zahn, had said she doubted there would be "much disagreement" with the idea that foreign-owned companies should pay more U.S. income tax. In response, Jay C. Kim of Diamond Bar, California, a Republican preparing to begin his first term on Capitol Hill, took exception:

"I disagree with that. I think it's—to me, taxing a certain group, especially the people who are succeeding in a free-market society, is penalizing those people, in my opinion. It's socialistic. I don't think it's right that this is—again, this is not the time for even thinking about raising taxes." [14]

It wasn't a question of raising taxes, of course, but merely of collecting taxes actually owed. Once more, bear in mind the tax rules. When someone else—individual or corporation—doesn't pay, you do. If you live in Maryland, Virginia, and Minnesota —and make less than $100,000 a year—it takes every dollar you pay in income tax to offset the lost revenue from foreign-controlled businesses. Every year.

In any case, to the extent that foreign-owned companies are

slicing their tax bills through transfer-pricing arrangements, inflated write-offs, and other practices, they are only doing what American-owned companies have been doing for years— except the foreigners are doing it better. And investors in some countries do it much better than those in others.

Of the 413 tax returns filed for 1989 by U.S. corporations controlled by investors in Saudi Arabia, 99 percent paid no U.S. income tax. Of the 224 tax returns filed by U.S. corporations controlled by investors in Ireland, 95 percent paid no income tax. Of the 1,661 tax returns filed by U.S. corporations controlled by investors in Panama, 92 percent paid no income tax. Of the 1,764 U.S. corporations controlled by investors in the Netherlands, 78 percent paid no income tax.

At the other extreme, of the 329 U.S. corporations controlled by Swedish investors, 78 percent paid some income tax. And of the 4,612 U.S. corporations controlled by investors in the United Kingdom, 44 percent paid income tax.

But what about the country whose investors control the largest number of U.S. corporations—Japan?

Of the 6,592 U. S. corporations controlled by Japanese investors, 73 percent paid no income tax. Overall, those Japanese-run companies reported revenue of $254 billion. That was 26 percent of the $967 billion in revenue reported by all foreign-controlled businesses together. The Japanese-owned companies paid $1.1 billion in U.S. income tax—or four-tenths of 1 percent of their revenue.

How does that compare with the taxes some U.S. companies are paying on their U.S. earnings? Let's add up the total tax and revenue figures of three companies for the three most recent years.

American Greetings Corporation, the Cleveland, Ohio, company that designs, produces, and sells greeting cards, paid a total of $111 million in U.S. income tax. That was 2.6 percent of the company's revenue of $4.3 billion—or more than six times the rate at which Japanese-controlled companies paid tax.

The Washington Post Company of Washington, which publishes the *Washington Post* and *Newsweek* magazine, paid a total of $225 million in U.S. income tax. That was 5.2 percent of the company's revenue of $4.3 billion—or thirteen times the rate at which Japanese-controlled companies paid tax.

Premier Industrial Corporation, a Cleveland company that supplies electronic components for industrial and consumer products and manufactures fire-fighting equipment, paid a total of $105 million in U.S. income tax. That was 5.3 percent of the company's revenue of $2 billion—or thirteen times the rate at which Japanese-controlled companies paid tax.

Looked at from a different vantage point, if Premier Industrial had paid U.S. income tax at the same rate as Japanese companies, its tax bill for the three years would have totaled only $8 million.

All this runs contrary to yet another set of claims by lawmakers back in 1986, when they promised that the Tax Reform Act would guarantee that businesses with comparable incomes would pay similar taxes. That turned out to be no more true than most other 1986 promises. As foreign control of U.S. businesses grows, and as the owners master the intricacies of the Internal Revenue Code, the rate at which they pay taxes declines.

In 1983, foreign-controlled U.S. companies reported $390 billion in revenue and paid $3.4 billion in U.S. income tax. Between 1983 and 1989, their revenue shot up 148 percent, climbing from $390 billion to $967 billion. But taxes paid rose only 82 percent—from $3.4 to $6.2 billion.

The rate at which foreign companies paid U.S. income tax fell from nine-tenths of 1 percent in 1983 to six-tenths of 1 percent in 1989. You might want to think of those numbers in terms of your personal tax situation.

Suppose that in 1983 you earned $25,000, roughly median family income that year. If your salary had gone up at the same pace as foreign corporate revenue, in 1989 your income would have totaled $62,000.

Your taxes, as always, would have gone up. In 1983, you would have paid about $2,700 in income tax on $25,000—a tax rate of 11 percent. In 1989, you would have paid about $8,500 in income tax on $62,000—a tax rate of 14 percent.

Look at the numbers closely. Your income and the revenue of foreign companies went up at the same pace. Tax rates were another matter. While the U.S. income tax rate of foreign companies fell 33 percent, yours went up 27 percent.

Enforcing the Tax Law by Bicycle

No one disputes that the job of tracking multinational corporations' income and expenses across national boundaries is a difficult task. In fact, it's an impossible one under the government's current audit procedures. In an article published by *Tax Notes,* a leading national publication on tax issues, Martin Lobel and Henry M. Banta, partners in the Washington law firm Lobel, Novins, Lamont & Flug, and Nicole Gueron, a law clerk in the firm, described the IRS enforcement practices this way:

"The current efforts to collect taxes from the multinationals are the equivalent of policing the New Jersey Turnpike on bicycles. Even with better bicycles, such efforts would be ludicrous. The cold fact is that under the current . . . procedures there is little possibility of being able to collect taxes from firms engaged in serious transfer pricing abuses." [15]

Which is not to say the situation is hopeless. Some strategies have been developed to deal with the problem. But so far, they have been thwarted. Why? An alliance between foreign governments and special interests in this country has blocked reforms. Look no further than California's ill-fated attempt to tax multinational corporations in the Golden State.

As always with taxes, the issue involves arcane terms, like "worldwide combined reporting" and "water's edge" and "domestic disclosure spreadsheet" and "unitary formula apportionment."

But the issue is not nearly so complex as the language. The question is actually quite simple: How does one state or one national government determine the amount of tax that should be paid by a multinational corporation with many subsidiaries in many different states and countries?

The answer already has resulted in your paying more taxes. And it's just the beginning. As the global economy grows, so, too, will your taxes, as the overall burden continues to be transferred from large corporations to small and medium-sized businesses and middle-income taxpayers.

To see how it works, let's create a business—say, the Multinational Toy Company (MTC), a British company with headquarters in London, that manufactures and sells a variety of toys and dolls.

Suppose a subsidiary, MTC Indonesia, makes dolls in Indonesia. It sells the dolls to another subsidiary, MTC Turks, a trading company located on the Turks and Caicos Islands. MTC Turks sells the dolls to yet another subsidiary, MTC California, which in turn sells them to toy stores and department stores throughout that state. One other note: The dolls, along with other toys, are shipped in a vessel owned by another subsidiary, MTC Shipping.

Let's assume, further, that it cost MTC Indonesia seventy-five cents to make the doll in Indonesia, and that MTC California sells it to retail outlets for $15.

Hence, the question:

What is the profit on each doll subject to California income tax? Or for that matter, U.S. income tax?

You might guess that after subtracting the seventy-five cents, and a reasonable amount for shipping and handling and other miscellaneous expenses, the balance would be income subject to tax. Let's say $10.

But you would guess wrong.

That's because back in London, Multinational Toy Company, the parent company, has many options. MTC Indonesia could sell the dolls to MTC Turks for $1. MTC Turks, in turn, could sell them to MTC California for $14. Thus, after deducting its expenses, MTC California would show a profit of less than $1 on each doll.

Meanwhile, back on the Turks and Caicos Islands, MTC Turks is sitting on a $13 profit. That's tax-free, since the islands have no income tax.

Those figures could be further manipulated by the other subsidiary, MTC Shipping, which is incorporated in Liberia, another country with no income tax. MTC Shipping could inflate its charges and siphon off yet more tax-free dollars.

So how do the U.S. government and state governments determine how much tax companies like MTC should pay?

Not very well.

For the most part, the IRS takes the word of multinational companies. Not because it is trusting, but because there is no choice. With thousands of global companies, and tens of thousands of subsidiaries, and millions upon millions of transactions each year, it is impossible to track each transfer of goods.

In those cases where the IRS does conduct audits, it seeks to compare charges with those levied in other businesses. How much did another trading company pay for a product? How much did another shipping company charge? The practice is imprecise, subject to interpretation, and requires an army of auditors and economists; it can be implemented in very few cases, and when it is, the legal proceedings drag on for a decade or more. All of which explains why many multinational companies—both foreign owned and U.S. owned—like it.

Some years ago, state governments sought a different approach to computing the amount of tax owed by a multinational subsidiary. A formula was created that compared the dollar amount of property, payroll, and sales of the subsidiary operating within the state to the dollar amount of property, payroll, and sales of the parent company worldwide. That ratio was applied to the parent company's taxable income to determine the amount of tax the subsidiary should pay within the state. This approach makes it more difficult for companies to hide their profits in a Turks and Caicos subsidiary.

Lawmakers and policymakers in Washington have never much cared for this method of assessing taxes, even though it requires fewer auditors, is more precise, and guarantees that companies pay the tax they owe. A succession of administrations and Congresses, Democrats and Republicans, have staunchly opposed adoption of the formula. The reason: Special interests—read: multinational corporations and foreign governments—will not permit it.

How can foreign governments veto tax policies within the United States?

Easily.

Reacting to pressure from foreign governments and global companies in the United States and overseas, federal officials through the 1980s pressured states to abandon the formula approach. One state after another caved in, until California remained the lone holdout.

Then in 1985, Barclays Bank International, Ltd., sued California, seeking a refund of the taxes it had paid, contending the formula violated a U.S. tax treaty with Great Britain. (It did not, but that's another matter.) When the California Supreme Court eventually upheld the validity of the assessment method, Barclays appealed the decision to the U.S. Supreme Court. At the same time, the British government mounted an intensive lobbying campaign aimed at convincing federal officials to persuade California to repeal its taxing system.

The Bush administration quickly fell in line and promised the British government it would support Barclays in its case before the Supreme Court. Then candidate Bill Clinton promised to support California. In a June 6, 1992, "Dear Brad" memo to Brad Sherman, a California tax official, Clinton wrote:

"I assure you a Clinton administration will be pro-California in this litigation." [16]

After the election, worried foreign business leaders, foreign government officials, and executives of some—but not all— U.S. multinational corporations began pressuring the new President to reverse his position. They created a public impression that California was collecting a tax on the worldwide income of corporations, instead of merely applying a formula to determine the share of that income subject to tax in California.

In any event, officials of governments and businesses deluged Washington with mail. They urged the new administration to oppose the California method and threatened to retaliate with taxes against American companies if it did not.

On April 15, 1993—appropriately enough, the deadline for filing tax returns—the Union of Industrial and Employers Confederations of Europe, an umbrella organization for European business and industry and European institutions, wrote to Treasury Secretary Lloyd Bentsen, suggesting that the new administration continue the Bush administration's support of Barclays:

"Worldwide unitary tax [the formula method] is a most serious issue, with the capacity to cause immense damage to international trade and investment. . . . Successive United States administrations have accepted the clear and cogent case against this tax." [17]

A similar letter to Bentsen followed four days later, from the

Confederation of French Industries and Services, warning that "it is necessary to avoid the damaging consequences of international retaliation in this area."[18]

At the same time, foreign business and political leaders suggested to American multinational companies that it would be in their best interest if they, too, lobbied against the California assessment method. Britain went a step further and said retaliatory taxes would be levied if the California formula was allowed to stand.

R. Madison Murphy, executive vice president of Murphy Oil Corporation in El Dorado, Arkansas, wrote to Bentsen:

> California's taxation of worldwide income of foreign multinationals has created a hostile environment for U.S. companies operating in foreign countries. The United Kingdom has been a vocal critic of the California unitary tax and has passed retaliatory legislation which would disallow advance corporation tax rebates to U.S. shareholders of U.K. corporations. This law has not been implemented but can be activated at any time. . . .
>
> Please assist us in our attempt to place this very important matter before the U.S. Supreme Court by urging and supporting the filing of an amicus curiae brief by the U.S. government in support of the position of Barclays Bank.[19]

And then there was the letter from Larry Thurston, vice president of Storage Technology Corporation. Remember, that's the company that Vice President Gore visited to promote support for NAFTA, the company that paid $300,000 in income tax to the U.S. government, the company that paid fifty-seven times that amount, or $17.1 million, in income taxes to foreign countries.

The StorageTek vice president wrote to Leslie B. Samuels in the Treasury Department's Office of Tax Policy urging the administration to throw its support to the British bank and oppose California:

"If a state of the United States, such as California, is allowed to use a different system internationally, foreign governments may retaliate against United States business. The United Kingdom has already enacted retaliatory legislation which could deprive United States businesses of substantial treaty benefits. Other foreign governments may follow suit. . . . Please continue supporting the taxpayer [Barclays] in this matter."[20]

Edgar S. Woolard, Jr., chairman of the board of Du Pont, recited a similar theme in a letter to President Clinton:

"Du Pont is concerned with reports that your administration is considering the reversal of the long standing and bipartisan position of previous administrations opposing the states' use of worldwide unitary taxation. We respectfully request that you continue the policy of opposing state tax systems that tax income earned beyond the borders of the United States."[21]

As the mail rolled in, Clinton backtracked and waffled on his earlier promise of support to California tax officials. At the same time, money poured into the offices of California state legislators. The legislature caved in and in September 1993 enacted legislation acceptable to the British. The old formula approach to collecting the state income tax was junked.

Nevertheless, in November 1993, the U.S. Supreme Court agreed to hear the Barclays case, even though the method of computing the tax was no longer used. Barclays is pursuing the matter in hopes of collecting a refund—and guaranteeing that no other state will one day implement the formula. If the Supreme Court should uphold the British bank, the decision could cost cash-strapped California $4 billion in tax refunds to all multinational companies doing business in the state.

The Supreme Court will hear arguments in 1994, and for California the outlook may be bleak for several reasons. First was the court's decision even to hear the dispute. A decade ago, in 1983, the Supreme Court upheld California's formula method in a case involving a U.S. corporation. Legal observers have speculated that the court agreed to look at the issue again because it was considering the possibility of reversing its earlier stance.

In addition, the British government has maintained an ongoing lobbying campaign, promising that if the Supreme Court hands down a decision against Barclays, it will retaliate against American companies operating in Great Britain.

And finally, there is the Supreme Court's record on tax matters over the last century. Given the choice between siding with special interests over the public interest, the court has most often sided with special interests.

Lest you have some doubt about this, you might want to think about the casualty deduction that a Pennsylvania businessman claimed on his personal tax return back in 1976. The U.S. Tax Court upheld the businessman's write-off for the loss of his place of business in a fire, a decision rooted in a Supreme Court ruling many years before.

The businessman's occupation?

He manufactured PCP and methamphetamine for distribution through a multimillion-dollar drug ring. During one of his manufacturing operations, a batch of volatile chemicals exploded and burned down his illegal drug laboratory.

Now You See It, Now You Don't

There are, to be sure, many other tax aspects to the global economy and the business of shifting taxes from them to you. But let's look at one more: the use of foreign trusts.

Foreign trusts are paper entities established in other countries to hold assets of U. S. citizens. The IRS doesn't get to look at their books. No one has the slightest idea how many foreign trusts exist. No one has the slightest idea of the number of such trusts established in any particular country. No one has the foggiest notion of who benefits from those trusts. And no one has the slightest idea how much money is channeled through the trusts to escape taxes.

It is safe to say, however, that the lost revenue can be counted in the billions of dollars every year.

Sometimes the tax-avoidance schemes are illegal. Sometimes they are perfectly lawful, structured through one of the myriad loopholes conveniently provided by Congress. At times, it seems, everyone—at least, everyone with serious money—has had a foreign trust. Or a dozen or more trusts.

Remember the Academy Award–winning movie *One Flew Over the Cuckoo's Nest*? The film, which depicted life in a mental hospital, swept the 1975 Oscars—best motion picture, best screenplay, best director (Milos Forman), best actor (Jack Nicholson), and best actress (Louise Fletcher). You may recall the movie and the cast. But do you remember its producer?

202   America: Who Really Pays the Taxes?

Saul Zaentz.

Zaentz, who lives in San Francisco, achieved success in the music field through his Fantasy Records Company, most notably after signing Creedence Clearwater Revival to a recording contract in 1968. In that same year, Fantasy Records became Fantasy, Inc. Two years later, all of Fantasy, Inc.'s stock was purchased by a Bahamian partnership called Argosy Venture. Had Saul Zaentz given up control? Hardly.

The partners in Argosy were five secret Bahamian trusts. One of those trusts—Trust T-6000—was the big owner, with 75 percent of Argosy. It was established first for Zaentz's wife at that time, Celia Zaentz, and later for his children. Other Caribbean companies and partnerships were formed to manufacture and distribute records and tapes.[22]

By the early 1970s, Zaentz had teamed up with actor Michael Douglas to translate *One Flew Over the Cuckoo's Nest,* the widely acclaimed Ken Kesey novel, to the screen. The film opened in November 1975 and, in the words of a spokesman for Zaentz's company, "Reviewer reactions were lavishly praiseful, and the response of the public was overwhelmingly positive."[23] So overwhelmingly that by October 1988, according to court records, Saul Zaentz's businesses had pulled in $46.5 million from the showing of the film.

And where, exactly, did the money go? Well, $1.2 million went to the Saul Zaentz Company. And $45.3 million flowed into a Caribbean company called N.V. Zwaluw.[24] Other Caribbean companies were involved, companies with names like Skylark Filmmaatschappij B.V. and Lataam N.V. and Obelix N.V., as well as Argosy Venture and a collection of trusts.

What followed was a blizzard of paperwork and money exchanges and loans back and forth, all blurring what was income and what was taxable, who received it and who didn't. Finally, in 1986, the IRS issued a deficiency notice, stating that Zaentz owed $26 million in back taxes for the years 1976 to 1982 and that the various corporations and trusts "are shams, and that you are the true earner of the income from the motion picture, 'One Flew Over the Cuckoo's Nest.' "[25]

Zaentz challenged the IRS claim in U.S. Tax Court. There the case dragged on until June 1990, when he agreed to pay

$1.5 million—or 6 percent of what the IRS originally said was owed. For several of the years in dispute, Zaentz, the producer of a movie that grossed more than $100 million, paid no income tax.

But in truth, Zaentz who later produced *Lord of the Rings* and *Amadeus,* was a minor leaguer in the foreign trust game. The major leagues are dominated by players like the Pritzker family of Chicago. Remember Royal Caribbean, the cruise line that pays no U.S. corporate income tax and is owned, in part, through Bahamian trusts formed for the benefit of the Pritzkers?

That's only one of the family's foreign trust arrangements. The Pritzkers have been using trusts outside the United States for years. The IRS contends that Abraham N. Pritzker, the family patriarch, who died in February 1986, managed to move $95 million into foreign trusts before his death to escape payment of estate taxes. When his estate's return was filed, it showed a taxable estate of—$3,000. The IRS says the family understated the value of the estate by $97.4 million and owes $53.2 million in taxes.[26]

The family has denied the claim and is contesting it in U.S. Tax Court. There the case joins many other proceedings in which the Pritzkers have been fighting other IRS claims for payment of millions of dollars in income taxes. In the other cases, too, foreign trusts are a central issue. As was the case with Zaentz, millions of Pritzker dollars poured into and out of trusts and corporations in other countries, blurring liability for taxes.

But wait, you say, Congress cracked down on the use of foreign trusts. There's even a line on the tax return labeled "Foreign accounts and foreign trusts," which requires taxpayers to acknowledge if they have an interest in such an account.

That ended the practice of tax avoidance through foreign tax havens? Right?

Not likely.

If you think so, you might want to ponder the purpose of the following classified advertisement, which appeared in a 1993 issue of *The Washington Lawyer,* the official journal of the District of Columbia bar:

"CALL THE CAYMANS or anywhere else (U.S., Canada) with no phone bill record. Traceless touch-tone telephoning via 1–900

STOPPER (786–7737). $1.95/min. Free information: 800–235–1414. Private Lines Inc. (operated by D.C. Bar member)."[27]

Actually, you don't have to use a "traceless" telephone and call someone on a Caribbean island to arrange favored tax treatment through a trust. You can call your friendly member of Congress, who will write a private tax law just for you. Like the following paragraphs from the Tax Reform Act of 1986, which were inserted in the Internal Revenue Code:

> (3) Special Rule for beneficiary of trust—In the case of an individual—
> (A) who is a beneficiary of a trust which was established on December 7, 1979, under the laws of a foreign jurisdiction, and
> (B) who was not a citizen or resident of the United States on the date the trust was established,
> amounts which are included in the gross income of such beneficiary under section 951(a) of the Internal Revenue Code of 1986 with respect to stock held by the trust (and treated as distributed to the trust) shall be treated as the first amounts which are distributed by the trust to such beneficiary and as amounts to which section 959(a) of such code applies. [Section 957(a)]

Those paragraphs provide special tax treatment for a certain unnamed beneficiary of a foreign trust. How, you might ask, did that provision end up in the Internal Revenue Code? Like so many tax breaks, apparently by immaculate conception. The people who wrote the tax law either say they do not know how it got there, or are not talking.

When Dan Rostenkowski, the Democratic chairman of the House Ways and Means Committee, and John J. Duncan of Tennessee, a Republican member of the committee, were asked about its origin, they replied:

"Members of the House have never been forced to divulge the names of constituents on whose behalf they sought transition relief. Some members choose to issue press releases announcing any transition rules in which they played a part.

Others choose to remain silent. We will continue to allow members to make that individual choice."[28]

In the case of the foreign trust beneficiary, every single member of the House Ways and Means Committee and Senate Finance Committee, Democrats and Republicans, chose "to remain silent." Rostenkowski and Duncan refused to identify the beneficiary. Others said they had no idea. Richard A. Gephardt, the Missouri Democrat and longtime Ways and Means Committee member, was typical. Said he:

"In response to your specific question relating to 'the identity of the unnamed individual who will benefit from a transition rule—"Special rule for beneficiary of (a) trust," ' my office had no involvement in this matter."[29]

Cutting Taxes, Cutting Jobs

None of this is to suggest that foreign trusts are the exclusive province of wealthy individual Americans seeking to ease their tax burdens. Large corporations make use of offshore accounts as well. Even the parent company of a dog named Tige.

You may not recognize the name Brown Group, Inc., but you're sure to have heard of the product: Buster Brown shoes, one of the country's oldest and best-known brand names. As American as apple pie, Buster Brown has been famous for nearly a century, personified by the little boy who delighted generations of adults and children with the slogan: "I'm Buster Brown. I live in a shoe. This is my dog, Tige. He lives in there too."

Founded in 1878, Brown has long been America's largest shoe company. At one time, it had more than thirty plants and employed some 30,000 workers, many at factories in small towns across Missouri, within a few hours' drive of Brown's corporate headquarters, in Saint Louis.

In the 1980s, with imported shoes surging into the United States, Brown began retrenching and embarked on a massive "restructuring" program. In 1985 alone, it closed nine plants and laid off or forced into early retirement thousands of employees. The company also shifted more of its production outside the United States. These moves, Brown assured stockholders, made 1985 a "year of progress" and would enable the company "to compete where we have a comparative advantage."[30]

As Brown cut jobs in the United States and created them overseas, it sought to transfer something else offshore as well— its tax liability. Early in 1985, Brown created a tax shelter in one of the world's many tax havens, the Cayman Islands.

On March 19, 1985, the company formed Brown Cayman, Ltd., a Cayman Islands corporation. Brown Cayman in turn became a wholly owned subsidiary of Brown Group International, Inc.—which for its part was owned by Brown Group, Inc. Three days after Brown Cayman was formed, papers were filed creating the Brinco Partnership in the Cayman Islands. Brown Cayman, Ltd., was Brinco's controlling partner.

Together, these various entities provided Brown with a conduit for revenue from its burgeoning Brazilian shoe operations without having to pay U.S. income taxes on all the earnings.

In going to the Caymans, Brown was following a stream of other tax-shy corporations and rich Americans who have flocked to the Caribbean islands for years. An hour and ten minutes from Miami, the Cayman Islands are one of the world's tax-free paradises. As a British crown colony, the Caymans are politically stable and congenial to North Americans—and they levy no income tax on foreign corporations or individuals who establish accounts there.

Equally important to foreign investors is the Caymans' code of financial secrecy, a practice that a local newspaper has described as "the lifeblood of this colony."[31] Virtually no one knows the identity of those who establish corporations and trusts in the Caymans, so tight is the security that governs the process. As a result, an estimated 25,000 corporations and trusts—a number equal to the entire population of the Caymans—have been formed on the islands.

The Cayman Islands are so dedicated to maintaining their reputation for financial secrecy that over the years they have resisted attempts by the U.S. government to break down the confidentiality barriers. Back in the 1970s, when U.S. tax authorities inquired about certain accounts, the Cayman government responded by passing the Confidential (Relationships) Preservation Law. That law made it a crime for a local bank officer or other official to divulge information relating to a customer or client account.

When the United States kept up the pressure, the Caymans finally agreed to cooperate with U.S. authorities on certain criminal investigations. But the kind of information they will provide and the circumstances under which they will provide it are still quite limited. As Alan B. Ratcliffe, the commissioner of the Royal Cayman Islands Police, explained, the cooperation "doesn't include tax offenses." [32]

Why not tax offenses?

". . . There are no tax offenses here," said Ratcliffe. [33]

In the case of the Brown Group, the various business entities created in the Caymans in 1985 were in theory organized to manage the company's Brazilian import business. For years, Brown had been importing into the United States a growing volume of shoes from factories in Brazil.

But Brown shipped no goods through the Caymans after Brown Cayman, Ltd., and the Brinco Partnership were formed. As it had done for years, the company continued to manage its Brazilian imports from its headquarters in Saint Louis. Shoes imported from Brazil were shipped directly to Brown distribution points in the States.

Brown's Cayman subsidiary and partnership had no real business purpose. In fact, Brown didn't even have an office in the islands. What it had there was a classic tax shelter, a paper business. The only product shipped through Brown's offshore subsidiaries was tax benefits.

The managing director of the Brinco Partnership later described the Cayman operation as a "money conduit" for Brown's Brazilian business. He said he understood it to have been created as a "tax shelter." [34]

The IRS described it this way:

"The restructuring of the business through the Brinco partnership . . . created significant tax advantages. . . . While Brinco earned substantial profits, there was no business purpose for the partnership to be domiciled in the Cayman Islands, other than tax savings." [35]

Exactly how much the Cayman subsidiary contributed to Brown's tax savings is unknown. What is known is that in 1985, Brown's U.S. tax payments worked out to 2.4 percent of the company's sales. The figure fell to 1.9 percent in 1986 and slipped to 1.7 percent in 1987.

At the same time Brown was cutting its federal tax bill through an offshore tax shelter, the company continued to cut its workforce back home. Plant closings and job layoffs that began in the 1980s continued into the 1990s. As before, the ax fell hardest in small towns across Missouri—communities where the shoe plant was the largest employer and only industry.

The shutdown hit one community, Dixon, in east-central Missouri, especially hard. In this hilly town of 1,585 on the edge of the Ozarks, the Brown Shoe Company was the largest employer. Many families—husbands and wives, parents and children, aunts and uncles—all worked or had worked at the plant since it was built, in 1956. With 350 employees, Brown accounted for 20 percent of the town's population.

The average wage was $7 an hour. Even though that was not high, few of those who were let go were able to find jobs paying comparable wages and benefits.

One of those who lost his job was Lloyd Henson.

A quiet, slightly built man, Henson, fifty-eight, had worked at the Brown plant for thirty-five years. He had gone there in 1957, shortly after he married.

He started on the production line, making one of the most famous products in America—Buster Brown children's shoes. "I ran an infill packer for twenty-two years," he said. "Before that I threw lathe and ran the heel sanding." More recently he was part of the maintenance crew—turning on the machinery in the morning, preparing the heating and air-conditioning, checking the equipment. The company trusted him, and he valued that trust. "I carried the keys to the factory," he said. "I had access to everything." [36]

After thirty-five years, Henson was making $6.65 an hour, or $265 a week, about $14,000 a year. "The pay wasn't terribly good," he said. "But it was close, just a few blocks from here." And Brown paid better than the few remaining factories in that part of Missouri, where wage rates were routinely $5 an hour. [37]

Most important, Brown provided a good health plan. "One of the best fringe benefits was the insurance. They paid most of our prescriptions. It was quite good. I think we only paid about $18 or $20 a month."[38]

Henson and his wife, Marie, raised two children, a boy and a girl. Although his pay fell short of median family income, he liked the area, where he had lived his whole life. He devoted off-hours to teaching Sunday school and to amateur photography.

In January 1992, Brown announced that it would close the Dixon plant in three months. Even though Brown had been folding plants in Missouri for years, the Dixon shutdown caught Henson by surprise: "I didn't think they were going to close it."[39] The company had recently upgraded the plant's air-conditioning system, and the quality of the factory's work, he felt, had never been higher.

"I think we made good shoes here," Henson said. "I'm sure I don't know as much about shoes as a foreman. But I was here long enough to know when a shoe really looks good—the heel heights are right, the back seams are straight, the elastic looks good. They really looked good to me. The shoes looked better to me than they did years ago. We had improved greatly over earlier years. We had to get the quality up in order to sell. There was a time when we just had to get the shoes out. It didn't make as much difference then. But in the last ten years the quality was very good."[40]

Brown blamed the shutdowns at Dixon and other Missouri plants in part on competition from imported shoes and in part on "high" labor costs at home.[41] B. A. Bridgewater, Jr., the president and chief executive of the Brown Group, said that foreign shoe manufacturers could pay their employees less than $1 an hour, while Brown Shoe's labor costs were about $8 an hour.

The shutdown in Dixon threw its 350 employees out of work. Most have not found new jobs, Henson said. Some did find work, only to be laid off again. As for Henson, he said he looked everywhere, but there were no jobs. He added: "We never see any ads for anything anymore. Never. The unemployment rate here is at 10 percent. It's been going up steadily the last two or three years. There are still some factories around here, but they never advertise. I'm sure they don't have to. I would guess they have a stack of applications. There are so many people looking for work." [42]

For months, he drew unemployment benefits while he looked for a job. Most employers would not even consider him because of his age, he said. He also learned that his years of dedicated work, strict attendance, and punctuality at Brown meant nothing in the 1993 job market:

"I had perfect attendance the last eight years. I was as trustworthy as anybody they had. And that meant nothing to any employer. It really amazed me. It just meant nothing to them." [43]

When his unemployment benefits ran out, he took a job in a window-manufacturing plant in Freeburg, Missouri—twenty-eight miles northeast of Dixon. To make windows and doors, he was paid $5 an hour. After paying for transportation to work ($10 a week), Social Security, and his health care costs—now running at nearly $300 a month—the Hensons don't have much left. But he says he is just holding on until he retires, at age sixty-two. If he had stayed at Brown until that age, he would have received a monthly pension of $350 to $400. After the plant closed, he lost some of those benefits too.

Brown gave employees the option of taking their retirement benefits in a lump sum or rolling them into an IRA account. For many younger employees, with small children, home mortgages, and household bills, there was only one choice. They took the lump sum. "A lot of people had to take theirs to pay their bills," Henson said. [44]

Henson put his retirement money in an IRA account, but he estimates he will receive only from $100 to $200 a month—depending on interest rates—when he retires. That's less than half the pension he was counting on if he had worked at Brown until age sixty-two.

What is happening in Dixon, Missouri, is happening across America. And for Dixon, and numerous communities large and small, the future does not look bright, what with the wholesale closing of manufacturing plants, the shipment of jobs offshore, and the failure to create new jobs that pay middle-class wages. No one is more concerned than Lloyd Henson.

"I'm not worried about me," he stressed. "I'm worried about the young people. Where are they going to get jobs? The young people in this country are in a worse financial condition than at any time in this country's history. You can see why. Low-paying jobs. They have no health care. No affordable housing. I think I was one of the lucky ones. I really do."[45]

The Hensons' house is paid off. Their children are grown. Lloyd Henson is a few years from retirement, though with an even more modest pension than he had planned. To him, the country's ongoing economic sluggishness is no surprise. A woman at the local bank, he said, put her finger on it:

"She told me the reason that people aren't buying and that things are as difficult as they are in the country is because there is no job security in America. She said that's why everything is as tight as it is.

"Everyone is afraid."[46]

So let's review the global economy's role in the U.S. tax system —the practices that have enabled individual foreign investors, foreign-controlled companies doing business in America, and U.S. companies doing business abroad to transfer their U.S. tax burden to you.

ONE. Foreign investors, both individuals and corporations, are paying U.S. income tax at an average rate of 2.5 percent on their investments in this country. Some are paying as little as six-tenths of 1 percent.

TWO. A growing number of American companies are paying more in income taxes to foreign governments than they pay to the U.S. government. They thereby ease the tax burden on residents of the other countries and raise the burden on Americans.

THREE. Foreign-controlled corporations operating in this country pay U.S. income tax at a rate well below that levied on American-owned businesses—as well as on you.

FOUR. Tax authorities in this country at both the federal and state level are woefully unprepared to audit the books of multinational corporations that use complex transfer pricing arrangements to escape payment of billions of dollars in taxes.

FIVE. Many longtime American corporations are systematically closing plants, shifting operations abroad, and eliminating middle-class jobs at home—all of which means a decline in tax collections from companies and individuals.

What, then, does the future hold?

More of the same—one tax law for the privileged, another for you.

CHAPTER 6

★ $ ★ $ ★

THE REVOLVING DOOR

The Right Connections

Here is your dilemma:

For many years, you have been excused from paying federal income tax. Now the President and some members of Congress have decided that isn't fair. They believe you should pay tax like everyone else. Worse still, they think you should pay tax at the same rate as everyone else.

Naturally, you like the existing system just fine. Because you must, however, you are willing to compromise, to pay some tax —but certainly not the full amount owed.

What to do?

Whom to turn to?

If you have to ask, you most likely are a member of the silent majority, the tens of millions of Americans whose income is derived from a weekly paycheck and whose connections in Washington are confined to obtaining a pass from their representative to watch proceedings on the House floor from the visitors' gallery.

If, on the other hand, you are knowledgeable in the ways of Washington, you won't have to ask. You understand exactly what must be done: Set up a lobbying machine. Pass out money to the favorite charities of friendly lawmakers. Contribute to their election funds. Fly them to sun-drenched islands. Hold testimonial dinners for them. And—most important of all— hire the people who help write the tax laws: not members of

Congress or their staffs, but special interests outside government.

Do all these things, and the odds are good that when you file your next tax return, you will be able to keep some of your income free of taxes and thereby ensure that your neighbor will have to pick up the difference.

That's what some of America's largest and most profitable corporations did in 1993.

In an intensive lobbying campaign to preserve one of the half-dozen most blatant tax-avoidance provisions in the Internal Revenue Code, an army of special interests descended on members of Congress and federal policymakers. Mixing cajolery and threats, they sought to guarantee their clients' right to pay less tax than others. In the end, the President and Congress capitulated, agreeing that at least 40 percent of the profits that U.S. companies earned in Puerto Rico would be exempt from the federal income tax.

Among the scores of beneficiaries: Merck and Company, Coca-Cola Company, Johnson & Johnson, Citicorp, Pfizer, Inc., Baxter International, Chase Manhattan Bank, American Home Products Corporation. Remember the names? Those are some of the companies that pay taxes at a rate below yours, or pay more taxes to support foreign governments than they do to support the U.S. government.

Call it the right connections.

The same kind of connections that earlier resulted in the following paragraphs being inserted into the Internal Revenue Code:

(38) The amendments made by section 201 shall not apply to—

(G) the expansion of the capacity of an oil refining facility in Rosemont, Minnesota, from 137,000 to 207,000 barrels per day which is expected to be completed by December 31, 1990.[1]

What those two paragraphs did was exempt the owner of the Rosemont oil refinery from paying taxes that others in a similar situation would be compelled to pay.

Who was the owner?

Koch Industries, the second-largest family-controlled business in the United States in terms of sales. The varied holdings of the Wichita, Kansas, company include refineries, pipelines, storage terminals, gas processing plants, drilling rigs, and cattle ranches. The company is run by two of the founder's sons, Charles and David Koch, longtime supporters of conservative causes. (Their father, Fred C. Koch, who died in 1967, was a founding member of the John Birch Society.) The Koch brothers, listed in the *Forbes* directory of the 400 richest Americans, are worth an estimated $1.5 billion each, according to the magazine.

In one of those tax ironies that abound in Washington, the private tax law for Koch Industries was enacted in 1986, six years after David Koch ran for vice president of the United States on the Libertarian party ticket. During the campaign, the Libertarians, who received substantial financial support from both Koch brothers, called for abolishing the Federal Bureau of Investigation and the Central Intelligence Agency, ending all government antipollution efforts and most regulatory programs—and eliminating Social Security and slashing federal income taxes.

How, you ask, do businesses and wealthy individuals go about securing a private tax law? How can you obtain one for yourself?

Well, you might try developing an interest in horses and racetracks.

Horses? Racetracks?

If it's the first Saturday in May, do you know where your congressman is?

If you live on the near northwest side of Chicago you do. He's in Louisville, Kentucky, for the 115th or 116th or 117th or 118th running of the Kentucky Derby. That's the place to find Dan Rostenkowski, the chairman of the House Ways and Means Committee, the one person who more than any other determines what new tax laws are enacted, what old ones are repealed, and which existing ones are amended.

In one of those coincidences of Washington life, each year Rostenkowski travels to Louisville during Derby week to speak to the American Horse Council.[2] In return for the speech, he collects a $2,000 honorarium. Until 1992, he could keep the money. Now it goes to one of his charities. The horse council picks up all expenses.

The American Horse Council represents the men and women in the horse business, or, more accurately, the new rich (Carl Icahn, who made his millions in the takeover wars of the 1980s and piloted Trans World Airlines into U.S. Bankruptcy Court) and the old rich (the du Pont family; Wilhelmina du Pont Ross, for one, paid her husband to run the stable and wrote off his salary on the couple's tax return).

In another one of those coincidences of Washington life, the Horse Council has proved remarkably adept in protecting the tax interests of horse owners. The council won new tax concessions for its members in the early 1980s and held on to their most prized ones during the so-called reform movement of 1985 and 1986. As a result, the horse set continues to enjoy favorable tax treatment today.

That may explain why horse people look so fondly on Rostenkowski. On his visit to Kentucky during Derby Week in 1989, he attended one of the perennial Derby social events, a luncheon at Spindletop Hall outside Lexington, which attracts the socially prominent and the rich and famous of the horse world. As they sought to show their appreciation for the congressman's efforts to lighten their tax loads, Rostenkowski "good-naturedly tried to ward off any accolades":

" 'Don't thank me for anything,' he said. 'I didn't do anything for you, and if I did, I don't want to know about it.' "[3]

All of which might explain why, if you have visited a track in recent years, you would have seen racehorses with names like My Deduction, Write Off (not to be confused with My Write Off), Tax Holiday, Another Shelter, Tax Appeal, and Justa Shelter. And the more pointed Tax Gimmick and Tax Dodge.

Horses have long had a good ride in the Internal Revenue Code. The code views horse breeding as a "farming business," on a par with raising pigs or cattle. A half century ago, when thousands of horses were at work on American farms, there was merit in that view. But with some exceptions, horses as work animals disappeared years ago. Yet the original tax deductions remain.

Owners can write off horse-related expenses—the cost of

food, housing, veterinarians, insurance, transportation, state and local taxes, interest charges, depreciation, and stud fees. They can write off the cost of going to horse shows or visiting other horse farms. An older horse can be exchanged for a younger, more valuable, horse tax-free. When a horse is sold, the profit is taxed not as ordinary income but at the lower capital gains rate.

No wonder the wealthy have a fondness for horses. Like the late William du Pont, Jr., of the famous Delaware family. Du Pont was a banker by trade, the president of Delaware Trust Company, a bastion of the family fortune. But at heart he was a country gentleman, who bred racehorses, hunted foxes, raised cattle, and dabbled in animal husbandry on two vast estates near Wilmington.

Du Pont's Fair Hill, Maryland, estate, in the rolling countryside west of Wilmington, was the center for a glittering series of social events organized around horseracing and foxhunting. Fair Hill was so vast it was said that du Pont could ride to hounds three days a week without retracing the route of a previous hunt. The centerpiece of Fair Hill was du Pont's personal grandstand, which could seat 12,500 spectators and was the largest private facility of its type in America.

Every year du Pont sponsored the Fair Hill Races, one of the most prized social events of the season, in which wealthy horse owners and society figures gathered to watch steeplechase races over a course du Pont himself had laid out. Modeled after the English Grand National Steeplechase, du Pont's Foxcatcher National Cup Steeplechase put horse and rider through a grueling three-mile, dog-legged course replete with nineteen formidable jumps. To compete at Fair Hill was to reach the pinnacle in American horse jumping. At all these events, the dapper, energetic du Pont—known as "Willie" to friends—was the star, reveling in the pageantry that equestrian events generated.

In addition to raising racehorses, du Pont bred cattle, designed racetracks, and gave money for research in animal husbandry. But his various agricultural ventures rarely, if ever, made money. His Foxcatcher Livestock Company ran in the red every year from 1945 to 1960. Du Pont could afford such losses. With a personal fortune estimated at $400 million, he was one of the world's richest men. Nevertheless, he deducted the losses on his income tax return. One year, the write-offs included the salaries of two professional foxhunters.

The IRS later challenged the deductions, arguing that du Pont's farming activities were a hobby and were not intended to earn a profit. Du Pont disagreed, claiming that simply because Foxcatcher lost money every year did not mean he did not intend to make money. His intent was to turn a profit; it just hadn't happened yet. A federal court agreed with du Pont and upheld his deductions.

To this long list of write-offs available to the horse crowd, a more valuable deduction was added in 1981. As tax writers prepared to put the final touches on the Economic Recovery Tax Act of 1981, the first major tax bill of the Reagan administration, lobbyists jockeyed at the finish line to get favorable treatment for their clients. Some of the most intense pressure centered on depreciation.

Depending on the number of years assigned to depreciate equipment, plant, or, in this case, horses, a lot of tax benefits were at stake. The shorter was the period of time allotted, the more taxes were saved. All the special interests sought to get their clients placed in the class requiring the shortest number of years possible.

When the final bill emerged from a House-Senate conference committee, all the attention went to parts that reduced individual and corporate tax rates and eliminated many shelters. But the bill also contained a provision that was a triumph for the horse lobby.

For depreciation purposes, the lobby managed to get racehorses and older breeding horses placed in the best of all possible categories—the so-called three-year class, along with "autos, light-duty trucks, [and] R & D [research and development] equipment."[4] This meant that horse owners could depreciate their steeds in three years instead of ten, as had previously been the case. If you bought a promising filly, say, for $30,000, the new law said that you could write off her value against your taxable income at the rate of $10,000 a year for three years, instead of $3,000 a year over ten years.

The tax break had an immediate impact. Horses—long thought of as risky though potentially lucrative ventures—suddenly had more appeal. The new cost-recovery rules brought what *Business Week* called a measure of "economic certainty" to investing in them.[5] So much certainty that even staid institutions like banks bought into the action. In Baltimore, the Mercantile–Safe Deposit & Trust Company invested $1.5 million of its clients' money on horses. A bank official said afterward that 50 percent of the investors made money, 25 percent broke even, and 25 percent lost money. "Those odds are pretty good," he said.[6]

Wall Street formed limited partnerships to invest in Thoroughbred racing and breeding. Horse breeders, dangling the tax savings as bait, attracted new investors into what one called the "horse racing manufacturing business."[7] You didn't need to own a ranch to become part of what a Texas promoter said was the "fastest growing, most exciting industry in the country today. HORSE RACING! The tax advantages and profit potential are unsurpassed. . . . You may have owned a yacht, a jet airplane or an island in the Caribbean; however, nothing will capture your mind like your own personal racehorse."[8] Still other promoters, realizing that some investors might be skittish about actually owning a horse, came up with a scheme that let them lease a horse, while at the same time reaping the tax benefits of horse ownership. "Some of the people breeding horses now are entrepreneurs who can barely tell a horse from a donkey but recognize a nice tax shelter," observed the *Wall Street Journal*.[9]

How, exactly, did horses end up being treated the same as cars for the purpose of depreciation in the 1981 tax law? As is so often the case, the people who wrote the law suffer from amnesia.

When a member of the House Ways and Means Committee staff, who was present during the conference, was asked who fathered the horse provision, he answered: "My memory is dim on that. It was a pretty informal session because they were meeting in a small room."[10]

A staff aide to Senator Walter D. Huddleston, the Kentucky Democrat, who tracked horse legislation on Capitol Hill, was no more enlightening: "I don't really know who did that. The conference occurred over a weekend. It was a rather slapdash thing, and I'm not really sure that it might be pinpointable to one person."[11]

When another Huddleston aide was asked the same question,

he replied: "I'll tell you who would be a better source, to be honest with you. He's a fellow by the name of Tad Davis." [12]

Tad Davis?

That's Thomas A. Davis, the senior partner of Davis & Harman, one of Washington's tax law firms and the registered lobbyist for the American Horse Council. In reports filed with the Clerk of the House in 1993, Davis described his current lobbying activities on behalf of the council:

"All legislation which would change the present tax law treatment of the equine industry." [13]

In short, preserving the tax advantages enjoyed by race horses and other breeding stock. What Davis & Harman do for horse owners is what they attempt to do for a lot of other clients —preserve their tax status or attempt to obtain new tax breaks for them. The law firm's lobby registration statements on behalf of various clients tell the story:

Chicago Board of Trade: "Legislation affecting the tax treatment of commodities."

General Aviation Manufacturing Association: "Investment tax credit and other tax issues concerning business aircraft."

Ad Hoc Committee of Life Insurance Companies: "Support an amendment to the Internal Revenue Code with respect to reserve treatment for annuities and life insurance contracts containing a market-value feature."

Stock Information Group: "Tax legislation affecting stock life insurance companies."

United States Sugar Corporation: "Legislation affecting the tax treatment of employee stock options, and other legislation relating to agricultural and environmental policies."

American General Life Insurance Company: "Banking and tax legislation which would change the present law treatment of life insurance companies and their products."

Florida Sugar Cane League: "Legislation relating to the FUTA tax exemption for H-2 workers, and trade legislation affecting the domestic sugar industry."

Underwriters of Lloyd's, London: "All tax proposals impacting on insurance syndicates." [14]

If Davis & Harman has done well for clients like the American Horse Council, the law firm itself has also done well. It has offices at one of the most prestigious locations in Washington—

the Willard Hotel complex near the Treasury Building. And that's only fitting. After all, the Willard itself is a tax break.

The oldest and grandest of Washington hotels—and, as legend has it, the place where the term "lobbyist" was coined in the days of President Ulysses S. Grant—the Willard underwent a major restoration in the 1980s. When the renovation work fell behind schedule, the wealthy investors risked losing some of their tax benefits. So they went to the tax-writing committees in Congress, which accommodated them with this clause in the Miscellaneous Revenue Act of 1988:

> (7) Special Rule.—In the case of the rehabilitation of the Willard Hotel in Washington, D.C., section 205(c)(1)(B)(ii) of the Tax Equity and Fiscal Responsibility Act of 1982 shall be applied by substituting '1987' for '1986.' " [15]

In plain English, this meant that a host of write-offs that had expired for countless other investors in other projects were extended for those who had put their money into the Willard. These people included a cross-section of Washington's political, social, and business worlds.

Among them: Oliver T. Carr, Jr., the Washington developer who oversaw the Willard's restoration; a flock of Roosevelts, including Kermit, the grandson of President Theodore Roosevelt and a former CIA operative; and John S. Nolan, the senior partner of Miller & Chevalier, which was organized in 1920 as "the nation's first law firm specializing in tax matters." [16] Before he went on to become one of the capital's most influential tax lawyers, Nolan served as assistant secretary of the U.S. Treasury for tax policy from 1969 to 1972.

Graduate School for Lobbyists

How did the Willard investors get such favored tax treatment?

The same way the American Horse Council does.

In one word—access.

Access to the congressional staff people on Capitol Hill who write the tax laws. Access to the important members of Congress who oversee the tax-writing process. Access to the Treasury Department officials who map out tax policies. Access to the people in the IRS who write the regulations and enforce the tax laws.

Access means those people know your name. It means they see a reason to take time out from their busy schedule to listen to you. Often, it means they are inclined ahead of time to try to accommodate you—because you have helped them or because you have helped their boss.

So how do you get that kind of access? Generally, by one of two routes: money or connections. Usually both. The money is passed out in honorariums, which lawmakers once were permitted to keep but now must donate to charity, and in campaign contributions.

The erosion of fairness in America's tax system has paralleled the growth in political action committees, or PACs—broadbased groups of special interests that band together to give money to politicians. From 113 PACs in 1972, the number had swollen to more than 4,000 by 1993. A Common Cause study found that as of 1992, the 431 members of the House of Representatives had received more than a quarter-billion dollars— $285 million to be exact—from PACs in the years from 1983 to 1992.

A disproportionate share of PAC money goes to members of the tax-writing committees. Dan Rostenkowski received more PAC money than all but one other House chairman, pulling in $2.2 million in the last ten years for his campaigns. Three others who were on the Ways and Means Committee for most of that time—Richard A. Gephardt, Robert T. Matsui, and Sam Gibbons—also collected large sums. Altogether, the four taxlaw writers received $9.1 million to help them get reelected. Over in the Senate, a Common Cause study found in 1990 that Lloyd Bentsen, then chairman of the Finance Committee and now Treasury secretary, had received more PAC money—$2.6 million—from 1983 to 1988 than any other senator.[17]

There's a good reason why tax writers get so much campaign money. It's cheaper and more certain for special interests to obtain preferential treatment through the tax code than by, say, getting the government to spend money on them. A tax break is a better investment. Once a preferential provision becomes part of the tax code, it doesn't require an annual review—unlike a program dependent on an appropriation. Thus, obtaining a tax break is, over the long run, money well spent, and one of the few areas where corporate America invests for the long term.

Just as important as campaign contributions to securing access are the connections made through Washington's revolving door. That's the practice whereby the people responsible for the tax system—the congressional staffers who wrote the laws, the lawmakers who oversaw the process, the Treasury officials who formed the tax policies, and the IRS people who implemented and enforced the laws—leave government and go to work for the special interests who want preferential treatment.

To put it bluntly: Your tax dollars pay the salaries of people who spend a few years in government acquiring skills and knowledge about tax law. They then take those skills and that knowledge outside government, where they earn large sums helping to gain favored tax treatment for their clients—and, therefore, higher taxes for you. A job training program underwritten by you.

The list of examples is endless. But let's begin with Davis & Harman, the firm that has been so successful in its tax efforts on behalf of horse owners.

The name partners, Thomas A. Davis and William B. Harman Jr., both got their start as attorneys with the IRS. Davis worked in the IRS chief counsel's office from 1966 to 1970. Harman was an attorney in that office's legislation and regulations division from 1958 to 1959; then he went on to Treasury, where he worked in the office of the tax legislative counsel from 1959 to 1961.

Another partner in the firm, Richard S. Belas, was tax counsel for Republican members of the Senate Finance Committee from 1980 to 1983; deputy chief counsel of the committee in 1983 and 1984; and chief counsel to Republican leader Robert Dole, a longtime member of the Finance Committee, from 1985 to 1989. Three other members of the firm, John T. Adney, John F. McKeever III, and Barbara Groves Mattox, were law clerks for judges in U.S. Tax Court or the U.S. Court of Claims, where a good deal of tax legislation winds up. One associate, Gail Wilkins, is married to William J. Wilkins, former staff director of the Senate Finance Committee and a member of the law firm of Wilmer, Cutler & Pickering.

Is Davis & Harman exceptional in having so many ex-government employees? Not at all. Washington is filled with their stories.

John J. Salmon was chief counsel and staff director of the House Ways and Means Committee from 1981 to 1985. Then he became a partner in the Washington office of a New York law firm, Dewey, Ballantine, Bushby, Palmer & Wood. Salmon represented Joseph E. Seagram & Sons, Integrated Resources, Inc., and Bear, Stearns, Inc., in 1986, when all three obtained special tax provisions in the Tax Reform Act of 1986.

Salmon has a list of corporate clients for whom he lobbies on taxes. Among them is Xerox Corporation, whose concern is "tax legislation relating to U.S. taxation of foreign source income." [18] And Household International, Inc., the diversified financial services company, whose concern is "tax legislation generally, and specifically foreign tax issues." [19] And the Union Pacific Corporation, which Salmon represents on "tax and other legislation affecting the company's various lines of business." [20]

Robert E. Lighthizer was chief counsel and staff director of the Senate Finance Committee from 1981 to 1983. Then he became a partner in the Washington office of Skadden, Arps, Slate, Meagher & Flom, another New York law firm. Lighthizer, too, represented a client who received a special tax break in the 1986 act, General Development Corporation. Among his other clients is the Sara Lee Corporation, which seeks help on "tax legislation relating to the foreign tax credit." [21]

William M. Diefenderfer III was chief of staff of the Senate Finance Committee during the drafting and subsequent passage of the Tax Reform Act of 1986. Then he joined Wunder, Ryan, Cannon & Thelen, a Washington law firm with a large tax practice, which became Wunder, Diefenderfer, Cannon & Thelen. Among the firm's clients and their concerns: the New York buyout firm of Kohlberg Kravis Roberts and "tax, banking, securities and investment issues." [22]

Mark L. McConaghy was chief of staff in 1981 and 1982 of the Joint Committee on Taxation, whose professional staff drafts most tax laws. McConaghy is now with the accounting firm Price Waterhouse. Among his clients: Du Pont Company, General Electric Company, General Motors Corporation, Hallmark Cards, Inc., Levi Strauss and Company, Merck and Company, the Pillsbury Company, Procter & Gamble Company, and Westinghouse Electric Corporation. Their legislative concerns: "tax reform proposals affecting corporations and individuals, which are favored in part and opposed in part by the client."[23]

Ronald A. Pearlman was in the IRS chief counsel's office from 1965 to 1969 and was assistant secretary for tax policy at Treasury in 1984 and 1985. Then he became a partner in Covington & Burling, one of Washington's largest law firms, and registered to lobby on tax matters. His clients have included a Saint Louis trust interested in "possible revision of Section 2612 (c)(2) of the Internal Revenue Code of 1986 (estate tax; generation-skipping transfers; transfers to grandchildren)."[24]

Catherine T. Porter was an assistant counsel to a subcommittee of the House Ways and Means Committee from 1981 to 1983, and the tax aide to Senator John H. Chafee, the Republican senator from Rhode Island, from 1983 to 1988. Then she became a partner in the Washington law firm of Miller & Chevalier, known for its tax practice. On January 9, 1990, Porter registered to represent the Organization for the Fair Treatment of International Investment, an umbrella group representing certain foreign companies. Their legislative interest: "provisions in tax law affecting foreign owned businesses in the U.S."[25]

Lawrence F. O'Brien III, the son of the former Democratic national chairman and postmaster general during the Kennedy presidency, worked in the office of the assistant secretary for legislative affairs at the Treasury Department from 1977 to 1979. Then he became a partner in Dewey, Ballantine, Bushby, Palmer & Wood, and later formed his own firm, O'Brien Calio. O'Brien has lobbied for many special interests on "tax legislative matters," including Beneficial Corporation, the financial services company.[26]

William J. Wilkins was staff director and chief counsel of the Senate Finance Committee in 1987 and 1988. Then he became a partner in the Washington law firm of Wilmer, Cutler & Pickering. He is registered to lobby on taxes for many large businesses, including McDonald's Corporation, whose interest is "foreign tax credit; treatment of royalties."[27]

Timothy M. Haake was an attorney with the IRS from 1973 to 1977, and tax counsel to members of the House Ways and

Means Committee and the Senate Finance Committee from 1977 to 1982. Then he became a partner with Wunder, Diefenderfer, Ryan, Cannon & Thelen. Among his clients: Grand Metropolitan PLC, the British conglomerate that owns Pillsbury. The legislative interest: "tax and trade issues . . . relating to foreign-owned companies and legislation affecting the food industry."[28]

Christine L. Vaughn was in the Office of Tax Policy at Treasury from 1981 to 1984. Then she joined the Washington office of Vinson & Elkins, a large Houston law firm. Among her clients: Merrill Lynch & Co., the nation's largest investment banking firm. The legislative interest: "various tax issues relevant to investment banking."[29]

Keith D. Martin was a tax aide to New York Senator Daniel Patrick Moynihan, now chairman of the Senate Finance Committee, from 1979 to 1982. Then Martin became a partner in the Washington office of Chadbourne & Parke, a New York law firm. Martin's clients have included Ruan Transportation Management Systems of Des Moines, Iowa, which was interested in "any tax legislation affecting truck leasing companies."[30] A Ruan company received its own private tax law in 1986.

Joseph K. Dowley was administrative assistant to Rostenkowski from 1976 to 1981, and assistant chief counsel and later chief counsel of the House Ways and Means Committee from 1981 to 1987. Then he became a partner in Dewey, Ballantine, Bushby, Palmer & Wood, lobbying for special interests on taxes. Among Dowley's clients is NYNEX Corporation, the regional telephone company based in New York, which Dowley represents on "legislation affecting the taxation and regulation of the client's business."[31]

J. Roger Mentz was assistant secretary for tax policy at the Treasury Department from 1985 to 1987. Then he became a partner with McClure, Trotter & Mentz. In 1993, he lobbied for Methanex, Inc., of Houston, Texas. The reason: "equal treatment of alcohol fuels under the Federal tax laws."[32]

Kenneth J. Kies was tax counsel for the Republican members of the House Ways and Means Committee from 1985 to 1986. Then he became a partner in the Washington office of the Chicago law firm Baker & Hostetler. A Kies client: California Independent Casualty Companies of America. Their legislative interest: "tax treatment of small property and casualty insurance companies."[33]

Jerry L. Oppenheimer was deputy tax legislative counsel at the Treasury Department in 1972. Then he became a partner in the Washington law firm of Mayer, Brown & Platt. His clients include the Brunswick Corporation, whose interest "is limited to amendments to the Internal Revenue Code and related acts."[34]

These are but a sampling of the people who moved from representing the government in tax matters to representing special interests seeking favored treatment in tax matters. While in government, most were at the working level. But some once held high-level positions.

Shirley D. Peterson was a partner specializing in tax law at the Washington law firm of Steptoe & Johnson when President George Bush named her assistant attorney general in the Tax Division of the Justice Department in 1989. Three years later, in 1992, she became commissioner of the Internal Revenue Service.

After Bill Clinton's election, Peterson resigned in January 1993 and returned to Steptoe & Johnson as a partner. The ink was barely dry on her resignation letter before she was registering to lobby Congress on behalf of the Los Angeles law firm of Gibson, Dunn & Crutcher. Her client's interest: "tax legislation that may be considered by the House and Senate."[35]

Peterson was following in the long tradition of other IRS commissioners. Like Donald C. Alexander.

Alexander headed the IRS under Presidents Nixon and Ford from 1973 to 1977. After leaving the agency, he stayed on in Washington to lobby. He is now a partner in Akin, Gump, Strauss, Hauer & Feld, and his clients in 1993 included: the Bechtel Group, Inc., of San Francisco, the private construction and engineering company headed by one of America's wealthiest families; the Freemont Group, Inc., a San Francisco–based affiliate of the Bechtel family, which invests heavily in real estate; the Association of Finance and Insurance Professionals; and Chiquita Brands International, Inc., the global food company. For each client, Alexander registered to lobby on taxes.

Another Alexander client was American Financial Corporation of Cincinnati, which was interested in "all hearings and legislation relating to federal tax legislation matters, specifically retention of dividends received deduction and similar corporate issues."[36]

American Financial is the holding company of Cincinnati financier Carl H. Lindner, Jr. A longtime presence on *Forbes* magazine's list of the 400 richest Americans, Lindner controls a variety of insurance and banking companies through American Financial, which is privately held. *Forbes* estimated his wealth at $650 million in 1993.

During the 1980s, Lindner's companies were major contributors to the Alliance for Capital Access, a Washington, D.C., lobby organized by junk bond king Michael Milken. The Alliance successfully headed off legislative proposals that would have limited the tax deduction for interest on corporate debt used in takeovers and leveraged buyouts.

Not all lobbying is on Capitol Hill. A good deal goes on before the tax bureaucracy, which is in a position in many cases to exert more influence on the amount of taxes paid than the average congressman. Here, too, we see the case of onetime government officials representing special interests in proceedings in which they formerly represented the government.

So it is with John E. Chapoton. From 1973 to 1977, Chapoton was assistant secretary for tax policy at Treasury. Now he's a partner with the Washington office of Vinson & Elkins, the large Houston law firm. In July 1993, while representing "ten large money center banks," Chapoton wrote a letter to Leslie B. Samuels, the person holding the job he once held, Treasury's assistant secretary for tax policy.

Chapoton explained that he was writing on behalf of the "Chemical, Chase, First Chicago, Citibank, Bank of America, Bank of Boston, Fleet, Norwest, Mellon and First Interstate" banks regarding a proposed change in the tax law dealing with their purchase of securities, which could result in higher taxes. Chapoton was having difficulty obtaining language in the proposed law that would suit his clients:

> We have proposed two solutions that have been reviewed by staff. . . . Based on our discussions with both Joint Committee and Treasury staff, my impression is that notwithstanding their agreement that something needs to be done

they are finding it difficult to reach agreement on the best solution.

This is not a run-of-the-mill tax issue and I can sympathize with the difficulties in reaching a final conclusion. Furthermore, the staff has been very generous with their time and attention in discussing this matter with us. However, time is running out. . . . After you have had a chance to read this and reflect on the matter, I would like the opportunity to discuss this matter by phone." [37]

Loophole Carvers

The revolving door between government staffers and tax lobbyists has been swinging almost from the day the income tax became law. Less than a decade after its enactment, some in Congress noticed a disturbing trend. Young staffers who had once prosecuted the government's tax cases were showing up as lawyers to defend wealthy taxpayers who were protesting the government's assessments. Thomas Lindsay Blanton, a Democratic congressman from Abilene, Texas, voiced his concern in 1924:

> We have down in the Treasury Department an army of agents and attorneys employed by the Government at fair salaries to prevent taxpayers from evading taxes, from escaping taxes, from dodging taxes, if you please.
>
> We educate these employees to do that. We pay the people's money to teach them how to keep the taxpayers from dodging taxes and just about the time we get them educated they find out that they can go out in the business world and hire themselves out, commercialize the education the government gives them at the expense of the Treasury, and help tax dodgers in showing them how to evade taxes by representing them in the department. [38]

One of the first graduates of this American School of Tax Avoidance was Ellsworth Chapman Alvord, who put his taxpayer-subsidized education to personal use. He became Washington's preeminent tax lobbyist from 1930 into the 1950s. Like generations that would follow him, Alvord got his start on Capitol Hill, in the Legislative Drafting Service, writing proposed tax legislation for members of Congress. Soon he moved to Treasury as a special assistant to Andrew W. Mellon, the powerful secretary of the Treasury. In 1930, with a background rich in the nuances of tax law, Alvord left Treasury for the greener pastures of tax lobbying.

Over the next three decades, Alvord was the lawyer to see in Washington when one needed a tax break from Congress. He represented wealthy individuals, large corporations, and powerful associations such as the U.S. Chamber of Commerce. Alvord secured many favorable tax breaks for clients or blocked legislation that would have harmed their interests. He perfected the practice, more widely used today, of getting special treatment for particular clients by having them written right into the law, while disguising their identity with language that was indecipherable to the average person. Like this section in the Revenue Act of 1951, which was written for one person:

Sec. 329. Receipts of Certain Termination Payments by Employee.

(a) Taxability to employee as capital gain—Section 1717 of the Internal Revenue Code is hereby amended by adding at the end thereof the following subsection:

(p) Taxability to employee of termination payments.— Amounts received from the assignment or release by an employee, after more than twenty years' employment, of all his rights to receive, after termination of his employment and for a period of not less than 5 years (or for a period ending with his death), a percentage of future profits or receipts of his employer shall be considered an amount received from the sale or exchange of a capital asset held for more than six months, if such rights were included in the terms of the employment of such employee for not less than twelve years, and if the total of the amounts received for such assignment or release are received in one taxable year and after the termination of such employment.

Got that? No? Well, the one it was written for surely profited handsomely by its obscurity.

Section 329 applied to one person: Louis B. Mayer, head of

Metro-Goldwyn-Mayer studios. Through a long-standing contract, Mayer was to receive 10 percent of the net proceeds from every picture made at MGM. On his retirement, in 1951, he had the option of either continuing to share in MGM's profits or taking his money in a lump sum. Mayer opted for the lump sum. The good news was that it came to roughly $2,750,000; the bad news was that under 1951 tax rates, he would have had to pay 90 percent of the proceeds in taxes.[39] Mayer asked whether Alvord couldn't help get his income classified as a capital gain, rather than ordinary income. That would cut his tax rate to about 20 percent.

With his intimate contacts on the Senate Finance Committee, Alvord had Section 329 slipped into the Revenue Act of 1951, and Louis B. Mayer saved nearly $2 million in federal income tax.

Many have since aspired to Alvord's example. A few have approached it. Like Charls Walker, for whom the stately door to the Treasury Department on Pennsylvania Avenue has truly revolved. A cigar-smoking, gregarious Texan, from a place called Possum Kingdom Lake, Walker has been in and out of the Treasury Department since 1959: one year guarding the accounts; the next year raiding them.

He first arrived in Washington in 1959 as an executive assistant to Robert B. Anderson, a Texas oilman, who was President Dwight D. Eisenhower's Treasury secretary in his second term. Working with Anderson, Walker saw firsthand how tax law was made and administered. Then he exited the Treasury in 1960 to become the chief lobbyist for one of the nation's most powerful lobbies—the banking industry.

As executive vice president of the American Bankers Association, Walker spent the next eight years working the other side of the street. In 1969, he returned to the Treasury as undersecretary after Richard M. Nixon was elected President. In that post and, later, as deputy secretary, Walker was responsible for helping to shape tax policy and practice fiscal restraint. When budget deficits began to climb in the early 1970s, he assured lawmakers that the administration was committed to reversing the trend as quickly as possible. As Walker told the Senate Committee on Appropriations on February 2, 1972: "I am sure that this committee is, as we are, deeply concerned about the large deficits in prospect for fiscal 1972 and 1973. No one can be happy about deficits of this size."[40]

But a year later, Walker resigned from Treasury and formed Charls E. Walker & Associates, a lobbying and economic consulting firm specializing in tax legislation. He then proceeded to boost the deficit by carving tax breaks out of the Internal Revenue Code. Walker later explained his goals: "I had knocked the dickens out of my estate when I came into government and I needed to catch up a little bit. So several of us got together and said let's hang out our shingle and see if anybody comes in."[41]

And come they did. General Motors Corporation, Ford Motor Company, General Electric Company, Gulf Oil Corporation, Procter & Gamble, Union Carbide Corporation, and Bethlehem Steel Corporation were among the *Fortune* 500 companies that flocked to Walker's door.

With his intimate knowledge of Capitol Hill and his ready access to the highest echelons of the Treasury Department, Walker emerged overnight as one of Washington's hottest lobbying properties. Perhaps his single most successful year came in 1981, when he was instrumental in securing a number of tax breaks that eventually cost the Treasury billions of dollars.

The first was something called the Accelerated Cost Recovery System (ACRS). It was the centerpiece of a series of corporate preferences in President Reagan's first major tax bill, the Economic Recovery Tax Act of 1981 (ERTA). ACRS featured a combination of rapid depreciation write-offs and investment tax credits. While he was pushing for it, Walker downplayed the potential revenue losses to the Treasury, saying that the new law would have "a relatively modest negative impact on Federal revenue."[42]

As it turned out, ACRS cost the Treasury billions of dollars. According to estimates, the losses were projected to hit $162 billion over a six-year period before Congress stepped in and scaled back the benefits.

Even more egregious was another tax giveaway that Walker helped put into the same tax bill. Once ACRS was in place, he realized that some of his clients would not be able to take advantage of it. Why? Because they were losing money. Only profitable companies could make use of the ACRS write-offs. If you weren't paying taxes, you couldn't cut your taxes. And some Walker clients in the airline and smokestack industries were in just that position.

So Walker and others, in extended conversations with Treasury officials, devised a way to get tax rebates for money-losing corporations that weren't even paying taxes. Officially, this was known as Safe Harbor Leasing. Washington pundits were soon calling it by another name—the Lease a Tax Break Law.

Into the Economic Recovery Tax Act went something called a "Special Rule for Leases." The rule was special indeed—it allowed money-losing companies to sell their unused tax credits to profitable corporations, which could then pay less in federal taxes. The formula was simple: The profitable company cut its taxes, and the tax revenue that would have flowed to the Treasury was rerouted to money-losing companies.

There was no counterpart for this in the lives of individual taxpayers. If there were, here's how it might work: A low-income couple who paid no taxes because they earned so little money and had so many dependents could lease the exemptions for two of their children to a wealthy childless couple. The children would stay with the parents, but the rich couple—in return for a cash payment to the parents—would get two additional personal exemptions on their income tax return. The poor family would get more money, the rich family would cut its taxes. The loser would be the American taxpayer.

As you might expect, Safe Harbor Leasing set off a stampede for tax breaks unlike anything Washington had ever seen. Ford Motor Company sold more than $1 billion in credits to IBM for $100 million. B. F. Goodrich sold a block of credits for $60 million. American Airlines, Pan American, and Scott Paper sold tax credits to Atlantic Richfield, Pepsico, and Standard Oil Company of Indiana.

General Electric Company, one of the nation's largest and most profitable corporations, bought so many credits that it not only eliminated its federal income taxes for 1981 but applied for $150 million in refunds for previous years.

Eventually, the hue and cry was so great that the giveaway was scaled back—but not before dozens of companies had cashed in, and Washington law firms had pocketed enormous fees from handling the transfers, and Charls Walker had established himself as one of the preeminent tax lobbyists of his time. Like most of those who have worked both sides of the street, Walker sees no problem. As he told an interviewer in 1987:

"Anybody who comes to me and says they want to be a tax lobbyist, I say, go get experience on the Hill." [43]

So if lobbying on tax matters has been around as long as the Internal Revenue Code, what's different about today? The answer, in one word, is volume.

Never before have so many people lobbied to secure preferential tax treatment for so many affluent individuals and influential businesses. One reason is the boom in employment on Capitol Hill. In 1954, the House and Senate had 5,600 staff members and other employees. By 1993, that number had swelled to 20,700—an increase of 270 percent. During the same period, the U.S. population rose from 162 million to 255 million—an increase of 57 percent. Employment on Capitol Hill shot up five times as fast as the population. The revolving door is spinning out more special-interest advocates than ever.

Washingtonians see nothing wrong with this process. The revolving door is an accepted, normal part of business in the capital, another branch of government. Nor do Washingtonians see anything improper about lawmakers dispensing tax breaks to those who are wealthy and influential enough to get a private hearing before them. That, too, is routine business. An aide to Representative Charles B. Rangel, Democratic congressman from New York and member of the House Ways and Means Committee, defended the hundreds of tax concessions written into the Tax Reform Act of 1986:

"The people who [got] relief . . . were those who had the greatest access. Now if you want to write about access, fine. But not about the abuse of the tax code. Because what they got was proper and just. It was just that justice was only available to those people with access." [44]

The Eternal Tax Break

And there it is. If you have sufficient influence, you have access. If you are an ordinary working person, you do not. For you, "justice" is not available.

Never was the power of access more amply demonstrated

than in 1993, when a coalition of special interests waged a lobbying campaign that successfully blocked efforts to require certain corporations to pay income tax on all their profits—just as
you must pay tax on all your earnings. The fight centered on
Section 936 of the Internal Revenue Code.

Like the rest of the code, Section 936 is written in the arcane
language of tax lawyers: "Except as provided in paragraph (3),
if a domestic corporation elects the application of this section
and if the conditions of both subparagraph (A) and subparagraph (B) of paragraph (2) are satisfied, there shall be allowed
as a credit against the tax imposed by this chapter an amount
equal to the portion of the tax which is attributable to the sum
of . . ."

And on it goes for several thousand words. But let's skip over
the legal language and look at the theory behind the law to see
how it might work if there were a counterpart to this at the local
level.

Suppose that you are the governor of New Jersey and want
to encourage new industry to move to Newark. You persuade
the legislature to enact a law exempting every business that
locates in Newark from the state corporate income tax.

Over time, many companies take advantage of the offer. Employment grows in Newark, although not nearly as fast as the
population. So even though the unemployment rate remains
high, at least some jobs are being created. That's the good news.
The bad news is that the state is losing tax revenue faster than
new jobs are being created. Before long, the state treasury is
losing $71,700 in corporate tax payments for every new job in
Newark. To offset the drain, taxes must be raised on everyone
living outside Newark and on businesses operating outside the
city.

Two questions arise:

Do you think you will be reelected?

Would it not be cheaper to pay every new worker in Newark
directly—say, $30,000 a year—and save the state $41,700 per
job?

This, in a nutshell, is the situation produced by Section 936,
except that it applies to Puerto Rico rather than Newark. Until
1993, companies doing business in Puerto Rico could avoid
all income tax on their profits there, even when the money

was sent home to the States. And scores did just that. The result: a bonanza for their stockholders, a devastating loss for the Treasury, and comparatively few well-paying jobs for Puerto Rico.

In 1992, Merck and Company, the New Jersey–based drug company, with annual sales of $9.7 billion, reported a tax savings of $181 million from its island operations. Johnson & Johnson, another New Jersey–based drug company, with annual sales of $13.8 billion, escaped paying $159 million in taxes. Pfizer, Inc., a New York–based drug company, with annual sales of $7.2 billion, avoided paying $126 million in taxes.

These companies and many others were benefiting from a tax law enacted in 1921 to apply to a wholly different island territory. Congress adopted the law at the request of certain business interests in the Philippines when those islands were a U.S. possession and American businessmen maintained that they needed the tax break to compete against the British.

By 1946, the Philippines had gained their independence. Nonetheless, the Philippines tax concession remained on the books and was seized on by Washington policymakers seeking to spur growth in Puerto Rico.

Which brings us to Tax Rule No. 6: Special interests abhor a tax-law vacuum. If the purpose for which a tax break originally was enacted no longer exists, new reasons will be found to perpetuate it.

And so it was in Puerto Rico, where political leaders launched a development program called "Operation Bootstrap." As part of it, Puerto Rico passed tax legislation that gave long-term exemption to American companies from "income, property and municipal taxes," plus an excise tax exemption for "raw materials, machinery, and equipment used in manufacturing for export or sold to other manufacturers in Puerto Rico."[45] But the chief appeal for U.S. corporations was a partial exemption from the federal income tax. That break, coupled with the Puerto Rican exemptions, produced a gradual response.

From 1950 to 1970, employment in the island's manufacturing plants rose 140 percent, from 55,000 to 132,000. The unemployment rate dropped from 12.9 percent to 10.7 percent. The number of persons without jobs fell from 88,000 to 79,000. For the American taxpayer, the costs remained fairly modest.

But in the 1970s, as U.S. companies discovered cheaper labor enclaves elsewhere in the world, the growth in Puerto Rican factory jobs leveled off. Worried island leaders and other special interests again turned to Congress, which rushed to the rescue and amended Section 936 in the Tax Reform Act of 1976. For the first time, companies operating in Puerto Rico could ship their profits back to the States tax-free.

Under the old Puerto Rican exemption, the U.S. Treasury lost an average of $300 million a year from 1970 to 1975. In the five years after "tax reform," from 1977 to 1981, the tax loss averaged $1.3 billion a year—an increase of 333 percent. More significantly, private employment on the island fell between those two periods, from an average of 590,000 jobs to 559,000 jobs. The hefty tax concession awarded to U.S. businesses was resulting in fewer—not more—jobs.

Still, a bad deal for one group of taxpayers—middle-class people and businesses that lack access—is a good deal for others. In this case, it was a terrific deal for the pharmaceutical industry. One pharmaceutical company after another set up operations or expanded existing plants on the island. And they transferred their patents and trademarks to Puerto Rico.

This meant that while the companies were developing new drugs, they wrote off those costs on their U.S. tax returns. Once they began producing the drugs, they claimed the profits, tax-free, in Puerto Rico. As Senator Robert Dole observed, "A clearer case of having your cake and eating it, too, has seldom existed in the U.S. tax law."[46]

Indeed not. By 1984, American businesses in U.S. possessions, mostly Puerto Rico, escaped payment of $2 billion in income tax. That was up from $838 million in 1977—an increase of 139 percent.

By comparison, the taxes paid by corporations operating in the United States during that period rose only 4 percent—from $55 billion in 1977 to $57 billion in 1984. So it was that taxes businesses were excused from paying—courtesy of just one provision in the Internal Revenue Code—went up thirty-five times as fast as taxes paid.

A few members of Congress, Democrats and Republicans, expressed concern. So, too, did some tax professionals inside and outside government. In May 1985, President Reagan issued a book-length report calling for an overhaul of the tax code "based on the principles of simplicity and fairness."[47] The report proposed replacing the tax credit with a wage credit.

The White House pointed out that although the original intent was to create jobs, companies were obtaining tax credits far in excess of the wages they paid. The report noted that employment levels "have been flat" and that "the credit rewards generating income in the possessions; it provides no direct incentive to generating employment." The report went on to say:

> The existing credit is very costly and inefficient. The average tax benefit per employee for all section 936 corporations was more than $22,000 in 1982, more than 50 percent more than the average wage of . . . $14,210.
>
> Fourteen corporations received tax benefits in excess of $100,000 per employee. Those fourteen companies accounted for 4 percent of the section 936 corporations for which employment data was available and derived 29 percent of the tax benefits.[48]

In other words, the U.S. Treasury—more precisely, you and all other taxpayers—was giving some companies more than $100,000 for every job they created, jobs paying an average of $14,210.

Weeks before Reagan's proposal was released—but after much of it had been leaked to the news media—the beneficiaries of Section 936 mounted a forceful campaign to preserve their multibillion-dollar tax break. Company executives, their lawyers, and lobbyists deluged Treasury Department officials with letters and telephone calls and requests for private meetings.

On April 30, 1985, H. L. Richardson, vice president of the pharmaceuticals and biomedical products department of E. I. du Pont de Nemours & Company, wrote to Treasury Secretary James A. Baker expressing his concern about the proposal to repeal Section 936. In his letter, Richardson raised four arguments that were central to the lobbying effort.

One argument was that it would be unfair to take away the tax break from companies that had built plants in Puerto Rico because of it: "The pharmaceutical industry has invested more than $800 million in Puerto Rico based upon the provisions of Section 936. . . . Stability is critical to this industry with a ten year product development cycle, since long-range decision making must be made on a firm basis."

A second argument was that the Puerto Rican economy was flourishing because of the tax break: "Today, Puerto Rico is the United States' showcase to Caribbean countries and all of Latin America. The Island's economic development, democratic institutions, and social progress are models of what can be achieved under the American system. One of the principal reasons for Puerto Rico's success is the incentives provided by Congress and the Government of Puerto Rico to attract mainland corporations to the Island. Of these incentives, Section 936 of the Internal Revenue Code is the most important."

A third argument was a warning that this flourishing economy would collapse without the tax break: "The passage of the Treasury Department's proposals would make the future economic outlook for Puerto Rico very bleak."

And the fourth argument was a not-so-veiled threat that if the provision was repealed, the companies would pack up and move to some other part of the world: "Recognizing the intensity with which foreign governments are using tax incentives to attract investment, multinational companies now operating in Puerto Rico would have little difficulty investing outside the United States. Therefore, the elimination of Section 936 would not shift Puerto Rico earnings to the United States but would result in a further decline in the U.S. balance of payments."[49]

The news media repeated the corporate warnings. Reported the *New York Times*: "Economists on and off the island have warned that if the tax privilege, Section 936 of the Internal Revenue Code, is phased out in five years as the White House proposes, dozens of corporations with thousands of jobs will leave the island."[50]

While du Pont's Richardson and others worked on Treasury officials, other business people and lobbyists worked the corridors of Congress. In a letter to Richard G. Darman, deputy secretary of the Treasury, Robert F. Dee, chairman of the board of SmithKline Beckman, wrote: "I thought you would be interested in seeing the effort that is being made by nine major pharmaceutical companies with Senator Bradley. The attached letter has been sent to Senator Bradley and will be followed up by a personal visit by several of the CEOs."[51]

The letter to Bill Bradley, the Democratic senator from New Jersey, was signed by the top officers of Johnson & Johnson, Schering-Plough, American Home Products, Merck & Company, Squibb Corporation, Hoffman-LaRoche, Pfizer, Inc., Warner-Lambert, and American Cyanamid Company.

The drug company executives worried about the plight of island residents—"our other concern is for the people of Puerto Rico who have been part of an economic miracle." And they warned that their companies could move elsewhere in the world —"recognizing the intensity with which foreign countries are using tax incentives to lure investment, multinational companies now operating in Puerto Rico would have little difficulty placing their funds outside the United States."[52] Yes—very nearly the same wording Richardson later used in his letter to Baker.

But the drug-company officials added one paragraph to their letter to Senator Bradley that was missing from similar letters to Treasury Department officials:

"We believe strongly in the principles and achievements of Section 936. We would welcome the opportunity of apprising the senior Senator from New Jersey, the nation's medicine-chest, of our position on this issue. We would also like to explore the possibility of your visiting the island in the near future under the aegis of the [Puerto Rico USA Foundation]."[53]

Whether Bradley took up the offer of an all-expenses-paid trip to Puerto Rico is not known, but other members of Congress already had, or would. Among them were Representative William R. Archer, Jr., Republican from Texas, and Senator Daniel P. Moynihan, Democrat from New York. Archer, a member of the House Ways and Means Committee, flew to San Juan courtesy of the Schering-Plough Corporation, one of the pharmaceutical companies that benefited from the tax concession. Moynihan, a member of the Senate Finance Committee, flew to San Juan courtesy of the Puerto Rico Chamber of Commerce. Their two committees would determine the final makeup of any tax bill.

While the lobbying machine was flying some lawmakers to Puerto Rico for "industry tax briefings," it was passing out honorariums to other lawmakers for delivering speeches.[54]

Malcolm Wallop, Republican senator from Wyoming, picked up $2,000 for speaking to the Puerto Rico USA Foundation, a tax-exempt organization comprising some seventy corporations that paid no taxes on their island profits. Senator Chafee from Rhode Island also collected $2,000 from the foundation and another $2,000 from the Pharmaceutical Manufacturers Association. Senator Moynihan, in addition to his trip to Puerto Rico, received $2,000 for a speech to the Puerto Rico Chamber of Commerce and another $2,000 for a speech to the Squibb Corporation, also a beneficiary of the tax break. Dan Rostenkowski, the Ways and Means chairman, collected $4,000 for a speech to Pfizer, Inc., yet another of the tax-free beneficiaries.

The all-out lobbying campaign succeeded. When it came time to vote on the Tax Reform Act of 1986, the possessions tax credit—one of the half-dozen or so most glaring tax breaks in the Internal Revenue Code—was preserved.

Not all members of Congress, to be sure, had to be persuaded of the wisdom of allowing corporations to pocket more than $35 billion in profits without paying taxes from 1977 to 1985. Some were longtime converts and vocal supporters. None more so than Charles B. Rangel, the New York Democrat who represented Harlem's poor blacks and Hispanics. The drug industry, in turn, was duly appreciative.

During the 1985–86 lobbying campaign, Bristol-Myers paid $2,000 to Rangel for a speaking engagement. The Squibb Corporation gave him another $2,000. And Pfizer, Inc., gave him $1,000. But it was later, in Puerto Rico, that the congressman received his most generous tribute.

It came from Rangel's own support group on the island, the Amigos de Charlie Committee, whose prime backers included drug-company executives. To show their appreciation for his efforts in preserving Section 936 through the years, the Amigos held one of their periodic testimonial dinners in March 1989. In a letter to an executive of Ayerst-Wyeth Pharmaceuticals, Inc., a committee member wrote:

Because of Congressman Charles B. ("Charlie") Rangel's continued staunch commitment to the defense of Puerto Rico's industrial development program and its indispensable partner, Section 936 of the Internal Revenue Code, the "Amigos de Charlie" Committee has reconvened to once again organize a reception honoring Charlie and his wife Alma.

Charlie's key position as a senior member of the House Ways and Means Committee enables him to play a key leadership role in the battle to prevent further erosion of Section 936 benefits. The reception will be an appropriate way to thank Charlie and encourage him to continue his most effective work.

The reception will be held at the Caribe Hilton on Friday, March 17, 1989. Tickets are $150 apiece.

I'm sure that you and several other key members of American Home [Products] who know the importance of Section 936 to your successful and profitable operations in Puerto Rico will want to join us in showing our appreciation and affection to Charlie and Alma.[55]

As for the cost of Rangel's flying to the reception honoring him for keeping a tax break intact, the bill was picked up by his campaign committee—the Rangel for Congress Committee.

While the proposal to repeal the credit in 1985 came from tax professionals in government and a Republican President, a second campaign, mounted in 1991, was initiated at the grassroots level. It had its start among pharmaceutical workers in the States who were losing their jobs as drug companies shifted production to Puerto Rico, where wages were lower and the profits tax-free. A Democratic President joined the campaign in 1993.

From 1980 to 1991, the number of production workers employed by drug companies in the States fell from 88,700 to 82,600. During that same period, the number of drug-company production workers in Puerto Rico rose from 7,500 to 14,100. What's more, from 1985 to 1990, the latest year for which statistics were available, the lost tax revenue had continued to climb, from $2.5 billion to $3.2 billion. Left unchecked, American companies would escape paying $40 billion or more in taxes during the 1990s.

In his economic message to Congress, President Bill Clinton drew applause when he said that "the tax code should not express a preference to American companies for moving somewhere else, and it does, in particular cases, today."[56] With that, the Democratic administration and tax writers on Capitol Hill dusted off the 1985 Republican proposal.

Once again, some lawmakers in both parties seemed sympathetic to the idea of at least drastically curtailing the tax break. The House version of the budget bill limited the Section 936 tax credit to a portion of the wages actually paid. Moreover, it contained a clause that for the first time would bar a company from claiming the credit if it closed plants in the States and moved jobs to Puerto Rico.

What followed was an extraordinary lobbying blitz by companies to protect their tax-free income. Among the lobbyists working the halls of Congress and the corridors of Treasury were Robert Leonard, former chief of staff of the House Ways and Means Committee; Beryl Anthony, Jr., a former congressman from Arkansas, who, until he left Congress in January 1993, had been a member of the Ways and Means Committee; Lawrence F. O'Brien III, formerly in the office of assistant secretary for legislative affairs at the Treasury Department; and Nicholas E. Calio, a former lobbyist for the National Wholesalers Association, who served as President Bush's assistant for legislative affairs from 1989 to 1991.

And then there was the ever present Puerto Rico U.S.A. Foundation, run out of the Washington law offices of Groom & Nordberg. The law firm, located atop an office building at 1701 Pennsylvania Avenue N.W., overlooking the White House, was the foundation's registered lobbyist and had played a key role in turning back the 1985–86 attack on Section 936. Carl A. Nordberg, the foundation's executive director, is another graduate of the federal government's tax-training school. From 1960 to 1963, he was in the chief counsel's office of the IRS, and from 1964 to 1967 he was a member of the staff of the Joint Committee on Taxation.

In addition to representing the foundation, Groom & Nordberg was looking after the tax interests of a number of large companies and trade groups, including some located in Puerto Rico. Among the firm's many clients: Eli Lilly and Company,

Westinghouse Electric Corporation, the American Petroleum Institute, Union Texas Petroleum, Prudential Insurance Company, Chevron Corporation, Murphy Oil U.S.A., Inc., Prudential Bache Securities, Cargill, Inc., and Amoco.

But it was the Puerto Rico U.S.A. Foundation that had played such a pivotal role in protecting the island's tax break. Over the years, it had arranged one trip after another to Puerto Rico for members of Congress and their staffs, usually coinciding with winter in Washington. In March 1989, for example, the foundation organized a congressional trip to the Cerromar Beach Hotel Dorado. Another trip was arranged in January 1990. Followed by two more in February 1990. And another in November 1991.

As the war to save Section 936 heated up, the foundation brought in another lobbyist, Stuart E. Eizenstat, a partner in the Washington law firm of Powell, Goldstein, Frazer & Murphy. From 1977 to 1981, he had served as assistant to President Carter for domestic affairs. In a lobbying registration report signed by Eizenstat, the firm said that "anticipated expenses will be legal fees and disbursements billed at standard hourly rates of the firm. Anticipated amount of expenses is $150,000 annually."[57]

Meanwhile, Puerto Rican government officials also were applying pressure on Treasury officials and lawmakers. So, too, were Hispanic members of Congress. In a letter to President Clinton, three Democratic representatives, Jose E. Serrano and Nydia M. Velazquez of New York, and Luis V. Gutierrez of Illinois, wrote: "There is ample evidence that the elimination of 936 could lead to the loss of thousands of jobs in Puerto Rico, and to the overseas flight of important high-tech, labor-intensive industries. There are, however, no assurances from representatives of the Department of the Treasury that the proposal will not devastate the island, both economically and socially."[58]

As they had done in 1985 and 1986, the drug companies fueled fears that jobs would disappear from Puerto Rico if they should be required to pay U.S. income tax. This time, the warnings sounded more like threats.

One came from Paul E. Freiman, chairman of Syntex Corporation, a company with annual sales of more than $2 billion, which was incorporated in Panama but whose headquarters are in Palo Alto, California. He put it this way: "We're manufacturing tiny pills down there. We can load them on 747s and ship them anywhere in the world. We can manufacture in Mexico or Europe. This is a world without boundaries."[59]

Irwin Lerner, chairman of Hoffman-LaRoche, the large Swiss-owned company with its U.S. headquarters in Nutley, New Jersey, sounded a similar refrain: "Manufacturing in Puerto Rico is an important part of drug industry profits. We can go to Singapore, Ireland, or any other tax haven that is begging us to come."[60]

The initial payoffs from the lobbying effort came when the Senate issued its version of the budget bill. Thanks to Daniel Moynihan, chairman of the Senate Finance Committee, and Bill Bradley, a Finance Committee member, the Senate bill preserved a good portion of the tax break. It also eliminated the House provision that would have prevented companies from claiming the credit if they had closed factories in the United States and moved jobs to Puerto Rico. The lobbying over this provision was at best curious, since many companies—the drug firms in particular—had insisted that the jobs they eliminated in the States were unrelated to the ones they created in Puerto Rico.

By the time a conference committee worked out the differences between the House and Senate bills, the companies operating on the island had achieved a significant victory. A headline across the top of page one of the *San Juan Star* summed it up:

FAVORABLE 936 PLAN PREVAILS

U. S. HOUSE ACCEPTS THE SENATE'S
LIGHTER CUTS OF THE TAX BREAK[61]

Although the tax concession was scaled back, the companies will still escape payment of $10 billion or more in income tax through the rest of the 1990s.

The companies will have two options to choose from in calculating their tax credits under the new law. They may claim the credit based on wages paid or on profits. Those industries that are labor-intensive, like apparel manufacturing—where the tax benefit already is a fraction of wages paid—will lose none of their credits.

The drug industry, on the other hand, where tax benefits are two to three times the amount of wages paid, will lose a portion of their credits. At a minimum, companies that based their credits on income rather than wages will be permitted to keep 40 percent of the tax credits to which they are currently entitled.

To put that $10 billion in tax savings in perspective: If you live in Kansas and make less than $50,000 a year, that represents every dollar you will pay in income tax for the rest of this century. Think of it as a transfer—from you to the American businesses operating in Puerto Rico. Just another piece of the jigsaw puzzle.

Beyond the issue of unfair tax policy is the question of whether such a tax credit creates the kinds of jobs its supporters claim. The Puerto Rico U.S.A. Foundation, for one, says that "the possessions operations of U.S. companies have created nearly 300,000 jobs for the relatively poor U.S. citizens of Puerto Rico and have been primarily responsible for the island's remarkable economic advancement over the past 40 years."[62]

To date, that "remarkable economic advance" includes what has become a permanent double-digit unemployment rate—running between 14 percent and 23 percent—and a per capita income that is two thirds the level of the poorest state, Mississippi. The employment rate in the manufacturing sector, which provides the highest-paid jobs, has gone down rather than up. That's the payoff since 1976 from the $35 billion in profits U.S. companies have been permitted to keep tax-free.

Lest there be any doubt about both the unfairness and the failed economics of the tax credit, consider what would happen if it was applied in the fifty states.

There are 16 million Americans who are either unemployed, so discouraged they have given up looking for work, or working part time because they have been unable to find full-time jobs. If, to create jobs for these 16 million people, companies in the States were provided with tax credits like those given the drug companies in Puerto Rico, it would cost the U.S. Treasury more than $1 trillion—that's trillion with a *t*—every year.

To pay for it, the U.S. government would have to abolish the

Defense Department—and with it the Army, Air Force, Navy, and Marines. It would have to abolish all other government departments—from the Department of Agriculture to the Veterans Administration. It would have to end interest payments on the national debt and eliminate all health care expenditures, including Medicare and Medicaid.

And it would have to eliminate Congress.

CHAPTER 7
★ $ ★ $ ★

AMERICA'S MOST UNPRODUCTIVE INDUSTRY

Perpetual Motion Machine

The newspaper headlines and television news reports tell the story:

> NATION'S LARGEST TAX PREPARATION FIRM
>   FILES FOR BANKRUPTCY
>
> FEDERAL GOVERNMENT FIRES 10,000 WORKERS
>
> ACCOUNTANTS NATIONWIDE DECLARING BANKRUPTCY
>
> RECORD NUMBER OF LAW FIRMS FOLD
>
> THOUSANDS OF POLITICAL FUND-RAISERS LOSE JOBS

What's that? You didn't see any of those stories?

Of course not.

Those are the stories you would read and hear about if the government ever decided to simplify the tax system. But don't worry about all those lost jobs. It will never happen. Which is why you will remain at the bottom of the tax pile for the foreseeable future.

The tax system that reaches into the pocket of every American is destined to remain incomprehensible to most people for two reasons.

First, those who work with the current system resist change because they don't want a comfortable boat rocked.

Second, the industry that has grown up around the existing system wields so much power and influence that it can—and does—do whatever it pleases.

This is the tax industry. It employs tens of thousands of people—accountants, economists, lawyers, academicians, think-tank analysts, lobbyists, brokers, computer programmers, government workers, and all their support personnel. It costs billions of dollars a year to operate. It is America's largest non-productive business.

It creates nothing. It makes nothing. It redirects creative energies away from innovation and job building to ever more sophisticated forms of paper shuffling. It drains money from the productive segments of the economy. It takes money from people who have little and gives it to those with much. It takes from the young and gives to the old. It takes from the thrifty who save and gives to speculators. It takes from some affluent people and gives to other affluent people. It takes from small and medium-sized companies and gives to multinational corporations. It takes from U.S.-owned businesses and gives to foreign-owned businesses.

What's the industry's secret?

One word: complexity.

But the industry calls it by a different name: simplification.

Long ago, tax people discovered how to guarantee a never-ending supply of complexity, so that their jobs would last forever and no one would ever understand what they were doing. They tell us all that they are engaged in simplifying the tax system. But the more the industry simplifies taxes, the more complex they become, thereby generating more need for simplification—and creating ever more work for those in the industry. It is a kind of perpetual motion machine.

The result?

After years devoted to simplifying the nation's tax laws, they are more complex than ever. They are longer than ever. They take more people to interpret than ever. They cost more money to enforce than ever. They waste more money than ever. But it is just within the last twenty-five years that the perpetual motion machine—with Congress at the controls—has truly run amok.

It began when Congress passed the Tax Reform Act of 1969. This was followed by the Tax Reform Act of 1976. And that was followed by the Tax Reform Act of 1986. In between and since, there has been a blizzard of other tax laws:

The Revenue Act of 1971, the Pension Reform Act of 1974, the Tax Reduction and Simplification Act of 1977, the Revenue Act of 1978, the Foreign Investment Real Property Tax Act of 1980, the Crude Oil Windfall Profits Tax Act of 1980, the Economic Recovery Tax Act of 1981, the Tax Equity and Fiscal Responsibility Act of 1982, the Subchapter S Revision Act of 1982, the Social Security Amendments Act of 1983, the Tax Reform Act of 1984, the Deficit Reduction Act of 1984, the Consolidated Omnibus Budget Reconciliation Act of 1985, the Miscellaneous Revenue Act of 1988, the Omnibus Budget Reconciliation Act of 1990, and the Omnibus Budget Reconciliation Act of 1993.

All this was not just tinkering. These laws included basic changes in the tax system, which continue to have enormous effects on Americans' livelihood and the nation's well-being. Plus, of course, the laws contributed more complexity than ever to the tax industry's perpetual motion machine.

The first tax law, in 1913, was 17 pages in length. The first complete revision, in 1938, was 140 pages. The current tax law runs more than 3,000 pages. All that complexity is good for the tax industry. It's bad for you, because you have to pay for it. And it's destructive for society overall.

It rewards the person who plays the tax lottery by filing a questionable tax return with the expectation that it will not be audited. (In 1991, one person in a hundred was audited.) It penalizes the honest taxpayer who has to pay for help to abide by a law that is unintelligible and subject to multiple interpretations.

It rewards tax attorneys and accountants who maintain their practices on the edge by making recommendations to their clients that they know the IRS and the courts might reject—if they were aware of them. It penalizes tax attorneys and accountants who follow the law and refuse to recommend questionable tax practices, knowing that clients may then leave for their less ethical competitors.

It rewards the dishonest person who claims a tax benefit that he or she is not entitled to receive. It penalizes the honest tax-payer who fails to claim a lawful benefit that he or she is un-aware of.

It rewards the influential people who can secure private tax laws from friendly members of Congress to remedy their personal tax problems or escape payment of taxes. It penalizes the politically powerless who have no access to lawmakers and are compelled to abide by the tax code, no matter how unjust its provisions may be.

It rewards the large company that can move money and expenses on paper from one subsidiary to another around the world. It penalizes the smaller company that operates in one geographical area.

All of which brings us to Tax Rule No. 7: When a member of Congress, or an official in the executive branch of government, talks about "simplifying" the tax code, hold on to your wallet.

In the years since enactment of the income tax in 1913, whenever those in Washington talked about the importance of "simplification," what they had in mind was a plan to raise your taxes and cut the taxes of their friends.

So it was in 1921, when, under the prodding of Treasury Secretary Mellon, Congress enacted legislation creating a Tax Simplification Board. Mellon's idea of "simplification" was to generously expand existing tax breaks, like the oil depletion allowance; introduce new breaks, like the capital gains tax; and slash the top tax rate on the country's wealthiest citizens from 73 percent to 25 percent.

Mellon was forthright: "The greatest simplification that can be made is in the reduction of the rates."[1] One of the Treasury secretary's first appointments to the Simplification Board was William M. Davis of Oklahoma, president of the Mid-Continental Gas and Oil Association. In 1934, Senator Kenneth McKellar, Tennessee Democrat, said he believed Davis remained on the board, "and I believe he is still 'simplifying.' A man does a good deal of 'simplifying' to get an exemption of 50 percent on the great oil industry of our land, or to secure its exemption from any taxation at all."[2]

Periodically, through the years, members of Congress would "simplify" the tax code. But it wasn't until the 1960s and 1970s that the work began in earnest, and they have been feverishly simplifying away ever since. Listen to them in September 1976 as one lawmaker after another, Democrat and Republican, urged colleagues to vote for the Tax Reform Act of 1976.

"This is a major effort to simplify the tax law and make it more equitable," said Al Ullman, Democratic representative from Oregon and chairman of the tax-writing House Ways and Means Committee.[3]

"The bill simplifies many of the provisions of existing law, particularly those frequently used by middle income taxpayers," said Carl T. Curtis, Republican senator from Nebraska.[4]

"The Tax Reform Act of 1976, which we are acting on today, contains no less than six provisions to simplify the tax system," said Hubert H. Humphrey, Democratic senator from Minnesota.[5]

"This legislation embodies not only a permanent reduction in tax liabilities for most Americans, it also substantially simplifies the code," said Dan Rostenkowski, Democratic representative from Illinois.[6]

But all that simplifying in 1976 was not enough. So lawmakers came back the next year with some more and even put the word into the act's title, calling it the Tax Reduction and Simplification Act of 1977.

Once more, Al Ullman explained: "This is the first major tax bill of this Congress and represents a serious response to two pressing problems in the country today: The need for an economic stimulus to reduce unemployment and ensure rapid economic growth and the need to simplify the individual income tax."[7]

Over in the Senate, Russell B. Long, the Finance Committee chairman, read from the same script: "[This bill] responds to two pressing problems facing the nation today: The need in the economy to reduce unemployment and spur economic growth, and the need to simplify our tax system so that more Americans can file their tax forms without using commercial services."[8]

In a report on the legislation, the Senate Finance Committee, which helped write it, reported that "the bill will considerably simplify income tax returns and the tax computation for almost all individual taxpayers."[9]

When he signed the bill on May 23, 1977, President Jimmy Carter was swept up in the simplification fever, saying proudly that "one of the most pleasant things for a member of Congress or a President is to be able to reduce taxes and, at the same time, to get our economy moving again and, also, to simplify the complicated tax codes."[10]

After back-to-back years of simplifying, Congress took a breather, waiting until 1986 to launch another simplification campaign. Once more, lawmakers assured colleagues that the pending bill would simplify the tax laws.

"It will have the effect of simplifying our tax system for most Americans. Our tax system has become too complicated and too burdensome," said Chalmers P. Wylie, Republican representative from Ohio.[11]

"All Americans win because the tax code is simplified and loopholes are closed," said William B. Richardson, Democratic representative from New Mexico.[12]

"Filing a 1040 form will be far simpler for the average taxpayer," said Robert K. Dornan, Republican representative from California.[13]

"When fully implemented, this act will meet the originally stated goals of the tax reform effort, namely to provide fairness, simplicity, and economic growth," said C. W. Bill Young, Republican representative from Florida.[14]

"The bill offers much desired simplification of the tax system," said James L. Oberstar, Democratic representative from Minnesota.[15]

"There is a third major benefit of this bill—simplicity. Americans may not be able to file tax returns on a form that fits on a postcard, but much of the needless complexity of the current law has been removed," said John H. Chafee, Republican senator from Rhode Island.[16]

"This bill will make great strides in restoring public confidence in our tax system by simplifying the tax filing process," said Mitch McConnell, Republican senator from Kentucky.[17]

Was *your* confidence restored?

The bill was just another act in the Capitol Hill Magic Show, in which, with deft sleight of hand, legislative magicians pretended to bestow the most generous tax cuts on the middle class and to give the smallest tax cuts to the wealthy, when they were doing the opposite.

As part of that same show, they waved the simplification

wand with one hand and, with the other, assured you that out of the goodness of their hearts they were going to make it possible for you to avoid a lot of paperwork by filing the short form and claiming the standard deduction. They were doing only you a favor—not the special interests, not the tax industry, not Congress.

Sure.

In fact, the short form and the standard deduction are staples of the two tax laws—one for the privileged person, one for the common person. That's why you may want to be wary when lawmakers talk about "simplification" and the "short form" and the "standard deduction" in the same breath. Listen, once more, as down through the years they extol the virtues of simplification and the standard deduction.

Representative John W. Byrnes, Republican from Wisconsin, in urging passage of the Tax Reform Act of 1969 in December 1969: "The final bill takes an important step in the direction of a goal that I have consistently worked for—simplification of our complex tax laws for the average taxpayer. . . . This [bill] will enable 8.4 million individuals who now itemize to utilize the standard deduction and file the simplified return. The percentage of taxpayers using the standard deduction will increase from 58 percent to 70 percent." [18]

Representative Wilbur Mills, the Arkansas Democrat who was chairman of the Ways and Means Committee, in December 1969: "This increase in the standard deduction will provide very substantial simplification in the preparation of tax returns by inducing large numbers of taxpayers to take the standard deduction instead of itemizing their deductions." [19]

And when President Nixon signed the bill, he said: "Over 19 million additional people who pay taxes will find their annual task easier because they will find it advantageous to use the simple standard deduction, which is being significantly increased, rather than listing each deduction separately." [20].

Seven years later, as Congress prepared to vote on the Tax Reform Act of 1976, lawmakers talked once more about the wonders of the standard deduction and the short form.

"The bill makes substantial simplification in some of the most complicated, widely used provisions of the tax law. . . . Perhaps the greatest simplification from the standpoint of the average taxpayer is the increase in the standard deduction that is made permanent in the bill. This will make it worthwhile for those who file 9 million tax returns to switch from itemizing their deductions to using the standard deduction," said Representative Al Ullman.[21]

The next year, when Congress came back with its Tax Reduction and Simplification Act of 1977, Ullman again asserted that "the increased level of the standard deduction will make it worthwhile for over 7 million taxpayers not to itemize their deductions, raising the fraction of taxpayers who do not itemize deductions to 76 percent."[22]

Nine years later, in 1986, Congress was back at it again, offering a still better and improved version of the standard deduction and the short form. Enthusiasm reigned.

"Is this bill simplification? Yes, major simplification. Approximately 80 percent of returns that will be filed will be the short form. Most taxpayers will not have to pay a fortune to an accountant or a tax lawyer to make out the return," said Senator Lloyd Bentsen.[23]

"Mr. President, what about simplicity? The argument has been made, 'Gee, it does not do much for simplicity.' For about 13 to 14 million Americans, it does a lot for simplicity, because those are Americans who are now itemizing their returns, and who, as a result of the increase in the standard deduction and the exemption, will be using a short form and will not have to itemize their returns," said Senator Bill Bradley, Democrat from New Jersey.[24]

"We have made it possible for the overwhelming majority of American taxpayers not to have to . . . itemize on the long form, but to just file a short form," said Representative Charles B. Rangel, Democrat from New York.[25]

"This reform bill will simplify our tax system, especially for those Americans who find it most difficult to cope with its complexities, in part by reducing the number of itemizers to only one out of four Americans," said Representative Dean A. Gallo, Republican from New Jersey.[26]

"Simplification is a virtue, and with the new tax bill, millions of Americans will be able to use the short, instead of the long form, and avoid many of the headaches which make us all dread the onset of April 15," said Representative John J. La-Falce, Democrat from New York.[27]

"More than two-thirds of all Americans will soon find that when it comes time to fill out their tax returns, they will only have to file a simple one-page 1040A or 1040EZ return. The higher standard deduction included in this measure will free another 13 million Americans from the annual chore of having to sort through shoe boxes full of receipts to justify their itemized deductions," said Senator David F. Durenberger, Republican from Minnesota.[28]

"The biggest beneficiaries of this bill are ordinary taxpayers who have no access to high-priced lawyers and lobbyists. These are the people who file the short form on April 15. They do not itemize, they take the standard deduction and their personal exemptions, and then they pay whatever tax rate the form says. . . . Far fewer taxpayers will be forced to hire lawyers and accountants to translate the arcane complexities of the present law into understandable English," said Senator John H. Chafee.[29]

"This bill contributes to tax simplification. As many as 10 million taxpayers will no longer need to itemize. Instead, they will use the short form. Millions of Americans can give up the part-time job of keeping records for the IRS," said Senator Paul S. Trible, Jr., Republican from Virginia.[30]

Congress's Little Secret

Why, you might ask, is it such a good deal to file a short form, to claim the standard deduction rather than to itemize deductions? Why is it so good that you will not be burdened with the need to keep records for the IRS?

It's not.

And that's Congress's little magic show secret.

If there be any doubt, ask yourself this question:

Why did 93 percent of individuals and families with incomes above $500,000 itemize their deductions in 1991—rather than claim the "simpler" standard deduction? Why did the members of Congress who said it was such a good deal for you to file a short form pass on that privilege themselves and instead file the long form?

A look at the tax return of one of those lawmakers, Senator (now Treasury Secretary) Lloyd Bentsen, provides the answer. On their 1987 tax return, Bentsen and his wife reported adjusted gross income of $919,566. Their itemized deductions totaled $261,294—or 28 percent of their income.

You may want to check those numbers against your own tax return to see how they compare. Let's say your family income totaled $40,000. If you claimed 28 percent in write-offs, that would add up to a deduction of $11,200. Unfortunately for you, the standard deduction in 1987 was $3,760. Even in 1993, it was only $6,200.

For the Bentsens, the write-offs ranged from $19,083 in charitable contributions to $95,049 for investment interest expense. After subtracting $261,294 in itemized deductions and $3,800 in personal exemptions, they were left with a taxable income of $654,472. On that sum, they owed $196,040 in income tax. (Self-employment taxes and the alternative minimum tax on tax shelter losses brought the tax bill to $211,411.)

What would the result have been if the Bentsens had taken the standard deduction?

It was $3,760 that year. Add in personal exemptions of $3,800, and the Texas millionaire and his wife would have been left with a taxable income of $912,006, instead of the $654,472 they reported. Their total tax bill with the standard deduction: $357,693. The Bentsens had a choice:

File Form 1040 with the standard deduction and pay $357,693 in income tax.

Or file Form 1040 with itemized deductions and pay $211,411 in income tax.

The Bentsens chose the long form. They saved $146,282.

Does this mean, then, that lawmakers are concerned about something other than the plight of the harried taxpayer, compelled to save receipts in a shoe box and labor over a 1040 Form with itemized deductions?

You bet.

The numbers tell the story. In 1960, a total of 24.1 million individuals and families filed itemized tax returns. By 1969, that number had swelled to 34.9 million—a 45 percent increase. What's more, when the decade began, itemized returns represented 40 percent of all returns filed. When it ended, they accounted for 46 percent. And the size of the deductions grew too. It shot up 127 percent, from $35.3 billion to $80.2 billion.

If this trend was left unchecked, sometime during the 1970s more than half of all taxpayers would be writing off deductions on their returns. This would mean not only more work for the IRS and more taxpayer error and fraud; it would mean less revenue for the Treasury.

But no member of Congress, at least no member who wanted to be reelected, would try to sell that to voters as a reason to rewrite the tax code. Hence the need for more salable explanations. Like simplification and the short form, or—in the case of the Tax Reform Act of 1969—what lawmakers could say was a tough new provision to make sure the rich pay their fair share.

The 1969 act had the desired effect. After rising to 35.4 million in 1970, the number of itemized returns fell back to 27 million in 1972—a decline of 8.4 million. Better still, itemized returns as a percent of all returns filed plunged from 48 percent in 1970 to 35 percent in 1972.

From the perspective of lawmakers and policymakers, both numbers now were going in the right direction—down. Another reform measure, the Tax Reform Act of 1976, would keep them going that way. From 1975 to 1977, itemized returns fell further, from 26.1 million to 22.9 million. And their percentage of all returns dropped from 32 percent to 26 percent.

As it turned out, 1977 was the low point. Both figures started back up in 1978. By 1986, itemized returns had reached a record 40.7 million—or 40 percent of all returns. Once again, tax reform and "simplification" would reverse the trend.

In 1988, itemized returns fell back to 31.9 million, or 29 percent of the total. Since then, the numbers have edged up only slightly, reaching 32.4 million itemized returns in 1991, or 28 percent of the total.

What's the bottom line for the lucky people whom lawmakers freed from record keeping and paperwork?

The answer, once again, needs to be put in historical terms. So let's look first at 1954, a time when the tax code encouraged the growth of an expanding middle class, a time, not incidentally, when the standard deduction and personal exemption contributed to that growth. A median-income family with three children who claimed the standard deduction that year paid 4 percent of its earnings in federal income tax.

Next look at 1993, a time when the tax code was contributing to the decline of the middle class, a time when the standard deduction and personal exemption furthered that decline. A median-income family with three children who claimed the standard deduction paid 8 percent of its earnings in federal income tax—a 100 percent tax rate increase over 1954.

That's the good news. Now add in Social Security taxes. When they are taken into account, the 1954 family paid out 5 percent of its earnings in combined federal taxes. The 1993 family paid out 16 percent. That represented a tax-rate increase of 220 percent.

If all this seems to suggest that Congress has used simplification—actually complexity—to stack the tax system against the person who depends on a weekly paycheck for income, that's because it has. Over time, the income tax has really become a tax on wages and salaries—not income. Because of withholding, most wage and salary income—95 percent or more—is taxed. But much income from other sources—capital gains, rental properties, interest, dividends, small businesses, foreign earnings—escapes tax. You can thank complexity—and the absence of real simplification. It's another piece of the jigsaw puzzle.

How complex has Congress made the Internal Revenue Code? Well, to start with, there's the language, which is utterly indecipherable to the ordinary person. Tax professionals, to be sure, often say the law is perfectly clear to them and that no one else need understand it. But if it really is clear, then how to explain the raging disputes over taxes paid and taxes said to be owed?

A professional tax preparer, working on behalf of an individual or a business, will file a tax return that reports no income tax owed, based on the preparer's interpretation of the tax code language.

Agents of the IRS will examine the return and, based on their interpretation of the very same tax-code language, conclude that the individual or business owes millions of dollars in income tax.

If you think that's a matter of overzealous government bureaucrats, think again. For the preparers are often unable to agree among themselves. Likewise, the government's auditors.

The tax industry thrives on such conflicts. Lawyers, accountants, and government auditors spend millions upon millions of hours every year seeking to justify their respective interpretations of the law. Consider one such dispute involving the Monex Corporation of Newport Beach, California.

The company sold precious-metals contracts, often to unsophisticated investors, through telephone boiler-room operations. When its various fees, commissions, and interest charges on loans to finance the contracts were added in, most investors lost money.

But Monex seemingly fared even worse than some of its clients. On its 1980 tax return, for instance, the company reported a loss and said it did not owe any federal income tax. However, after conducting an audit, the IRS concluded that Monex had a profit and owed $21.1 million in income tax.[31]

And so it went on Monex's 1981, 1982, 1983, and 1984 returns. The company said it lost money in each of those years. The IRS later contended Monex was profitable in those years. Monex said it owed no tax; IRS said the company owed $151.3 million.[32] The company is contesting the IRS claims in U.S. Tax Court.

Monex is run by a Newport Beach millionaire, Louis E. Carabini, Jr., a onetime drug-company salesman and coin-shop operator. Over the years, his commodities companies have been the target of legal actions by disgruntled investors and by state and federal regulators.

In September 1992, the Federal Trade Commission filed a lawsuit in U.S. District Court in Los Angeles in which it accused Carabini, two associates, and two of his companies, Unimet Trading Corporation, which buys precious metals, and Unimet Credit Corporation, which finances metals contracts, of engaging in "numerous unfair or deceptive acts or practices."[33] The commission said that Carabini and the others had "falsely" represented "that an investment in precious metals or currencies financed by defendants is low in risk," when in fact such an investment "carries a high risk that investors will lose some or all of their investment." In addition to the FTC legal action,

Carabini and his companies are defendants in class-action lawsuits brought by a number of investors who make similar allegations.

Whatever the outcome of the civil litigation over Carabini's business practices, the disputes in U.S. Tax Court have produced documents that amply illustrate the distance that can exist between a taxpayer's view of the law and the IRS's view. For instance: As we have seen, over the five years from 1980 to 1984, Monex reported that it lost money every year and owed no federal income tax. The IRS, on the other hand, said Monex earned substantial profits and owed $172.4 million in income tax.

Monex said that the $85.5 million in interest expenses it incurred in trading Treasury securities with the Goldman Sachs, Dean Witter, and Oppenheimer firms was a legitimate business deduction. The IRS disagreed, saying that the transactions "were prearranged shams in substance which were undertaken for the primary purpose of tax avoidance." [34]

Monex said that the $68.7 million it lost in trading in Treasury bill options was another legitimate deduction. The IRS disallowed the deduction, saying the transactions "were prearranged factual shams and shams in substance which were undertaken for the primary purpose of tax avoidance." [35]

Monex said that the $213.2 million it lost trading in options, futures, and forward contracts on the London Metals Exchange and through brokers in London and Bermuda were legitimate business deductions. The IRS said no to that one too.

How can such an extreme disagreement come to be? Some might attribute it to Monex's seemingly questionable business practices. But securities and commodities brokers working for Wall Street's most prestigious investment firms have been locked in similar disputes with the IRS for years.

Surely, though, reality is not so difficult to discover. How is it possible for a company to say it lost money for five years and owed no income tax, and for the IRS to say the company had ample profits and owed $172.4 million in income tax, and for both claims to have such an appearance of legitimacy that a court may take years to decide between them?

The answer, again, is one word: complexity.

The tax law is sutured together with thousands of definitions and redefinitions, qualifications and exceptions and contingencies, to the point that sometimes profits do become losses, and wasted money turns into an asset, and black becomes white, or gray or green.

Which is why business is booming in U.S. Tax Court.

A Court for the Oppressed?

The court started on a modest scale. After adoption of the income tax, stories abounded about the power of tax authorities to impose unjust assessments and the lack of an adequate appeal process. James A. Reed, a Democratic senator from Missouri, summed up the problem in May 1924:

> There is nothing in the whole tax law that, in my opinion, has been a subject of greater criticism and that has resulted in more unjust oppression of our people than the right of some subordinate in the tax department to arbitrarily raise the assessment duly sworn to by a citizen, and thereupon require that citizen either to put up the money to pay the tax and then get it by such laborious processes as are provided in the law, or in default of the payment of the cash, which he frequently can not raise, to have his property seized and held under a distraint process which frequently results in bankruptcy and always in great oppression.[36]

Tax court was created to remedy the problem. Originally called the Board of Tax Appeals, it was formed by the Revenue Act of 1924 "to afford the taxpayer his day in court." Reed and others saw the board as a way to balance the power of government bureaucrats against the interests of the average taxpayer.

In its first twenty-five years, the court decided about 5,500 cases a year. As recently as 1970—nearly a half century later—the number of cases filed was little more than 7,000 a year. Then, as with the rest of the tax industry, things began to change.

By 1975, the number of cases filed had climbed to more than 11,000. By 1980, there were 22,000. And by 1992, more than 30,000.

The increase has had a dramatic effect on the court's operations. Once housed in a modest series of offices in the basement of the IRS building on Constitution Avenue in Washington, the court moved in 1975 to its own courthouse in Washington, which was intended to handle space requirements for many years to come. Within eight years, the court had outgrown its new quarters. The building, as Chief Judge Theodore B. Tannenwald, Jr., put it, was "filled to the brim."[37] To handle the overflow, the court has since leased additional office space in neighboring federal buildings for use as courtrooms.

Perhaps more significant than the overall volume of tax cases is the growth in large, complex cases. Tax court people refer to these as "jumbo cases." They often involve international tax matters, lengthy records, voluminous written arguments, and long, complex trials, with transcripts that run into the thousands of pages, and take years to resolve, like the dispute involving the ARAMCO partners—Exxon, Texaco, Chevron, and Mobil.

In recent years, the amount of tax money at stake has climbed sharply too. In 1989, the unpaid taxes disputed in tax court totaled $18.3 billion. By 1991, that figure had shot up to $32.3 billion. And in 1992, it reached $33.9 billion.

Back when the court was first established, the issues, like the tax law, were comparatively simple. Like whether money deposited in Max Kass's bank account represented income or reimbursement from a relative for the purchase of junk.

Kass was an Albuquerque, New Mexico, junk dealer who bought and sold used goods, sometimes for himself, sometimes for his uncle, who was in the same line of work. After Kass purchased merchandise for his uncle, the latter would deposit money in Kass's bank account to pay for the goods Kass had bought for him. The IRS took the position that this money was income to Kass and sent him a deficiency notice saying he owed $4,557 in federal income taxes for the years 1919 through 1922. Kass appealed to the Board of Tax Appeals, which sided with him: "No profit was made by the taxpayer upon merchandise purchased for his uncle's business and he acted only in the capacity of buyer for him. . . . The deficiency determined by the Commissioner is disallowed."[38]

Today, the court is clogged with complex cases dealing with such issues as transfer pricing, intangible assets, trusts, passive losses, and foundations. Consider the cases of Charles F. Dolan and the Joseph E. Seagram Corporation.

Dolan is one of the nation's leading cable television entrepreneurs and a perennial member of the *Forbes* directory of the 400 richest Americans. In 1993, the magazine estimated his worth at $735 million. As chairman of Cablevision Systems Corporation on Long Island, Dolan heads one of the nation's largest, most lucrative cable networks. It serves 1.4 million subscribers in eleven states and generates $570 million in revenue a year.

Dolan began wiring parts of Manhattan for cable in the early 1960s. He launched Home Box Office in 1970, and he later pioneered regional sports cable channels and the country's first twenty-four-hour cable channel for local news.

Dolan lives on Long Island, on a five-acre waterfront estate in the Cove Neck section of Oyster Bay, where he sails his seventy-three-foot-long sloop, the *Encore*.

Dolan is in tax court contesting the IRS's attempts to collect $234 million in back taxes and penalties for the years 1984, 1986, 1987, and 1988, which the government says he owes. In two of those years, Dolan—whose salary and bonuses exceed $1 million a year—paid no income tax at all.

According to the IRS, in 1984 Dolan had an adjusted gross income of $157.6 million from partnership interests and trusts. But on his tax return that year, he reported a loss of $13.1 million. Federal income taxes paid: zero. The agency contends that Dolan "understated" his income by $169.3 million, which it said was the value of interests he received for "personal services" he rendered in the formation, development, and operation of various cable companies.[39]

The IRS also said Dolan failed to report $19.1 million in income earned by various trusts he established for himself or members of his family. Describing the trusts as "shams," the agency said that their income should have been included on Dolan's personal tax return. The IRS also contested a $1.6 million charitable contribution that Dolan made to his own foundation. The deduction was disallowed because Dolan "failed to establish the fair market value of the contribution." At the end of 1993, Dolan's case was still pending.[40]

For Dolan, who is challenging the IRS claims, the tax issues revolve around personal service income, trusts, and a foundation. For the Joseph E. Seagram Corporation, it's the value of stock.

The Joseph E. Seagram Corporation is the U.S. subsidiary of Seagram Company, Ltd., the global producer and marketer of distilled spirits, wines, coolers, fruit juices, and mixers. The parent company has subsidiaries and affiliates in thirty countries, 16,000 employees worldwide, and annual revenue of $6.1 billion. It boasts the world's largest distribution system in the spirits and wine industry.

Seagram is controlled by the Bronfman family, whose principal members, Edgar M. Bronfman, Sr., and Charles R. Bronfman, are two of the world's wealthiest individuals. *Forbes* magazine estimated their worth in 1993 at $2.3 billion *each*.

The U.S. subsidiary of their liquor empire is in U.S. Tax Court, trying to save $160 million in taxes. That's what the IRS says Seagram owes because of its 1981 takeover bid for Conoco, Inc., a medium-sized oil company that the Bronfmans wanted.

After a Seagram affiliate offered to purchase 40 percent of Conoco's stock, both the Du Pont Company and Mobil Oil Corporation entered the contest, driving up the price of Conoco's shares. Eventually, Du Pont won out and acquired Conoco, but not before Seagram had purchased 27.7 million shares. Subsequently, the two companies worked out a deal in which Seagram exchanged all those Conoco shares for 164 million shares of Du Pont—or 24 percent of Du Pont's stock.

During the bidding war, Seagram had paid a higher price for some of the Conoco shares it bought than Du Pont ultimately paid in the winning offer. Seagram entered a short-term capital loss on its 1982 federal income tax return of $545 million.

The IRS disallowed the deduction, stating that the merger between Du Pont and Conoco was essentially a tax-free reorganization, and thus Seagram did not sustain any loss. It would do so only if Seagram sold its Du Pont shares, which it had no intention of doing.[41]

If Seagram enjoys the same kind of success in tax court that it does on Capitol Hill, the company will fare quite nicely. That success is evident in the following paragraphs buried in the Tax Reform Act of 1986:

> (8) TREATMENT OF CERTAIN INSTALLMENT OBLIGATIONS.—
> Notwithstanding the amendments made by subtitle B of title III, gain with respect to installment payments received pursuant to notes issued in accordance with a note agreement dated as of August 29, 1980, where—
> (A) such note agreement was executed pursuant to an agreement of purchase and sale dated April 25, 1980,
> (B) more than ½ of the installment payments of the aggregate principal of such notes have been received by August 29, 1986, and
> (C) the last installment payment of the principal of such notes is due August 29, 1989,
> shall be taxed at a rate of 28 percent.[42]

Gibberish to you, no doubt, but gold to Seagram. This custom-designed provision exempted the company from a section in the new law that raised the capital gains tax rate for all other corporations. The clause is estimated to have saved Seagram $40 million in taxes.

Now, you might wonder how provisions that grant tax exemptions for select businesses and individuals escape the close scrutiny of lawmakers, how they are enacted into law.

That's easy.

Few members of Congress ever read the tax legislation they vote on. From time to time, they even acknowledge as much.

When it came time to cast votes on the Tax Reform Act of 1969, William J. Randall, Democratic representative from Missouri, observed:

"You will recall the bill which passed the House several months ago contained 363 pages. The Senate bill contained 600 pages. Today, by an extraordinary relaxation of House rules, we will have two hours for explanation of this bill instead of the usual one hour. Then as representatives of the people we are expected to cast an enlightened vote. . . . It may be repetition but I repeat once again when we get a printed copy of a conference report just a matter of three to four hours before we have to vote on that conference report the only conclusion can be this is no way to run a railroad."[43]

It was the same in 1986, during debate on the Tax Reform Act that year. David O. Martin, Republican representative from New York, put it this way:

"This has to be one of the most complex documents that has ever been put together in the history of man in one volume. Trying to read and understand it is virtually impossible. I would suggest that there is no member who truly understands it. It was delivered to my office less than ninety-six hours ago and here we are debating this fundamental change of thirty years of social policy in three hours at the rate of 308 pages an hour."[44]

Stan Parris, Republican representative from Virginia, said: "Very frankly, Madam Speaker, I respectfully submit there is not a person alive who knows what is in this bill."[45]

Philip M. Crane, Republican representative from Illinois, was more blunt: "The truth of the matter is, there will not be a single member of this body who will have read these documents when we are asked to vote on them tomorrow any more than the conferees, the people responsible for reconciling House and Senate differences, had anything to look at when they cast their vote last August. There was no document.

"We have the document now and considering the time constraints, even if one were to sit up the remainder of tonight in anticipation of that debate tomorrow, there is not going to be any member who has read it, and that is not as disturbing as it sounds, because we would not understand it if we read it anyway."[46]

And it was the same in 1993, as Congress prepared to vote on the budget bill containing many tax-law changes. Said Gerald B. H. Solomon, Republican representative from New York:

"Who has had time to read this? Look at it. Several thousand pages. Not one member knows what he or she is voting on here today."[47]

The Lawyers' and Accountants' Relief Act

If Congress doesn't know what's in the tax code, how can lawmakers expect average taxpayers to know?

The answer, of course, is they can't.

And there's no better example of this confusion than the fact that even tax-return preparers—the professionals who go to school and who are paid to understand the intricacies of the code—are as baffled as the average person when it comes to filling out tax returns.

Every year, *Money* magazine publishes a feature in which fifty tax-return preparers volunteer to compute the federal income tax owed by a hypothetical American family. And every year, only a handful of the professionals pass the test.

Year in and year out, most preparers flunk even the basic parts of Form 1040—failing to compute certain deductions or overestimating others. In 1988, the first year *Money* conducted this survey, the fifty preparers came up with fifty different figures for the tax owed by the hypothetical family.

Even though the preparers were working with the same set of basic numbers—the family's earnings, taxes withheld, charitable contributions, mortgage interest deductions, and so forth —they produced wildly differing results for the tax owed, ranging from $7,202 to $11,881. In following years, it has been much the same story. In 1992, not a single one of the preparers "turned in an error-free return." [48]

In 1993, only a few of the preparers who entered the *Money* contest avoided significant mistakes. The magazine noted that the "contestants' calculations of tax due ranged from $31,846 to $74,450, a 134% variance and the second widest dollar spread in the test history. That means our hapless hypothetical family could have underpaid their tax by $3,797—or overpaid it by nearly $40,000." [49]

As befits a perpetual motion machine, the complexity that baffles tax professionals has generated an ever growing number of—yes, more professionals. In 1952, membership in the tax section of the American Bar Association totaled 3,200 lawyers. By 1993, that number had ballooned to 22,500. If the overall population of the United States had increased at the same rate as tax lawyers, it would total 1.1 billion. New York City alone would have a population of more than 30 million.

And then there's H & R Block, Inc., the Wal-Mart of the tax industry. The company dates from shortly after World War II, when the three Bloch brothers—Henry, Richard, and Leon—

started a bookkeeping and tax service for small businesses in Kansas City, Missouri. From its origins in a $50-a-month rented office at the rear of a real estate company, H & R Block—the brothers gave the company a slightly different spelling than their name—has grown into a nationwide company of 8,000 offices, whose stock is traded on the New York Stock Exchange. "We never envisioned the business would be this big when we started out," Henry W. Bloch, the president and chief executive officer, once told an interviewer.[50]

But then no one envisioned that Congress in simplifying the tax code so many times since 1969 would render the document virtually incomprehensible. Proponents of the "simplification" provisions in the Tax Reform Act of 1986 predicted that H & R Block's business would be hurt by the law. Henry Bloch, who has a better grasp of taxes than the people who write the laws, knew better and said so. He also at the same time warned that many middle-income taxpayers would pay more—rather than less—under the bill. He was right on both counts.

Rather than being harmed by tax reform, H & R Block's tax-preparation business continued to boom. In 1986, the year of tax reform, the company prepared 9,215,300 returns in the United States. The next year, the total went up to 9,668,200 returns, a 4.9 percent increase. Then in 1988, returns prepared rose to 10,487,000, an all-time high. What was the reason? "Taxpayer confusion created by the Tax Reform Act of 1986 contributed to this 8.5 percent increase," the company told stockholders in the annual report.[51] Since then, the total returns prepared by H & R Block has continued to increase. In the 1993 tax-filing season, the company prepared 12,964,400 returns—up 41 percent from the tax reform year.

As you might expect, the ever growing number of tax professionals, along with the ever increasing complexity of the code, have been accompanied by an ever growing number of books on taxes. Books for professionals. Books for the Form 1040 do-it-yourself person. Books on how to avoid paying taxes. Books on how to survive an IRS audit. Books on how to reform the tax system. Books on esoteric sections of the tax code. Books on how to pass your estate to your grandchildren tax-free. And on and on. How many books are there?

Thumb through the annual *Books in Print* catalog of R. R.

Bowker, and the entries under a half-dozen headings alone (Tax Planning, Tax Returns, Tax Shelters, Taxation—Law and Legislation, Taxation, and Income Tax) come to more than a thousand titles. To that figure must be added all the books under various subcategories, like Tax-Exempt Securities and Corporate Tax Law.

And then there's the burgeoning computer segment of the tax industry. To help both the professional and the amateur navigate their way through the Internal Revenue Code, software developers are turning out computer programs almost as fast as Congress adds new sections to the tax code, with names to match: A-Plus Tax, EasyGo OnPoint, Flash1040, JetTax 1040 Express, Master 1040, PREPaTAX92, RAM-1040, Tax Commissioner, TaxCut, Tax Machine, and Tax Partner 1040.

Three quarters of a century of simplifying the tax code has begot one tangible thing—complexity.

So much complexity that the backlog of paperwork confronting just one division of the tax industry is sufficient to keep an army of lawyers and economists at work well into the next century. These are the people in the IRS and the Treasury Department who write the regulations that implement the tax laws Congress passes.

You might think that would be simple—a matter of routine.

You would be wrong.

The regulations process is one of the main cogs in the perpetual motion machine, a full-employment guarantee that Congress provides for the tax industry. That's why every tax bill has not only an official title, the one you see in the newspapers, but also a decidedly unofficial—and much more accurate—title, which Washington insiders joke about.

Thus, what was known formally as the Tax Reform Act of 1969 was commonly referred to as the Lawyers' and Accountants' Relief Act. The Tax Reform Act of 1976 was known around Washington as the Tax Practitioners Act of 1976. And the Tax Reform Act of 1986 was, informally, the Accountants Relief Act.

Here is how the regulations process works:

First, Congress passes a tax law. Next, the IRS drafts rules spelling out how the law is to be applied. The IRS sends the draft to technicians in the Treasury Department for review.

When staffers at the IRS and the Treasury have agreed on wording, the draft is sent to the highest levels of both agencies for approval. Then it is published in the *Federal Register*, the daily journal for all federal government regulations.

Now the fun starts. Instead of ending, the regulations work is only beginning. The proposed regulations become a lightning rod for the tax industry. For months, they are picked apart by lawyers, accountants, and lobbyists for various special interests, who flood the IRS with position papers, letters, and briefs on highly technical aspects of tax law in the proposed changes.

This sends the regulation writers back to the drafting table to start all over again. The IRS reviews the comments, drafts a revised version of the regulations, and submits the new draft to Treasury for review. When the revised language is agreed upon, the proposed draft is sent once again to high-level officials at Treasury and the IRS for approval. Then the second version of the proposed regulations is published in the *Federal Register*.

And the whole process is repeated.

In 1969, Congress ordered the Treasury Department to prepare regulations that properly defined the difference between debt and equity. For most people, at least those employed outside the tax industry, this would not appear to be a daunting task. If you are buying the house in which you live, and you originally paid $100,000 for it and the balance on the mortgage is $50,000, you have $50,000 worth of equity. If, on the other hand, you borrowed $10,000 from the bank to finance an around-the-world trip, you have a debt of $10,000. The debt is the $10,000 you owe to the bank. The $50,000 already paid on the mortgage is your equity.

But the tax industry thrives on making simple matters complex. When deliberations began shortly after the congressional directive in 1969, teams of lawyers labored over the subject for thirteen years. In the end, they produced "110 single-spaced pages of densely complex regulations addressed to this single issue."[52]

Sometimes the IRS either decides regulations aren't necessary or never gets around to publishing the final version. This is why the agency still carries on its books regulations dating as far back as the Tax Reform Act of 1976.

Things haven't always been this way. When Congress adopted the Internal Revenue Code of 1954, one of the three largest rewrites of the tax code in history, all the regulations were written and implemented within two years.

Why doesn't that happen anymore? There are two reasons.

First, the huge volume of tax legislation over the last two decades has placed an enormous burden on the IRS, hampering its ability to produce timely regulations.

Second, Congress increasingly uses vague language in writing tax laws. Instead of drafting precise bills, the legislative tax writers sketch a broad outline and leave the IRS to fill in the blanks.

The result has been a growing backlog of unissued regulations. In 1970, the IRS had 250 regulations projects in the works. By 1980, the number had risen to 300. By 1985, it was up to 450. By 1993, the number stood at 597—an all-time high.

Even if Congress passes no new tax legislation in the near future—an unlikely event—the Treasury and the IRS would still have to work until the next century to complete the regulations now under review.

In short, the whole process is out of control—and you are picking up the tab.

What are you paying for?

For lawyers and accountants to argue—sometimes for years at a time—over arcane points of tax law. A brief review of a few IRS regulations projects gives the flavor of what they are debating:

- Basis Following Triangular Reorganization.
- Outbound Section 361 Transfers.
- Accumulation Trusts.
- Affect of Acquisitive Reorganizations on E&P Pools.
- Treatment of an Affiliated Group of Corporations as a Selling Consolidated Group for Purposes of Elective Recognition Under Section 338(H) (10).
- Sourcing of Pass-Through Payments and Fees Paid in International Short Sales of Stock.
- The Use of GAAP Earnings as E&P of Foreign Corp.
- Amendments to DASTM.
- Change in Method of Accounting to QBU's That Are No Longer Hyperinflationary.

- Partial Suspension of the Application of Section 1248(E) and the Limitation of Section 1248(F) Nonrecognition Provisions.
- Update Existing Regulations by Removing Obsolete Provisions and Adding New Provisions to Reflect Statutory Changes Since the Publication of the Existing Regulations.
- Treatment of Designated Hedges by RIC's.
- Final Regulations Under Section 166 Relating to the Express Determination Requirement for the Conclusive Presumption of Worthlessness for Bad Debts of Banks.[53]

If the titles of the regulations seem a bit obscure, how about the actual text, like this excerpt from a regulation on commodity futures contracts:

> Section 1.1092(b)-IT sets forth the general loss deferral rule and wash sale rule applicable to positions of a straddle. Generally, 1.1092(b)-IT(a) provides that if a taxpayer disposes of less than all of the positions of a straddle, any loss sustained with respect to the disposition of that position or positions will be disallowed to the extent that there is unrecognized gain in (1) successor positions, (2) offsetting positions to the loss positions, and (3) offsetting positions to the successor positions.[54]

If none of this makes much sense to you, that's fine with the tax industry. The industry's lawyers, lobbyists, and accountants like the tax code that way: complex, baffling, ambiguous, beyond the comprehension of average taxpayers—written in a language that only they understand. That way, they can charge big fees for years on end, while debating fine points of tax law that should be resolved easily. Like how to define an "S corporation."

S corporations are closely held, private companies—often family-owned businesses. Remember the Beverly Hills Gun Club? The term comes from a section in the tax code called subchapter S. The regulations project "defining" S corporations has been dragging on for well over a decade. It wasn't supposed to be this way.

Congress updated the law on these companies in 1982, liberalizing the rules for S corporation status. Lawmakers hailed the measure because—as you might guess—it would "simplify the tax rules." Dan Rostenkowski of the House Ways and Means Committee told the House in April 1982:

"This bill represents a further effort to simplify the Internal Revenue Code in order that taxpayers and their advisers may plan and conduct business and financial transactions in a rational manner without the tax laws duly impeding or complicating the conduct of these transactions." [55]

Over in the Senate, Bob Dole, the ranking Republican on the Senate Finance Committee, was equally proud of lawmakers' work on the Subchapter S Revision Act of 1982, saying it would "simplify and modify the tax rules" and make things easier for taxpayers and the government alike.[56]

Twelve years later, the IRS has yet to issue final regulations defining S corporations. This is good for the tax industry. The ongoing debate has generated a lot of work for lawyers, some of whom want to write, for tax purposes, their own definition of the American family.

When subchapter S was first enacted in 1958, it placed the number of shareholders who could constitute an S corporation at ten. This is because subchapter S was originally intended to help small-business owners. Ever since, special interests have lobbied to raise the number. The Revenue Act of 1978 increased it to fifteen. The Subchapter S Revision Act of 1982 more than doubled it to thirty-five. All those small businesses—the neighborhood hardware store, the corner grocery—whose images lawmakers like to invoke were getting larger all the time.

In May 1993, two Washington tax lawyers suggested a way to get around the thirty-five-shareholder limitation. Barbara Groves Mattox, of Davis & Harman, and Gregory F. Jenner, of the Washington office of Will, McDermott & Emery, a Chicago law firm, spelled out their proposal in a letter to G. Barksdale Penick, associate tax legislative counsel of the Treasury Department. It would allow an "unlimited number of shareholders" in an S corporation so long as all were members of the same "family." [57]

And what is a family? According to Mattox and Jenner:

". . . a family is defined as a common ancestor and his or her lineal descendants. To prevent unrelated persons from claiming common ancestors which are far removed or untraceable, the proposal requires that the youngest generation of share-holders cannot be more than four generations removed from the common ancestor at the time the family test is applied." [58]

Mattox and Jenner declined to disclose the identity of their client or clients. But already support was being lined up in Congress. In their letter to Penick, the two lawyers said that Representative E. Clay Shaw, a Republican member of the House Ways and Means Committee, and two other lawmakers —Representative Benjamin L. Cardin, a Democrat from Mary-land, and Mel Reynolds, a Democrat from Illinois—planned to introduce legislation to amend the subchapter S limitation.

By the end of 1993, several senators, not to be outdone by their colleagues in the lower chamber, drafted their own legis-lation along the lines recommended by the two tax lawyers. Introduced by S. David Pryor, Arkansas Democrat, and John Danforth, Missouri Republican, the bill offered yet another def-inition of a family: Whatever the number of family members, it never exceeds . . . one.

The Pryor-Danforth bill not only would raise the number of shareholders in an S corporation from thirty-five to fifty; it would count all relatives as one person. However many uncles, aunts, nephews, nieces, cousins, children, parents, and grand-parents in the business, for tax purposes they would be re-garded as one person.

Even when the IRS writers issue regulations promptly, there are often unforeseen consequences, thanks to the way Congress drafts tax legislation. The problems arise when lawmakers seek to apply a tax law to some people, and to exempt others from it, as they so often do. So it was with the Clinton budget bill of 1993, which raised the tax on diesel fuel from 20.1 cents a gallon to 24.4 cents. The tax increase was a key element in the President's budget deficit reduction program. But bowing to pressure from farmers and other interests, Congress retained an exemption from the tax for farmers, certain construction workers, and other off-road consumers of diesel fuel, including home owners who burn kerosene.

Thereby the question: how to differentiate tax-exempt fuel from tax-paying fuel?

Lawmakers provided the answer: dye.

Congress instructed the regulations writers to "allow an individual choice of dye color approved by the Secretary [of the Treasury] or chosen from any list of approved dye colors that the Secretary may publish." [59]

When the IRS laid out the rules for the dye process ordered by lawmakers, it touched off a firestorm among the affected businesses and individuals. Fuel oil dealers, home heating oil suppliers, consumer groups, and other parties complained that the proposal would be costly, complex, impossible to administer, harmful to consumers, hazardous to home owners, and destined to generate mountains of paperwork.

Besides that, there was the matter of the color picked by the IRS.

Red.

For one thing, red was already in use as a premium dye by many diesel fuel distributors.

"The use of red dye has historically been a voluntary way to distinguish higher fuel quality," wrote Ken White of Retrofit Specialties of Haddon Heights, New Jersey. "If the regulations are not amended there will be no easy way for the end user to be sure that they are receiving a premium diesel product." [60]

Some suppliers worried about abuses.

"We believe this opens up a vast potential for consumer fraud by unscrupulous operators if the consumer cannot tell whether the fuel is treated with Premium Additive," wrote Jamie Duke of Schaeffer's Specialized Lubricants of Saint Louis, Missouri. "We also believe our sales of Premium Diesel will fall drastically. . . . Our suggested regulations: Fuel destined for non-taxable use be dyed blue and have a marker added." [61]

Other suppliers said it was a tricky business to depend on accurate coloration of fuel oil.

"Experienced operators who have dealt with dyes advise that whatever color of dye is selected by the IRS, the color will not necessarily be the color of the diesel fuel that has been dyed," warned the Independent Liquid Terminals Association, a Washington, D.C., trade association of terminal storage operators. "For example, a blue dye added to a fuel with a yellow cast may turn the fuel a pale green color." [62]

Still others suggested that the IRS drop the entire idea and let exempt users apply for refunds from the Treasury.

"Please charge the diesel fuel tax as you do the gasoline tax," wrote Larry Edwards of Sterling Oil and Gas Co., of Sterling, Colorado. "Charging the tax to everyone with no exceptions and letting the end user apply for the refund would be the fairest way to handle this."[63]

But the Virginia Petroleum Jobbers Association, Inc., disagreed, arguing that such a move would place too great a burden on low-income consumers:

"Handling the paperwork involved in applying for refunds would be a difficult chore for this class of customer. The initial outlay would be a hardship in itself for these consumers. If they are to master the paperwork needed to apply for refunds, the Internal Revenue Service will find itself swamped with a flood of small claims."[64]

Even other government agencies weighed in to condemn the proposal. Like the Department of Health and Human Services, which administers the Low-Income Home Energy Assistance Program for poor people. Laurence J. Love, acting assistant secretary, wrote to the IRS:

We have grave concerns about the environmental, health, and safety effects of the proposal to require that dye or markers be added to diesel fuel destined for certain nontaxable uses. . . . We are concerned about the effects of your proposal on households that heat with kerosene.

Because kerosene oil used for home heating purposes is exempt from the tax, it would be subject to the proposed dye requirement. As a result, the health and safety of numerous low-income individuals and families would be placed in serious jeopardy. Since kerosene heaters often are not vented, toxic fumes from the dye would be released into their homes."[65]

Then lastly, of course, there was the question of the cost of the program to small businesses. As Conrad N. Bagne of the Arctic Slope Regional Corporation, Point Barrow, Alaska, complained: "Any requirement to keep dyed and undyed fuel separate would require the construction of additional tankage and distribution facilities."[66] Not to mention the purchase of special equipment in which to inject the dyes, as well as the chemical dyes themselves.

Taking Care of Friends

In time, the IRS presumably will work out the varied dye conflicts in a final set of regulations. But on occasion, the agency,
after years of laboring over the fine points of tax law, closes
projects without ever issuing final regulations. That's what happened with commodity tax straddles.

Straddles were one of the go-go tax-avoidance devices of the
1970s. By manipulating contracts to buy certain commodities,
investors could straddle two tax years and use paper losses from
one to offset real income and lower their taxes. Most of these
deals had no economic substance and were crafted solely to
avoid payment of taxes.

In that, they were similar to the book-juggling routine employed in the 1930s by the J. P. Morgan partners to escape
payment of taxes. After the Morgan disclosures, Congress enacted legislation that it said would put an end to such practices.
As customary, Congress allowed sufficient room for new ap-
proaches.

Throughout the 1970s, tax-shelter promoters peddled one
kind of straddle after another—gold, silver, Treasury bills, lin-
seed oil, cocoa beans, crude oil, platinum, soybeans, and about
every commodity conceivable. Finally, Congress cracked down
in the Economic Recovery Tax Act of 1981. The new law spec-
ified that "commodity futures transactions be taxed on their
economic substance." The IRS was now free to try to collect
billions of dollars in back taxes.

That made some people unhappy. Especially some politically
well-connected people, like commodity traders and dealers in
Chicago, home of the country's largest and most aggressive
commodities exchanges. With IRS agents poring over their returns, the traders turned to a friend in Congress—Dan Rostenkowski.

A recipient of campaign contributions and speaking fees
from the Chicago Board Options Exchange, the Chicago Board
of Trade, and the Chicago Mercantile Exchange, Rostenkowski
was sympathetic to the traders' plight. He inserted a clause in
the Deficit Reduction Act of 1984 that exempted professional
traders and dealers from the provisions of the 1981 anti-strad-
dle legislation.

As a result of Rostenkowski's action, straddle investors, depending on who they were, were treated in diametrically opposite fashion. If you were a private investor who had put money into tax straddles before 1981, you had to pay the back taxes and penalties. If, on the other hand, you were a professional trader, you were excused from paying them because you were in the commodities business. The amnesty for the 300 Chicago traders cost Treasury an estimated $500 million.

Actually, it cost a great deal more in terms of complexity and turmoil. Rostenkowski's amendment set off a new wave of litigation over straddles, with individual investors contending in U.S. Tax Court that they, too, were exempt from the IRS claims. They argued that the Rostenkowski amendment, while supposedly intended to help only professional traders, applied to all straddle investors.

And the tax court, in a 1985 ruling, agreed. As proof, the court cited the language of the 1984 amendment, which had been hastily drawn and written into the tax bill at the last moment.

The decision set off shock waves at the IRS. If allowed to stand, it would undercut the agency's efforts to collect an estimated $8 billion in unpaid taxes and penalties. That was too much to lose. So another amendment was whipped up and folded into the Tax Reform Act of 1986. It did the same thing Rostenkowski had tried to do in 1984—exempt only the professional traders from back taxes on straddles. But it did so in clearer, more precise language, emphasizing that the exemption applied only to "those taxpayers in the business of trading commodities."[67] Translation: Dan Rostenkowski's commodity-trading constituents in Chicago.

All this fooling around with straddles played havoc with the process of writing regulations. Soon after Congress enacted the first straddle legislation in 1981, lawmakers had asked the IRS to hurry up and get the regulations written. In a letter to Treasury Secretary Donald T. Regan, Senator Richard Lugar, a Republican from Indiana, urged him to press the IRS "to expedite the promulgation of regulations dealing with the tax straddle provisions" of the 1981 act.[68]

Two years later, in 1983, Assistant Secretary for Tax Policy John E. Chapoton said that the Treasury Department intended

"to make every effort to publish regulations on several important issues in the tax straddle area before the end of the year." [69]
Then Rostenkowski struck.

Five years later, in 1988, the IRS said it was on the verge of
issuing the straddle regulations. When an interviewer asked
deputy chief counsel Peter K. Scott how much longer his agency
would be grappling with the matter, he answered:

"Not long, I hope. Every day is one more day that we
shouldn't be grappling with it. It's hard for me to believe that
this thing has hung on for as long as it has. . . . It is long since
overdue to be resolved, that's for sure." [70]

The IRS never did issue final regulations on the 1981 straddle cases. Although temporary regulations were published, the
agency disclosed early in 1993 that there would be no final ones.
The same fate may ultimately befall a series of other straddle
regulations projects that are still pending.

While the 1981 straddles are dead, as far as IRS regulations
writers are concerned, they are alive and well in U.S. Tax
Court, where some 5,000 cases are still pending.

Meet Morris Krumhorn, a commodity trader on the Chicago
Mercantile Exchange, who, like many fellow traders, has been
active in the options and futures market. Working through the
Chicago Board of Trade, the New York Mercantile Exchange,
and the Commodity Exchange (COMEX), Krumhorn bought
and sold commodity futures contracts in cocoa, coffee, sugar,
lumber, copper, nickel, tin, various currencies, and other commodities.

Krumhorn was also a horse-racing enthusiast. He had his
own horse-racing and breeding operation—MDK Stables,
where he kept as many as thirty horses. They raced at tracks
from Hialeah Park to Churchill Downs to the Meadowlands.

According to documents filed in U.S. Tax Court, in 1978
alone Krumhorn earned $4.4 million in capital gains income
from his commodity-trading business. But by executing trades
in commodity straddles through a London trader and using
other deductions, he avoided all federal income tax that year.
In fact, his tax return showed a loss of $149,096. For 1979, it
was much the same story, with Krumhorn writing off $339,034
in losses from his horse-racing and breeding operation, enabling him to report a tax loss for that year too.

The IRS had a different view. It had one word for the $4.1 million in commodity straddle losses that Krumhorn contended he sustained on the London market: "shams."[71] According to the IRS, the records of the trades were haphazard and some of the trading dates did not track. The agency concluded that they were "fictitious" and had "no economic substance." It added:

"The record is clear that the trading was exclusively tax motivated. . . . Because the disputed trades are sham transactions, [Krumhorn] incurred no losses."[72]

Krumhorn disputed the IRS findings in tax court, asking a judge to reject the agency's claim that he owed $3.1 million in back taxes and penalties.

His reasoning?

He was exempt from such claims because of Dan Rostenkowski's amendment to the tax law.

And so go America's two tax systems. Some people who speculate in commodities can write off their losses. Most can't. Some businesses can secure their own private tax laws from friendly members of Congress. Most can't. Some people can enjoy the benefit of itemized deductions. Most can't. Some people can route their income through partnerships and trusts and foundations. Most can't.

The only constant is the two congressional committees that make it all possible. Every year, the House Ways and Means Committee and the Senate Finance Committee hold annual hearings, ostensibly in pursuit of an ever better tax system, an ever simpler Internal Revenue Code. But the annual rituals were perhaps best described a half century ago by a witness who said:

"This is the twenty-fifth anniversary of my appearance before the Ways and Means Committee and, due to my long experience, I have come to regard the hearings of this Committee and of the Senate Finance Committee as annual meetings of the Amalgamated Association of Tax Dodgers."[73]

CHAPTER 8

★ $ ★ $ ★

THE UNFAIREST TAXES OF ALL

The Unequal Burden

You are standing in the supermarket checkout line, express lane, with your one pound of ground beef. You notice that the two people ahead of you, a man and a woman, each have ground beef too.

The woman is first. The cashier runs her beef across the scanner, and the price comes up at $1.78 a pound. Next, the man slides his ground beef onto the conveyor, it crosses the scanner, and the price registers $3.12 a pound.

Now it's your turn. The cashier pulls the beef across the scanner. The price: $4.45 a pound.

Is this a great way for a supermarket to make money, or what?

But wait, you say—no supermarket could stay in business if it charged one customer 158 percent more for a product than it charged the next customer in line. There are laws against such practices.

This is true. Supermarkets can't.

But state and local governments can. And do.

The amount of money at stake is not a few dollars but tens of thousands of dollars for an individual or a family over a lifetime. If you are the lucky person in the checkout line, you are saving that much money. If you are the unlucky person, you are overpaying by a comparable amount.

Almost anywhere in the United States, if you own a home you may fairly assume that someone who owns a home of equal value is paying much less in real estate taxes than you are, and someone else is paying much more. The disparities exist within communities and between communities, within states and between states. In certain areas the disparities are lawful—indeed, they have been approved by the U.S. Supreme Court. In other areas, the disparities are illegal, but the politicians in charge choose not to correct the situation. They do so on the assumption that the overwhelming majority of home owners will do nothing to challenge the inequities.

You might think of taxes as the handicap in a marathon race that has been rigged by its sponsors—federal, state, and local governments. Before the runners start out, the federal government hands certain participants a ten-pound weight to carry in one hand. Then local and state governments give those same runners a twenty-pound weight to carry in the other hand. Other runners receive a lighter weight from the federal government and a still lighter one from local and state governments.

Guess who's going to win.

Whatever the tax imposed by local and state governments—. and they are many—it weighs more heavily on Middle America, and in some cases the working poor, than on anyone else. Whether it's a sales tax or an occupation tax. A wage tax or an excise tax. An income tax or a real estate tax. It's not necessarily the type of tax that's so onerous, but rather the way local and state governments administer it.

And the taxes are everywhere. If you get your shirt laundered or your dress dry-cleaned in Washington, D.C., you're taxed. If you get your swimming pool cleaned or use a dating service in Iowa, you're taxed. If you replace the worn tires on your car with a new set in Georgia, you're taxed on the old ones. If you buy snack foods in Maryland, you're taxed. If you're a patient in a nursing facility in Oklahoma, you're taxed. If you make a 900 telephone call in Minnesota, you're taxed. And if you buy a car almost anywhere, you're taxed.

Let's say the sales tax is 7 percent in your state. If you earn $30,000 a year and buy a Ford Escort for $10,000, you will pay

$700 in taxes. That's 2.3 percent of your income. If, on the other hand, your neighbor earns $1 million a year and buys a Lincoln Continental for $40,000, he will pay $2,800 in tax. That's three-tenths of 1 percent of his income.

You have contributed eight times as much, proportionately, to the support of state government as your neighbor—and his car cost four times as much as yours.

Or suppose that you finally had to buy a new refrigerator. You settled on a model that cost $900, and you paid $63 in tax. That was 10.9 percent of one of your weekly paychecks. Your neighbor purchased the deluxe model for $2,500 and paid $175 in tax. That was nine-tenths of 1 percent of one of his weekly paychecks.

You have contributed twelve times as much, proportionately, to the support of state government as your neighbor—and his refrigerator cost three times as much as yours.

And then there's the state income tax. You have to pay it. Your neighbor doesn't.

Not possible, you say.

Remember President Bush and his wife, Barbara? While they were living in the White House, you may recall, the President and the First Lady owned a home in Maine—a state with an income tax that carries a top rate of 9.89 percent. The Bushes also rented a hotel room in Texas—a state without an income tax. Naturally, they declared Texas as their official residence and paid no state income tax.

Remember Joe Allbritton, the Washington banker who eliminated much of his federal income tax bill with huge investment interest deductions? He runs the Riggs National Bank in the District of Columbia. He owns a television station in the District. He lives in an exclusive section of the District—which has an income tax with a top rate of 9.5 percent. But Allbritton also owns a home in Texas, so he declared Texas as his official residence and paid no District of Columbia income tax.

For the most affluent individuals, local and state taxes are often optional. But not for you.

So that you may better appreciate the tax weight you are carrying in life's marathon, let's look at the real estate taxes on two properties—one in California, the other in New Jersey.

We'll begin in California, a state where disparities are perfectly legal. This house, located in the Holmby Hills section of Los Angeles, is owned by Charles Z. and Mary Jane Wick.

It's a nice neighborhood.

Down the street a few blocks is the home of television producer Aaron Spelling and his wife, Candy. Spelling is the producer of so many hit television shows (*The Love Boat, Dynasty, Fantasy Island, Charlie's Angels*, and *Beverly Hills 90210*, among others) that he has earned a niche in *The Guinness Book of World Records:* It would take 108 days of nonstop viewing to watch all his programs.[1] Five years in the building, the Spelling house has 56,500 square feet of living space. Among the amenities are a bowling alley, a swimming pool, a private screening room, tennis courts, a French-style wine and cheese room, an ice rink, a forty-foot lily pond, and a formal rose garden planted on top of the garage. It even has a gift-wrapping room, "lined with custom-built shelves for ribbon, rolls of paper, boxes of trim."[2]

A little closer to the Wick house is the gray-stone mansion that *Playboy* founder Hugh M. Hefner calls home, with its thirty rooms, Botticini marble floors, and hand-carved oak paneling. Hefner's landscaped lawn, featuring a lagoon, waterfalls, and the Woo Grotto, used to provide a relaxed setting for nude swimming and sexual encounters at his once famous weekend parties attended by everyone from Linda Lovelace (star of the classic porn film *Deep Throat*) to Warren Beatty.

On the same street is the new home of Norman E. and Irene C. Friedmann. He's chief operating officer of Herbalife, a company that markets health and nutrition supplements. She's better known as Irene Kassorla, a popular psychologist, television personality, and author of several books, among them *Nice Girls Do—And Now You Can Too!* (Kassorla wrote that "in this book you will learn a step-by-step process for achieving complete sexual gratification. It's called the pleasure process."[3]) Before Friedmann and Kassorla could build their home, described as a $35 million project, they had to demolish a multimillion-dollar house once occupied by the late comedian Jack Benny and his wife, Mary Livingstone. It was noted at the time that although the Bennys had renovated the house, Friedmann and Kassorla found that it "needed updating and was too small for them."[4] The replacement house has seven bedrooms, sixteen bathrooms, eleven fireplaces, and five kitchens.

And a little closer still to the Wicks is the home of Elizabeth Avery Keck, horsewoman, art collector, and member of the Keck oil family. Her father-in-law, William Keck, founded Superior Oil Company and her husband, Howard B. Keck, ran the company until it was sold to Mobil Oil Corporation. Mrs. Keck's horse, Ferdinand, won the Kentucky Derby in 1986 and went on to earn more than $3 million. Through the years, she has assembled a museum-quality collection of French paintings and tapestries worth millions. The house, according to Los Angeles County property records, has eight bedrooms and nine bathrooms.

By now you have some feel for Holmby Hills, a section of Los Angeles west of Beverly Hills and south of Bel Air. It's on the south side of Sunset Boulevard, which winds through Hollywood, Beverly Hills, Bel Air, Westwood, and Pacific Palisades on its way to the Pacific Ocean. If you live outside California, the name Holmby Hills may not be as recognizable as Bel Air or Beverly Hills, long synonymous with California wealth. But there is wealth and there is wealth. And there are distinctions among the neighborhoods.

A longtime Bel Air resident, Zsa Zsa Gabor, once described the difference between her neighborhood and Beverly Hills: "Bel Air is not like Beverly Hills at all. It's very chic, elegant. Underplayed people live here. Beverly Hills is all showoff, showoff, showoff."[5] As for the difference between Beverly Hills and Holmby Hills, it once was put this way: "Beverly Hills is a holding pattern for people hoping to be rich enough to land in Holmby."[6]

Which brings us to the home of Charles and Mary Jane Wick. You may have heard of the Wicks: they are the closest of friends with Ronald and Nancy Reagan. Mary Jane, a former Goldwyn girl, sometimes served as liaison between the First Lady and her San Francisco astrologer, Joan Quigley, adviser to the First Family.

Charles Wick was a piano player in the big-band era, who went on to become a Hollywood booking agent, investor (he made money in nursing homes), motion picture producer *(Snow White and the Three Stooges),* and fund-raiser extraordinaire, teaming up with William E. Casey, the former spymaster and tax-shelter entrepreneur, to raise millions of dollars for Ronald Reagan. After the 1980 election, the Wicks went to Washington as part of an advance party to help ease the transition from the Carter White House and to arrange the most ostentatious inaugural celebration ever.

At the time, some critics drew a contrast between the opulence and the luxuries of the Reagans and their friends—all the furs and jewelry on display at ten inaugural balls—and the lot of many hard-pressed working Americans. Wick dismissed this peevish reaction, saying that ordinary people in the 1980s were just like those in the 1930s; they enjoyed seeing the glitz and the glamour:

"During the Depression, when people were selling apples and factories were still and guys were jumping out windows because they lost everything, people would go to the movies. They loved those glamour pictures showing people driving beautiful cars and women in beautiful gowns, showing that people were living the glamorous good life." [7]

Wick went on to serve as director of the United States Information Agency. Dressed in $1,000 Savile Row suits, with a tie clip and cuff links stamped with the presidential seal, he jetted first class ("I'm not going to fly coach to Europe and Africa and that kind of thing and ruin my health") from one world capital to another, dedicating an art exhibit here, speaking to foreign dignitaries there, staying in the best hotels. [8] Along the way, Wick became embroiled in several embarrassing incidents, including charges that his staff maintained a blacklist of people who should not be invited to speak to foreign audiences because they were too liberal. Among the banned speakers: Walter Cronkite, Coretta Scott King, and John Kenneth Galbraith.

But back to the Wick house in Holmby Hills. According to Los Angeles County real estate records, it is 7,558 square feet in size, the equivalent of three to four typical suburban tract houses. It has six bedrooms and eight bathrooms. So what's the Wick house worth? The market value of expensive California homes is difficult to pinpoint. But given the selling price of homes in the surrounding area, a conservative estimate—even in a declining real estate market—would put the value at upwards of $1 million. Possibly two or more times that amount.

And what is the real estate tax bill for a $1 million house surrounded by houses worth $5 million or $10 million or $35 million?

In 1992, it was $5,756.

Percentagewise, that's far less than the real estate taxes paid by millions of middle-class individuals and families across the nation who own homes worth a fraction of that amount.

Like Bruce and Dawn Firus.

The Firuses and their four children live in Millville, a town of 25,000 in southern New Jersey. The family owns a five-bedroom, 2,800-square-foot, split-level house on two acres in a pleasant, well-kept neighborhood. The house had an estimated market value of $155,000 in 1993. The real estate tax bill: $4,800.

If the Firuses were paying real estate taxes at the same rate as the Wicks out in California, their bill for the year would total $930. It would be even less than that if the Wicks house were worth more than $1 million.

For Firus, a senior corrections officer at a New Jersey state prison, real estate taxes take a big bite out of the family budget. Indeed, a bigger bite than any other federal, state, or local tax they pay. Firus considers the real estate tax the most inequitable.

"Nobody likes taxes, but the only fair way to go about it is income taxes," said Firus. "The more you make, the more you pay. The less you make, the less you pay. And that would allow people when they retire or when they get hurt at work—that would allow people to still keep their house if something happened to them. If I got hurt at work and there was no way I could work again, the tax bill still comes. The property tax is not an equitable way to determine taxation. It's not right."[9]

What has proved especially frustrating to the Firuses is that they thought they had done everything possible to avoid the real estate tax burden with which they are now saddled.

When they outgrew a previous house in Millville, the couple decided that the only way they could have a house the size they wanted in the neighborhood of their choice was to build it themselves.

So in June 1988, they purchased a two-acre lot in a wooded area in the northern part of town. Fully aware of the high real estate taxes in New Jersey—they were paying $1,000 for an 1,100-square-foot house—they began driving around looking at houses, trying to settle on a type on which the taxes would not exceed $3,000 a year. "We felt that was our limit," Firus said. "It was three times what we were paying." [10]

They wrote down the addresses of various properties, then checked the assessments with the city. Based on those findings, they settled on a house plan similar in design to houses that were being built in the area. After some preliminary site work, the Firuses began building their dream home in September 1988.

"I laid the first block over Labor Day weekend," said Firus. "Nineteen months later, we moved in. In that nineteen months, the only time I stopped was for Christmas. I worked every day. I worked out here, Dawn worked out here, even the kids worked. I would lay the cement, and the kids would trowel it for the steps. When I was doing the block walls, I was down in a hole next to the foundation, I would raise the trowel up to them, and they would put cement on it." [11]

When the days grew short, Firus would set up lights on stands so he could lay blocks in the dark. "There are 3,458 blocks in that basement, and they were all laid one at a time," he said. "It took me eight weeks to do it." [12]

Other family members, including Firus's father, a carpenter, also invested a lot of time in building the house.

"When we had to stand the walls up, we got coffee and doughnuts for everyone," Firus recalled. "Everybody came out and pushed the walls up, plumbed 'em up, nailed them in place, and had doughnuts and coffee. While they were doing that, I was putting the next one together." [13]

After the house was completed, in March 1990, an assessor hired by the city came by to inspect it. Weeks later, the couple was stunned by his proposed assessment, which translated into an annual tax bill of $5,662.

Thus began a series of appeals. The Firuses marshaled evidence, including a report by the city that showed similar houses nearby with much lower taxes. Ultimately, their tax bill was reduced slightly—they'll pay $4,800 in 1993–94—but remains much higher than they ever budgeted for.

What accounts for this?

"When I objected to our assessment and compared our assessment with nearby similar properties," Firus recalled, "I was told by the city that assessing is an art form. What's so arty about counting bathrooms? Is that part of the new creativity?" [14]

Raising Taxes—Behind Your Back

So what does it all mean—this contrast between the real estate taxes paid by the Firuses, a hardworking middle-class family that lives in a typical suburban setting on the East Coast, and the real estate taxes paid by the Wicks, a prosperous family that lives in one of the nation's richest communities on the West Coast?

It means that local and state politicians have perfected their own tax magic act. And at least in one area—real estate taxes— they have outperformed their colleagues in Washington. They have taken what once was the only local and state government levy even loosely based on a person's ability to pay, and converted it, in some cases, into a tax that falls lightly on those at the top and, in other cases, into a kind of tax lottery, in which some working folks win and some lose.

To make matters worse, the real estate tax has long been a principal source of revenue for local governments. In South Carolina in 1991, real estate taxes accounted for 92.1 percent of local government revenue. In Mississippi, 94.5 percent. In Minnesota, 94.6 percent. In Iowa, 96.1 percent. In New Jersey, 98.2 percent. While the national average has slipped through the years, dropping from 86.9 percent in 1965 to 75.3 percent in 1991, local governments still rely on property taxes for three fourths of their money. The change has been barely perceptible in some states. In 1965, for example, property taxes accounted for 98.2 percent of revenue in Wisconsin. Twenty-six years later, in 1991, it was 97.1 percent. In Massachusetts, it was 98.9 percent in 1965 and 97.2 percent in 1991.

Because of this dependence on real estate taxes, the growing inequities have been matched by growing public resistance to higher taxes. So much resistance that pressures in some states are leading to tax anarchy. Michigan, for one, in the fall of 1993 jettisoned its property tax, which provided funding for the state's schools, without having a replacement. By year's end, the state legislature agreed to a plan that will either raise the state sales tax from 4 percent to 6 percent, or raise the state income tax from 4.6 percent to 6 percent. Voters will be asked to take their pick in an election in 1994. Whatever the choice, low and middle-income people will pick up a disproportionate share of the cost of running the state's schools. In other areas, opposition to real estate tax hikes is forcing cutbacks in programs and services that have been a staple of American life. Like public libraries.

All across the country, cash-strapped cities, counties, and states have slashed library budgets. To make do with less, libraries once open seven days a week are now open only six, or five, or four. Libraries once open twelve hours a day are now open only eight. Literacy programs have been curtailed. Bookmobile services to remote areas have been eliminated. Librarians have been dismissed and full-time workers have been converted to part-time. Branch libraries have been closed. Money for buying books, the whole reason for the existence of libraries, has been dramatically reduced. So, too, money for subscriptions to newspapers, magazines, and other periodicals.

In Los Angeles, Sue Cowen, the public affairs officer for that county's library system, spoke of the telephone call she received from a person asking how much money the library spent on Japanese materials.

"We don't spend any money on Japanese materials," she replied.

"How much are you spending for Spanish materials?" the caller pressed.

"The same as Japanese—nothing," Cowen answered, adding, "We don't spend any money for Japanese, Spanish, Vietnamese, or English materials. We don't have any money."[15]

It's much the same everywhere, in big cities and small towns. A sampling of cutbacks compiled by the American Library Association ranges from a 49 percent reduction in the materials budget in Syracuse, New York, to a book-buying budget that "barely meets the state-mandated minimum" and staff short-ages "so severe that emergency closings are commonplace" in Philadelphia, to the closing of the venerable Municipal Reference Library, which housed a nearly century-old collection of local government documents, in Chicago. And on it goes.

For much of what is happening at the local and state level, in spending and program cuts, and higher taxes to provide fewer services, you may thank members of Congress.

Congress?

Over the last two decades, Congress has shifted programs and services from the federal government to local and state governments. But not the money to pay for them. In addition, it has enacted one piece of legislation after another creating new programs—and then ordered local and state governments to pay for them.

Federally mandated programs will cost cities alone an estimated $54 billion for the years 1994 through 1998. For just 1993, the bill came to $5.6 million for Berkeley, California; $582 million for Los Angeles; $49 million for Atlanta; $3 million for South Bend, Indiana; $84 million for Baltimore; $3 million for Rocky Mount, North Carolina; $476 million for New York; $7 million for Alexandria, Virginia; $3 million for Cheyenne, Wyoming.[16]

Keep in mind, the $54 billion cost estimate for 1994–98 is just for cities. Add to that $34 billion for counties. Again, for just 1993, the bill came to $56 million for Orange County, Florida; $11 million for Gwinnett County, Georgia; $3 million for Lake County, Illinois; $9 million for Johnson County, Kansas; $59 million for Prince George's County, Maryland; $25 million for Erie County, New York; and a whopping $1 billion for Los Angeles County.[17]

Add to those numbers additional billions of dollars in costs that many cities and counties are spending for health care, education, and other social services for a growing wave of illegal immigrants, as well as skyrocketing costs to build and staff new prisons.

These costs and others growing out of programs initiated by Congress, or by Congress's failure to deal with what are national problems like illegal immigration, have had a direct impact on your local and state taxes. The statistics tell the story.

From 1980 to 1991, the latest year for which complete figures are available, local and state tax collections soared from $223 billion to $525 billion—an increase of 135 percent.

Meanwhile, federal tax collections climbed at little more than half that rate during the same period, from $351 billion to $642 billion—an increase of 83 percent.

Local real estate tax collections between 1980 and 1991 spiraled from $66 billion to $162 billion—an increase of 145 percent.

Local sales tax collections shot up from $12 billion to $32 billion—an increase of 167 percent.

State individual income tax collections ballooned from $37 billion to $99 billion—an increase of 168 percent.

And federal income tax collections from individuals? They went up from $244 billion to $468 billion—an increase of 92 percent.

As for federal income tax collections from corporations, they rose from $65 billion to $98 billion—an increase of 51 percent.

But once more, let's look at the numbers in contrast with the 1950s, the period of sustained middle-class growth.

In 1950, all local and state tax collections amounted to 45 percent of federal tax collections. Eleven years later, in 1961, that figure had edged up to 50 percent.

By contrast, in 1980, all local and state collections amounted to 64 percent of federal tax collections. Eleven years later, in 1991, that figure had surged to 82 percent.

If this trend continues, local and state government tax collections will exceed federal tax collections in the early part of the next century. That brings us to Tax Rule No. 8: When members of Congress talk about cutting federal spending and enacting new federal programs, they are raising your local and state taxes.

What difference does it make?

Local and state taxes are weighted far more heavily against middle-income people and the working poor. Some states even have constitutional prohibitions against levying taxes according to a person's ability to pay. Michigan, which scrapped its property tax to pay for schools, imposes a flat 4.6 percent personal income tax. The state constitution prohibits more than one rate. It also limits the amount of tax collections to a formula tied to personal income at the 1979 level. Other states have similar tax limitations. In short, the overall local and state system treats those at the top far more lightly than the federal tax structure. Everyone else is stuck.

Meet the Lord family of West Linn, Oregon.

Jerry D. Lord is a pulp tester at a commercial recycling plant in Oregon City, Oregon, that processes newspapers and glossy magazines into recycled paper. Lord, his wife, Linda, and their four children live in a middle-class suburb of Portland. The Lords are typical of Middle America today as they find themselves paying an increasingly larger share of the family income in state, local, and federal taxes.

In 1992, the Lords' total state and local tax bill came to $5,329. Of that, $1,991 went to Oregon in state income taxes and $3,338 was for local real estate taxes. In addition, the couple paid $2,869 in federal income tax and $3,221 in Social Security and Medicare taxes. Overall, the family paid $11,419 in federal income and Social Security taxes, state income and local real estate taxes. That was 26 percent of their adjusted gross income of $43,690—well above the tax rate imposed on many millionaires. And that does not take into account all the miscellaneous levies, like gasoline taxes and the telephone excise tax. Thirty years ago, a comparable middle-income family would have paid taxes at less than half that rate.

Like most middle-income families, the Lords are falling behind. In 1992, Jerry Lord earned $42,710 in regular wages and overtime at the recycling plant. Although he believes he earns a good hourly wage by current standards, he, like an increasing number of working Americans, is actually earning less per hour than he was six years ago, when a previous employer—a trucking company—folded and left him unemployed for the first time in seventeen years. His hourly rate in 1987 was $14.80. In 1993, it was $14.69. When the dollars are adjusted for inflation, he is doing even worse.

Lord poses the same question raised by other middle-income families:

"In a sense, I feel I make pretty good money, but not by today's standards, not for what you need; $40,000 isn't that much, and what gets me is that they want everybody to go out there and basically go into the service industry, and they want you to make less. How are we going to live, have any kind of life, if we are making 1950 wages?"[18]

And he sounds the same frustrations:

"We are sitting here right now with total savings of maybe $5,000 in the bank. We watch every penny, everything we do. We are just barely making it. I'm not getting ahead. My whole net worth is in my house."[19]

Many of the politicians responsible for the Lords' tax rate pay taxes at about the same rate or at a lower one, even though they have much higher incomes.

Take former President Bush, who championed the federal tax cuts through the 1980s and supported many of the federal programs that passed the costs along to local and state governments.

For 1989, the Bushes reported income of $466,244. They paid a total of $127,201 in federal income tax, Social Security tax, real estate tax, personal property tax, and state and local income tax.

Their tax rate: 27 percent.

That was 1 percent above the Lord family tax rate of 26 percent—although the Bushes' income was ten times greater.

And 1989 was not a particularly good year, taxwise, for the Bushes. In 1991, with an income of $1,324,456, they paid $239,083 in federal, state, and local taxes, for a tax rate of 18 percent. The First Family's state and local income and personal property taxes totaled $4,312—or three-tenths of 1 percent of their income.

The Lords, on the other hand, saw 4.5 percent of their earnings go to the Oregon income tax—a tax rate fifteen times greater than the Bushes'.

Like most states, Oregon derives revenue from an income tax that is most generous to those at the top. In 1992, for example, a single person with a taxable income of $40,000 paid taxes at a rate of 8.7 percent. An individual with a taxable income of $1 million paid taxes at a rate just three-tenths of 1 percent higher.

The Oregon income tax has three brackets, with the first $2,000 in income taxed at 5 percent, the next $3,000 at 7 percent, and all income over $5,000 at 9 percent. This places a middle-income family in the same top tax bracket as a millionaire.

That's the way it is in most states. Even those where government officials establish multiple brackets to create the illusion
of a progressive tax—one in which rates rise along with income.
Because the brackets are so closely bunched at the bottom, or
in the middle-income range, there is little difference between
the effective tax rate of an average worker and the effective tax
rate of the state's wealthiest resident. In this, the states have
merely refined the federal government's practice of treating
someone with a taxable income of $55,000 the same as someone
with a taxable income of $110,000. As a result, there is little or
no relationship between the amount of tax levied and a person's
ability to pay it.

Virginia, for example, has four brackets. The tax-rate schedule begins at 2 percent on the first $3,000 and reaches a maxi-
mum of 5.75 percent on all income above $17,000. Thus, a
Virginia family with $40,000 taxable income pays tax at a 5.1
percent rate. A family with two and one-half times that income,
or $100,000, pays at a rate of 5.5 percent. And a family with
twenty-five times that income, or $1 million, pays at a 5.7 per-
cent rate. The tax-rate difference between the middle-income
family and the rich family is six-tenths of 1 percent. Or viewed
from another perspective: A family with a taxable income of
$20,000 is in the same tax bracket as Middleburg, Virginia,
resident Jack Kent Cooke, a millionaire investor and the owner
of the Washington Redskins, who, worth an estimated $800
million, is among the *Forbes* 400 richest Americans.

Kentucky goes Virginia one better, with five brackets. The
bottom rate of 2 percent applies to the first $3,000 of taxable
income. The top rate of 6 percent is imposed on income above
$8,000. A family with a taxable income of $40,000 pays tax at
an effective rate of 5.5 percent, while a family with an income
of $1 million pays at a rate one-half of 1 percent higher, or 6
percent. This puts a Kentucky family with a taxable income of
$15,000 in the same top tax bracket as the members of Louis-
ville's Brown family, owners of Brown-Forman Corporation—
which makes Jack Daniel's and Southern Comfort—who, worth
an estimated $1 billion, are among the *Forbes* 400 richest Amer-
icans.

Georgia adds to the deception with six brackets, taxing the

first $1,000 at 1 percent and everything over $10,000 at 6 percent. A person with a taxable income of $40,000 pays tax at a rate of 5.5 percent, while an individual with an income of $1 million pays at a rate one-half of 1 percent higher, or just under 6 percent. A single Georgia worker with a taxable income of $15,000 is in the same tax bracket as Anne Cox Chambers, part owner of the Cox newspaper (*Atlanta Journal*) and television empire, who, worth an estimated $2.4 billion, is among the *Forbes* 400 richest Americans.

And then there's Missouri, which boasts ten brackets. The bottom rate of 1.5 percent is applied to the first $1,000 of taxable income. The top rate of 6 percent is imposed on income over $9,000. A family with a taxable income of $40,000 pays tax at a 5.4 percent rate, while the family with $1 million in income pays at a rate three-fifths of 1 percent higher, or slightly under 6 percent. This puts a family with a taxable income of $10,000 in the same tax bracket as August Busch III of Saint Louis, and other members of the Busch beer family, who, worth an estimated $1.1 billion, also are among the *Forbes* 400 richest Americans.

Other states dispense with the pretense of progressive taxation. They levy a flat tax so that poor and rich alike pay at the same rate. Pennsylvania, for one, imposes a flat 2.8 percent rate on most income, with no personal exemptions and few deductions. This means that the working-poor person earning $12,000 a year is in the same tax bracket as Richard Mellon Scaife, Pittsburgh-area newspaper publisher, a descendant of Treasury Secretary Andrew Mellon, and, worth an estimated $750 million, among the *Forbes* 400 richest Americans.

The consequences of a system like Pennsylvania's can be seen by comparing state and federal tax statistics. In 1991, about 1.3 million individuals and families in Pennsylvania with adjusted gross incomes below $15,000 paid federal income tax.

By contrast, about 1.8 million individuals and families in that income group paid state income tax. The state income tax hit about a half-million more persons at the bottom than did the federal income tax.

Other local taxes, like wage taxes, add to the disproportionate burden on those in the middle and at the bottom. Philadelphia imposes the nation's highest and most regressive tax of all—a 4.96 percent tax on weekly wages. In Detroit, it's 3 percent; in Pittsburgh, 2.875 percent; in Louisville, 2.2 percent.

Now add in both local and state sales taxes, which also fall more heavily on middle-income and lower-income people. Mississippi, the nation's poorest state, has a 7 percent sales tax, as does Rhode Island. It's 6.25 percent in Illinois, 6 percent in Florida and Connecticut.

In Louisiana, the state sales tax is 4 percent. But Baton Rouge has a 2 percent sales tax, and the parish of East Baton Rouge a 4 percent tax, bringing the total to 10 percent. New York State has a 4 percent sales tax. But Erie County, New York, where Buffalo is, has a 4 percent tax, bringing the total for its residents to 8 percent. Tennessee has a 6 percent sales tax. But Shelby County, where Memphis is, has a 2.25 percent tax, bringing the total to 8.25 percent.

Whatever the type of tax levied by state and local governments—real estate tax, per capita tax, occupation tax, gasoline tax, sales tax—it is almost always weighted against middle-income people and the working poor.

In that, state and local governments are merely imitating the federal government by extending favorable tax treatment to those at the top of the economic ladder. They also are emulating the federal government by excusing corporations—some businesses more than others—from paying their share of the cost of governments. Once more, the statistics tell the story.

Between 1961 and 1991, the size and cost of local and state governments grew astronomically across America, and the taxes assessed to pay for it grew astronomically too. But taxes went up a lot more for some than for others.

Over the thirty years, revenue from state sales taxes, paid largely by low-income and middle-income people, rose from $4.5 billion to $103 billion—an increase of 2,189 percent. Money collected from state income taxes, which with few exceptions hit the same groups hardest, climbed from $2.4 billion to $99 billion—an increase of 4,025 percent.

For corporations, though, the income taxes paid to states went up much more slowly, from $1.3 billion to $20.4 billion— an increase of 1,469 percent.

Those percentages are so large they may seem meaningless.

But you might want to think of the 2,189 percent increase in state sales tax collections this way: If you were a typical middle-income family in 1961, earning $5,737, and your income had gone up at the same rate, today you would be earning more than $130,000.

In any event, the corporate tax situation is more grim in certain states. In New York State, corporate income taxes accounted for 13 percent of all tax collections in 1961. By 1991, that figure had plunged to 7 percent.

In Wisconsin, corporate income taxes accounted for 13 percent of all tax collections in 1961. By 1991, the corporate share had dropped to 6 percent.

In Pennsylvania, corporate income taxes accounted for 13 percent of all tax collections in 1961. By 1991, the corporate share had fallen to 8 percent.

It wasn't supposed to work this way. When Congress passed the Tax Reform Act of 1986, which slashed the federal corporate tax rate from 46 to 34 percent, it was suggested that states would reap a financial windfall. Just the opposite has happened. Corporate income tax payments to states peaked at $23.9 billion in 1989, and it's been downhill since. They dropped to $21.8 billion in 1990 and to $20.4 billion in 1991—the two largest percentage declines in back-to-back years.

The War Between the States

What accounts for corporate America's lagging support of state and local governments?

Two factors:

One, the same practice that has allowed corporations to shave their federal income tax bills—shifting income among states and countries to reduce or eliminate tax payments.

Two, the consequences of what might best be summed up as the fallout from the war between local and state governments.

All are competing to see who can give the most tax breaks to corporations that promise to move to an area and create jobs, or that promise not to move from an area and take away jobs. The phenomenon, to be sure, is not a new one. States have been competing with one another for years to lure prospective commercial or industrial businesses. Southern states, in particular, have long done quite well by promising major tax breaks while holding out the prospect of a union-free environment with lower wages and workers' compensation charges.

But in recent years this rivalry has given way to something wholly different and more destructive—a competitive frenzy, fueled by fear, that will have ominous consequences for state and local taxpayers for years to come.

Now the fighting isn't simply between northern states and southern states. It's between one southern state and another southern state. Between one northern state and another northern state. Between counties within states, and between counties among states. Between cities and suburbs. Between cities within states and among states. Between a city in one part of a metropolitan area and a city in another part of that same metropolitan area.

The state and local governments are offering ever larger tax breaks and other incentives to attract or keep companies and jobs. The manic bidding has come to resemble the scramble among professional sports franchises that compete to see which can come up with the most lucrative combination of salary and benefits for the latest hot property in baseball, football, basketball, or hockey. Except that in this case, the states and cities are giving away tax dollars. The result is a continuing erosion of corporate tax collections—with you making up the lost revenue, in either higher taxes or reduced programs and services, such as shuttered libraries.

For the most part, this is an outgrowth of America's declining middle-class job market. The struggle for jobs is so intense, the fear of losing corporate employers so pervasive, that governors, legislators, and mayors will do almost anything to try to "create" or keep jobs.

And corporations, like professional athletes, have become adept at playing the game. A company need only hint that it is moving somewhere else to prompt state and local officials to pony up a package of "tax incentives" and other taxpayer-funded breaks to induce it to stay. Meanwhile, if the company suggests an interest in some other locale, officials there counter with more and better offers.

For corporations, the best of all possible scenarios is to incite a bidding war among several states.

Here's how the game is played: Let's say the Acme Tool Company has picked out the state where it wants to build. That state, eager for the jobs, is already offering tax incentives for the company to make the move. But Acme Tool executives wonder whether they couldn't get more. So the company president tells officials in State No. 1 that he likes their proposal, but at the same time tells the news media that the company is exploring possibilities in other states.

This brings a flood of new tax concessions from other states and cities. Alarmed, State No. 1 decides it had better increase its bid. The governor, the legislature, and other government agencies quickly put together a new offer, which surpasses those from competing states—as well as their own original proposal.

Then Acme Tool's president announces the site of the new plant—State No. 1, just as the company had planned all along.

Sound unlikely? Not at all. That's what happened in South Carolina, which provided an extravagant bundle of tax concessions to lure German automaker BMW to the state in 1992. This in a state that has long imposed most of its tax burden on working individuals and families. It was already one of those states that seek to create the impression of a progressive tax by having several brackets. The bottom rate of six begins at 2.5 percent on taxable income of $2,160. The maximum rate is fixed at 7 percent on income over $10,801. A family with a taxable income of $40,000 pays state income tax at a 6.2 percent rate, just four-fifths of 1 percent below the 7 percent rate paid by families with incomes of $1 million. To view it a bit differently, South Carolina families with taxable incomes of $12,000 are in the same tax bracket as Roger Milliken of Spartanburg, head of the textile company bearing the family name, who, worth an estimated $600 million, is among the *Forbes* 400 richest Americans.

The state has for some time excused corporations from having to pay a significant share of the costs of government. This was not always so. In 1961, South Carolina received 9 percent of its total tax collections from corporate income taxes. This placed the state No. 10 among the thirty-six states that imposed a corporate income tax.

By 1991, the corporate share of South Carolina tax collections had plunged to less than 4 percent, and the state had plummeted to No. 42 among the forty-six states that levied a corporate income tax. Only Rhode Island, Colorado, Oklahoma, and New Mexico collected a smaller share of taxes from corporations. Working people, of course, make up the difference.

South Carolina is destined to maintain that low ranking for generations if it grants many more tax packages like the one it handed out to BMW, after Germany's largest auto maker let it be known that it wanted to build a plant in the United States.

Word surfaced in early 1992 that BMW was considering South Carolina for its first auto assembly plant outside Germany. The disclosure set off a wave of economic excitement in the state, one of the nation's poorest. The prospect that the German car maker—a company with annual sales of $18.7 billion—would locate in South Carolina electrified state officials. "I can tell you that we'll do everything we can to get them," Governor Carroll A. Campbell told reporters.[20] Indeed they would.

By looking at South Carolina, BMW, too, was heading down a new road. The company had never built a plant outside Bavaria, its home base. But it was drawn to the United States now by lower labor costs: German auto workers were paid $23 an hour, on average, excluding benefits; U.S. workers got $17 an hour. And although BMW had never before played the American game of pitting one state against another to extract maximum advantage, the company was a quick study.

First reports indicated that BMW was focusing on a site in Anderson County, South Carolina, for an assembly plant that might cost upwards of $1 billion to build. Asked about its intentions, BMW was coy. A spokesman said that the company was looking at a number of places: "[South Carolina] is just one alternative, and the United States isn't the only place we've looked."[21]

No sooner had word leaked out about BMW's interest in South Carolina than similar stories began appearing about sites in Nebraska. Now, it was said, officials in Omaha were putting together a collection of incentives. Soon the reports got more specific. BMW was said to be considering a site near Omaha's airport. Nebraska was promising subsidized "air cargo ship-

ments of parts from Germany," lower fuel costs, a more edu-
cated and trained population, and tax and economic benefits
valued at $100 million.[22]

In what must have warmed the hearts of BMW negotiators,
South Carolina newspapers poured out stories about the Nebraska offer and why it posed a threat to South Carolina's bid.
At the same time, other states, from Massachusetts to Arizona,
were jumping into the contest, promising BMW lavish incentives.

South Carolina promptly upped the ante. Officials pulled
together an improved mix of tax breaks and other economic
incentives. Governor Campbell flew to Munich, BMW's headquarters, in late March 1992, with a delegation of economic
development officials to discuss matters further. They report-
edly came back discouraged. BMW had suggested, according to
local press reports, that "South Carolina's incentive package was
inadequate."[23] Days after the visit, BMW Chairman Eberhard
von Kuenheim did little to raise the state's hopes. When asked
if the car maker was about to announce the site for its North
American plant, von Kuenheim replied: "The world is big.
When we should decide, we will choose a place that is most
favorable for us."[24]

Next, BMW informed state officials that the original Anderson County site was inadequate. The company was leaning instead to a tract in adjoining Spartanburg County, because it was
adjacent to the Greenville-Spartanburg airport and had more
direct access to the port of Charleston, through which BMW
could export cars. This complicated the bargaining for South
Carolina. The state controlled the Anderson site but not the
Spartanburg property.

Nevertheless, South Carolina wanted that plant. So, working
with state legislators, Governor Campbell assembled a new "incentive" package and hurriedly pushed it through the state senate and house. The cost to taxpayers started at $25 million to
acquire the plant site and moved up through millions of dollars'
worth of infrastructure improvements. A *Spartanburg Herald-
Journal* account described the furious pace of lawmaking:

A $25 million section of a three-pronged BMW incentive
package raced through the Legislature Wednesday as the

House made minor adjustments to a version already approved by the Senate.

The Senate is expected to go along with the changes. House fiscal leaders predicted the remaining two parts of the Senate-passed package also will sail through the House by Tuesday with no opposition.

Gov. Carroll Campbell's aides have been hastily guiding the package through the General Assembly, anticipating an announcement in the next few weeks by the German automaker BMW about whether it will locate a $1 billion factory in Spartanburg County.

The package is intended to give South Carolina the upper hand against a few other competing states." [25]

BMW held out for still more. In the weeks following, the company deftly played off Nebraska against South Carolina. BMW officials pointed to such Nebraska plusses as lower utility costs. One Spartanburg trade consultant later marveled at the shrewdness of von Kuenheim, the BMW chairman: "He knew quite well he had a lot to offer, and he sold it well." [26]

South Carolina kept coming up with more. On June 10, Spartanburg County passed a measure that cut in half the real estate taxes BMW would owe on the Spartanburg plant.

Finally, on June 23, 1992, BMW announced that it would, after all, build in South Carolina. Von Kuenheim made the announcement from Munich in a broadcast televised before a festive group of South Carolina and BMW officials at the factory site. There, on a 900-acre tract adjacent to the Greenville-Spartanburg airport, BMW would erect a 1.9-million-square-foot plant that would turn out its first cars in 1995. BMW's initial investment would be from $250 to $300 million, and employment would expand gradually to about 2,000 persons by the year 2000.

The company cited three reasons why it picked South Carolina—a qualified labor force, a good quality of life, and "a positive relationship between business and government." [27]

Positive it was. BMW came away with some of the most lucrative state and local tax breaks ever bestowed on a corporation by any state.

Just what was the final tab?

All told, state officials said, the tax breaks and other incentives added up to $130 million. Actually, it was more. The $130 million figure did not include the cost of another state commitment—its pledge to produce 2,000 trained workers for BMW. Nor did it include the interest payments on $25 million in bonds the state sold to acquire the Spartanburg site.

To attract a $250–$300 million plant, South Carolina gave away tax breaks and other taxpayer-funded benefits equal to half the value of the plant.

For BMW, South Carolina's generosity was a dream come true. At home, the German car maker doesn't get deals like that. German companies pay a corporate income tax of up to 50 percent on profits. That compares with 35 percent in the United States. German corporations pay an additional municipal trade tax—the equivalent of state income taxes in this country—of up to 25 percent. In South Carolina, the corporate income tax is 5 percent. Thus, even had BMW received no tax breaks or government subsidies at all from South Carolina, it would have paid lower taxes there than it does on its German operations.

After giving away roughly $150 million in tax breaks, South Carolina found out that BMW was investing far less than it had been led to believe. Rather than employing 4,000 workers, as initial reports suggested, BMW was talking about maybe 2,000 by the end of the decade. If all went well, the company said, it would add more jobs later.

And then there was the pay those 2,000 workers would receive. Attractive as the tax incentives had been for BMW, the company left little doubt that the main reason it came to South Carolina was for low wages. As Bernd Pischetsrieder, a member of BMW's board, had put it: "We aren't here to pay what we pay in Germany."[28]

South Carolina had assumed that BMW would pay the prevailing wage of U.S. auto workers—roughly $17 an hour, or $6 an hour less than German auto workers were paid. But soon after the plant was announced, BMW hinted that it was looking at the prevailing manufacturing wage in South Carolina—which was $10 an hour. If so, the BMW deal will be even costlier to taxpayers than originally estimated, because the state had calculated the economic return on the assumption that the auto workers would earn $17 an hour.

As for BMW, the company could not be happier about the deal. At groundbreaking ceremonies in September 1992, Eberhard von Kuenheim, the BMW chairman, after turning a spade of earth with Governor Campbell, took a moment to reflect on the significance of the event: "This is a moment charged with emotion for all of us. I am certain that this day will be remembered in the history books of South Carolina just as it will be in the chronicles of BMW." [29]

Tax Subsidy for a Plant Closer

The thumbscrew that BMW used on South Carolina officials was the same that many American corporations have used on other states: jobs. South Carolina wanted to attract new ones. In other states, officials want to hold on to what they have. In both cases, the average taxpayer picks up the tab for the tax giveaways.

Other states, in a never-ending quest for a shrinking number of jobs that pay middle-income wages, are deploying the tax money in a wholly different way: They are taking the taxes of workers who have been dismissed to subsidize the companies that laid them off.

Witness Pennsylvania's taxpayer-subsidized assistance to the Keebler Company, the nation's second-largest baking business. You may know Keebler through its products on supermarket shelves, products with names like Town House crackers, Chips Deluxe, Zesta saltines, or Deluxe Grahams. Or you may know Keebler for its lovable elves, the industrious make-believe bakers who advertise Keebler products on television.

For 132 years, Keebler baked some of its well-known cookies or crackers in Philadelphia, where the company began in 1853. A German immigrant, Godfrey Keebler, opened a bakeshop that year in downtown Philadelphia. Nine years later, Keebler hit it big when he began supplying bread to the Union Army during the Civil War. The Keebler Company eventually evolved into a business with bakeries in more than a dozen cities, supplying consumers in all fifty states. In 1974, the company was acquired by United Biscuits Holdings PLC, a $4.6 billion Scottish corporation headquartered in London.

Still, Keebler continued to bake in Philadelphia. Or it did until 1985, when the company closed its Northeast Philadelphia bakery, throwing 500 longtime employees out of work. The closing came as a shock to employees, many of whom lived in nearby working-class neighborhoods and considered the bakery a second home.

Ernest Dunn, Jr., will never forget the day. A fourteen-year veteran of Keebler, Dunn was at home, preparing to report for the night shift, when he got the news. "My mother called me at home at night and she said, 'How come you didn't tell me Keebler's was closing?' " he recalled. "I didn't know they were closing. She said, 'Turn on Channel 3.' So I turned on the TV, and there were these people from Keebler's, crying on camera. I said, 'No, Mom. I didn't know about it.' That's how I found out about it. On the news. They told the people on day work they were closing in November. So when I came to work that night I knew my job was gone." [30]

Keebler blamed the shutdown on excess capacity, saying that the company's bakeries were running at only 60 percent of capacity. Yet that very same year the company had record sales of $988.6 million and grabbed a larger share of the U.S. cookie and cracker market. As Keebler's parent, United Biscuits noted in its 1985 annual report: "Keebler's share of the U.S. cookie market by the end of 1985 was 13.5 percent. This was its highest ever achieved and the fourth consecutive year of increase in market share." [31]

Whatever the reason for closing the Philadelphia bakery, the shutdown was painful for longtime employees like Dunn. A Vietnam veteran, Dunn had been wounded by a land mine during the war and afterward suffered severe stress, an ailment for which he continues to receive treatment. He had gone to work at Keebler shortly after he was discharged from the service, and the bakery had been a rock of stability—providing a steady paycheck and good benefits.

"When I first started working there I was in general help—sweeping floors, whatever had to be done," he said. "From there I went into the cleaning department, where I cleaned up the lines, cleaned up flour, washed the walls, stuff like that.

Then I went into the paper-stocking department. We stocked the paper for the boxes that the cookies actually go into. From there I went to the baking department, where they baked the cookies. I was an oven man. From there I went to the mixing department. I mixed the doughs. I made every dough they had at one time or another. That's where I lost my job." [32]

The layoff sent him into a deep depression, Dunn said, adding that "I thought many times of taking my own life." No longer able to provide for his family as he had before, he felt "degraded as a human being." Dunn credits his wife, Jane, with helping him in the darkest moments: "She pulled me through." Then Jane Dunn became ill, suffering a major heart attack in 1989. She died of another attack in the summer of 1993, at the age of thirty-nine, leaving Dunn to raise the couple's four children—ages thirteen to seventeen. [33]

When Keebler closed, Dunn received $1,300 in severance pay —or roughly $93 for every year he'd worked there. He paid off a truck loan and had a couple of hundred dollars left when he enrolled in a program to learn a new trade—air-conditioning repair, installation, and design.

Upon completing the course, Dunn soon discovered he wasn't likely to find a job with the kind of pay or benefits he'd had at Keebler. He sent résumés everywhere, he said, but the only jobs available paid around $7 an hour—or $5 less than the $12.10 an hour he was earning when Keebler closed.

With four children at home, Dunn had no choice. He took what he could get. He held a succession of maintenance jobs earning from $7 to $10.50 an hour. Each required him to pay for part of his health coverage. In the summer of 1993, Dunn was laid off from the $10.50-an-hour job because of a sluggish economy and had to collect unemployment again.

As Ernest Dunn and many of his former coworkers at Keebler moved from one low-wage job to another, collecting unemployment in between, Keebler made plans to bake again in the Philadelphia area—not at its old plant in the city, but in a newer one in a little town nearby.

In 1991, Keebler's U.S. parent—UB Foods U.S., Inc.—disclosed that it had acquired a never used bottling plant in Oxford, Pennsylvania, about thirty-five miles southwest of Philadelphia. UB Foods said it had paid $4.2 million for the plant, with the intention of remodeling it and making snack foods there. It would be called Emerald Industries and would employ 155 people.

In Oxford, an area of high unemployment, the news that the small town had attracted a large multinational company was greeted with jubilation. Chester County Commissioner Joseph J. Kenna said it showed how the county could compete with other regions in enticing major corporations. "The county will get to be a competitor in an area where it's been difficult in the past," he said.[34]

Just how did tiny Oxford, population 3,700, manage to lure Keebler back to Pennsylvania?

With help from Pennsylvania taxpayers.

For starters, the state provided Keebler with a $2 million loan, repayable over fifteen years at 2 percent interest. Yes, 2 percent. The money came from the Pennsylvania Industrial Development Authority (PIDA), an arm of the state Commerce Department, chartered to promote jobs.

Another Commerce Department program lent the company $500,000, also at 2 percent interest, to purchase machinery. Then there were less direct subsidies. The town of Oxford received a $750,000 interest-free loan from yet another state program, to pay for a sewage pumping station, a twelve-inch water line, a rail spur, an access road, and other improvements to serve the Keebler plant.

For the icing on the cake, Oxford received a $750,000 Urban Development Action grant from the U.S. Department of Housing and Urban Development to improve its sewer and water systems so they could accommodate Keebler.

In seeking the federal money, Oxford said that the food-making plant Keebler proposed was crucial to "provide employment opportunities for many of the former mushroom industry employees who recently have been unemployed due to foreign mushroom imports."[35]

All together, United Biscuits, with $4.6 billion in revenue and an operating profit of $298 million in 1992, received $4 million in various state and federal taxpayer-subsidized incentives to locate in Oxford.

Which means that Ernest Dunn and his fellow Keebler co-workers, who lost jobs that paid middle-income wages in 1985, and who have paid income taxes to Pennsylvania while working at low-wage jobs ever since, have subsidized the company that eliminated their jobs so that it could create new, lower-paying jobs for others.

Dunn deeply resents this: "I do not want this state of Pennsylvania to give Keebler a dime of my tax money to open wounds that I have been working for seven years to close."[36]

Pennsylvania had no qualms about doing just that. As the state viewed it, a job was a job, wherever it was created, at whatever wage it paid. On November 11, 1991, Governor Bob Casey pointed with pride to the state's role in bringing the Keebler affiliate and other companies to the state:

"Even in tough economic times, the best companies in America are investing in Pennsylvania. The bottom line is that the climate for economic growth is excellent in Pennsylvania and business knows it because we're willing to roll up our sleeves and make it work. . . . We're putting together the kind of deals that are recession busters, deals that save marginal businesses and attract new ones that generate jobs and added revenues for localities across the state."[37]

At the same time, Pennsylvania claims it has strict guidelines against subsidizing a company that closes a plant in one location, then reopens it somewhere else in the state. "You can't take a facility in Philadelphia, Pennsylvania, and uproot it and move it anywhere else and expect to receive state financing," Andrew Greenberg, state commerce secretary, testified before a Pennsylvania legislative committee in 1992.[38] Then how could the state provide aid to Keebler?

Well, for one thing, state officials said, several years had passed since the Philadelphia plant closed. More important, it was said, the company would be making different kinds of snacks in the new plant than it made in the old. The Oxford plant also would be more advanced technologically than the old facility. Wrote one state official in recommending the loan to Keebler:

"[The] Keebler Company meets the criteria we have established for designation of companies as advanced technology companies. Keebler is a very large company that has a significant research and new product/process development effort in place. . . . This company is one of the technology leaders in the snack food industry, in which new products must always be in development to maintain market share. In addition, the facility under consideration for the Oxford site is intended to be a pilot facility for many of the new products that Keebler hopes to move from research into production." [39]

What kinds of jobs were being created in Keebler's high-tech snack plant in Oxford?

Most of those eventually hired were called "production attendants," which sounded like the "production workers" who operated the line at the old plant in Philadelphia. But there was a difference. Back in 1985, many veteran employees in Philadelphia had been earning, after years of representation by the bakery workers union, from $12 to $14 an hour, a wage that translated into an annual income of roughly $27,000. Most of the new employees at Keebler's "high-tech" Oxford plant started at about $9 an hour, or $19,000 a year.

Even so, Ernest Dunn would love to work at one of the low-paying, "high-tech" jobs. He and other onetime Keebler employees in Philadelphia have applied for work at the Oxford bakery and would gladly relocate if they got the job. But they have not been hired or even interviewed.

Nor for that matter have most who have applied there. In what is increasingly a sign of the times, Emerald Industries was swamped with applications by job seekers. A local employment agency that processed the applications received 1,200 résumés for the first forty-five jobs. When the company began production in the spring of 1993, it had on file job applications from more than 1,000.

In recent years, similar scenes have been played out in scores of cities and towns across America as a growing number of workers compete for a shrinking number of jobs that pay middle-income wages. Just as corporations play off one state against another for tax breaks, so, too, do they play off younger workers against older workers, non-union workers against union workers, the unskilled against the skilled, to further drive down wages—often with the help of tax subsidies from local, state, and federal governments.

Ernest Dunn knows there is little hope he will ever work in

Oxford. What angers him most is that he believes Keebler closed the Philadelphia bakery to lower its wage costs, then tapped Pennsylvania taxpayers for a handout to start up again.

"Some companies do have to close," Dunn said. "They have financial problems. But these people didn't. There was no waste in that plant. When they closed, that plant was making money. Everybody knows they didn't have to close."[40]

Bailing Out a Dealmaker

In still other states, the pressure by corporations for tax subsidies is less subtle, the demand for a handout more direct. In some of these cases, companies are resorting to what can only be described as economic intimidation to extract tax breaks under threat of cutting jobs or pulling out of the state altogether. This even occurs in cases where the company's financial crisis is largely of its own making. We need look no further for an example than the multimillion-dollar subsidy Minnesota taxpayers bestowed on Northwest Airlines.

The bailout of Northwest was an especially difficult pill for many Minnesotans to accept, because the airline had long been one of the state's good corporate citizens. Founded in 1926, Northwest grew into the nation's fourth-largest airline, with 37,000 employees and a route system covering the United States and Asia. In an industry noted for red ink and large debts, Northwest was an exception. In 1988, a year of record earnings, Northwest posted its thirty-ninth straight profitable year. And its long-term debt, $385 million, was remarkably low by industry standards.

Then the trouble started. In 1989, the airline fell victim to the leveraged buyout craze sweeping Wall Street, as takeover artist Marvin Davis sought to buy the carrier. In the end, Davis and others were outbid by another dealmaker, Alfred A. Checchi, who, with a partner, Gary Wilson, acquired Northwest in a $3.65 billion deal.

A graduate of Harvard Business School, the charismatic, forty-one-year-old Checchi had experienced a meteoric rise in the business world. At age thirty, he was treasurer of the Marriott Corporation, where he arranged the sale and leaseback of hotels to pump up the chain's bottom line and thereby win the undying praise of J. W. Marriott, Jr., who described him as "one of the two or three smartest men I've ever dealt with—absolutely brilliant."[41] Checchi went on to become financial adviser to the billionaire Bass brothers of Texas before he was forty, and to accumulate a personal fortune estimated at $50 million when he acquired Northwest.

As with all leveraged buyouts, Checchi financed the Northwest takeover with borrowed money—more than $3 billion. He put together a consortium that included KLM Royal Dutch Airlines and a San Francisco investment group headed by Richard C. Blum, the investment-banker husband of Dianne Feinstein, the Democratic senator from California. Although some industry observers doubted that Northwest could generate the cash to make the interest payments on its huge debt, Checchi dismissed skeptics. He had grand plans. By attracting high-paying business travelers, he said, he would double the airline's $5.6 billion annual revenues within five years.

"This is the beginning of a new era at Northwest," he predicted. "We have a strong foundation to build on. We are determined to make this the most exciting era for everyone connected with the airline."[42]

It was exciting, all right. Northwest began losing money almost from the day the Checchi group took over. In the last quarter of 1989—Checchi's first as chairman—the airline lost $7.1 million. Northwest downplayed the numbers. "We feel very good about our forecast for 1990," said John Dasburg, a former Marriott executive brought in by Checchi as an executive vice president.

Actually, matters got worse. In 1990, Iraq's invasion of Kuwait sent fuel prices soaring for all airlines, and Northwest—a perennially profitable airline under its former management—lost $302 million.

Not to worry. The sudden surge of red ink provided a new opportunity, strengthening Northwest's position on another front: negotiating tax breaks from state and local authorities in Minnesota.

Although Northwest could barely pay its bills in 1991—and was on its way to posting a loss of $316.9 million that year—the airline decided to go forward with a long-discussed plan to build a multimillion-dollar maintenance base for a new fleet of

European-built airbus jets it was buying. Prior to the Checchi takeover, Northwest had hinted that the maintenance facility would be in the Minneapolis–Saint Paul region, the airline's home base, where it employed 17,000 people.

Now Northwest saw a way to extract concessions from Minnesota taxpayers. The first tactic: Scare elected officials. Early in 1991, the airline disclosed that it was reviewing offers from other state and local governments that wanted the maintenance base, which ultimately would employ 1,500 persons. Northwest said it was trying to decide on one of six areas—the Twin Cities; Duluth, also in Minnesota; Detroit; Memphis; Kansas City, Missouri; and Atlanta. Now the rush was on to see who would hand out the most tax breaks and loans.

Soon stories began appearing that Northwest was leaning toward the economically depressed Duluth region, 150 miles north of Minneapolis and Saint Paul. But why would Northwest, whose aircraft already congregated at Minneapolis–Saint Paul International Airport, choose to place the overhaul facility that far away? The answer: politics.

To secure tax breaks and cash incentives from the State of Minnesota, Northwest needed all the political muscle it could get. Minnesota's governor, Arne Carlson, favored Duluth. More important, Duluth just happened to be represented in Congress by James Oberstar, the Democratic chairman of the U.S. House Aviation Subcommittee, which oversees the airline industry.

Minnesota officials scrambled to come up with an offer and push it through the legislature. In May 1991, state lawmakers approved a controversial $740 million package of tax breaks, government-backed loans, and cash for Northwest.

The bill authorized the state to sell $350 million in revenue bonds to build an aircraft maintenance base in Duluth and an engine repair facility in neighboring Hibbing. Northwest would pay off the bonds through lease payments on the hangars. The bill also exempted construction materials purchased in building the bases from the state's sales tax and gave Northwest a $5,000 tax credit for each new employee.

More significantly, but little understood at the time, the bill gave Northwest authority to negotiate a loan from the Metropolitan Airports Commission, which managed Minneapolis–

Saint Paul International Airport, where Northwest was the dominant airline.

In the public's mind, the bill was to build aircraft maintenance hangars in Minnesota's depressed far north. But only $350 million of the $740 million price tag would go for hangars. What was the remaining $390 million slated for and where would it come from? It was to be a low-interest loan to Northwest, the one from the Metropolitan Airports Commission. In short, it was a loan from taxpayers to help Northwest through tough financial times arising from the leveraged buyout.

After the bill was signed, Northwest, its financial fortunes still sagging, pressured Minnesota officials to come through with the loan. Northwest claimed it had to complete negotiations by the fall so the overhaul bases could be built and opened on schedule by April 1993. In fact, the airline's own pressing cash needs were driving the deadline.

When negotiations went slower than Northwest liked, the airline broke off talks and threatened to cancel plans to build the bases in Minnesota. A representative was dispatched to Louisiana to meet with Governor Buddy Roemer about the possibility of converting two existing hangars in Lake Charles, Louisiana, into maintenance bases. Roemer told reporters that a Northwest official had told him the airline was terminating discussions with Minnesota, and that Lake Charles "was the airline's preferred site."[43]

The threat brought all the parties back to the bargaining table in Minnesota, and in November, agreement was reached to provide Northwest with the cash it was seeking. The pact called for the airport authority to convey $270 million in cash from the sale of revenue bonds to the public. In turn, Northwest would sell to the airports commission its flight training center and subsidiary operations at Minneapolis–Saint Paul International, where it had been training pilots and other personnel for years. Northwest would then lease back the facilities.

By any standard, it was a most unusual transaction. Here was an airline that had long owned and operated its own flight training center selling the facility to a government agency for $270 million. Then leasing back the same facility for an annual fee to cover the interest on the bonds. A memorandum from Jeffrey W. Hamiel, executive director of the airports authority, to the airport commissioners, recommending that they approve the arrangement, took note of the special circumstances:

"As you know we recognized from the outset that this financing was not a typical commercial lending request. However, MAC consented to consider the unique request by Northwest because of the significant economic impact that its operations and presence have on the region."[44]

An independent financial appraisal of Northwest prepared for the State Department of Finance said the "proposed transaction appears to be a 'win-win' situation for the state and Northwest Airlines."[45] The otherwise upbeat report warned, however, that the deal was not without risk:

"While Northwest's strategies and business plans call for significant financial improvement, the carrier lacks the 'financial safety net' a strong balance sheet would provide and could be more vulnerable than financially stronger carriers as it must rely on credit lines to weather unexpected events."[46]

That risk was never spelled out clearly to Twin Cities taxpayers. It meant this: If Northwest defaulted on its lease payments, the airports commission would have to make payments on the bonds it sold to investors. And to make the payments, it might have to impose a property tax in the seven-county metropolitan area that constituted the airport district.

While a citizens group formed to protest the loan, the deal was approved. Even state legislators who had qualms about it felt they had no choice but to go along. A special legislative commission gave final approval in December.

With all the pieces of the rescue in place, Minnesota politicians hailed the result, which they said had kept Northwest Airlines with its 17,000 employees there and assured 1,500 well-paying jobs on the way.

"States have to do those things that are necessary for their long-term best interests," said Governor Carlson. "You do it for jobs. You do it because you have a vision of a growth economy for the state."[47]

"This is a vote for new jobs in Minnesota," said Senator Doug Johnson, whose district would benefit if the hangars were built. "This is a vote that guarantees the new jobs are not going to Texas or Georgia or Louisiana."[48]

Representative James Oberstar, whose Minnesota congressional district would also benefit from the new bases, said the transaction "means a new breath of life for a generation of young people in northeastern Minnesota. They now have an opportunity that eluded most of us."[49]

Northwest said a ceremonial groundbreaking would take place before the end of 1991 and construction would start the following spring. But construction never started in 1991 or 1992. By the time the airports commission came through with the cash for Northwest in 1992, the airline was on its way to losing $1.1 billion for the year. When this was added to losses of $316.9 million in 1991 and $302 million in 1990, Northwest had run up total losses of $1.7 billion under Checchi.

Throughout this period, Northwest laid off workers, extracted wage and benefit givebacks from remaining employees, instituted stringent cost-cutting measures, sold assets, and restructured its debt. Checchi also forced out scores of top and midlevel managers who had helped build Northwest, replacing them with associates he had worked with previously, many at Marriott, most of whom had no experience managing an airline. The executive turmoil contributed to the image of a company in a tailspin.

By April 1993, when Northwest said the bases would be in operation, construction still had not started. As 1993 gave way to 1994, not a spade of earth had been turned, and though Northwest continued to say it would build the bases, many Minnesotans were skeptical.

Bob Covington, a computer consultant who was active in a citizens group that tried unsuccessfully to stop the loan, believes there is a message for taxpayers everywhere arising from the Northwest bond deal.

"Don't be stampeded into one of these," he warned. "Northwest was very clever, tying the air bases and the loan together in one package, when the two had no relationship to each other. Nobody knows what the money was used for. They could have used it for anything. There was no accountability."[50]

Let us summarize. A profitable multinational corporation sets off a bidding war among several states to see which will come up with the most generous tax concessions to subsidize construction and operation of a new plant. A profitable multinational corporation closes a plant with higher-paid workers in one city, and the state arranges subsidies to help it open a new plant that will employ lower-paid workers in another city. Corporate-takeover artists, who acquired an airline and transformed it from a moneymaker to a money loser, pit state against state to see which will finally hand over the most tax subsidies.

For taxpayers everywhere, and society as a whole, it is the ultimate lose-lose situation. The new jobs that are created in one state when a company opens a plant, courtesy of tax breaks, are offset by the loss of jobs in another state, where the company closes a plant. One community gains tax revenue. Another loses it. What's more, the new jobs often pay less than the old, and they have fewer benefits. Even the tax breaks offered foreign companies to move to the United States produce illusory benefits. In 1978, Volkswagen, the German car maker, opened a plant in New Stanton, Pennsylvania, just south of Pittsburgh. It was built after the state came up with $70 million in incentives, including tax abatements and money for new infrastructure. Ten years later, in 1988, the plant closed. The 5,000 people who were once employed there were out of work.

No one keeps a running count of the value of all the tax concessions and assorted incentives that local and state governments extend to corporations. But it is easily in the tens of billions of dollars. If you are a typical middle-income or working-poor taxpayer in any of the fifty states, its your tax money that state and local officials are handing out. And they are handing it out in ever larger amounts.

Legalized Inequities

What makes it all possible?

The absence of any higher authority that might put an end to the bidding wars corporations provoke among state and local governments. Congress, partly for constitutional reasons, mostly for political reasons, watches the warfare from the sidelines. That leaves only the judicial system to act as an arbiter. But when it comes to taxes, the federal courts' sense of fairness is little different from Congress's. But then fairness and the law often have little in common. Lest you have any doubt, look no further than California's system for levying real estate taxes.

You may want to dismiss the California real estate tax as just another example of how the state of fads is disconnected from the rest of the country. But you would be making a mistake. Such real estate tax inequities abound in most states. What's more, many states—Arizona, Massachusetts, Michigan, Missouri, New Jersey, Oregon, South Carolina, and Washington, to name a few—have imposed some kind of limitation on overall state tax collections. It is a device that, no matter how well intended, ultimately leads to the kind of injustices produced by California's real estate tax.

Furthermore, it may take years for the effects of such tax and economic changes to work their way through the system. Such was the case with the product of the California tax revolt called Proposition 13, which placed a limit on real estate taxes. In 1979, Howard Jarvis, the leader of the movement, wrote:

"Contrary to what the opposition had predicted during the 13 campaign, the impact of 13 on government services was 'generally minimal,' according to State Finance Director Richard Silberman, one of Brown's closest aides. In February 1979 —eight months after 13 went into effect—Silberman said that the state had not been hurt by 13."[51]

A little more than a decade later, as a result of Proposition 13 and other economic forces, California ran up the largest deficits ever recorded by a state government, essential services were slashed, the quality of life was deteriorating, and residents were fleeing the state as never before. By the time the fallout could be tabulated, Howard Jarvis was dead and Richard Silberman—the state official Jarvis cited as an expert on tax and economic policy—was in prison for money-laundering.

To better understand how the California system works, and the role of the courts in it, let's return to Los Angeles—this time not to Holmby Hills, the richest of the rich enclaves, but to neighboring Bel Air and Beverly Hills, merely very rich, and to Baldwin Hills, a solid middle-income neighborhood. As was the case with the Wick property, the fair market value of these large homes in Bel Air and Beverly Hills is difficult to determine. But again, based on selling prices of other homes in the area, a conservative estimate would seem to be $1 million. Some are probably worth several times that amount. Let's look not only at the houses but at the stories of the people who own them. We'll begin in Bel Air.

Bel Air is situated on the north side of Sunset Boulevard, just opposite Holmby Hills. There, the narrow roads wind up and down and around the hills, past secluded estates guarded by stone walls and private security forces. During the day, the stillness is broken only by the chugging of tour buses filled with camera-laden passengers straining to catch a glimpse of Elizabeth Taylor and Tom Jones coming out of their homes.

This house is not on the tour map. It's one of the homes of William A. and Betty Wilson, who, like the Wicks of nearby Holmby Hills, are old friends of Ronald and Nancy Reagan. A millionaire investor and rancher, William Wilson was another member of the California kitchen cabinet that bankrolled Reagan's rise to the White House, one of three trustees who managed the Reagans' financial affairs, helping the President fulfill what he perceived as the dream of every American: to become rich.

Wilson once described himself and others in the Reagans' circle this way: "I don't read much, none of us do. We like to ride, look at Western art, Andrew Wyeth, that kind of thing. . . . None of us are really politically minded. Most of us just play tennis, ride horseback." [52]

After the 1980 election, Wilson moved into an office next door to the White House to screen presidential appointments. In 1981, Wilson was appointed as the President's personal envoy to the Vatican, and in 1984 he became the first U.S. ambassador there in more than a century.

In May 1986, Wilson resigned as ambassador when it was disclosed that he had met secretly with Libyan leader Mu'ammar Gadhafi. The unauthorized meeting took place after Libyan-backed terrorists attacked passengers at airport ticket counters in Rome and Vienna. Eighteen persons, including five Americans, were killed and 120 were injured. When he stepped down, Wilson, who had served as director of the Pennzoil Company at the same time he served as a U.S. ambassador, denied he had met with Gadhafi to discuss business dealings.

The Wilsons' home is in keeping with Zsa Zsa Gabor's assessment of much of Bel Air—understated. About 6,200 square feet in size, it has four bedrooms and five bathrooms, according to records in the Los Angeles County assessor's office. The value, naturally, is upwards of $1 million.

The 1992 real estate tax bill: $4,326. That's below the real estate taxes paid by many middle-income home owners elsewhere in California and in other states. As a percentage of the house's value, it falls below the tax paid by working-poor home owners in some parts of the country.

Not far from the Wilson home is the Bel Air residence of Earle M. and Marion Jorgensen, two other longtime friends of the Reagans. In Reagan's two campaigns for governor of California, and in his two presidential campaigns, he and Nancy spent each election night at the Jorgensen house, awaiting the returns.

Jorgensen made his fortune in steel and aluminum, in a company that bears his name. Like Wilson and Wick, he was a member of Reagan's kitchen cabinet. When Reagan was midway through his second term in Washington, Jorgensen and about twenty friends chipped in to buy the First Family a retirement home in Bel Air.

The transaction was carried out through a company called Wall Management Services, Inc. Jorgensen was chairman of the board. In August 1986, Wall Management purchased a 7,192-square-foot ranch house in Bel Air for $2.5 million, a price that, in the words of one real estate agent at the time, "makes it practically a fixer-upper." [53] The three-bedroom, six-bathroom house is on a one-acre-plus lot near the homes of Elizabeth Taylor, Burt Bacharach, and Joanne Carson.

Wall Management leased the property to the Reagans for an undisclosed amount and sought an opinion from the Government Ethics Office as to the propriety of turning the house over to the Reagans as a gift. The Ethics Office said it was OK. Los Angeles County records show that it was transferred to the Reagans in June 1993. [54]

In any case, the Jorgensen Bel Air house has 6,067 square feet of living space, four bedrooms, and six bathrooms. Its value: well over $1 million. Its 1992 real estate taxes: $6,666.

A few miles from the Wilson home, in Beverly Hills, is the home of William Belzberg. That's Belzberg as in the Canadian Belzberg brothers—Hyman, Samuel, and William—a family of corporate raiders who made millions through the 1980s, sometimes merely by threatening a takeover, sometimes by carrying through the threat, dismantling the business and eliminating jobs.

They made money the latter way by taking a Connecticut company that had been in business for nearly 200 years, Scovill Inc.—whose subsidiaries included such household names as Yale locks and Hamilton-Beach small appliances—and dismantling and selling off the corporation piece by piece in just four years.

Samuel and Hyman Belzberg both live in Canada, but William long ago established residence in Beverly Hills. The 7,792-square-foot home has six bedrooms and six bathrooms. The 1992 real estate tax bill on the property: $10,167.

Calculated on the basis of the size of the house and its value —let's say $1 million, although the true worth is certainly much higher—the Belzberg real estate taxes worked out to $1.30 a square foot. That's 24 percent less than the $1.70 in real estate taxes paid by Stephanie Nordlinger.

Stephanie Nordlinger?

Some miles distant from the multimillion-dollar mansions of Holmby Hills, Bel Air, and Beverly Hills lies the real world of Baldwin Hills, a middle-class, integrated neighborhood with lots of green lawns and trees. The single-family homes, mostly one story, were built in 1947 by the Baldwin Hills Development Company. Some residents have lived there for more than two decades.

One of the more recent arrivals is Stephanie Nordlinger, a native Los Angeleno whose family roots in the area go back to the 1850s. After receiving a master's degree in economics from the University of California at Berkeley in 1962, Nordlinger joined the U.S. Agency for International Development in Washington, D.C., where she worked four years. Later, after returning to Los Angeles, she earned a law degree from the Loyola University School of Law (Los Angeles), joined the public defender's office, and then went into private practice.

Although she had always rented, Nordlinger said that from time to time she would look at possible houses to buy. When she saw a newspaper advertisement for Baldwin Hills and visited the neighborhood, she immediately liked it. "It's the kind of West Side area that I had grown up in," she said, and the streets are lined with "liquidambar trees, the only trees in Los Angeles that look like the East, with bright reds and yellows." [55]

It was against that background that Nordlinger, "after many years of saving," purchased her first home in November 1988. [56] The 1,114-square-foot house has three bedrooms and one bathroom. With the exception of a storage room added to the garage by previous owners, the size of the house remains unchanged from the day it was built, nearly a half century ago.

Nordlinger paid $170,000 for the house. Her real estate taxes in 1992 totaled $1,896, or $1.70 a square foot. That's more than the $1.30 paid by the Belzbergs. More than the $1.10 paid by the Jorgensens. More than the seventy-six cents paid by the Wicks. More than the seventy cents paid by the Wilsons. Millionaires all. And a millionaire Nordlinger is not.

At $1.70 a square foot, she pays more in real estate taxes than convicted junk bond king Michael R. Milken, who remains a fixture in the *Forbes* magazine directory of 400 richest Americans, with an estimated worth of $400 million. The Milkens live in a seven-bedroom, eight-bathroom, 6,388-square-foot house in Encino that was once part of the Clark Gable and Carole Lombard estate. Their $8,088 tax bill for 1992 works out to $1.27 a square foot.

Nordlinger pays more in real estate taxes per square foot than Peter S. Bing, a millionaire investor, trustee of Stanford University, and member of the *Forbes* 400. The Bing family made its money in real estate and is worth an estimated $600 million. Peter Bing owns a home two blocks from Belzberg in Beverly Hills. The 5,941-square-foot home has seven bedrooms and seven bathrooms. The 1992 real estate taxes totaled $4,743. That works out to eighty cents a square foot, less than half Nordlinger's tax rate.

At $1.70 a square foot, Nordlinger pays more in real estate taxes than Zsa Zsa Gabor, who owns a 6,393-square-foot home with four bedrooms and five bathrooms in Bel Air (Zsa Zsa pays ninety-two cents a square foot). More than Eva Gabor, who owns a 6,414-square-foot house with six bedrooms and four bathrooms in Bel Air (Eva pays seventy-six cents a square foot). More than Charlton Heston, who owns a 5,082-square-foot home with five bedrooms and six bathrooms in Beverly Hills (Heston pays $1.13 a square foot).

She pays more than Metro Galaxy Productions, Inc., the company that owns a Hollywood landmark on Sunset Boulevard—the one-story bar with flashing neon lights that say LIVE NUDE GIRLS GIRLS GIRLS. Galaxy pays $1.63 a square foot.

Lastly, Nordlinger pays much more than the owner of the Beverly Hills Gun Club (twenty-nine cents a square foot).

There are, to be sure, other ways of comparing real estate taxes paid by home owners in different Los Angeles neighborhoods beyond the square-foot measure. The results, though, are largely the same.

How about the bathroom index? In southern California, there seems to be a correlation between economic status and the number of bathrooms in a house.

With only one bathroom, Nordlinger paid $1,896 in real estate taxes in 1992. That was 128 percent more than the $833-per-bathroom tax paid by Larry Gelbart, the Hollywood scriptwriter (the movie *Tootsie* and the television show *M*A*S*H*), who owns a 6,724-square-foot house with six bedrooms and eight bathrooms in Beverly Hills. And she paid 168 percent more in taxes than the $707-per-bathroom tax paid by Franklin O. Booth, Jr., a member of the family that controls the Times Mirror Company (publisher of the *Los Angeles Times* and *Newsday*), who owns an 8,097-square-foot house with seven bedrooms and nine bathrooms in Bel Air.

By now you get the idea.

Stephanie Nordlinger is not faring too well, taxwise.

How is this possible? How can a single woman buying a home in a middle-class neighborhood pay comparatively more in real estate taxes on a three-bedroom, one-bathroom house than the millionaire friends of the former President of the United States and the millionaire corporate takeover artists and businessmen and the millionaire Hollywood types who live in the most exclusive communities in the country?

Simple. Remember the supermarket checkout counter?

Stephanie Nordlinger was the last one in line. As a result, she pays the highest price for her pound of ground beef. In this case, it's not beef. It's a home.

And it's all perfectly legal. Nordlinger found that out the hard way.

The assessment system is a product of California's 1978 tax

revolt and Proposition 13. As so often happens with taxes, the problem was genuine, the solution a disaster. When real estate prices ran wild in California through the 1970s, fueled by inflation and a soaring demand for housing, longtime home owners found their tax bills going up just as fast. At the time, real estate taxes in California, as in most other states, were tied to a property's current market value. With house prices spiraling, so, too, did tax bills. Government officials could have lowered tax rates, but didn't. They could have granted broad-based exemptions, but didn't. Instead, they allowed the money to roll in. And governments, being governments, spent it.

This set the stage for the tax revolt led by Howard Jarvis and Paul Gann. It ended with Proposition 13, which amended the California constitution to state that real estate taxes could not exceed 1 percent of a property's value. More important than the 1 percent figure was the definition of "value." For properties acquired prior to 1975, value was defined as the 1975 assessed value. For properties acquired after that date, value meant the selling price.

Middle-income families who owned their homes at the time, to be sure, benefited the same as wealthier home owners. The real losers were members of the next generation of home buyers, many of whom would be shut out of the market.

This was Stephanie Nordlinger's welcome to the neighborhood.

The previous owners had paid tax based on an assessment of $121,500. Nordlinger would pay based on her purchase price of $170,000. Others in the neighborhood, who had lived in their houses for years, paid on the basis of assessments running generally about $30,000.

Nordlinger thought it wasn't fair. She paid the first installment of her taxes due under protest and filed a request to have the assessment reduced to $30,000. The Los Angeles County Board of Assessment Appeals rejected her request.

Then she sued, pointing to the gross disparities in assessments on surrounding streets. A house one block away, the same size as hers but situated on a larger lot, was assessed at $35,280, based on its 1975 value. The tax bill for that house was $358. Another three-bedroom, one-bathroom house, slightly larger than Nordlinger's and on a bigger lot, was assessed at

$36,107. That tax bill: $361. Nordlinger's tax bill was $1,701. In all, she was paying taxes about "five times higher than the average paid by the owners of . . . eighteen neighboring properties." [57]

The same was true across Los Angeles—indeed, across all of California. The new owner of a home in Venice paid $3,350 in real estate taxes, or thirteen times more than the $260 paid by a longtime resident in an identical house. The former owners of a Malibu house paid taxes based on an assessed value of $170,000, the new owners paid taxes based on the selling price —$2.1 million. A 1989 buyer of a home in Santa Monica paid $4,650 in real estate taxes; his neighbors, who lived in a comparable home, paid $270. The disparity even existed in Watts, where a new arrival paid $800 in real estate taxes while a longtime owner paid $160 on the identical property.

In fact, some residents of crime-plagued Watts were paying taxes at a higher rate than people living in Beverly Hills, where properties "appreciated by as much as 1,600 percent [and] longtime homeowners pay an effective tax rate of only $1/12$th of 1 percent of the present value of their homes. By contrast, longtime owners in Watts pay an effective tax rate more than double the Beverly Hills rate, $1/5$th of 1 percent of their home's value." [58]

California jurists were unpersuaded.

Nordlinger lost in the California Superior Court. She lost in the California Court of Appeal. The California Supreme Court refused even to hear her case. Finally, she went to the U.S. Supreme Court. There, Nordlinger spelled out the results of California's decidedly unequal application of real estate taxes:

"Long-time owners of the most luxurious mansions in the wealthiest neighborhoods have become so advantaged by [Proposition 13] that they now pay lower taxes than recent buyers of humble bungalows in the poorest parts of Los Angeles County." [59]

What's more, she pointed out, studies showed that new home buyers had paid 95 percent of the increased taxes since 1978, meaning that they were subsidizing public services used by long-time residents who paid a fraction as much.

The League of Women Voters of California, which supported Nordlinger's position, submitted a brief saying that while Proposition 13 was enacted in response to what were perceived to be unfair property taxes, "there is nothing fair or equitable in requiring a new property owner to pay 10, 15, 17 and even 583 times more taxes than his or her neighbors solely because the neighbors have owned their property for a longer period of time."[60]

But "fairness" has little to do with the U.S. tax system, whether it is the federal income tax or the California real estate tax. In a brief supporting the California tax structure, Kenneth Hahn, the Los Angeles County assessor, said that "the method of taxation chosen by California need not be the best choice—indeed, it need not even be a wise choice—but our federal system leaves such choices to the political processes of the states," and besides, "all legislation benefits some group at the expense of another."[61]

A friend-of-the-court brief filed by Governor Pete Wilson, members of the state legislature and members of the California congressional delegation also endorsed the existing system, saying that "it is not unconstitutional to tax properties differently that are identical."[62]

The Supreme Court agreed, by an eight-to-one vote. Harry A. Blackmun delivered the court's opinion. While acknowledging that over time the California system had "created dramatic disparities in the taxes paid by persons owning similar pieces of property," the court concluded that it mattered not.[63] The only question to be answered, the justices said, was whether "the difference in treatment between newer and older owners rationally furthers a legitimate state interest."[64]

The court said it did.

What was the "legitimate state interest"?

There were two, the court said. First, higher taxes on newcomers would preserve neighborhoods and encourage stability. Second, if everything came down to whether to compel existing owners to sell their properties because of a high tax burden, or to prevent a younger generation from buying properties because of a high tax burden, the choice was clear:

"The state may decide that it is worse to have owned and lost, than never to have owned at all."[65]

The lone dissenter, Justice John Paul Stevens, delivered a stinging rebuke, labeling the beneficiaries of the California tax system "squires." Stevens took special note of a particular exception to the assessment rules, one that allows parents to transfer a property to their children without any change in the assessed value. This is sort of like allowing you to pay federal income tax on the salary your father or mother earned thirty years ago, instead of the one you earn today. Wrote Stevens:

"Such a law establishes a privilege of a medieval character: Two families with equal needs and equal resources are treated differently solely because of their different heritage."[66]

With its nearly unanimous decision, the Supreme Court gave its approval to the concept of separate and unequal taxation—affirming, albeit indirectly, America's two-tiered tax system.

CHAPTER 9

★ $ ★ $ ★

CAN IT BE FIXED?

In Congress's Best Interest

So what to do?

Is it possible to write a tax law that is free of special-interest provisions?

Is it possible to write a tax law that affords the same benefits to all taxpayers—regardless of income?

Is it possible to write a tax law that can be so clear, logical, and uncomplicated that Form 1040 could be reduced to a single page?

Is it possible to write a tax law that does not place people with widely divergent incomes in the same bracket?

Is it possible to write a tax law that requires businesses to pay a fair share of the nation's taxes, without the disparities in treatment that now give some an unfair advantage over others?

Is it possible to write a tax law that will generate sufficient revenue not only to meet the government's day-to-day obligations but to end the budget deficit—rather than merely reduce its growth rate?

Is it possible to write a tax law that could do this without raising the taxes of the vast majority of American individuals and families, and possibly providing a very modest tax cut for many?

Is it possible to do all these things in one tax law?

The answer, in one word:

Yes.

What is the likelihood that Congress will do it?

Virtually none.

None, that is, unless enough people demand it.

The reason: The existing tax structure works to the best interest of members of Congress, not you.

Before explaining how a simplified tax system could be crafted to achieve the varied goals, it's important to recall the power of special interests, the pervasive influence of the tax industry, and the reluctance of Congress to enact tax legislation that is tied to a person's ability to pay.

To begin with, supporters of every preference in the Internal Revenue Code justify their privilege with variations of one argument: If the tax break is ended, Western civilization as we know it will collapse.

Thus, without a preferential capital gains tax, all investment will come to an end, no new businesses will be created, working Americans will lose their jobs, investment dollars will gush overseas, unemployment will rise, risk taking will be discouraged, and the rich will sit on their money.

Without the transfer-pricing mechanism that allows foreign-owned corporations to pay less U.S. income tax than many small businesses, those companies will either pack up and leave the United States or raise their prices and hurt poor American consumers.

Without the itemized deduction for home mortgage interest and real estate taxes, all home building will come to a halt, millions of Americans will be forced out of their homes, others will be unable to buy homes, and the construction industry will collapse.

Without the preferential tax exemption for U.S. corporations operating in Puerto Rico, all those companies will abandon Puerto Rico, the island's economy will disintegrate, unemployment will soar, welfare payments will spiral.

Without the tax exemption for bonds issued by local and state governments, highway construction will end, homes for the poor will not be built, local and state taxes will roar out of control.

Without a low corporate tax rate, companies will not flourish, they will be unable to hire workers, they will lack the funds to make long-term investments, they won't be able to pay dividends, and no one will buy their stock.

Without the itemized deduction for charitable contributions, the destitute will go unaided, churches will close, the religious fabric of society will unravel, victims of natural disasters will have to fend for themselves, and colleges will shut their doors.

To understand just how nervous lawmakers get when such threats are made—and how skewed are their assessments of what tax-law changes really mean—let's look at two tax provisions. One was enacted despite claims that massive unemployment would follow. The other was repealed because of claims that it had led to unemployment.

First, the tax provision supposedly destined to result in the loss of jobs. During debate on the Tax Reform Act of 1986, several lawmakers tried to eliminate a section of the bill that would limit the amount of the business-expense deduction for meals and entertainment. Under prior law, companies could deduct 100 percent of such costs. The proposed law limited the deduction to 80 percent. If a company spent $5,000 to entertain clients at a banquet, it could deduct only $4,000 on its tax return.

As lawmakers so often do when crusading for or against a tax provision, opponents of this change claimed it would be harmful to lower-income working persons. Listen to the words of two members of Congress who sought—without success—to delete the provision.

Paul Laxalt, then a Republican senator from Nevada: "Statistics that I have seen demonstrate that the proposed limitations will have a devastating impact on establishments and workers in the restaurant, hospitality, and entertainment industries. According to the National Restaurant Association, up to half a million—500,000 people—could lose their jobs. A lot of these people—the waiters and waitresses, the busboys and dishwashers—are people in the income range whom we presumably are trying to protect with a lower tax rate."[1]

Daniel K. Inouye, the Democratic senator from Hawaii: "I also believe that reducing the deductibility for business meals will not only handicap businessmen and women, it will have a devastating effect on restaurants and their employees. The Japanese or German businessman will continue to be able to write off his entertainment expenses; while his American counterpart will have to compete over a fast food counter. And, according to statistics I have seen, if we adopt the provisions under consideration there will be: A $56 billion decline in total business meals outlay over five years; permanent loss of 40,000 jobs. Many of those jobs are held by the least skilled and least employable in our work force."[2]

The business meal and entertainment expense limitation survived the Laxalt-Inouye challenge and took effect in 1987. In the years since, business people have continued to eat, they have continued to entertain. The job losses—whether 40,000 or 500,000—never occurred. And in 1993, the amount of the allowable deduction was further reduced to 50 percent.

Next, let's look at another tax-law change, in which the response from Congress was just the opposite. In the 1993 budget bill, lawmakers repealed the 10 percent luxury tax on boats selling for more than $100,000. It had been enacted just three years earlier. Listen as one lawmaker after another says the attempt to tax the rich only hurt the poor and resulted in job losses.

Bill Archer, Republican representative from Texas: "Perhaps we should remember the so-called luxury tax from the 1990 budget deal. It is repealed in this bill because that misguided class warfare scheme backfired and killed the boat-building industry. Try to sock the rich and you drown working men and women."[3]

Christopher H. Smith, Republican representative from New Jersey: "In one of the only wise actions in the conference report, the misguided luxury tax will be repealed. In New Jersey, we learned how the luxury tax—designed to tax the rich—failed miserably. Instead of raising revenues by hitting the wealthy yacht buyers, the tax destroyed the jobs of the middle-class Americans who build yachts."[4]

Connie Mack, Republican senator from Florida: "Everyone knows today that the luxury tax does not work, that it was not the wealthy who ended up paying more in taxes. Instead, the American working people—the boat manufacturers, the plane manufacturers—lost their jobs. They are the ones who paid the real tax."[5]

William V. Roth, Jr., Republican senator from Delaware: "In the last few years . . . we saw Congress levy higher taxes on risk-taking, investment, and reward. We saw it with the luxury tax, a tax that destroyed thousands of jobs; threw families into economic chaos, and depressed important industries."[6]

Edward M. Kennedy, Democratic senator from Massachusetts: "The tax was enacted in November 1990 by Congress as one of numerous deficit reduction measures. . . . It quickly became clear, however, that the tax was counterproductive. It has been the cause of significant job losses in the boat industry in Massachusetts and many other states, and has only made the recession worse."[7]

Claiborne Pell, Democratic senator from Rhode Island: "This tax has been a disaster for Rhode Island and other states whose economies depend on a healthy boat building industry. This tax has not raised the revenue it intended. All it has accomplished has been what was not intended: it has put hundreds of workers in my state and other boat building states out of work."[8]

There was but one nagging problem with all this hand-wringing over how the luxury tax eliminated middle-income jobs.

It wasn't true.

Hard times had started in the boat-building industry in the late 1980s—before the luxury tax was enacted. Like other businesses, some boat builders were swept up in the takeover craze. Some owners made millions when they sold out. The new owners took on too much debt and eliminated jobs. Companies were scaled back. Some entered bankruptcy court. Profits dropped. And overlying all that was the gradual transformation of a mom-and-pop business into one dominated by several large companies. All this before there was even a hint of a luxury tax.

Some members of Congress who supported repeal of the luxury tax are the same people who advocate a consumption tax to replace or supplement the income tax. That, of course, was precisely what the luxury tax was—a consumption tax. Except it hit the most prosperous consumers, the people with the greatest access to Washington. This would suggest that when lawmakers and policymakers talk about a consumption tax, what they really have in mind is a tax on everyday products that would be targeted at middle-income and lower-income consumers.

Sometimes special interests can successfully pressure Congress to repeal a tax law, as they did with the luxury tax. And sometimes they can block enactment of a tax, not for years, but for decades—even when members of both parties over time have urged its adoption.

So it is with the capital gains tax at death.

Call this the invisible tax break. Invisible, that is, to everyone except the very wealthy. For among all their tax privileges—the ability to invest in tax-exempt bonds, to shift income offshore, to convert personal expenses to business deductions, to inflate the value of charitable deductions—this is one of the most cherished: the right of the very rich to pass along their accumulated wealth in stocks, bonds, and other assets to heirs free of capital gains tax.

This break goes back to the beginning of the income tax, and it has never been seriously threatened. And almost nobody, except the very rich, knows about it. Because only they can make significant use of it.

Most taxpayers who sell stocks or bonds—to pay for a child's education, to care for an elderly parent, or to provide for their own retirement needs—must pay tax on the profits earned from the sale. Say you purchased 1,000 shares of AT&T in 1985 for $19 a share and you sold those shares for $53 in 1993. Your gain would be $34,000. Your tax on that gain, at 28 percent, would be $9,520.

But the very rich have found a way to avoid paying that tax. Here is how they do it.

Pretend you come from a wealthy family and in 1950 your father purchased 1,000 shares of General Electric Corporation stock for $20 a share. His total investment: $20,000. He holds on to those shares throughout his life and wills them to you upon his death in 1993.

Over the forty-three years, the original investment has multiplied in value many times. GE stock split three ways in 1954 and had two-for-one splits in 1971, 1983, and 1987. As a result, the original 1,000 shares has grown to 24,000 shares by 1993. With GE stock trading at $105 a share at the end of 1993, your father's original $20,000 investment now is worth $2,520,000.

That means the stock had a total increase in value of $2,500,000 by the time the shares passed to you. Ordinarily, when stock changes hands, a capital gains tax must be paid. So what was the income tax on that $2.5 million you inherited?

The answer: zero.

Under tax law, shares of stocks, bonds, and other capital assets can be passed along at death and escape all capital gains. If your father had sold the GE stock before his death, he would have paid capital gains taxes of $700,000. But you are getting the stock for free—and no capital gains tax is due.

Better still, when you inherit the stock it gets a new "original" value—the price at which it was selling on the day you received it. Thus, the $2 million in appreciated value is forgiven and forgotten by the tax code.

Now you can turn around and sell the stock—on the same day you get it, if you like—and pocket the entire proceeds without paying any capital gains tax. Or hold on to it, collect the dividends on the 24,000 shares, and pass the stock on to your children.

If this doesn't sound like something that happens often in your family, don't feel left out. Very few American families have this deal.

In large part, this is how the rich stay rich—by passing on from generation to generation assets that have appreciated greatly in value but on which they never pay capital gains taxes.

How much is this costing you?

One estimate by the Treasury Department and Office of Management and Budget put the lost revenue at $24 billion for 1991 alone.[9] If you made less than $50,000 that year and lived in Michigan, Missouri, South Carolina, Virginia, Wisconsin, and Maryland, that was every dollar you paid in income tax.

Perhaps most remarkable, given the amount of revenue lost and the blatant inequality it promotes, is that the exemption from capital gains taxes at death has never seriously been threatened.

During the 1980s, the Treasury Department, the Joint Committee on Taxation, and numerous Washington experts talked of the need to reform the tax code, to close loopholes, and to make more income subject to tax. As a Treasury Department report put it in 1984:

> In order to broaden the base, simplify the tax system, and eliminate special preferences and abuses, the Treasury Department proposals would modify or repeal a number of itemized deductions, exclusions, and special tax credits.

These changes generally involve special preferences which are not used by the majority of individual taxpayers and include various fringe benefits, wage replacement payments, preferred uses of income, business deductions for personal expenses such as entertainment, and other areas of abuse.[10]

Among the Treasury recommendations that later became law were proposals to tax unemployment compensation, repeal the marital deduction for two-income families, revoke tax-deductible Individual Retirement Accounts, and impose higher taxes on the college savings accounts of small children. There were even proposals calling for a modest tax on some tax-exempt bonds, one of the holiest of the sacred cows.

Conspicuously absent from Treasury's attack on "special preferences and abuses" was any suggestion to tax capital gains at death.

Indeed, in the history of the income tax there has been only one serious assault on the exemption, and it was soundly defeated by Congress. In 1963, President John F. Kennedy, as part of a tax overhaul plan, urged Congress to "impose a tax at capital gains rates on all net gains accrued on capital assets at the time of transfer at death or by gift." [11] By doing so, Kennedy said, "the ability to avoid all capital gains taxes on assets held until death will be eliminated." [12]

When the proposal reached Capitol Hill, tax writers on the House Ways and Means Committee, besieged by special interests, killed the provision, and the full House of Representatives never even had a chance to vote on it.

"We deleted some of the most objectionable features of the President's proposals," Representative Howard H. Baker, a Republican congressman from Tennessee, told House members in September 1963. Baker cited Kennedy's capital gains at death proposal as one of the "objectionable" features.[13]

C. Douglas Dillon, Kennedy's Treasury secretary, tried to resurrect the provision during an appearance before the Senate Finance Committee one month later:

. . . gains which are unrealized at the time of death are never subject to income taxes. A man who accumulates an estate from salary or dividends, or business profit, pays income tax on the accumulation during his lifetime and then if the estate is large enough, his estate may be liable for estate tax when he dies. The same is true of a man who builds up a valuable business and sells it before he dies.

However, the individual who holds appreciated assets until death, as well as his heirs, escape all income and capital gains tax applicable to their gains, since the tax cost or basis to the heir is stepped up to the value of the property, the gross estate of the decedent.[14]

Dillon's appeal failed.

The exemption for the capital gains tax at death is typical of the special-interest provisions that are woven through the tax code. Its supporters, namely the rich and those they hire, would no doubt argue that the exemption fosters basic American values by encouraging investment, promoting stable capital markets, and strengthening families. In this they would reflect the prevailing view of all special interests—that the tax system exists to promote the personal objectives of each. That view was summed up in a letter that an official of a Drexel Burnham Lambert subsidiary wrote to an assistant Treasury secretary in 1985 concerning proposed tax-law changes. The letter began this way:

"While no one denies that our tax code needs simplification, it appears that the original reasons for much of the code—fostering capital formation—have been overlooked."[15]

The "original" purpose of the Internal Revenue Code was to foster capital formation?

Hardly.

Indeed, you won't find any mention of capital formation in the debate that led to enactment of the income tax.

Nonetheless, the Drexel Burnham official has lots of company.

Many people believe that the tax code should have some kind of social or economic purpose besides gathering money—namely, the purpose of helping them, their businesses, or institutions.

College and university presidents and art museum directors believe the tax code's purpose is to encourage donations of securities and artworks.

Wealthy investors believe the tax code's purpose is to reward them for buying stock.

Home owners believe the tax code's purpose is to subsidize their purchase of houses.

Officials of state and local governments believe the tax code's purpose is to subsidize their building projects.

Corporate executives believe the tax code's purpose is to bail out their failed business ventures.

A Modest Proposal

These beliefs, and many others like them, have led to the two tax laws. It need not be that way. There are alternatives. Here is one way the tax system could be restructured:

INCOME. Define income to be taxed in the concise terms of the Sixteenth Amendment—"lay and collect taxes on incomes, from whatever source derived." A dollar is a dollar, whether earned in a factory, by speculating in stock options, or by selling real estate. No exceptions. No special treatment for anyone.

ITEMIZED DEDUCTIONS. Eliminate all itemized deductions, from mortgage interest to state and local taxes, from gambling losses to medical expenses. Every exception to tax law, no matter how well intended—remember Mother Drexel—leads to inequities.

TAX RATES. If all the itemized deductions were gone, it would be possible to restore a truly progressive tax structure. The bottom rate, now fixed at 15 percent, could be lowered to 5 percent. The top rate, on the other hand, would be boosted back up to 70 percent—but instead of beginning on taxable income above $250,000, as it does now, it would not kick in until taxable income reached several million dollars. There should be at least a dozen different rates in between, so that people in dissimilar economic situations no longer occupied the same tax bracket. The brackets would be indexed for inflation.

CAPITAL GAINS. Eliminate the preferential rate for capital gains. All capital gains would be taxed as normal income.

EXCEPTIONS. The only exception would be a return to income averaging, so that windfall income in a single year—such as that from the sale of investments held for many years—would not be subject to tax at the highest rate. (This was the original purpose of the capital gains preference.)

CAPITAL GAINS TAX AT DEATH. Impose the income tax on the increase in value of all holdings at death.

TAX-EXEMPT SECURITIES. End the tax exemption for local and state government securities. While the community that issues the tax-exempt bonds may benefit because it pays less interest, the cost to the country at large exceeds the savings. And the damage in terms of fairness is incalculable. To ease the anxieties of state and local governments over the loss of the tax exemption, Congress could grant those governments the authority to tax U.S. Treasury securities.

WITHHOLDING. To help curtail tax avoidance, begin withholding on all income—from Wall Street brokerage accounts to interest on savings accounts to stock dividends. And require withholding on everyone—including foreign investors.

PERSONAL EXEMPTIONS. The only holdover from the current system would be the personal exemption, which would assure that people living below the poverty level are not taxed.

SOCIAL SECURITY. Remove Social Security from the unified budget, return it to a pay-as-you-go system, and lower the tax rate from its current 6.2 percent level. At the same time, impose the tax on all wage and salary income, rather than limiting it to $60,600, the maximum amount subject to tax in 1994. In addition, raise the retirement age and end payments to people whose other income exceeds, say, two to three times median family income, but only after they have gotten back what they have paid in. (Either Social Security will be fixed in an orderly way in the 1990s or more drastic action will be forced shortly after the turn of the century.)

MEANS TESTING. To reduce conflicts and injustices between generations, begin means testing for all government benefits. A Philadelphia physician summed up the issue this way: "I have patients who come to my office in chauffeur-driven limousines. They own three or four homes. And Medicare pays their bills. Does this make sense?"

NEW TAXES. Throughout this century, a wide range of products and services used by low-income and middle-income people have been subject to excise taxes—from the telephone to gasoline. With the exception of a brief period during the Depression, one item has escaped untaxed—Wall Street securities transactions. An excise tax of up to 1 percent should be imposed on the value of all securities and options trading. At the same time, the investment income of retirement plans should be taxed. With $3 trillion—that's trillion—in assets, these plans represent the largest pool of untaxed wealth in the country.

ENFORCEMENT. At present, the federal government makes little or no use of the electronic tools at its disposal for tracking financial transactions in a global economy. Those tools, once devoted to the cold war, should be used to guarantee compliance with the tax laws. That they are not is another reflection of the existence of two tax systems, in which enforcement efforts are more heavily concentrated in the middle-income brackets than at the top.

PENALTIES FOR TAX FRAUD. Junk the current system of criminal penalties for tax crimes. Instead, make the penalty an economic one, to remove the profit motive from tax evasion. Anyone convicted of tax fraud would risk losing most or all of his assets—including homes, cars, and investment holdings.

CORPORATE TAXES. This is perhaps the most complex and difficult to reform. It might be worth scrapping the entire net-income approach and replacing it with a graduated gross-receipts tax. The tax rates should be set to generate revenue equivalent to 25 percent of total income tax collections from individuals and businesses. In the case of multinational corporations, the tax could be calculated on the formula basis once used by California. (One argument against such a tax would be that unprofitable companies would be obliged to pay it. On the other hand, it would force the kind of discipline that business schools and Wall Street analysts like to preach.) Such an approach would also render meaningless the tax-avoidance devices used by corporations, such as transfer pricing.

SPENDING CUTS. Any attempt to tax the country out of its annual deficits would prove futile. Therefore, a new and more just tax code should be accompanied by a reduction in federal spending amounting to at least 10 percent of general fund outlays. That spending is running upwards of $1.1 trillion a year.

What would the results of such a system be?

- A very slight tax cut for many working poor and middle-income people; a substantial tax hike for those at the very top.
- A tax hike for some corporations, especially multinational businesses; a tax cut for others, notably smaller businesses.
- A truly progressive system, in which taxes would be imposed according to a person's ability to pay.
- An end to the two tax laws.
- An end to the federal deficit—not just a reduction in its growth rate—which would lead to lower interest payments and, in time, tax cuts.
- An end to most of the tax industry.
- A truly simplified system in which most tax returns could be completed on a postcard and none would require more than one side of an eight-and-one-half-by-eleven-inch sheet of paper. Almost all schedules would be eliminated.

You will hear a litany of reasons why such a simplified system will never work. Members of the tax industry will tell you so. Members of Congress will tell you so. Special-interest groups will tell you so. Academicians will tell you so. Economists will tell you so.

They have one thing in common: a vested interest in preserving two tax laws—one for the privileged person, whom they represent, and another for the common person, who has no representation.

They will tell you, for example, that an increase in the corporate income tax, no matter how it is levied, will be passed along to consumers.

If this is true, you might ask these questions:

Why do corporations spend so much money lobbying to keep their taxes low, if they merely pass the taxes along to you?

Why do they oppose a higher corporate income tax, which they say is passed along, yet support as its replacement a value-added tax—the equivalent of a national sales tax—which most definitely would be passed along?

Why do they rail against the taxation of dividends at both the corporate and the individual levels, if they really are just passing the corporate taxes along to you?

And why did the system work so well in the 1950s, when the corporate tax rate was 52 percent, compared with 35 percent in 1994?

The tax industry will also tell you that tax rates should not be raised on the affluent because they are already paying a larger share of the income tax than they once did.

As with many of the claims for preserving the status quo, there is a kernel of truth in this one.

In 1971, the top 1 percent of taxpayers accounted for 18 percent of the total income tax paid. By 1991, they accounted for 22 percent—an increase of four percentage points over two decades.

Now, here is what they don't tell you. That increase is due to two factors:

First, more wealth is concentrated at the top, which translates into additional tax revenue. More important, the number of people with large incomes has grown substantially. For 1971, just 883 returns were filed by people reporting income of more than $1 million. By 1991, that number had ballooned to 51,555. Similar increases occurred in the $500,000 to $1 million income group, and in the $200,000 to $500,000 class. As a result, while the top 1 percent collectively accounted for a larger share of taxes paid in 1991 than in 1971, their individual tax bills were much lower.

People with incomes over $1 million paid, on average,

$960,430 in income tax in 1971. In 1991, those people—who included numerous billionaires as well as multimillionaires— paid $628,973. That was a tax cut of 35 percent. And to put the 51,555 million-dollar-plus returns in perspective, they represented just one-twentieth of 1 percent of the 97.5 million tax returns filed by working Americans.

Would there be inequities in a greatly simplified system?

Undoubtedly there would.

But that's not the sole issue. It is this:

The United States can retain its current tax system—riddled with inequities, built on the wasteful expenditure of billions of dollars every year by a nonproductive tax industry, and stacked against the middle-income individual and family.

Or it can institute a new tax system, which, while not perfect, will favor the growth of a broad-based middle class; will eliminate much of the tax industry and thereby, hopefully, divert that spending to more productive purposes; free up members of Congress and other officials to work on the serious problems in U.S. society; end the practice by which members of Congress's tax-writing committees collect millions of dollars in campaign contributions from people and businesses seeking preferential treatment; and, perhaps most important, restore fairness and trust.

The importance of such a system goes beyond the raising of revenue. It goes, in fact, to the question of just what kind of society the United States will have in the next century.

In an economy in which workers are no longer employed by the same company for life, in which all previous commitments between employers and employees have been junked, in which millions of Americans are being forced into lower-paying jobs, in which millions will never recover the losses sustained from a falling standard of living, in which millions will never achieve the American dream of moving up the economic ladder—in such an economy, a tax system that further widens the gap between those at the top and everyone else is a system that will be flouted and will have far-reaching consequences beyond taxes.

Following publication of *America: What Went Wrong?* we spent more than a year traveling across the country, listening to people from all walks of life express their frustrations about what's gone wrong with the United States. They were blue-collar workers and professionals. Men and women. Young and old. Rich, middle class, and poor. White, black, Hispanic, and Asian.

There was a strong sense that the problems, while serious, were not insurmountable and could be corrected. There was an equally strong sentiment that the lawmakers and policymakers in Washington, whether Democrat or Republican, and for whatever reason, lacked the necessary resolve.

More disturbing was a question posed over and over again, in one variation or another, by a cross-section of people, from Cherry Hill, New Jersey, to Portland, Oregon, from Boston to Miami. The question was asked not by radical students but by a grandmother and a professional person and a blue-collar worker and a white man in a three-piece business suit in Philadelphia, who stated it most bluntly:

"Do you really believe these problems can be solved without people taking to the streets?"

Notes on Sources

The tax and government-finance statistics used throughout this book are based on data from the following sources: the Internal Revenue Service's annual Statistics of Income for individuals and corporations and the quarterly *SOI Bulletin;* the Annual Budget of the U.S. Government; the Economic Report of the President; the Federal Reserve Board; and the Advisory Commission on Intergovernmental Relations.

Chapter One: Where Did All the Money Go?

1. *Congressional Record,* Aug. 5, 1993, p. H-6156.
2. Ibid., p. H-6118.
3. *General Explanation of the Tax Reform Act of 1986,* prepared by the staff of the Joint Committee on Taxation, May 4, 1987, p. 6.
4. Interview with authors, May 28, 1993.
5. Ibid.
6. Ibid.
7. Ibid.
8. Ibid.
9. Lexington, Ky., *Herald-Leader,* Sept. 5, 1991.
10. *Wall Street Journal,* Nov. 17, 1977.
11. U.S. Tax Court, Docket No. 7516-92, *Joe L. Allbritton and Barbara B. Allbritton* v. *Commissioner of Internal Revenue.*
12. *Congressional Record,* Feb. 26, 1981, p. H-711.
13. Senate Committee on Finance, *Tax Reduction Proposals,* 97th Cong., 1st sess., May 13, 14, 18, 1981, Part 1 of 3, p. 17.
14. *Congressional Record,* May 19, 1981, p. H-2317.
15. Ibid., July 17, 1981, p. S-7854.
16. U.S. Treasury Department, *Tax Reform for Fairness, Simplicity, and Economic Growth,* vol. 1 (Nov. 1984), p. 75.
17. "The President's Tax Proposals to the Congress for Fairness, Growth, and Simplicity," May 1985, p. 340.
18. *This Week with David Brinkley,* May 11, 1986.
19. *General Explanation of the Tax Reform Act of 1986,* prepared

by the staff of the Joint Committee on Taxation, May 4, 1987, pp. 625–26.

20. *Business Week,* Nov. 25, 1991, p. 5.

21. U.S. Tax Court, Docket Nos. 14574-90, 11144-91, *Wachtell, Lipton, Rosen & Katz* v. *Commissioner of Internal Revenue.*

22. Ibid.

23. Statement by Joseph W. Barr, secretary of the Treasury, before the Joint Economic Committee, Jan. 17, 1969.

24. Ibid.

25. *New York Times,* Jan. 18, 1969, p. 15.

26. *Wall Street Journal,* Jan. 20, 1969.

27. *Time,* April 4, 1969, p. 84.

28. Report of the Senate Committee on Finance, *Tax Reform Act of 1969,* Nov. 21, 1969, p. 1.

29. *Congressional Record,* Aug. 6, 1969, p. 22563.

30. Ibid., Dec. 22, 1969, p. 40896.

31. Ibid., p. 40880.

32. Ibid., p. H-40899.

33. *Public Papers of the Presidents,* Dec. 30, 1969, p. 1044.

34. *Congressional Record,* Sept. 16, 1976, p. 30823.

35. Ibid., p. 30720.

36. *Public Papers of the Presidents,* Oct. 4, 1976, p. 2396.

37. U.S. Congress, Joint Committee on Taxation, *General Explanation of the Tax Reform Act of 1976,* Dec. 29, 1976, p. 105.

38. *Congressional Record,* Sept. 25, 1986, p. H-8387.

39. Ibid., Sept. 27, 1986, p. S-13892.

40. Ibid., Sept. 25, 1986, pp. H-8369–70.

41. Ibid., Sept. 27, 1986, p. S-13869.

42. Ibid., Sept. 25, 1986, p. H-8381.

43. Ibid., Sept. 25, 1986, p. H-8388.

44. Ibid., Sept. 25, 1986, p. H-8388.

45. Ibid., Sept. 27, 1986, p. S-13926.

46. Ibid., Sept. 26, 1986, p. S-13785.

47. CNN, *Larry King Live,* June 16, 1993.

48. Ibid.

49. Reuters Transcript Report, June 9, 1993.

50. U.S. Securities and Exchange Commission, Storage Technology Corporation, 1992 Annual Report.

51. Ibid.

52. Lobby Registration Report, Liz Robbins and Associates, Clerk of the House of Representatives, Office of Records and Registration, Sept. 13, 1992.

53. *Congressional Record,* Sept. 27, 1986, p. S-13922.

54. 41 U.S. Tax Court 419.

55. 29 TCM 1257.

56. U.S. Tax Court, Docket No. 22619-80, *B. Gerald Cantor and Leona Palmer* v. *Commissioner of Internal Revenue.*

Chapter Two: The Tax War You Lost

1. House Committee on Ways and Means, *General Revenue Revision,* 85th Cong., 2d sess., 1958, p. 1990.

2. *Congressional Quarterly Almanac,* 1981, p. 11-E.

3. *Congressional Record,* Jan. 30, 1894, pp. 466–67.

4. 158 *U.S. Reports* 601.

5. *The Annals,* American Academy of Political and Social Science, vol. XLVIII (July 1913), pp. 56–7.

6. House Committee on Ways and Means, *Report No. 5,* to accompany H.R. 3321, April 21, 1913, p. xxxvii.

7. Harry M. Daugherty, *The Inside Story of the Harding Tragedy* (New York: The Churchill Company, 1932), p. 74.

8. Andrew W. Mellon, *Taxation: The People's Business* (New York: Macmillan, 1924), p. 83.

9. Ibid., p. 16.

10. Jack Kemp, *An American Renaissance* (New York: Harper & Row, 1979), p. 53.

11. Mellon, *Taxation,* p. 13.

12. *Congressional Record,* June 18, 1986, p. S-7778.

13. Mellon, *Taxation,* p. 18.

14. House Committee on Ways and Means, *General Revenue Revision,* 1958, p. 1983.

15. *Annual Report of the Secretary of the Treasury,* 1924, p. 4.

16. Speech before Orange County (Calif.) Press Club, July 28, 1961, *Vital Speeches of the Day,* Sept. 1, 1961, p. 677.

17. *Annual Report of the Secretary of the Treasury,* 1924, p. 4.

18. Ibid., 1925, p. 350.

19. Letter from Albert H. Wiggin to Andrew W. Mellon, May 8, 1924, *National Archives,* Record Group 56, Box 208.

20. Letter from Andrew Mellon to Sigmond Palmer, Oct. 8, 1924, *National Archives,* Record Group 56, Box 208.

21. *New York Times,* Feb. 27, 1926, p. 1.

22. *Congressional Record,* May 27, 1993, p. H-2946.

23. Ibid., p. H-2943.

24. Ibid., Aug. 5, 1993, p. H-6142.

25. Ibid., p. H-6103.

26. *Atlantic Monthly,* August 1952, p. 76.

27. *Congressional Record,* Aug. 15, 1951, p. 10070.

28. House Committee on Ways and Means, *President's 1961 Tax Recommendations,* 87th Cong., 1st sess., 1961, p. 4.

29. Roper Organization, Inc., *The American Public and the Federal Income Tax System,* vol. I (June 1986), p. 32.

30. *Congressional Record,* Feb. 16, 1934, p. 2662.

31. Ibid., Aug. 16, 1937, p. 9019.

32. Ibid., July 28, 1954. p. 12426.

33. Ibid., Aug. 6, 1969, p. 22577.

34. Ibid., Sept. 16, 1976, p. 30823.

35. Ibid., Sept. 27, 1986, p. S-13931.

36. Ibid., Aug. 5, 1993, p. H-6231.

37. *New York Times,* June 8, 1937, p. 1.

38. *Philadelphia Inquirer,* Feb. 5, 1936.

39. *Congressional Record,* Feb. 16, 1934, p. 2662.

40. Joint Committee on Tax Evasion and Avoidance, 75th Cong., 1st sess., June 29, 1937, p. 227.

41. Ibid., June 17, 1937, p. 12.

42. U.S. Tax Court, Docket No. 4163-81, *Ben W. Heineman and Natalie G. Heineman* v. *Commissioner of Internal Revenue.*

43. Ibid.

44. Ibid.

45. Ibid.

46. Ibid.

47. U.S. Tax Court, Docket No. 11747-92, *Earl O. Bergersen and Evelyn K. Bergersen* v. *Commissioner of Internal Revenue.*

48. Ibid.

49. Ibid.

50. Ibid.

51. Ibid.

52. Ibid.

53. Ibid.

54. *Congressional Record,* Dec. 22, 1969, p. H-40866.

55. Ibid., p. H-40886.

56. Ibid., p. H-40880.

57. *Congressional Record,* 1969, p. 22577.

58. *Public Papers of the Presidents,* Dec. 30, 1969, p. 1044.

59. *Congressional Record,* Sept. 26, 1986, p. S-13816.

60. Ibid., Sept. 27, 1986, p. S-13868.

61. Ibid., Sept. 25, 1986, p. H-8392.

62. Ibid., p. H-8434.

63. Ibid., p. H-8425.

64. Ibid., Sept. 27, 1986, p S-13962.

65. *Congressional Record,* Sept. 25, 1986, p. H-8404.

66. Ibid., Sept. 27, 1986, p. S-13894.
67. Ibid., p. S-13917.
68. Ibid., p. S-13936.
69. Ibid., Sept. 26, 1986, p. S-13805.
70. Ibid., Sept. 25, 1986, p. H-8377.
71. Ibid., Sept. 27, 1986, p. S-13875.
72. Ibid., p. S-13935.
73. Ibid., Sept. 25, 1986, p. S-8382.
74. Ibid., p. H-8366.
75. Ibid., Sept. 27, 1986, p. S-13880.
76. Ibid., Sept. 25, 1986, P. H-8389.
77. Ibid., p. H-8412.
78. Ibid., Sept. 27, 1986, p. S-13901.
79. Ibid., Sept. 25, 1986, p. H-8357.
80. Ibid., p. H-8370.
81. Ibid., p. H-8406.
82. Ibid., Sept. 26, 1986, p. S-13804.
83. Ibid., Sept. 27, 1986, p. S-13962.
84. Ibid., Sept. 25, 1986, p. H-8397.
85. Ibid., p. H-8440.
86. Ibid., pp. H-8440–41.
87. *Public Papers of the Presidents,* Oct. 22, 1986.
88. *Congressional Record,* Sept. 25, 1986, p. H-8389.
89. Akio Morita and Shintaro Ishihara, *The Japan That Can Say "No": The New U.S.–Japan Relations Card* (Kobunsha Kappa-Holmes).
90. *Congressional Record,* Aug. 5, 1993, p. S-10531.
91. Ibid., Aug. 6, 1993, p. S-10704.
92. Ibid., June 30, 1993, p. S-9438.
93. Ibid., p. S-9102.
94. Ibid., Aug. 5, 1993, p. H-6148.
95. Ibid., July 28, 1993, p. H-5365.
96. Ibid., Aug. 4, 1993, p. E-1976.
97. *Wall Street Journal,* June 1, 1993.
98. CNN, *Inside Business,* June 27, 1993.
99. CNN, *The Capital Gang,* June 26, 1993.

Chapter Three: Why You Pay More

1. Federal Reserve Board, Prepared testimony of Alan Greenspan before the Committee on the Budget, House of Representatives, Feb. 28, 1990.
2. *The Conference on Inflation: Health, Education, Income Security and Social Services,* Sept. 19–20, 1974, Washington, D.C., pp. 804–5.

3. Social Security Administration, "Old-Age and Survivors Insurance for Workers and Their Families" (pamphlet), January 1940.

4. *Public Papers of the Presidents,* Jan. 29, 1968, p. 83; *Congressional Quarterly Almanac,* 1967, p. 323.

5. *Congressional Record,* Jan. 29, 1968, p. 1250.

6. Ibid., Jan. 31, 1968, p. 1689.

7. *Public Papers of the Presidents,* Jan. 15, 1969, p. 1273.

8. Ibid., May 8, 1977, p. 836.

9. *Congressional Record,* Oct. 26, 1977, p. 35239.

10. Ibid., Dec. 15, 1977, p. 39148.

11. *Public Papers of the Presidents,* Dec. 20, 1977, p. 2153.

12. *Congressional Record,* March 24, 1983, p. H-1780.

13. *Public Papers of the Presidents,* April 20, 1983, p. 560.

14. *Congressional Record,* Feb. 20, 1934, pp. 2913–14.

15. Ibid., Dec. 22, 1969, p. 40892.

16. Speech to Women's National Democratic Club, Oct. 9, 1986.

17. *Congressional Record,* Aug. 6, 1993, p. S-10709.

18. *Public Papers of the Presidents,* Aug. 14, 1935, p. 324.

19. "Tax Proposals: Message from the President of the United States," Jan. 23, 1978, House Document No. 95-283, p. 13.

20. *New York Times,* Nov. 28, 1982, p. 29.

21. Ibid., Nov. 26, 1982, p. 24.

22. Ibid., Nov. 28, 1982, p. 29.

23. U.S. Treasury Department, *Tax Reform for Fairness, Simplicity, and Economic Growth, Report to the President,* vol. 2 (Nov. 1984), p. 52.

24. *Tax Reform Act of 1985,* Report of the House Ways and Means Committee on H.R. 3838, Dec. 7, 1985, p. 98.

25. Interview with authors, Aug. 9, 1993.

26. Ibid.

27. Ibid.

28. Ibid.

29. Ibid.

30. Ibid.

31. Ibid.

32. Ibid.

33. Ibid.

34. Ibid.

35. *Congressional Record,* Sept. 7, 1917, p. 6728.

36. *Washington Post,* Aug. 25, 1917.

37. *Boston Transcript,* June 29, 1917.

38. *New York Times,* Aug. 24, 1917.

39. Katherine Burton, *The Golden Door* (New York: Kenedy, 1957), p. 51.

40. *Congressional Record,* 1944, p. A-2012.

41. Ibid., 1943, p. A-4964.

42. John Ensor Harr and Peter J. Johnson, *The Rockefeller Conscience: An American Family in Public and Private* (New York: Scribner, 1991), p. 215.

43. House Committee on Ways and Means, *Tax Reform, 1969,* 91st Cong., 1st sess., Part 4 of 15, Feb. 26 and 27, 1969, p. 1564.

44. Ibid.

45. Ibid., p. 1567.

46. Ibid.

47. *Congressional Record,* May 19, 1978, p. 14590.

48. Ibid.

49. Ibid., p. 14591.

50. Ibid.

51. Senate Committee on Finance, *Revenue Act of 1978,* 95th Cong. 2d sess., Part 5 of 6, Aug. 25 and Sept. 6, 1978, p. 1130.

52. Ibid., p. 1116.

53. *Tax Notes,* Aug. 3, 1981, p. 297.

54. "The President's Tax Proposals to the Congress for Fairness, Growth, and Simplicity," May 1985.

55. Ibid., p. 70.

56. Ibid., p. 71.

Chapter Four: Why Corporations Pay Less

1. *Financial World,* June 22, 1993, p. 22.

2. *Congressional Record,* Aug. 6, 1993, p. S-10712.

3. Ibid., Aug. 5, 1993, p. H-6149.

4. Securities and Exchange Commission, Amendment No. 1 to Royal Caribbean Cruise Lines Registration Statement, filed March 30, 1993.

5. Ibid.

6. Ibid.

7. Royal Caribbean brochure, Bermuda, 1993.

8. U.S. District Court, Miami, Case No. 92-CV-2767, *Sergio Joaquim* v. *Royal Caribbean Cruises Ltd.*

9. Royal Caribbean Registration Statement.

10. Ibid.

11. *Congressional Record,* Sept. 27, 1986, p. S-13876.

12. Ibid., Sept. 26, 1986, pp. 13785–86.

13. Ibid., Sept. 27, 1986, p. S-13922.

14. Ibid., p. S-13901.

15. Ibid., p. S-13918.

16. Ibid., p. S-13921.

17. Ibid., p. S-13880.

18. Ibid., Sept. 25, 1986, p. H-8398.

19. Ibid., p. H-8434.

20. Securities and Exchange Commission, prospectus, Darling-Delaware Company, Inc., March 16, 1989.

21. Ibid.; Connie Bruck, *The Predators' Ball* (New York: The American Lawyer–Simon & Schuster, 1988), p. 84.

22. Prospectus, Darling-Delaware, March 16, 1989.

23. Ibid.

24. Ibid.

25. Ibid.

26. *Forbes,* Aug. 1, 1983, p. 76.

27. *Chicago Tribune,* Aug. 27, 1985.

28. *Forbes,* Oct. 7, 1985, p. 100.

29. Hearings before the House Ways and Means Committee, June 9, 1986, p. 11.

30. Ibid., June 30, 1987, p. 27.

31. House of Representatives, *Report of the Committee on the Budget on H.R. 3545, the Omnibus Budget Reconciliation Act of 1987,* p. 1066.

32. Securities and Exchange Commission, prospectus, Plum Creek Timber Company, L.P., June 1, 1989.

33. Ibid.

34. *Wall Street Journal,* June 18, 1990.

35. Paul F. Ehinger & Associates, *Forest Products Industry Report on Mill Closures, Operations and Other Related Information,* May 1993, Eugene, Ore., pp. 3–5.

36. Office of U.S. Trade Representative, Fact Sheets on (1) Super 301 and (2) Special 301, May 25, 1989.

37. Prospectus, Plum Creek Timber Company, L.P., June 1, 1989.

38. Securities and Exchange Commission, Plum Creek Timber Company, L.P., 1992 Annual Report.

39. Louis Eisenstein, *The Ideologies of Taxation* (Ronald Press, 1961), p. 123.

40. *Financial World,* Sept. 14, 1993, p. 14.

41. Ibid.

42. *Congressional Record,* Sept. 26, 1986, p. E-3299.

43. Ibid., p. S-13837.

44. Ibid., Sept. 25, 1986, p. H-8396.

45. Ibid., p. H-8440.

46. *Wall Street Journal,* Aug. 18, 1986.

47. *Business Week,* Aug. 25, 1986, p. 24.

48. *Congressional Record,* Aug. 5, 1993, p. H-6266.

49. Ibid., p. H-6135.

50. Ibid., p. H-6127.

51. Ibid., p. H-6150.

52. Assorted literature distributed at Beverly Hills Gun Club, authors' files.

53. *Time,* July 3, 1944.

54. 42, U.S. Board of Tax Appeals, p. 1266.

55. Ibid.

56. *Los Angeles Daily News,* April 11, 1993.

57. Los Angeles County Recorder's Office, Document No. 83-1228508, First Amendment to Agreement and Certificate of Limited Partnership of High Caliber Enterprises Ltd.

58. Ibid., Document No. 84-1448370, Third Amendment to Agreement and Certificate of Limited Partnership of High Caliber Enterprises Ltd.

59. U.S. Tax Court, Docket No. 17340-82, *Arthur M. Kassel v. Commissioner of Internal Revenue.*

60. Securities and Exchange Commission, Beverly Hills Gun Club, Inc., registration statement, May 27, 1993.

61. *Miami Herald,* Dec. 2, 1990.

62. Beverly Hills Gun Club, registration statement.

63. Ibid.

64. Permanent Senate Subcommittee on Investigations of the Committee on Governmental Affairs, *Crime and Secrecy: The Use of Offshore Banks and Companies,* March 15, 1983, p. 155.

65. *Congressional Record,* Sept. 25, 1986, p. H-8403.

Chapter Five: Foreign Tax Breaks

1. Securities and Exchange Commission, prospectus, Texaco Capital LLC, Oct. 21, 1993.

2. Securities and Exchange Commission, Form 10-K, Warnaco Group, Inc., Year Ending Jan. 2, 1993.

3. Ibid.

4. *Financial World,* Jan. 21, 1992, p. 72.

5. Subcommittee on Multinational Corporations, Senate Committee on Foreign Relations, Part 7, 93rd Cong., 2d sess., Feb. 20, 1974, p. 81.

6. *Time,* Jan. 15, 1951, p. 69.

7. Commerce and Monetary Affairs Subcommittee, House Committee on Government Operations, 95th Cong., 1st sess., Sept. 26, 1977, p. 482.

8. *New York Times,* Jan. 3, 1951, p. 1.

9. U.S. Tax Court, Docket Nos. 18618-89, 24855-89, 18432-90, *Exxon Corporation and Affiliated Companies v. Commissioner of Internal Revenue,* Respondent's Trial Memorandum, Feb. 21, 1991.

10. Subcommittee on Oversight, House Committee on Ways and

Means, *Department of the Treasury's Report on Issues Related to the Compliance with U.S. Tax Laws by Foreign Firms Operating in the United States,* 102d Cong., 2d sess., April 9, 1992, p. 9.

11. Ibid., p. 9.

12. Ibid., p. 22.

13. Ibid., pp. 52–53.

14. *CBS This Morning,* Jan. 5, 1993.

15. *Tax Notes,* June 28, 1993, p. 1841.

16. *National Journal,* Aug. 7, 1993, p. 1973.

17. U.S. Treasury Department, FOIA correspondence file.

18. Ibid.

19. Ibid.

20. Ibid.

21. Ibid.

22. U.S. Tax Court, Docket No. 3273-86, *Saul Zaentz and Lynda Zaenta* v. *Commissioner of Internal Revenue.*

23. Los Angeles County Superior Court, Case No. C-747745, *The Saul Zaentz Company* v. *MGM/UA Entertainment Co. et al.*

24. Ibid.

25. U.S. Tax Court, Docket No. 3273-86.

26. U.S. Tax Court, Docket No. 16867-90, *Estate of A. N. Pritzker* v. *Commissioner of Internal Revenue.*

27. *The Washington Lawyer,* Sept.–Oct. 1993, p. 59.

28. Letter from Representative John J. Duncan and Don Rostenkowski to authors, May 17, 1988.

29. Letter from Representative Richard A. Gephardt to authors, May 18, 1988.

30. Securities and Exchange Commission, Brown Group, Inc., 1985 Annual Report.

31. Permanent Senate Subcommittee on Investigations, 98th Cong., 1st sess., March 15, 1983, p. 44.

32. *New York Times Magazine,* March 29, 1992, p. 46.

33. Ibid.

34. U.S. Tax Court, Docket No. 104-92, *Brown Group, Inc.* v. *Commissioner of Internal Revenue.*

35. Ibid.

36. Interview with authors, Aug. 9, 1993.

37. Ibid.

38. Ibid.

39. Ibid.

40. Ibid.

41. *St. Louis Post-Dispatch,* Jan. 9, 1992.

42. Interview with authors, Aug. 9, 1993.

43. Ibid.
44. Ibid.
45. Ibid.
46. Ibid.

Chapter Six: The Revolving Door

1. Internal Revenue Code, Sec. 168(i).
2. U.S. Congress, Clerk of the House, Financial Disclosure Reports.
3. *The Blood Horse,* May 13, 1989, p. 2637.
4. Summary of H.R. 4242, Economic Recovery Tax Act of 1981, Joint Committee on Taxation, Aug. 5, 1981, p. 14.
5. *Business Week,* May 10, 1982, p. 147.
6. Ibid., Jan. 18, 1982, p. 98.
7. "A Breed Apart," booklet published by 440 Ranches, p. 3.
8. Ibid.
9. *Wall Street Journal,* March 1, 1982.
10. Interview with authors, Aug. 3, 1982.
11. Ibid.
12. Ibid.
13. Lobby Registration Report, Davis & Harman, Clerk of the House of Representatives, Office of Records and Registration, Jan. 15, 1993.
14. Ibid., April 12, 1993, April 13, 1993, July 9, 1993, July 12, 1993.
15. Internal Revenue Code, Sec. 168(i).
16. *Martindale-Hubbell Law Director* (District of Columbia, 1993), p. DC605B.
17. Common Cause press release, April 24, 1990.
18. Lobby Registration Report, Dewey, Ballantine, Bushby, Palmer & Wood, Clerk of the House of Representatives, Office of Records and Registration, July 28, 1993.
19. Ibid.
20. Ibid.
21. Ibid., Skadden, Arps, Slate, Meagher & Flom, July 6, 1993.
22. Ibid., Wunder, Diefenderfer, Cannon & Thelen, April 5, 1993.
23. Ibid., Price Waterhouse, May 14, 1993.
24. Ibid., Covington & Burling, July 9, 1993.
25. Ibid., Miller & Chevalier, Jan. 9, 1990.
26. Ibid., Dewey, Ballantine, Bushby, Palmer & Wood, April 8, 1988.
27. Ibid., Wilmer, Cutler & Pickering, July 20, 1993.
28. Ibid., Wunder, Diefenderfer, Cannon & Thelen, April 5, 1993.
29. Ibid., Vinson & Elkins, April 9, 1993.

30. Ibid., Chadbourne & Parke, April 23, 1986.

31. Ibid., Dewey, Ballantine, Bushby, Palmer & Wood, July 29, 1993.

32. Ibid., McClure, Trotter & Mentz, March 23, 1993.

33. Ibid., Baker & Hostetler, July 9, 1993.

34. Ibid., Mayer, Brown & Platt, July 7, 1993.

35. Ibid., Steptoe & Johnson, June 25, 1993.

36. Ibid., Akin, Gump, Strauss, Hauer & Feld, July 9, 1993.

37. U.S. Treasury Department, FOIA correspondence file.

38. *Congressional Record*, Feb. 22, 1924, p. 2951.

39. Stanley S. Surrey, "The Congress and the Tax Lobbyist—How Special Tax Provisions Get Enacted," *Harvard Law Review*, May 1957, p. 1147.

40. Hearings before the Senate Committee on Appropriations, Feb. 2, 1972, p. 177.

41. *Washington Post*, Aug. 22, 1982.

42. Hearings before the Subcommittee on Taxation and Debt Management, Senate Finance Committee, 96th Cong., 1st Sess., p. 98.

43. *Washington Post*, Jan. 19, 1987.

44. Interview with authors, March 1, 1991.

45. U.S. Treasury Department, *The Operation and Effect of the Possessions Corporation System of Taxation, Fourth Report*, February 1983, p. 23.

46. *Congressional Record*, July 21, 1982, p. S-8802.

47. "The President's Tax Proposals to the Congress for Fairness, Growth, and Simplicity," May 1985.

48. Ibid., p. 308.

49. U.S. Treasury Department, FOIA correspondence file.

50. *New York Times*, Aug. 25, 1985, p. 35.

51. U.S. Treasury Department, FOIA correspondence file.

52. Ibid.

53. Ibid.

54. House of Representatives, Annual Disclosure Reports.

55. Letter from Robert W. Van Kirk of the Amigos de Charlie Committee to Angel J. Seda Comas, Feb. 14, 1989, authors' files.

56. *Congressional Quarterly Weekly*, Feb. 20, 1993, p. 404.

57. Lobby Registration Report, Powell, Goldstein, Frazer & Murphy, Clerk of the House of Representatives, Office of Records and Registration, June 24, 1993.

58. U.S. Treasury Department, FOIA correspondence file.

59. *Financial World*, June 22, 1993, p. 35.

60. Ibid.

61. *San Juan Star*, July 24, 1993, p. 1.

62. News release, May 28, 1992.

Chapter Seven: America's Most Unproductive Industry

1. *Annual Report of the Secretary of the Treasury,* 1921, p. 25.
2. *Congressional Record,* Feb. 1, 1934, p. S-1777.
3. Ibid., Sept. 16, 1976, p. 30807.
4. Ibid., p. 30718.
5. Ibid., p. 30721.
6. Ibid., p. 30811.
7. Ibid., May 16, 1977, pp. 14802-03.
8. Ibid., p. 14866.
9. Senate Finance Committee, *Report No. 95-66,* to accompany H.R. 3477, March 28, 1977, p. 3.
10. *Public Papers of the Presidents,* 1977, p. 962.
11. *Congressional Record,* Sept. 25, 1986, p. H-8367.
12. Ibid., p. H-8370.
13. Ibid., p. H-8429.
14. Ibid., p. H-8433.
15. Ibid., p. E-3299.
16. Ibid., Sept. 27, 1986, p. S-13869.
17. Ibid., p. S-13936.
18. Ibid., Dec. 22, 1969, p. H-40880.
19. Ibid., p. 40866.
20. *Public Papers of the Presidents,* 1969, p. 1044.
21. *Congressional Record,* Sept. 16, 1976, p. 30808.
22. Ibid., May 16, 1977, p. 14803.
23. Ibid., Sept. 27, 1986, p. S-13876.
24. Ibid., Sept. 26, 1986, p. S-13817.
25. Ibid., Sept. 25, 1986, p. H-8372.
26. Ibid., p. H-8412.
27. Ibid., p. H-8430.
28. Ibid., Sept. 26, 1986, p. S-13822.
29. Ibid., Sept. 27, 1986, p. S-13869.
30. Ibid., p. S-13886.
31. U.S. Tax Court, Docket No. 24251-92, *Monex Corporation* v. *Commissioner of Internal Revenue.*
32. Ibid.
33. U.S. District Court, Los Angeles, Case No. 92-CV-5759, *Federal Trade Commission* v. *Unimet Credit Corporation et al.*
34. U.S. Tax Court, Docket No. 24251-92, *Monex Corporation* v. *Commissioner of Internal Revenue.*
35. Ibid.
36. *Congressional Record,* May 8, 1924, p. 8109.
37. House Subcommittee on Appropriations for the Treasury, Postal Service and General Government, March 4, 1983, p. 32.

38. U.S. Bureau of Tax Appeals, *Reports,* vol. 2, p. 1116.

39. U.S. Tax Court, Docket No. 27550-92, *Charles F. Dolan and Helen A. Dolan* v. *Commissioner of Internal Revenue.*

40. Ibid.

41. U.S. Tax Court, Docket No. 6112-92, *J. E. Seagram Corporation* v. *Commissioner of Internal Revenue.*

42. U.S. Congress, Conference Report, *Tax Reform Act of 1986,* H.R. 3838, vol. 1, p. I-303.

43. *Congressional Record,* Dec. 22, 1969, p. H-40897.

44. Ibid., Sept. 25, 1986, p. H-8375.

45. Ibid., p. H-8398.

46. Ibid., Sept. 24, 1986, p. H-8334.

47. Ibid., Aug. 5, 1993, p. H-6111.

48. *Money,* March 1992, p. 88.

49. Ibid., March 1993, p. 98.

50. *Kansas City Star,* April 1, 1979.

51. Securities and Exchange Commission, H & R Block, 1988 Annual Report.

52. *Tax Lawyer,* vol. 36, no. 1, p. 9.

53. U.S. Internal Revenue Service, Office of Chief Counsel, Regulations Projects Status and Disposition Reports, 1992 and 1993.

54. *Federal Register,* Jan. 24, 1985, p. 3319.

55. *Congressional Record,* April 1, 1982, p. 6345.

56. Ibid., Sept. 30, 1982, p. 26444.

57. U.S. Treasury Department, FOIA correspondence file.

58. Ibid.

59. Conference Report of the House Committee on the Budget, *Omnibus Budget Reconciliation Act of 1993,* to accompany H.R. 2264, Aug. 4, 1993, p. 214.

60. U.S. Internal Revenue Service, Advance Notice of Proposed Rulemaking, 58 Fed. Reg. 45,081, Aug. 26, 1993 (Dyeing Diesel Fuel), letter, Retrofit Specialties, Oct. 1, 1993.

61. Ibid., Schaeffer's Specialized Lubricants, Sept. 22, 1993.

62. Ibid., Independent Liquid Terminals Association, Sept. 27, 1993.

63. Ibid., Sterling Oil & Gas Co., Sept. 25, 1993.

64. Ibid., Virginia Petroleum Jobbers Association, Sept. 27, 1993.

65. Ibid., Lawrence J. Love, acting assistant secretary for children and families, Department of Health and Human Services, Sept. 28, 1993.

66. Ibid., Arctic Slope Regional Corp., Sept. 27, 1993.

67. *Report of the House Committee on Ways and Means,* 99th Cong., 1st sess., p. 911.

68. *Tax Notes,* Nov. 2, 1981, p. 1028.

69. Ibid., Oct. 24, 1983, p. 347.

70. Ibid., May 23, 1988, p. 924.

71. U.S. Tax Court, Docket No. 4397-90, *Morris Krumhorn and Adrian Krumhorn* v. *Commissioner of Internal Revenue*.

72. Ibid., pp. 48, 60.

73. *Bulletin of the National Tax Association*, vol. 28 (1942–43), p. 205.

Chapter Eight: The Unfairest Taxes of All

1. *The Guinness Book of World Records* (Enfield, Eng.: Guinness Publishing, 1993), p. 170.

2. *Los Angeles Times*, April 16, 1993.

3. Dr. Irene Kassorla, *Nice Girls Do—And Now You Can Too!* (Los Angeles: Stratford Press, 1980), p. 4.

4. *Los Angeles Times*, Oct. 7, 1990.

5. Gil Reavill, *Los Angeles* (Oakland, Calif.: Compass American Guides, 1992), p. 144.

6. Walter Wagner, *Beverly Hills: Inside the Golden Ghetto* (New York: Grosset & Dunlap, 1976), p. 172.

7. *New York Times*, Aug. 16, 1981, p. 1.

8. *Washington Post*, July 13, 1983.

9. Interview with authors, Nov. 27, 1993.

10. Ibid.

11. Ibid.

12. Ibid.

13. Ibid.

14. Ibid.

15. Ibid., July 1, 1993.

16. Price Waterhouse, *Impact of Unfunded Federal Mandates on U.S. Cities*, Oct. 26, 1993.

17. Price Waterhouse, *The Burden of Unfunded Mandates: A Survey of the Impact of Unfunded Mandates on America's Counties*, Oct. 26, 1993.

18. Interview with authors, June 3, 1993.

19. Ibid.

20. Columbia, S.C., *State*, Feb. 6, 1992.

21. Ibid., Feb. 5, 1992.

22. Ibid., April 17, 1992.

23. Ibid., June 24, 1992.

24. Ibid., April 2, 1992.

25. Spartanburg, S.C., *Herald-Journal*, April 23, 1992.

26. *Business Atlanta*, January 1993, p. 42.

27. Press release, BMW North America, Inc., June 23, 1992.

28. Columbia, S.C., *State*, June 24, 1992.

29. Ibid., Oct. 1, 1992.

· 30. Interview with authors, Oct. 25, 1993.

31. Securities and Exchange Commission, United Biscuits Holdings PLC, 1985 Annual Report.

32. Interview with authors, Oct. 25, 1993.

33. Ibid.

34. *Philadelphia Inquirer,* Oct. 10, 1991.

35. Borough of Oxford (Pa.), Urban Development Action Grant Application, UB Foods U.S., Inc., amended, Sept. 20, 1991.

36. Commonwealth of Pennsylvania, House of Representatives, Hearings before House of Labor Relations Committee, Oct. 14, 1992, p. 23.

37. Commonwealth of Pennsylvania, Department of Commerce, press release, Nov. 11, 1991.

38. Commonwealth of Pennsylvania, House of Representatives, Hearings before House Labor Relations Committee, Oct. 14, 1992, p. 15.

39. Commonwealth of Pennsylvania, Department of Commerce, memorandum, William J. Cook to Herb Packer, Sr., Governor's Response Team, Sept. 20, 1991.

40. Interview with authors, Oct. 25, 1993.

41. *Washington Post,* June 20, 1989.

42. St. Paul, Minn., *Pioneer Press,* July 28, 1989.

43. *Minneapolis Star-Tribune,* Oct. 18, 1991.

44. State of Minnesota, Department of Finance, memorandum from Jeffrey W. Hamiel, executive director of Metropolitan Airports Commission (MAC) to MAC Commissioners, Nov. 10, 1991; included in memorandum of John Gunyou, Commissioner of Finance, to Legislative Commission on Planning and Fiscal Policy, Nov. 11, 1991, re Northwest Airlines Financings.

45. State of Minnesota, Department of Finance, Report to the State of Minnesota, *The Economics of the Airline Industry and the Financial Condition of Northwest Airlines,* September 1991, The Arvai Group.

46. Ibid.

47. *Minneapolis Star-Tribune,* Dec. 17, 1991.

48. Ibid.

49. Ibid.

50. Interview with authors, Nov. 5, 1993.

51. Howard Jarvis with Robert Pack, *I'm Mad as Hell* (New York: Times Books, 1979), p. 163.

52. Joel Kotkin and Paul Grabowicz, *California Inc.* (New York: Rawson, Wade, 1982), p. 62.

53. *Los Angeles Times,* Mar. 31, 1988.

54. Los Angeles County Recorder's Office, Document No., 93-1058780.

55. Interview with authors, Jan. 2, 1994.

56. U.S. Supreme Court, No. 90-1912, *Nordlinger* v. *Hahn,* Petitioner's Brief on the Merits.

57. Ibid., Joint Appendix, p. 18.

58. Ibid., Petitioner's Brief on the Merits.

59. Ibid.

60. Ibid., Motion of the League of Women Voters of California for Leave to File Brief as Amicus Curiae in Support of Petitioner.

61. Ibid., Brief of Respondents.

62. Ibid., Brief of Governor Pete Wilson at al.

63. 120 L. Ed. 2d 1.

64. Ibid.

65. Ibid.

66. Ibid.

Chapter Nine: Can It Be Fixed?

1. *Congressional Record,* June 18, 1986, p. S-7801.

2. Ibid., p. S-7802.

3. Ibid., Aug. 5, 1993, p. H-6125.

4. Ibid., p. H-6259.

5. Ibid., Aug. 6, 1993, p. S-10645.

6. Ibid., p. S-10665.

7. Ibid., March 3, 1993, p. S-2270.

8. Ibid.

9. Budget of the U.S. Government, Fiscal Year 1993.

10. U.S. Treasury Department, *Tax Reform for Fairness, Simplicity, and Economic Growth,* November 1984, vol. 1, p. viii.

11. "Tax Reduction and Reform"—Message from the President of the United States (H-Doc. No. 43), *Congressional Record,* Jan. 24, 1963, p. 969.

12. Ibid., p. 970.

13. *Congressional Record,* Sept. 24, 1963, p. 17917.

14. Senate Committee on Finance, 88th Cong., 1st sess., Part 1, Oct. 15, 1963, p. 144.

15. Letter dated Feb. 25, 1965, from Pamela Adam to Ronald A. Pearlman. U.S. Treasury Department, FOIA correspondence file.

Index

ABOUT THE AUTHORS

Donald L. Barlett and James B. Steele are investigative reporters for the *Philadelphia Inquirer* who have worked together as a team since 1971. Their specialty is researching, analyzing, and writing in-depth series on the complex issues and institutions that profoundly affect American life.

Over the years, Barlett and Steele have received virtually every major national journalism award for their investigative reports, including two Pulitzer Prizes for their writings on the federal tax system. They are the authors of three other books.

The University of Missouri in 1983 presented Barlett and Steele with its Honor Award for Distinguished Service in Journalism, citing them for "their standard-setting development of investigative techniques and documentation, including their pioneer use of computers." And the National Council of Teachers of English honored them in 1988 for having turned into everyday English the deliberately obfuscatory language of Congress's tax-writing committees.

Mr. Barlett was born in DuBois, Pennsylvania, on July 17, 1936, and grew up in Johnstown, Pennsylvania. He attended Pennsylvania State University and served three years as a special agent with the United States Army Counter Intelligence Corps. He has been a full-time investigative reporter since 1965, first at the *Cleveland Plain Dealer* and then at the *Chicago Daily News*. He joined the *Philadelphia Inquirer* in 1970.

Mr. Steele was born in Hutchinson, Kansas, on January 3, 1943, and grew up in Kansas City, Missouri. A graduate of the University of Missouri at Kansas City, he began his journalism career at the *Kansas City Times,* where he covered labor, politics, and urban affairs before joining the staff of the *Philadelphia Inquirer* in 1970.